The Presence of the Past

THE OXFORD MUSIC / MEDIA SERIES
Daniel Goldmark, Series Editor

Tuning In: American Narrative Television Music
Ron Rodman

Special Sound: The Creation and Legacy of the
BBC Radiophonic Workshop
Louis Niebur

Seeing Through Music: Gender and Modernism
in Classic Hollywood Film Scores
Peter Franklin

An Eye for Music: Popular Music and the
Audiovisual Surreal
John Richardson

Playing Along: Digital Games, YouTube, and
Virtual Performance
Kiri Miller

Sounding the Gallery: Video and the Rise of
Art-Music
Holly Rogers

Composing for the Red Screen: Prokofiev and
Soviet Film
Kevin Bartig

Saying It With Songs: Popular Music and the
Coming of Sound to Hollywood Cinema
Katherine Spring

We'll Meet Again: Musical Design in the Films of
Stanley Kubrick
Kate McQuiston

Occult Aesthetics: Synchronization in Sound Film
K.J. Donnelly

Sound Play: Video Games and the Musical
Imagination
William Cheng

Sounding American: Hollywood,
Opera, and Jazz
Jennifer Fleeger

Mismatched Women: The Siren's Song Through
the Machine
Jennifer Fleeger

Robert Altman's Soundtracks: Film, Music and
Sound from M*A*S*H to A Prairie Home
Companion
Gayle Sherwood Magee

Back to the Fifties: Nostalgia, Hollywood Film,
and Popular Music of the Seventies and Eighties
Michael D. Dwyer

The Early Film Music of Dmitry Shostakovich
Joan Titus

Making Music in Selznick's Hollywood
Nathan Platte

Hearing Haneke: The Sound Tracks of a
Radical Auteur
Elsie Walker

Unlimited Replays: Video Games and
Classical Music
William Gibbons

Hollywood Harmony: Musical Wonder and the
Sound of Cinema
Frank Lehman

French Musical Culture and the Coming of
Sound Cinema
Hannah Lewis

Theories of the Soundtrack
James Buhler

Through The Looking Glass: John Cage and
Avant-Garde Film
Richard H. Brown

Sound Design is the New Score: Theory, Aesthetics,
and Erotics of the Integrated Soundtrack
Danijela Kulezic-Wilson

Rock Star/Movie Star: Power and Performance in
Cinematic Rock Stardom
Landon Palmer

The Presence of the Past: Temporal Experience
and the New Hollywood Soundtrack
Daniel Bishop

The Presence of the Past

*Temporal Experience and the New
Hollywood Soundtrack*

DANIEL BISHOP

OXFORD
UNIVERSITY PRESS

Oxford University Press is a department of the University of Oxford. It furthers
the University's objective of excellence in research, scholarship, and education
by publishing worldwide. Oxford is a registered trade mark of Oxford University
Press in the UK and certain other countries.

Published in the United States of America by Oxford University Press
198 Madison Avenue, New York, NY 10016, United States of America.

© Oxford University Press 2021

All rights reserved. No part of this publication may be reproduced, stored in
a retrieval system, or transmitted, in any form or by any means, without the
prior permission in writing of Oxford University Press, or as expressly permitted
by law, by license, or under terms agreed with the appropriate reproduction
rights organization. Inquiries concerning reproduction outside the scope of the
above should be sent to the Rights Department, Oxford University Press, at the
address above.

You must not circulate this work in any other form
and you must impose this same condition on any acquirer.

Library of Congress Cataloging-in-Publication Data
Names: Bishop, Daniel, 1982– author.
Title: The presence of the past : temporal experience and
the new Hollywood soundtrack / Daniel Bishop.
Description: [1.] | New York : Oxford University Press, 2021. |
Series: Oxford music/media series | Includes bibliographical references and index.
Identifiers: LCCN 2021008104 (print) | LCCN 2021008105 (ebook) |
ISBN 9780190932695 (paperback) | ISBN 9780190932688 (hardback) |
ISBN 9780190932718 (epub) | ISBN 9780190932701 (updf) | ISBN 9780190932725 (oso)
Subjects: LCSH: Motion picture music—History and criticism. |
Film soundtracks—History and criticism. | Nostalgia in motion pictures. |
History in motion pictures.
Classification: LCC ML2075 .B57 2021 (print) |
LCC ML2075 (ebook) | DDC 781.5/42—dc23
LC record available at https://lccn.loc.gov/2021008104
LC ebook record available at https://lccn.loc.gov/2021008105

DOI: 10.1093/oso/9780190932688.001.0001

1 3 5 7 9 8 6 4 2

Paperback printed by Marquis, Canada
Hardback printed by Bridgeport National Bindery, Inc., United States of America

The publisher gratefully acknowledges support from the AMS 75 PAYS Fund of
the American Musicological Society, supported in part by the National Endowment for
the Humanities and the Andrew W. Mellon Foundation.

Contents

Acknowledgments   vii

Introduction: The Presence of the Past in the New Hollywood   1

1. *Bonnie and Clyde* and the Aural Imagination of American Counterculture   28
2. The Revisionist Western and the Mythic Past   60
3. The Mythic Elements of *Chinatown*   93
4. Radio, Memory, and the Past in the Nostalgia Film   126
5. *Badlands* and the Music of Temporal Immanence   157

Notes   197
Bibliography   231
Index   243

Acknowledgments

This project began its life as my dissertation, and the debts of gratitude engendered by that project were so numerous that, although the present book would not otherwise have come into being, they cannot all be recapitulated here. I would like to try, however, even if sometimes in admittedly broad strokes. The Musicology Department at the Jacobs School of Music at Indiana University, its faculty, and my graduate school cohort helped to nourish and support much of this work in its initial form. In particular, thanks go to my former graduate student colleagues Kerry O'Brien, Lisa Cooper Vest, Amanda Sewell, and Kate Altizer. An early version of the material on *The Last Picture Show* benefitted from conversation with Virginia Whealton, who shared several ideas. More recently, a kind thank you goes to Mark Francis, whose knowledge of *Schulwerk* discography helped to untangle the soundtrack of *Badlands*.

Over the last several years, much of the material in this book was hashed out and refined through presentations at conferences of the American Musicological Society and the Society for Cinema and Media Studies. In particular, however, the Music and the Moving Image conference at NYU Steinhardt, and the community of scholars fostered there by Gillian Anderson and Ron Sadoff, have both facilitated invaluable feedback as the project continued to evolve.

I would also like to thank Phil Ford, who, well after serving as my advisor, has continued to be an invaluable mentor, friend, and sounding board for strange ideas.

Portions of Chapter 1 appeared in an earlier form as an essay in *Critical Insights: Bonnie and Clyde*, edited by Rebecca Martin and published by Salem Press in 2016. Many thanks go to Salem Press for their kind permission to republish this material, and to Laura Mars at Salem / Grey House for her help in navigating this process.

Norm Hirschy at Oxford University Press has been an invaluable guide, generous with time and information, and patient with the inexperience and numerous questions that are inevitably part of a first book. Many thanks also go to my production manager, Haripriya Ravichandran at Newgen Knowledge Works.

Teachers learn innumerable things from their students, and in this respect a large, collective debt of gratitude must go to my students, who have regularly shown me that the most difficult (and most valuable) skill in teaching is to imagine beyond one's own experience and assumptions. Thanks also go to Constance Cook Glen for her mentorship of my teaching, and the Music in General Studies program and the Musicology Department at the Jacobs School of Music for facilitating this work.

And thanks, finally, go to my family—my parents, Bill and Eleanor Bishop and my sister Katharine Wilson, for their incalculable support over the years. And to Sherri and Madelyn Bishop, for being my world.

Introduction

The Presence of the Past in the New Hollywood

A Tale of Two Critics

In 1967, critic Pauline Kael published a celebrated and lengthy review that has come to exemplify how critical culture grapples with the nature of cinematic violence. In addition to passionately defending the recent film *Bonnie and Clyde* (1967) against several high-profile critical detractors, however, Kael took note of more than just the film's controversial violence, appraising the way in which *Bonnie and Clylde* "[plays] upon our attitudes toward the American past by making the hats and guns and holdups look as dated as two-reel comedy." For Kael, *Bonnie and Clyde* offered not just "the past," but the past as if it were filtered through silent film comedy: a jokily iconic, even campy past, in which the filmmakers, by "emphasizing the absurdity with banjo music . . . make the period seem even farther away than it is."[1] Later in the review, Kael continued to explore the film's use of the past alongside an awareness of the contemporary moment, linking the film's sense of period style both to a mythically "primordial" American imaginary and the in-the-moment iconicity of contemporary pop art:

> There's something new working for the Bonnie-and-Clyde legend now: our nostalgia for the thirties—the unpredictable, contrary affection of the prosperous for poverty, or at least for the artifacts, the tokens, of poverty, for Pop culture seen in the dreariest rural settings, where it truly seems to belong. Did people in the cities listen to the Eddie Cantor show? No doubt they did, but the sound of his voice, like the sound of Ed Sullivan now, evokes a primordial, pre-urban existence—the childhood of the race. Our comic-melancholic affection for thirties Pop has become sixties Pop, and those who made Bonnie and Clyde are smart enough to use it that way.[2]

A few years later, in response to the austere coming-of-age drama *The Last Picture Show* (1971), critic Andrew Sarris would draw upon the seeming expressive opposites of gritty realism and Hollywood fantasy to describe that film's evocation of the fifties:

> Why then is "The Last Picture Show" so popular? I suppose at least partly because [director] Peter Bogdanovich establishes a realistic mood and sticks to it. . . . With what seem to be ghostly wind machines from the abandoned sets of "The Magnificent Ambersons" (Welles), "My Darling Clementine" (Ford), and "The Ox-Bow Incident" (Wellman), Bogdanovich manages to give his real-life location the resonance of an old-movie lot.[3]

In American film culture of the sixties and seventies, Kael and Sarris were two critics frequently at odds with one another. Nevertheless, in these passages both writers seem to be rooting out a related sensibility in recent cinematic representations of the American past. This sensibility draws, on the one hand, upon a sense of realistic, affective immediacy, and on the other, an aesthetic of self-conscious artifice or nostalgic distance. For Kael, the setting of *Bonnie and Clyde* is not merely a tacit function of genre, nor is it simply an excuse to indulge in production values for their own sake. Instead, the historical setting of rural America in the thirties engages in a play of familiarity and distanciation—overlapping fond cultural memories of Eddie Cantor with the fetishized icons of popular culture. For Sarris, the use of location shooting in *The Last Picture Show* combines with a classical sense of realism to disclose a deeper artificiality. Paradoxically, by capturing actual, real locations in the world, the film conjures up a studio-bound illusionism reminiscent of a vanished Old Hollywood past.

Both Kael and Sarris also touch, albeit in passing, upon the role of the soundtrack. For Kael, the use of the banjo both creates the feel of a corny, overdone put-on and ultimately establishes a subversive counterpoint to the film's gradual descent into brutal violence. For Sarris, in turn, *The Last Picture Show*'s prominent use of wind effects constitute a "ghostly" sense of presence, ideal for a film whose characters ache with nostalgia for a vanishing way of life. But these ghosts belong not just to an ostensibly "real," or rather, to a *historical* rural America of the early fifties—surprisingly, for Sarris, they are also the ghosts of old *films*, a lost Hollywood past swept aside by a new era of filmmaking. As it is presented in both films, a construction of "the past" collapses together self-conscious distance and visceral immediacy, blurring the lines between reality, fantasy, and memory. This sense of "pastness" not only is channeled through images and narrative dialogue, but also is enacted, in perhaps an even more direct way, by the work of music and sound.

It is a larger contention of this book that Kael and Sarris were on to something, and that they were not alone, even if contemporaneous film culture rarely gave this "something" fully self-conscious articulation. While critics, scholars, and audiences of the late sixties and seventies periodically noted the number of prominent films not just set in, but to some extent *about* the past, this development was more typically understood as a fashionable fad, and at most as a reaction (whether politically engaged or escapist) to a complex and troubled contemporary present. The idea of the past as a subject in its own right thus tended to be subsumed into discussions of genre, commercial production cycles, or cultural allegory, whereas the importance of the past *itself*, a past that is necessarily interwoven with particular representational forms but nevertheless exists in excess of these forms—what we might call not just "the past," but rather a quality of "pastness"—could easily be overlooked. The presence of the past could be attributed to the generic setting of a Western, to the fact that gritty, revisionist Westerns were "in" following the success of *The Wild Bunch* (1969), or to the traumatic impact of the Vietnam War on American culture. Politically, *Bonnie and Clyde* could be read as representing an increasingly radicalized youth counterculture, while *American Graffiti* (1973) could be understood as advancing a culturally infantile yearning for a pre-countercultural era. While such viewpoints represent important facets of these films' cultural reception, it is the work of this book to examine other ways in which a particular sensibility of "pastness" was active in the films themselves, in film culture, and in American culture more broadly.

Bonnie and Clyde and *The Last Picture Show* are often viewed as representative examples of a distinct era in Hollywood filmmaking, roughly occupying an interval between the mid-sixties and the mid- to late seventies. This hybrid of popular and modernist film has become known as the New Hollywood Cinema.[4] While more mainstream, stylistically traditional films continued to be made, several of Hollywood's most prominent and critically celebrated films—the films that initially emerged as canonical when critics began to take assessment of this era—engaged in striking formal, aesthetic, and thematic experimentation.[5] At the end of the day, such films were still identifiable as commercial Hollywood cinema, but they were nevertheless trying very hard to be legible as *something else*, borrowing from styles of independent and art cinema and subverting cultural norms in affinity with a developing American counterculture.[6]

The decades after World War II brought extensive industrial, technological, and expressive transformations to American film production and culture. In this sense, the New Hollywood that came to popular attention during the cultural storms of the late sixties had historical roots stretching back, arguably, to the late forties. Throughout the postwar era, Hollywood weathered periods of increasing economic instability and declining audiences. Changing social values also led to shifts in how the industry regulated the portrayal of sexuality, violence, and criminality. As early as the mid-fifties, Hollywood was adapting to these changes, attempting to balance tried and tested formulas with appeals to niche audiences, including both younger demographics and more cosmopolitan viewers increasingly familiar with the imported international art house fare whose American exhibition culture had burgeoned in the fifties. Despite this broader context, however, the epochal cultural turns of the later sixties and early seventies have made its cinema arguably stand alone. In defining a New Hollywood Cinema, traditional narratives of the sixties and seventies—narratives of social crises and activism, conflicting generational values, political radicalization, political defeatism, the collapse of the New Left and the emergence of the Reaganite right—have all become central.

In the manner of an artist who declares all their paintings, regardless of formal visual content, to be self-portraits, "the past" in cinema can usually, in one way or another, be argued to be *about* the present in which the film was created. This is generally true of all of the films discussed in this study, as their reception in journalistic and scholarly culture has routinely emphasized. Critics have never had difficulty interpreting *The Wild Bunch* to be, on some level, *about* the Vietnam War. In addition, there is a thriving scholarly literature on the topic of how *history* is represented in film, recently encompassing the first monograph specific to the New Hollywood historical film.[7] But such films are also frequently about the past *itself*, exceeding the boundaries of either contemporary allegory or historiographic construction. It is important, in other words, not to simply reduce the New Hollywood's representations of the past to allegory for its present or to a positional statement on historical significance. In an era in which artistic culture was marked by a highly self-conscious sense of its own *presentness*, it is all the more vital to recognize that many films of the New Hollywood were also deeply involved in representing the past *itself*—the past as an imagined, yet irreducibly experiential reality.

The imperatives of *the Now* have tended to dominate our understanding of this era, and the late sixties in particular—not just in terms of understanding cinematic pasts, but as a way of thinking about the demands of political activism, as well as the nature of experience, spontaneity, and actuality—all key aesthetic buzzwords of the era. But what about the *then* of this *now*? How does an aesthetic worldview heavily invested in presentism understand the nature of the past? Or perhaps, to reverse the equation, what about the *now* of this *then*? How does a cinematic past create a sense of the immediate, experiential present? A contextualized view of these films should also be capable of examining how they reflect upon the past *itself* as something that, through the filmic imagination, could be (as philosopher Stanley Cavell has characterized cinematic ontology) "simultaneously present and absent."[8] The film world is "present" through the unique capacity of cinema to manifest phenomenal experience. It is, however, absent as well, and this absence is tangible not just because cinematic representations lack material reality, but also due to the inevitable distance between us (the experients of the film world) and a *real* temporal past that is inaccessible as a result of the human experience of time.

A constellation of ideas on the nature of vanished or otherwise materially insubstantial temporal experiences, what we might call "sensibilities of the past," intertwine in some of the most representative of New Hollywood films—ideas related to nostalgia and cultural memory, to the relationship between myth and history, and to the phenomenal experience of the physical world. While the so-called nostalgia boom of the early seventies has received considerable critical attention, the investments of New Hollywood Cinema in the idea of the past extended beyond fifties nostalgia and the films (such as *American Graffiti*) with which it was most closely associated. Sometimes this sense of the past was engaged *through* the topoi of genre. Traditional genres such as the Western or film noir might be both set in the past *and*, independently, individual films might also be reflective of "the past" as a conceptual subject. Some filmmakers also turned to their own generational past, nostalgically evoking the experience of coming of age in the late fifties and early sixties in an effort to cultivate a shared space of cultural memory. Elsewhere, the past was a site of an ambiguous historical revisionism, a coming to terms with the past as a construction of a mythic American imaginary. In an age in which many traditional myths had come to seem deeply suspect, it was increasingly perceived as vital to cultivate new, sometimes melancholy, sometimes disturbing understandings of myth's persistence within a revisionist context. In all of these ways of understanding the presence of the past, a key role was played by the expressive use of music and sound, which became an ideal vehicle for conveying a range of temporal sensibilities. While these sensibilities manifested in diverse ways, they nevertheless share a central quality—a dialectical portrayal, on the one hand, of the immediacy and experiential actuality of the past, and on the other, of the mediating distances that inevitably separate us from this experience.

The Presence of the Past: Contextual Histories

A fascination with a sensibility of pastness and its meanings, of course, is not unique to the New Hollywood era, but is rather rooted in significantly older discourses of modernity, some of which bear useful comparison to the later historiography of the sixties and seventies. For example, writing about the aftermath of the French Revolution and the Napoleonic Wars, historian Peter Fritzsche has traced the origins of what he calls a "melancholy of history." In the world Fritzsche describes, the contemporaneous historical moment was increasingly understood to be *radically new*. Two results of this newness were that, first, the past correspondingly came to be viewed as a field of both irrecoverable loss and uncanny otherness; second, this dislocation of past opened it up to a sense of possibility and re-reading, a reservoir of unprecedented and unpredictable subjectivities.[9] In this way, Fritzsche's newly alienated Europeans began not only to understand, but also affectively to *feel* history differently as a phenomenal experience, self-consciously viewing themselves as actors on the stage of history—sharing universal stakes in a present moment while simultaneously feeling cut off from the tangible reality of their past. The more this sense of radical contemporaneity became a subject of discourse, the more the past could be imbued with a drama and variant readings, as well as with a sense of nostalgic loss, frequently realized in meditative fixation upon the image of abandoned ruins.

In this era, which of course also cultivated the aesthetics of Romanticism, radical newness represented an originating point for the modern political-social concept of permanent revolution, even if this concept also remained tied in complex ways to an idealization of the past. Despite more than a century's remove, similar correspondences between the revolutionary impulse and historical self-consciousness would become central to the counterculture of the sixties. The popular narrative of this era (a complex mythology in its own right) customarily identifies the mid- to late sixties as a period of radicalization and increasingly utopian politics, emphasizing the tumult of the Civil Rights, Black Power, and antiwar movements, alongside broader shifting attitudes toward sexuality and drug use and other lifestyle values and practices. Yet beyond these thoroughly mainstreamed narratives of tangible social progress was an often surprisingly *aestheticized* worldview. In a new introduction for a 1995 reprinting of his classic text, *The Making of a Counter Culture* (1969), historian Theodore Roszak reflected upon the sixties from the vantage point of a writer who had helped to initiate its mythology. In this way, Roszak is especially illuminating as a latter-day commentator on the counterculture's self-conscious relationship to its unique place and time. As "the product of plenty and societal success, not of misery and failure," sixties counterculture, in Roszak's summation, was an elite, bourgeois political moment that built specifically upon a *lack* of concrete historical tradition. Whereas "Europe had a long tradition of left-wing insurgency ... America didn't," a distinction that Roszak views, ultimately, as a *productive* limitation, as it was this "very weakness of conventional ideological politics in the United States [that] lent the counterculture its unique insight."[10] The uniqueness of American counterculture, for Roszak, was its focus on the role of consciousness and, especially, of *imagination* in radicalization, developing a perspective—in essence, a magical one—in which altered states of consciousness would produce altered states of society.

In comparing Fritzsche's post-Napoleonic Europe with Roszak's considerably later moment in Western modernity, a contemporary (non-Indigenous) American might ask, in turn: where were *our* ruins? Where were the tangible traces of *our* cataclysm and ensuing alienation? *Our* basis for a radically antiestablishment history? "We" had folklore, the frontier, the Indians, and the Civil War. Instead of the physical ruins of ancient edifices with whom we could trace, however interrupted, some form of continuous identification, we had nebulous spaces, peoples, and events—easily effaced, obliterated, or forgotten. Instead of the remnants of vanished empires, we had the legacies of transplanted and enslaved peoples, or decimated and forcibly assimilated nomadic and agrarian societies. The emphasis on radical newness in the countercultural imagination, as Roszak understands it, might well be compared to that of Fritzsche's moderns, but the past that was comparably dramatized and rendered the object of melancholy was, perhaps from the start, even *more* prone to fantasy and invention—to the sense of "enchantment and playfulness" that Roszak attributes (with a mix of fascination and frustration) to "technocracy's children."[11] This needful condition may well be seen as underpinning the importance of what film critic J. Hoberman (following Norman Mailer) has called the "Dream Life," in which American culture increasingly understood and created itself through images drawn from the movies. A comparably important facet of this Dream Life, as music critic Greil Marcus has speculated, was the American countercultural imagination's self-projection into a surreally anachronistic utopia of archaic magic and radical communitarianism—what Marcus has called the "Old, Weird America."[12] Europe had its communards. We had snake oil salesmen.[13]

By contrast with the sixties, the seventies have tended to be marked as a "problem decade."[14] Traditionally, the decade has struggled to be interpreted on its own terms, rather than as either the burnout following the collapse of the New Left, or the interval preceding the pendulum's return swing into the neo-conservatism understood to define the eighties. The seventies have also been viewed as a site of regressive nostalgia for the era that had preceded the cultural turmoil of the late sixties—a seventies of economic recession, social breakdown, paranoia, and narcissistic self-development (epitomized by Tom Wolfe's concept of the "Me" Decade). The aestheticized, utopian sensibilities of radical newness Roszak describes came, we must imagine, with an inevitable letdown in the face of immutable, everyday realities. But it is also fascinating to trace the degree to which this pessimism, in popular film at least, was not unique to the seventies, but had already been present in the most celebrated countercultural films of the sixties. It is certainly present in several of the films studied in this work, such as Arthur Penn's *Bonnie and Clyde* (1967), and Robert Altman's *McCabe and Mrs. Miller* (1971). It is also epitomized by Peter Fonda's cryptic and much-dissected climactic *bon mot* ("We blew it") in *Easy Rider* (1969), a film routinely identified as among the first to fully articulate a New Hollywood ethos. If this is the case, then the New Hollywood may well have been born with the inevitable failure of its utopian project already lurking in the corners of its mind.[15]

While Roszak observes this current of cynicism, he dodges its implications, stating, "I was first asked 'whatever became of the counter culture' in 1970, within six months of this book's publication . . . I have always taken this eagerness to bury the protest movement as an indication that the counter culture touched a very raw nerve."[16] Unlike Roszak, I am less interested in validating or invalidating any particular narratives of the sixties, and more interested in the effect of such narratives upon the cultural imaginary and its understanding of the past. Building upon Marcus's notion of the "Old, Weird

America," it is fascinating to imagine that this shape-shifting trickster's utopia might have represented not just an imagined alternative to "straight" society, but also a refuge from a tumultuous present—a refuge all the more melancholic for bearing an implicit awareness of its unsustainability within a larger social reality. Utopianism, while it could easily be understood to radically remake the present, could just as easily manifest as a nostalgic retreat, not merely the progressive and regressive ends of a spectrum, but two faces of a single coin.

Moving into the seventies as an era of Hollywood filmmaking, we encounter what David Cook has described as a necessarily temporary coexistence of an experimental auteur cinema and a blockbuster mentality—temporary in the sense that, eventually, from Cook's perspective, one or the other of these two cinemas needed to "win," or at least to acquire enough normative power to be able to restructure the other within a newly reconfigured industry.[17] When (or if) the New Hollywood, in its countercultural sense, ever ended is a point of contention. Some critics have argued, in fact, that it never actually *began*, but had rather been illusory all along. But as Cook also points out, the process of industrial conglomeration that had begun in the early sixties had already accelerated drastically, lifting the industry out of its recession by 1973, fairly early in the decade.[18] Conglomeration diversified risk and ensured a steady flow of capital, but it also made inevitable a shift of industrial attitudes toward the "product," discouraging interest in artistic experiment and encouraging a view of film as a calculated marketing investment.

Extending our broader reading, then, the optimistic frontier metaphors of the late sixties translate in the seventies into a turn toward interiority and self-cultivation (when read positively), or (when read negatively) toward fragmentation and narcissism. But there are other ways of reading this turn. Historian Andreas Killen, for example, has re-examined these tropes and found in them considerably more complexity by taking the fragmentation of the unified self as a meta-narrative for society, politics, and art in the seventies, thus showing how fragmentations might in some cases be read as sites of fascinating, unpredictable social transformation.[19] Musicologist Mitchell Morris, in his study of seventies pop, similarly identifies the decade as marked by fragmentation, but cultivates an understanding of this fragmentation as, in the moment, opening up the possibility of solutions whose novelty and value have traditionally been overlooked in cultural criticism. The fragmentation of the unified self could thus *also*, in a different way, facilitate negotiations of social representation that were radically diverse to the point that they challenged the ability of a singular cultural identity to contain them. To epitomize this diversity, Morris memorably cites network television's side-by-side packaging of fantasy and realism, in the simultaneous coexistence of such cultural offerings as *Green Acres* and *All in the Family*, separated only by a click of the remote control.[20]

In the seventies, in other words, the fractured remnants of fragmented cultural narratives remained, to an unprecedented degree, simultaneously available to audiences.[21] In such an environment it is easy to imagine reality and fantasy not only coexisting, but interpenetrating each other, producing complex and productive contradictions. This was troubling territory, however, for social critics who preferred more tangible, even black-and-white narratives. As regards rock music criticism in particular, Morris writes:

> The burst of conflicting styles and genres that began the 1970s made it impossible for listeners to imagine a unified generational audience hearing a naturalized music that spoke truth to power. Popular music subsided into its bad old ways, hustling its multiple audiences for a buck. Where had its antinomian potential gone?[22]

In critical film culture of the late seventies and early eighties, similar expressions of disappointment were frequent, particularly following the success of a string of blockbusters whose unprecedented financial returns permanently altered the industrial logic of risk and payoff—*The Godfather* (1970), *The Exorcist* (1973), and *Jaws* (1975), culminating in *Star Wars* (1977). The seventies also saw film studies move toward an increasingly formalized academic stance informed by Marxist, psychoanalytic, and feminist currents of thought. These emerging traditions, and their critiques of the ambivalent cynicism of many New Hollywood films, were often predicated upon a desire for ideological clarity and agency that was rarely embraced in this cinematic moment.

Robin Wood's 1986 book *Hollywood from Vietnam to Reagan* helped both to solidify this tradition of critique and to extend it to the author himself, with Wood actively disavowing and revising his earlier critical work as having been *too* auteurist, a stance that, by the mid-eighties, Wood viewed as glorifying "a myth of the bourgeois artist."[23] *Hollywood from Vietnam to Reagan* is a fierce, deliberately polemical work, but it is one whose urgent tone of Late-Cold-Warrior interventionism inevitably limited the conceptual territory that Wood was able to empathetically navigate. Setting a precedent for later scholars of the era such as Robert Kolker, Wood centralizes the notion of "the incoherent text"—a work that confronts ideological problems, yet lacks the ability to offer ideological solutions, dwelling instead on stylistic and thematic engagements with paralysis, paranoia, and impotency.[24]

Wood's larger point, to be fair, is that incoherent texts offer complex experiences and provoke questions—and when they offend, they at least do so in a rich and often intellectually rewarding way. Wood also values the New Hollywood as a departure from an even more ideologically pernicious Old Hollywood, whose "requirements, passively accepted by studios and audiences, corresponded neither to the films people wanted to make nor the films people wanted to see."[25] But from the perspective of the mid-eighties, Wood ultimately viewed the New Hollywood Cinema as having been full of blockages that, annoyingly, go unfixed by radical thought within the film itself because in Hollywood, at the end of the day, "radical alternatives remain taboo." Incoherency isn't inherently bad—but it is, from Wood's perspective, inherently regressive. The best of these films thus function for Wood as something akin to time capsules, radical promises that are "stored away for the future," when we might finally be able to make their crooked roads straight again.[26]

In Mitchell Morris's view, the "positive social alternatives" that Wood laments not finding in the New Hollywood Cinema were important components of popular music, although they played a game unfamiliar to critics rooted in a particular idealization of the counterculture, attached as they were to the image of rock music as a uniquely authentic and transgressive mode of expression. In black, female, and gay audiences, Morris locates a progressive adoption of musical styles that were frequently viewed as aesthetically regressive and highly commercialized.[27] And yet Morris also deploys a type of musical hermeneutics that goes beyond the creation and reception of music by particular historical and social groups. In addition to showing how marginalized audiences appropriated and recoded mainstream music, Mitchell also engages with how this music itself might have cultivated states of interiority and imaginative fantasy in its listeners, as well as examining the meanings of this interiority and fantasy as subtly political gestures. I cannot argue that the negotiation of marginalized identities plays a similar role the films analyzed in this study. In fact, to the contrary, the films that most immediately represent the aesthetic sensibility examined in this book—like the *auteurs* who have unfairly dominated many typical narratives of this era—are largely white, male, and heteronormative affairs. The first and most obvious explanation for this disparity is that the aestheticized view of the past traced in this book is a luxury made possible by a position of privilege.[28] This is a view with which, one imagines, Robin Wood might have been largely in agreement, although he perhaps would have been more likely than a contemporary commentator to reach for the word "bourgeois."

Nevertheless, I find considerable value in—and will attempt in this work to adopt—a perspective on the seventies as a decade in which fragmentation, interiority, and the historical imagination played roles in popular film that can productively belie overly familiar ideological readings. Such criticism, I feel, might benefit *from adopting the perspective of the seventies itself*, at least as Morris has characterized this perspective. Describing how the culture wars of the eighties functionally reduced our culture's sense of its social choices to a frustratingly banal binary of "identity politics" vs. "universalism," Morris speculates that

> what the denigration of identity politics during the 1980s and 1990s surrendered is the sense of possibility that such notions created during the 1970s. There was no reason to suppose that the rise of one or another form of "power" always meant the decline of others. It was hoped during much of the 1970s that social negotiation was not a matter of "either/or" but rather a matter of "both/and." As a result, I see the musical representations of the songs in this book as fundamentally optimistic. Even at their most melancholy, they hope for something better.[29]

Melancholy will indeed occupy much of the present study. The irreducible differences between canonical New Hollywood filmmaking and seventies pop music, however, will mean that social optimism, unfortunately like social diversity and equity, remain decidedly underrepresented.[30] The fact that I am largely hewing, in my case studies, to such films should not be taken as an espousal of the qualitative values that led to their canonization in the first place. Rather, the selection of case studies is intended to show that the ideas I suggest can productively apply to canonical films, even ones that have already been interpreted through numerous other frameworks. In such texts, which already tend to bend toward ambiguity in narrative and stylistic terms, there is ample room for a more productive approach to fissures, fragmentation, and ideological inconsistencies. It is here that the study of sound and music in the New Hollywood might make useful contributions to a broader historiography of this cultural moment: by moving away from a tendency toward ideological critique without necessarily abandoning critical engagement, we might engage sound and music in a "both/and" reading of the New Hollywood. Here, too, there might be a productive role for an expressive understanding of the past as engaged with a sensibility of present-tense actuality. We might imagine this past not as *inherently* apolitical (its articulations and their implications were frequently quite political) but rather as a sort of open space beyond the restrictive shoehorning of allegorical, historical, or ideological determinism. In this sense, the past becomes an open text, perhaps refreshingly so.

One way of reconsidering Wood's "coherent" and "incoherent" texts is to reframe them instead as "closed" and "open." For a variety of overlapping historical, industrial, and aesthetic reasons, the classical Hollywood film, for example, tends toward textual closure. But even here, as Wood himself admits, upon closer (or more eccentric) inspection, cracks, fissures, and inconclusiveness can emerge.[31] Sound and music can play important functions in facilitating this openness, as they—being non-linguistic elements within what is typically understood as a medium driven by dialogue—are potentially among the most spectral, intangible, or otherwise polysemic elements of film experience.[32] Peter Franklin's recent study of classical film music, for example, has opened up a rich space for reading potential cracks and fissures that allow the experiences of both classical film and its music to be far more open to "against-the-grain" readings than previously assumed by critical thinkers concerned with using film music to advance the modernist project of critiquing mass culture.[33]

Sounding the Past: Theory, Criticism, and Industry

In addition to exploring alternatives to the traditional limitations of ideological criticism, the present book also attempts to take account of two recent trends in film music scholarship. First, it approaches the soundtrack as a whole, embracing both music and sound design as interacting phenomenal and expressive elements worthy of close interpretive reading. Second, it attempts to weave some of the concerns of film theory into musicological discussion—not just in order to contest the traditional visual biases of film theory with aurally sensitive readings, but also to find in film-theoretical and philosophical traditions a conceptual reciprocity with my framing of the "presence of the past." These points of contact include the realist film theory of André Bazin and his more recent interpreters, philosopher Gaston Bachelard's understanding of elemental matter as imaginal phenomena, as well as more recent work in film philosophy—in particular, authors such as Daniel Frampton and Daniel Yacavone who attempt to understand film as a uniquely expressive type of "mind" or "world." This is not merely a matter of selecting an analytical model, like a pair of tinted spectacles through which to view cultural objects as they lie there, inert and uncommunicative on their own. Rather, concerns of film theory and philosophy were already historically present within the cultural background and stylistic registers of the New Hollywood, particularly with respect to the influence of modernist European New Waves on American cinema.

One important historical-theoretical shift in film aesthetics contextualizing this project is what film historian Paul Monaco has characterized as a modern "cinema of sensation," which began in the sixties to rival (and, in the blockbuster spectacles of the seventies, eventually to trump) a contrastingly classical "dialogue-based cinema."[34] Monaco's distinction highlights the importance in this transition of stylistic elements that create a direct affective impact upon the viewer. A foregrounded sense of sensory impact was critical to developments in the aesthetics of the non-musical soundtrack (anticipating the later expressive category of "sound design") and in visuals (in the manipulation of classical continuity editing). Film thus began to emphasize the "feel" of time upon the viewer, and to play provocatively with temporality—fragmenting it, overlapping it, or presenting it in long takes to convey undifferentiated or unmediated experience. The historical film, as a genre, does not enter into Monaco's discussion, and his representative example of the "cinema of sensation" is Alfred Hitchcock's *Psycho* (1960), which is neither a period piece nor, later perspectives might argue, part of the "New Hollywood" moment as it is most commonly defined.[35] Nevertheless, it is easy to imagine concerns of sensation and temporality acquiring a distinct resonance within representations of the past, allowing cinema to represent a new *type* of past, one that moves away from the monumentality of the epic, or the clichés of historically located genres, and instead emphasizes an awareness of its ephemeral present.

In terms of shifting audience tastes, Monaco and other historians, such as Tino Balio, have also highlighted the importance of the expanding niche market for foreign art films in the United States.[36] In part, the existence of this demographic helped to convince Hollywood filmmakers of the possibility that mainstream film could similarly draw upon stylistic experimentation and adult content, and that these might even be markers of an authentic (and marketable) artistic vision. Gerald Mast, writing in the second edition of his *A Short History of the Movies*, tied the cinema of sensation (although he does not use this term) directly to the influence of international art film and to broader industrial changes, in the sense that a concern with stylism frequently went hand in hand with a concern for authenticity in films that

> [require] accident and imperfection for their visual style and human credibility. This demand for authenticity is the result of the conversion of the American cinema to a uniquely European cinema value—to render the experiential nature of a human event. The new films do not depict action so much as how the action *feels*.[37]

Part of this focus on "depicting how an action *feels*" is certainly attributable to the influence of the exploration, by a variety of European modernist cinemas of the post–World War II era, of the relationship between film and reality. These included postwar Italian neorealism and its focus on capturing an uninflected, undramatized sense of objective reality, as well as the French New Wave, which, with playfully self-conscious stylism, challenged the traditionally literary qualities of French mainstream cinema.[38]

A perhaps even more proximate influence, as Jay Beck has argued, is the British New Wave of the early sixties, from which several directors (such as John Schlesinger and Tony Richardson) would migrate into the Hollywood orbit, bringing with them a stylized approach to sound that was de-theatricalized and often experimented with non-synchronicity.[39] At the same time, new styles of documentary cinema, such as direct cinema and *cinema vérité*, took advantage of the new technologies of easily portable cameras and sound equipment (such as the Nagra III) to explore the complexities and ambiguities of capturing raw, documentary reality in an uninflected form.[40] When the New Hollywood Cinema drew upon the stylistic referents of art cinema and documentary, it was thus also, to an extent, drawing upon a body of ideas regarding the aestheticized presentation of reality and temporality, ideas that would inflect the representation of the past. Following this logic, we might imagine a sort of *vérité* past, one that emphasizes its own tangible (albeit imagined) reality through its use of audiovisual gestures that we might call "reality effects."

Likewise, while Italian neorealism and the French New Wave had largely waned or redirected their energies by the late sixties, characteristically associated filmmakers such as Roberto Rossellini, Francois Truffaut, and Jean-Luc Godard were still active, and their influence on films such as *Bonnie and Clyde* was critical.[41] Discussions fostered by this body of film continued to be active in film criticism and, to an extent, in a burgeoning body of film theory. Both stylistic currents were concerned with the ability of the camera to capture, in however stylized or mediated a form, something essential to the tangible physical reality of human experience. As these ideas were absorbed into New Hollywood filmmaking, with them came a dialectical concern with conveying both direct, unmediated reality and stylized artificiality—two seeming polarities that are always, in fact, deeply intertwined.

The first thing to acknowledge in any discussion of realism is that we are dealing with an "-ism"—not "the real" itself, but rather a set of aesthetic gestures that are understood to expressively convey some varying quality of "the real." Paul Monaco, for example, has pointed out the shifting role of color cinematography over time, signifying fantasy and artifice through the forties, but gradually flipping places with black-and-white cinematography to signify realism.[42] Similarly, in terms of sound, John Belton has shown how the ostensibly "realistic" soundscape of stereophonic theatrical sound in the fifties became a "frozen revolution" when it failed to signify immersive verisimilitude to a generation for whom the small, black-and-white screen and monaural sound of broadcast television had become much more strongly associated with the representation of reality.[43] Thus, to say a film such as *Bonnie and Clyde* is more "realistic" than a more mainstream film of the same year would be to make an ideological move, positioning *Bonnie and Clyde*'s visceral aesthetics not just as "more realistic," but as more "authentic." And yet—because classical style had become readable as a signifier of realism—the techniques through which this new realism was articulated exist as varying forms of stylization, encompassing both *vérité* naturalism (such as the use of non-actors, direct sound recording, and the foregrounding of durational time), and self-consciously "non-realistic" effects (such as self-reflexivity, expressionism, the fantastic and oneiric).

The tradition of so-called realist film theory, especially as it was developed in the forties and fifties by André Bazin, offers an important context for the way in which certain New Hollywood films represented the historical past. Bazin's basic claim was that film's mechanically photochemical process, by way of "capturing" the actuality of what was in front of the camera, allowed film to possess a privileged relationship to reality.[44] Although Bazin was fully aware of the constructed, artificial nature of film, he nevertheless viewed indexical realism as the element that granted the film medium its uniqueness within his evolutionary view of art history, as well as its potentially expressive, political, and even spiritual agency. Beginning with the flourishing of academic film studies in the seventies, however, Bazinian realism began to be viewed as hampered by its evolutionary assumptions, technological determinism, ideological naiveté, and selectivity—creating a general theory of cinema that lionized a certain group of historically and culturally contingent films toward which Bazin was biased.[45] Nevertheless, by the late sixties, Bazin's place in a larger discussion was assured. A small but significant portion of his theoretical work had been translated into English and circulated within a burgeoning American film culture. His writings were regularly understood to be one foundational current within film theory, as demonstrated by his prominent position in theoretical anthologies and by his familiarity among several prominent film critics. In his survey *The Major Film Theories* (1976), Dudley Andrew also viewed Bazinian theory as part of a lineage leading to the experiments in documentary film, such as D. A. Pennebaker's work with direct cinema, a style influential on New Hollywood aesthetics.[46]

More recently, neo-Bazinian film theory has been experiencing a resurgence, fueled by interest in phenomenology and film philosophy, as well as by Bazin's complex place in the aesthetics of mid-century European modernism.[47] Trends in both film history and theory have also been moving away from the "high theory" of the seventies and eighties to embrace different means and ends—some more pluralist or cognitivist, others more experimental or even playful.[48] One direction in which this latter has been evident is in a broader renewed interest in cinephilia. Several scholars have explored cinephilia as a historically situated cultural phenomenon, whether located in an American "golden age of cinephilia" of the fifties to seventies, or in the more recent "post-filmic" context of fan communities and remix aesthetics.[49] Others, such as Christian Keathley and Robert B. Ray, have advocated for radical critical approaches that meld historical and theoretical objectivity with an unconventional privileging of the subjectivity of the viewer.[50]

In Keathley's case, the construct of cinephilia is central, in a way that engages not just with Bazin as an influential historical figure, but also as a model for neo-Bazinian thought. Keathley's book *Cinephilia and History* traces cinephiliac culture and its impact on filmmaking. More radically, it pursues cinephilia not just as an object of study, but as a methodological model.⁵¹ Instead of simply connoting a love of film, Keathley's cinephilia is a radically subjective mode of spectatorship, a style of viewing so familiar with traditional narrative codes that it is compelled to look beyond them in search of subjective and contingent meaning—the fugitive details that hover on the border of meaningless accidents, but which nevertheless somehow acquire a deep significance for the viewer.

Keathley thus establishes a precedent for discussing the film codes of post–World War II European art film with regard to their representation of fleetingly tangible realities, both in their self-reflexive stylization and in their capturing of unmediated presence. By showing how Bazinian realism and the New Wave's paradoxical love of unaffected artifice interacted with technological thresholds such as wide-screen cinema and the auteur theory, he traces a feedback loop in which the accidental details of film, seized upon by non-traditional spectatorship, could also become the conscious aesthetic vocabulary that might characterize a filmmaking practice, as well as a film culture. The present study will attempt to develop these insights, drawing them into a later American context, and directing them more specifically toward the relationship between sound, music, and the representation of the past.

The protagonists of Keathley's *Cinephilia and History* worked to popularize a French concept of auteurism that would eventually migrate to the American cultural sphere, to be supported by critics such as Andrew Sarris and contested by others, such as Pauline Kael. At the same time, American film critics of the sixties and seventies were also building upon developments in postwar film culture that manifested in idiosyncratic "cult" viewing strategies and performative writing of critics such as Parker Tyler and Manny Farber.⁵² As we saw in the writing of Sarris and Kael that opened this chapter, whether they appreciated the ethos of auteurism or not, intellectually adventurous American critics of the sixties (particularly those, like Kael, with a colorful writing style) increasingly adopted a mode of responding to cinema that located pleasures in moments of subjective imagination, sensual tangibility, and evocations of sensory presence.

To be clear, the position I am maintaining here requires a broader application of the term "aesthetic"—a term which Keathley pointedly contrasts with the objectives of Bazinian realism, which he identifies less as an aesthetic and more as a *psychological* category.⁵³ Keathley is correct in that "aestheticism," understood as a self-conscious commitment to "quality" filmmaking as the production of beauty, was in fact a point of departure for the French New Wave, who sought by contrast to capture not the traditionally "beautiful," but rather an improvisatory sensibility invested in fleeting sensory details. Nevertheless, although I depart from Keathley's prioritizing of psychology, I do so in order to explore the implications of a Bazinian "real" for the aural gestures in New Hollywood Cinema that signify a sense of presence. The "reality" of the past in such representations is not the "aestheticized" storybook past of the traditional historical film. Instead of simply serving the purpose of a generic setting or a presentist allegory, the past becomes an exposed nerve—a site of raw sensory experience (*Bonnie and Clyde*), nostalgic memory (*American Graffiti*), or sensualist deconstructions of traditional mythology (*McCabe and Mrs. Miller*).

While the elements of film culture discussed thus far have primarily related to *interpretations* of New Hollywood Cinema and its broader historical era, many other historical changes in the American film industry offered a context in which a "cinema of sensation" might flourish. These changes pertained to both musical and non-musical soundtrack work in film, and they locate this study within not just an aesthetic context, but within an era of industrial history that saw the rise of sound design and the pop score. Shifts in film training and production contributed to this larger picture, as well as shifts in popular taste and the perceived commercial marketability of music in film.

Although the sixties and seventies saw commercial American filmmaking, in general, remain closely tied to Hollywood studios in terms of financing and distribution, the industry also saw a broader decentralization of knowledge, ideas, and talent, as well as a gradual breakdown of the geographic centrality of Hollywood to film production. In addition to earlier trends of location shooting and runaway production (i.e., shooting internationally for economic reasons) the growth of other centers of filmmaking and culture was critical—especially New York City, whose theatrical, documentary, and independent film scenes were influential on New Hollywood aesthetics. This decentralization was also tangible in the training of filmmakers, with relevance for the soundtrack, newly understood as an extension of film style. Several older, established filmmakers of a more traditional background, such as Arthur Penn, Robert Altman, and Sam Peckinpah, found new niches and more industrial leeway for their unique sensibilities. Others, such as Peter Bogdanovich and William Friedkin, were of a younger generation but still received their formative training in the performing arts—such as theater and television. A third group, the so-called Film School Generation (or, less charitably, the Movie Brats) included George Lucas and Terence Malick, as well as Steven Spielberg and Francis Ford Coppola.[54] These were younger artists who, rather than (or in addition to) the traditional path of industrial apprenticeship also received formative training in the recently developed academic study of filmmaking, a course of study that gave them an unprecedented degree of immersion in film history, European art cinema, and the theoretical study of film. In general, the Film School Generation was also trained in elements of production and post-production that, under the old system, would have been the domain of self-contained studio departments, bureaucratically centralized and not necessarily in direct creative dialogue. Far from the model of an older studio director who might view anything beyond staging and shooting the film as somebody else's labor, these younger filmmakers were more inclined to embrace a culture of auteurism in which directors were sometimes deeply involved in the creative editing of both image and sound.

The creative, expressive use of sound in film is, of course, as old as film itself. It did not "begin" at any one point at which the pragmatic concerns of sound engineering were replaced with aesthetic ones. At issue, however, is a conceptualization of sound within filmmaking practice that has often rendered terms such as "creative" or "expressive" categorically inappropriate. As film scholar James Lastra has traced, since the beginnings of film sound, complex negotiations have varyingly located film sound as either an "art" or a "craft."[55] During the classical studio era, practitioners of sound recording, mixing, and editing tended to think of their work more as a craft—one that was commonly understood to be successful to the extent that it achieved a culturally determined benchmark of fidelity and unobtrusive stylistic transparency. This resulted in a generally accepted hierarchy of importance, favoring voice, sound effects, and music, usually ranked in this order of decreasing narrative privilege. Although we should be wary of this somewhat reductive view of studio era sound, this model had real staying power, and for good reason. The division of labor both from above (studio production) and below (trade unions) stood to benefit from institutional regularity and from unadventurously stable categories of "good" and "bad" sound.

In historical narratives tracing the development of film sound into the post–World War II era, the technologies of Dolby stereo are generally seen as perhaps the single most important technical breakthrough facilitating a new expressive model for the use of sound, particularly following the massive success of *Star Wars* (1977).[56] Dolby allowed for higher-fidelity sound, wider dynamic range, and increased potential for complex mixing, and was a central component of the increasingly complex soundscapes of the new era of blockbuster films. Dolby is also closely linked to the emergence of the professional category of the "sound designer," a credit first officially claimed by Walter Murch for his work on *Apocalypse Now* (1979). The term "sound design," used in contrast to traditional categories of recording, editing, and mixing, bore implied connotation of creative composition (along with the labor involved in managing the spatialized deportment of stereophonic sound), rather than classical associations of functional craftsmanship.

It is important to realize, however, that technology facilitating new directions in film sound existed prior to both the widespread industrial adoption of Dolby and the concept of the "sound designer" as specifically identified. In dealing with creative sound work prior to the mid- to late seventies, scholars have tended to focus on sound *auteurs*, or directors with a unique authorial approach to sound.[57] But broader, frequently overlooked technological changes also began to impact film style in the fifties, related to both stereophonic sound and to the adoption of magnetic tape recording. Initially, these two innovations were directly connected: widescreen projection formats used larger film gauges (such as 65 or 70 mm), allowing more room on the film itself, onto which multiple strips of magnetic recording could be printed, facilitating multichannel encoding for stereophonic exhibition prints. As interest in stereophonic exhibition formats temporarily faded, however, the use of magnetic tape for *recording* persisted, even though these recordings were eventually mixed down and printed as a single track of monaural optical sound.[58] Magnetic sound recording could also be layered into a soundtrack with less noise, encouraging more complex, layered mixing, innovative recording practices, and, gradually, a more creative, compositional approach that would become identified as sound design.[59]

Contemporaneous with these shifts in film sound aesthetics, long-gestating developments in film music were also brought to a head in the context of the New Hollywood Cinema, its economic realities, and its stylistic values. Throughout the postwar period, the characteristic sounds of jazz, pop, and post-tonal art music had gradually made inroads into film music composition, hybridizing with the syntax of the classical score.[60] In admittedly broad and relative terms, film music style became more diverse, frequently favoring idiosyncratic instrumentation and textures, and often more modernist in its larger aesthetic outlook. Filmmakers drew upon new musical sounds to give films a modern feel appreciable to new (and often younger) audiences. Pop theme songs and eventually entire soundtrack albums became an increasingly important part of film marketing. By the late sixties and early seventies, it had also become common for the traditional place of classical underscoring to be held by pop songs (whether original or compiled) or by original underscoring composed in a recognizably popular style.

Older and more established composers often looked upon such practices with suspicion or even unconcealed disdain. The reasons for these attitudes were diverse, including perceptions of lazy commercial opportunism on the part of the film industry, as well as by the conviction that contemporary pop music could not possibly approach the artistic quality and universal dramatic signification possible in the classical score. This latter concern was sometimes motivated by composers' desire for aesthetic and cultural capital comparable to that of concert music. On a practical (and perhaps empathetically understandable) level, many composers were also all too aware that the late sixties and early seventies were a time of economic recession and strain in the film industry, an environment that tended to amplify careerist instincts. But a tone of condescension toward contemporary popular music is frequently tangible in this literature, and all too frequently went uncontested by its readers and critics.[61]

More recently, scholars such as Jeff Smith, Julie Hubbert, and K. J. Donnelly have attempted to escape these biases, coming to terms with the pop score as a unique and complex aesthetic entity unto itself. Smith, in particular, has broadened our understanding of the hybrid relationship between the original composed pop score and classical film music style. With the growing importance throughout the fifties and sixties of soundtrack album marketing, Smith has shown, composers began to adapt the precepts of classical style to a variety of popular music styles. However, rather than devolving into hyper-commercialized expressive emptiness, this development enabled film music to speak in complex new forms, blending together older expressive formulas with contemporary sounds.[62] Compiled pop scores, as Smith's discussion of *American Graffiti* shows, can similarly adapt preexisting music to the traditional narrative strategies of film music, while maintaining unique forms of expressivity resulting from the recognizability of the musical material. This aesthetic came to participate reciprocally in the music video genre and, in many cases, to play cannily upon preexisting cultural affiliations.[63] Throughout the films studied in this work, we will see these dynamics of historical and contemporary, as well as classical, popular, and modernist musical styles play out in a variety of ways in relation to the topic of the past.

Overview of Chapters

It is the contention of this study that the use of sound design, popular music (whether original or compiled), and combinations of more traditional film music with these innovative elements could have profound effects on the representation of the past as an experiential present. Recognizably compiled music, as well as the use of the discrete, self-contained musical artifact of the pop song (as opposed to the more flexible, dramatically adaptable classical score) could manipulate an audience's subjective identification with the film world in a ways that had distinctly temporal implications. These could range from creating a tension between imagined positions of dramatic interiority and exteriority, to oscillating between objective and subjective modes of expressivity to convey alienating distance or empathetic closeness to the film characters and their worlds. It is this "frame-like" quality of the musical soundtrack that this study will trace in terms of its use in representing the past. What does it mean, for example, for music on the one hand to draw its audience empathetically into a time other than their own, while on the other hand pushing them outside of the representation, reminding them of their own temporal distance from what is being depicted? In this way, music can playfully manifest "reality effects" by oscillating between sensibilities of dramatic immediacy and mechanized, ironic distance.

Chapter 1 explores these issues in *Bonnie and Clyde* (1967). I characterize the film's sound design as a self-reflexive meditation on the photo- and phonographic capturing of human presence through mechanical mediation. This capturing, I argue, functions as a metaphor for historical narrativity, a confining discourse to which the film seeks alternatives through a stylistic language that conjoins visceral realism and ephemeral abstraction. Contributing to a developing scholarly discourse on the aesthetics of the pop score, I also read *Bonnie and Clyde*'s bluegrass score as an extension of the film's concerns with sensory immersion and mechanized, alienating distance. Ultimately, these readings are grounded within the film's countercultural reception, which drew upon shifting perception of both bluegrass and the concept (borrowed from avant-garde theater) of the "Happening," to draw out the paradox of articulating the contemporary self *through* the actuality of the historical past. *Bonnie and Clyde*'s status as a popular narrative film fiction, rather than a product of "authentic" avant-garde or underground cinema might seem to limit the role of the Happening to that of an appropriative, superficial buzzword. I argue, however, that within the aesthetics of New Hollywood Cinema, however mainstreamed, *Bonnie and Clyde*'s soundtrack nevertheless evidences a striking investment in the immediacy of sensory experience.

It is a critical commonplace that the genre of the Western engages with myth. But the topic of what myth actually *does* in the Western remains far from exhausted. Most frequently, myth has been read as a gesture of cultural mystification, obscuring the systemic violence that accompanied America's westward expansion. Within the critically self-conscious style of New Hollywood, the genre of the revisionist Western was thus understood to intervene with a "counter-mythic" discourse. In Chapter 2, I test the conceptual limits of this counter-mythic discourse with readings of two seemingly very different revisionist Westerns, *Butch Cassidy and the Sundance Kid* (1968) and *McCabe and Mrs. Miller* (1971). In doing so, I position the category of myth not in its more familiar designation as a cultural narrative, but rather as a spatiotemporal form of experience, a sensibility concerned with conveying an imagined time-outside-of-time. Despite a tendency in critical literature to perceive the highly successful *Butch Cassidy* as ersatz fluff and *McCabe and Mrs. Miller* as an authentic work of counter-Hollywood resistance, I argue that these two films might be revealingly compared for the underlying similarities in their approach to conveying a mythic experience of the past. In this sense, Burt Bacharach's pop score for *Butch Cassidy* and the use of Leonard Cohen's songs in *McCabe and Mrs. Miller* distinctly position each film within a mythic space of timelessness, in which the immediate present of a contemporary experience and the distancing effects of historicity might be imagined to blur and freely flow into one another.

From a consideration of myth and sound in the revisionist Western, I pivot in Chapter 3 to a consideration of a related, yet distinct body of American myth: the image of Southern California as framed through the genre of film noir—specifically the Los Angeles of Roman Polanski's *Chinatown* (1974). This chapter examines the role of Jerry Goldsmith's celebrated jazz-modernist score as a negotiation of mythic temporality and expressive immediacy. Mirroring the futurist primitivism of his earlier work on *Planet of the Apes* (1968), Goldsmith's *Chinatown* score embraces sounds characteristic of avant-garde music, a "presentist" gesture that helps to allegorize the film's tale of corruption for the world of the seventies, negating the "period" quality often associated with genre pastiche. At the same, however, Goldsmith's jazz-inflected theme and Polanski's neoclassicist formalism balance its seventies allegory with a paradoxically "present" sense of the past.

This chapter attempts to explore this dimension of the film through a phenomenological reading of timbre in film music, drawing upon philosopher Gaston Bachelard's understanding of elemental images and the poetic imagination. Extending and developing the reading of myth in Chapter 2, I argue that in *Chinatown* the mythic suspension of time doesn't locate us in a ruefully impossible, imagined time outside of time. Rather, building upon film scholar Dana Polan's reading of the film, I argue that *Chinatown*'s soundtrack illustrates the crumbling of a comprehensible, historical rationality defined by political corruption, and instead reveals the incomprehensible mythic irrationality of paranoia. By drawing upon jazz and the avant-garde, two registers complexly associated with both the primitive and the cosmopolitan, Goldsmith's score delimits the edges of a vortex, at the bottom of which lurks something worse than mere corruption—an archaic, primal chaos at the root of civilization itself. Rather than offering an imagined escape from modernity, the elemental sounds of *Chinatown* allows us to imagine modernity's repressed terrors.

As Julie Hubbert has shown, in the New Hollywood era, several prominent filmmakers conspicuously limited their use of underscoring, relying upon the use of radio, jukeboxes, and other playback devices as source music, in order to articulate an aesthetic of realism indebted in part to documentary aesthetics. Often, in films such as *Mean Streets* (1973), the device of compiled scoring via diegetic radio became a way to emphasize contemporaneity, using the conspicuous variety of popular music to break down the stylistic homogeneity of the classical score and extending the aesthetics of the *auteur* director into the soundtrack. At the same time, however, films set in the past have traditionally used the temporal specificity of diegetic popular music as a narrative and aesthetic tool to suggest a historical setting. In Chapter 4, I explore what happens when these two trajectories overlap, with compiled pop scoring represented as mediated by radio transmission in *The Last Picture Show* (1971) and *American Graffiti* (1973). Both films are set in the precountercultural fifties and early sixties, and both are complexly invested in the aesthetics of nostalgia. As in Chapter 2, I compare two films that bridge critical thresholds of perceived countercultural authenticity, with the earlier film frequently understood as authentic American art cinema, and the latter often reductively criticized as a conservative idealization of the precountercultural era. Both films, however, adopt the image of the radio signal as a technological-aesthetic metaphor for melancholy temporal distance. The image of the transmitted signal in these films thus belongs to an aesthetics of sound, music, and presence that is not reducible to binary logic of progression and regression. Rather, they articulate an attitude to the past defined by the nostalgic desire to preserve, conjure, or otherwise re-experience what has been lost to time—a desire that paradoxically exists only within a melancholy awareness of the impossibility of recovery outside of imagined experience.

Chapter 5 engages director Terrence Malick's philosophical and aesthetic preoccupations in a reading of his first feature, the "lovers-on-the-run" drama *Badlands* (1973). Malick's concerns with sensory immersion, eccentric irony, and the relationship between history and human experience all cultivate in *Badlands* a sensibility of phenomenal presence as a complex ontological ground for the characters' (and audiences') sense of being in the world. My goal is to focus on *Badlands* as a specifically audiovisual exploration of these existential and phenomenological concerns, exploring how the film's two primary sources of compiled non-diegetic classical music (the pedagogical music of Carl Orff and Gunild Keetman and the early compositions of Erik Satie) function in the film as active philosophical agents, cultivating embodied states of play and ambiguous melancholy as we strive to create meaning from the raw temporal immediacy of experience. The past, in *Badlands*, is practically non-existent, paradoxically akin to a sense of pure immanence in material reality.

In the impoverished language of commercial advertising, the array of reality effects with which this book is concerned might serve to express the past in touristic terms: offered up to us "as if we were there"—locating the past as if it were a spectacle of exotic realism mounted for our pleasure and consumption. But in the far richer language of poetic hermeneutics, the past may be conceived of as an undiscovered world that we can imaginatively explore, both within and, potentially, beyond of the boundaries of historical narrativity. We are given in these films a sense of the past that conveys an effect of sensual, tangible presence. This past is not "history," per se, as much as it is "that-which-once-was." Of course, given that these are fictional films, we might rather characterize their worlds as "that-which-once-*wasn't*." In this way, all of the films discussed in this work, to varying degrees, are overlaid with the darker, more pessimistic sensibilities of their era. The various escapes provided by myth or nostalgia, or by fleeing into the redemptive utopian spaces outside of historical narrativity, may all be understood as temporary, fleeting, or simply the deceptions of false consciousness. But it is through this paradox that the idea of temporal experience, as it is pursued in the chapters that follow, maintains a unique critical dynamic: truly empathetic to the desires and dreams of the film world, yet not allowing for mystical absorption into it. This dynamic, in fact, might not be a bad conceptual model, not only for approaching the aesthetic, ethical, and cultural legacies of the New Hollywood era, but also, in a broader sense, for negotiating the various legacies of America in the sixties and seventies.

1
Bonnie and Clyde and the Aural Imagination of American Counterculture

The Breakdown as a Happening

What is a breakdown? Musical etymologies would point us first to a traditional concluding dance in African American celebrations of the antebellum era (and their minstrel show imitations), distinguished by the propulsive rhythms of feet hitting the ground. Another use of the word, more direct to our purpose, points toward the term as a synonym for the hoedown— referring both to a tradition of rural American social dance itself and to the related musical genre. This genre was marked by aggressive tempos and ornate figuration, an Americanized version of the Old World "reel."[1] In both of these etymologies, the expectation is for speed, rhythmic complexity, and drive. The literary and pop-psychological connotations of the word itself suggest both uncontrollable forward motion and the moment when that motion comes to a sudden halt. It might bring to mind Bob Dylan's popular anecdote describing the playing of Appalachian banjo virtuoso Roscoe Holcomb as possessing "an untamed sense of control"—dexterity that teases its own limits, a spectacle of abandon.[2]

The most famous breakdown in *Bonnie and Clyde* (1967) is a 1949 recording of "Foggy Mountain Breakdown," by bluegrass stars Lester Flatt and Earle Scruggs, which is used multiple times as compiled underscoring over the course of the film. But we might extend the concept even further: machines break down in *Bonnie and Clyde*—stolen cars crash or are shot to pieces; characters break down as well, confronting their mortality and dying in inglorious, nervy spasms. And yet these breakdowns are governed by a larger sense of order and structure, always existing on a line dividing chaos from order, raw realism from stylistic mannerism. These dramatic dynamics were clearly important to screenwriters Robert Benton and David

Newman, who in their pre-shooting script, even without identifying the specific selection by Flatt and Scruggs that had accompanied their writing sessions and would eventually appear in the finished film, nevertheless included the phrase "wild country breakdown music" (or some variant) periodically throughout the script.[3] Aside from these notes, however, the pre-shooting script doesn't place much emphasis on music, and the emphasis that is there often serves to specify an intended *lack* of music at places where it might be perceived as too "Hollywood." The opening credits, for example, are specifically described as silent in the script.[4] Perhaps Benton and Newman were trying—in a script consciously adapting stylistic devices of the French *nouvelle vague*—to emulate that cinema's sense of musical restraint.

In particular, the early films of François Truffaut and Jean-Luc Godard often de-emphasized two characteristics that defined dramatic film scores in the classical Hollywood tradition: the close dramatic welding of leitmotifs to narrative development, and the unambiguous emotional amplification of image and narrative through a neo-Romantic musical language. In *Bonnie and Clyde*, we perceive that, by 1967, this common practice had itself begun to break down, infiltrated by other sounds and styles. *Bonnie and Clyde*'s underscore, by Broadway veteran Charles Strouse, plays by some of the inherited Hollywood rules, but also leaves ample room for hearing *Bonnie and Clyde*'s score against the grain, locating in its traditional forms of dramatic expressivity, but something else, as well—something wild and "untamed," but still very much part of a larger "controlled" style. The film thus represented in its soundtrack a characteristic New Hollywood blending of traditional genre filmmaking with sensibilities broadly suggestive of modernist art cinema, an overlap that would endear it to a growing American counterculture.

Although set in the past, *Bonnie and Clyde*'s aural world is self-consciously in the present tense. In historical films a quality of "pastness," or the past framed as historicized past, is perpetually in tension with a quality of "presentness," or the past as present—with the latter realized both as the film's narrative diegetic present and, often, as an allegory of the present moment in which the film is created and viewed. How might sound and music construct these forms of temporality in film? And how might this aural sensibility of the past situate *Bonnie and Clyde* within a broader context of American counterculture? My contention is that in *Bonnie and Clyde*, the soundtrack stages pastness and presentness in a state of dialectical tension. On the one hand, the film conveys the past as a visceral, raw present—a sort of "reality effect." On the other hand, it stages the past as a site of unrecoverable, lost materiality. This dialectical quality ideally suits a film that pushes boundaries of both self-conscious stylism and raw, often extremely bloody, realism—a "breakdown" that blends self-conscious stylistic abstraction with a sense of the wild, untamable Real. *Bonnie and Clyde* offers us a sort of *vérité*, fly-on-the-wall vision of the past. The nature of this past seems to resist the abstraction of lived experience into recorded history. Through a set of stylized gestures, the film suggests the presence of an uninflected existence seemingly situated beyond the view of historical mediation. It is this quality, I will argue, that locates *Bonnie and Clyde* within the context of the countercultural phenomenon of the Happening. Yet the past of *Bonnie and Clyde* is also, at the same time, "a foreign country."[5] This past is defined by a quality of temporal otherness in which compositionally crafted soundscapes and a modern musical sensibility locate us, as listening subjects, outside of its frame, reminding us of this inevitable externality.

Bonnie and Clyde's temporal sensibility plays out in both musical and nonmusical dimensions of the soundtrack. Through its sound design, the film embodies past actualities, drawing upon the unique possibilities of cinema to represent the past in a present tense. Strouse's pop score, with its bluegrass emulations of "Foggy Mountain Breakdown," despite being empathetically—even classically—fit to many scenes, also employs sudden, disorienting musical shifts and a mechanized, non-developmental approach to thematic material. As a result, music frequently confuses the viewer's investments of emotional empathy, creating an alienating frame around the historical diegesis. As compiled music, "Foggy Mountain Breakdown" gradually shifts from being an empathetically expressive musical artifact toward more "broken down" uses—interrupted, destabilized, or deeply ironic. In such moments, we are reminded that compiled film music is a sound object potentially both externalized and externalizing, an object that—as it recurs—draws our attention to the way in which it remains mechanically the same while the rest of the film changes around it.

A common creative gesture shared, to some degree, across a broad spectrum of the postwar American avant-garde was the attempt to transcend representation and engage with actuality. Extending this historical-aesthetic dynamic into the sixties, we might see the same concerns at play in various ways in avant-garde theater and film.[6] My intention in extending such readings to *Bonnie and Clyde* is not somehow to reclaim *Bonnie and Clyde* as a product of any specific avant-garde movement. Although the present reading will eventually consider *Bonnie and Clyde* alongside event-art characteristic of the decade in the theatrical genre of the Happening, a more proximate, and more popular sensibility, that nevertheless engages comparable ideas, may be found in screenwriters Benton and Newman's notion of mid-sixties American pop culture as an emergent ethos they termed "New Sentimentality." By focusing on Benton and Newman, however, I am not claiming that any one source of authorial agency intentionally created *Bonnie and Clyde*'s aural sensibility of the past. Rather, my reading adopts a diffuse, collective sense of authorship. In this way, I adopt film critic J. Hoberman's concept of the "Dream Life"—an imaginal cinematic topos that is both shaped and shared between a film and its culture at large, including the various forces involved in creating and interpreting film. My intention is to disentangle a variety of authorial strands as they claim importance including walk-on roles for players as diverse as star-producer Warren Beatty and session musician Doug Dillard. In addition to the more obvious agency of composer Charles Strouse, at certain points the film's larger soundscape was also inflected by director Arthur Penn's sense of mythic resonance and contemporaneity, by editor Dede Allen's connection to a New York School of filmmaking, and by screenwriters Benton and Newman, both of whom admired the French New Wave and whose journalistic work engaged a modish fascination with new understandings of experience.[7]

The notion of *auteur* cinema, imported from French criticism, became increasingly important to American film culture of the sixties. Auteurist interpretation also became a dominant lens through which the developing culture of American art house cinema defined creative, adventurous filmmaking.[8] Declaring their affinity with foreign art house cinema, Benton and Newman initially sent their draft of *Bonnie and Clyde* to director François Truffaut himself, in the hopes that he might consider making the film. In addition to the cool, romantic gangsterism of Truffaut's *Shoot the Piano Player* (1960), Benton and Newman specifically cited his *Jules and Jim* (1962) for the way in which it weaves a sense of immediacy and contemporaneity into its evocation of the historical past.[9] This latter idea draws our attention to *Bonnie and Clyde*'s exploitation of the critical attitude of "New Sentimentality."

Coined by Benton and Newman in the July 1964 issue of *Esquire*, "New Sentimentality" assessed recent cultural history as transitioning into a seemingly contradictory attitude: a modern, hip romantic sensibility that spoke to Benton and Newman's perception of the values of the Kennedy era as it progressed into the mid-sixties. Key New Sentimental concepts were the cynical valuation of the cultural "operator," as well as a sense of coolly unapologetic self-centeredness, privileging direct experience over traditional political or ethical values. Key New Sentimental couples freely crisscrossed between film and real life, encompassing JFK and Jackie, as well as Jean-Paul Belmondo and Jean Seberg's outlaw couple from Jean-Luc Godard's *Breathless* (1960). Benton and Newman would later acknowledge how the idea of the New Sentimentality had underscored *Bonnie and Clyde*, which they had begun to write soon after the response to their article convinced them that they had hit a nerve.[10] In particular, the New Sentimental blend of hipster existentialism and Pop-Art coolness—as well as its tightrope negotiation of ironic and sincere emotional investment—may be seen in the outlaws' media-savvy manipulation of their own celebrity, their romantic fatalism, and in the film's larger approach to the presence of the past. The past itself forms yet another point of New Sentimental engagement in the *Esquire* article, where the authors compare the pasts of Tolstoy ("Old") and Proust ("New"):

> The Motherland, the adulteress, the man of the soil, the intellectual, the Hero—these are Tolstoy's creations in Old Sentimentality. The operator, the manipulation of people in love, the vision of love as a fleeting episode in which any commitment brings pain and ineptitude, and most important now, the sense of the past as no different from today in terms of human behavior—that is all in Proust. He was the visionary of the New.[11]

The New Sentimental approach to the past thus bears a cool distrust toward traditional gestures of grand historical narrativity, favoring instead an emphasis upon the *experience* of the past through small, unmarked details.[12] As a writer practically synonymous with re-experiencing the past through memory, Marcel Proust is thus a particularly apt figurehead.

Appearing in 1964, the "New Sentimentality" article reads today more as a product of the early, rather than the later sixties: under "Politics," for example, Benton and Newman list as Old: "Marxism, Pacifism, SANE, Reform movements . . ." and as New, they identify "The C.I.A.," continuing, ". . . no longer shocked by corruption and stupidity in high places, we now admire the smoothie who didn't botch it up, the *coup* that worked."[13] By late 1967, when *Bonnie and Clyde* was released, this provocatively cynical celebration of Realpolitik would no longer hold sway in a counterculture increasingly informed by the antiwar movement and the politics of anticolonial liberation. Benton and Newman would themselves later reflect upon how their film had become a Vietnam text, appreciating this facet of the film's reception but remarking just how little Vietnam had been on their minds at the time of the film's initial creation.[14] Nevertheless, viewed as a context for *Bonnie and Clyde*, the New Sentimentality article demonstrates the roots of the film's attitude toward the past, forming a authorial thread running through these distinct cultural climates—a mode of conceptualizing experience that, allowing for some adaptive flexibility, links the sensibilities of the Beat era, the Kennedy era, and the era of the Happening.

Period Source Music and the "Deep Night" of the Past

Bonnie and Clyde's opening credits begin in silence, followed by the "click" of a camera and the sudden appearance of an anonymous photograph. A wearied woman sits with an infant. The woman wears a checkered blouse and the top of her forehead is in sharp relief to a black background. The left side of the child's face is slightly blurry, making the eyes appear uneven. The expressions are neither happy nor sad but are instead indefinable, as if—despite the obviously posed shot—they have been caught in the midst of some private everyday action (Figure 1.1).

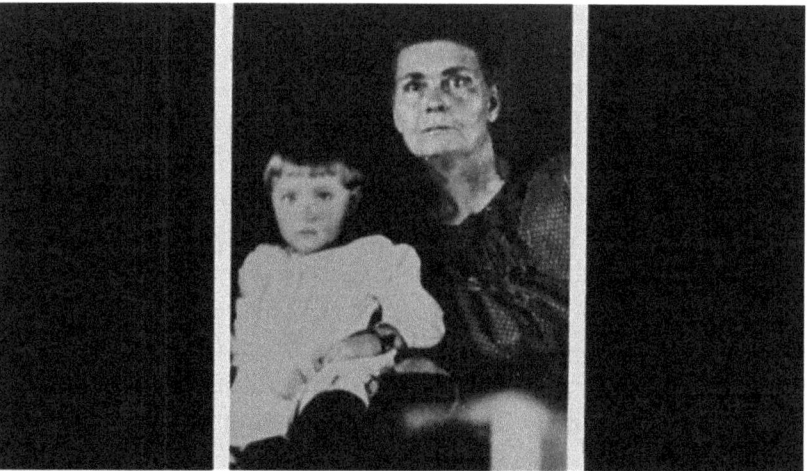

Figure 1.1 Opening credits sequence of *Bonnie and Clyde* (1967) at (0:00:10).
Screen capture from *Bonnie and Clyde*. Warner Bros. Home Video, 2008. DVD.

Of course, the viewer will probably not get all this in the cinema, where, at the mercy of projection, the image flashes for slightly longer than a second before vanishing.[15] New photographs continue to appear and then vanish in a slightly accelerating rhythm until a title screen appears, its letters gradually reddening as if blood were seeping through the fabric of the screen (0:00:10).[16]

Nearly all commentators on this sequence recognize the influence of photographers Walker Evans and Dorothea Lange, whose work has acquired a privileged status in the iconography of the Great Depression. Many also discuss the narrative patterns that the images articulate. Photographs of gradually older boys precede Beatty's name and girls for Dunaway's, establishing our hero and heroine's rural upbringing as an abstractly implied background. Themes also emerge: images of hunting and gunplay locate violence as an element characteristic of American life; images of impoverished families introduce a layer of social commentary, playing again upon Depression-era cultural iconography, as well as collectively establishing what Carolyn Geduld has identified as the film's "tribal" aspect, positioning the extended family unit, or clan, in conflict with the collectivized whole of modern civil society.[17]

The temporal structure of the sequence also draws our attention to its specifically photographic nature. The photographs hardly appear before they disappear. They linger most tangibly, perhaps, as retinal afterimages on the black leader that engulfs them—fragments of a past that, even as they are made manifest, are already gone. The sequence reminds us of the ways in which the photographic image is a locus of both indexical reality and fragile ephemerality. A photograph is an image created by the action of light waves on chemically treated paper, exposed for only a brief interval of time. The photographer traditionally *frames* an image but does not *create* the image in the manner of a painter with a brush and palate. The photograph's indexical nature thus allows it to hold a privileged relationship to objective reality, not just an image, but a trace of something that has been. The mechanically created image and its unique ontology, a persistent theme in the reception and theory of photography since its origins, would come to inform film theory as well, in particular the realist theories of André Bazin. For Bazin, the narrative fiction film—despite the inevitable artifice of filmmaking, of which Bazin was well aware—nevertheless draws upon a sense of objectivity, a *there-ness* to both image and, if we stretch our imaginations, to sound, as well. In the initiatory blackness, the "click" of the camera may be perceived as not just simultaneous to the image—it seems to create the image, calling it into existence.[18]

Bonnie and Clyde is a film in which characters are constantly creating, posing for, and exchanging photographic images. Throughout the film, the photographic click becomes an aural motive for the act of memory and image-creation. Unlike a classical leitmotif, however, it is marked more by a sense of mechanical, objectifying sameness than by its capacity for dramatic development. As the title sequence continues, gradually, Rudy Vallée's recording of the song "Deep Night" (1929) fades into audibility (0:00:48). Lacking any narrative explanation (such as a visualized diegetic source) "Deep Night" seems to be serving the mood-establishing function traditionally held by original main title music, but it also strikingly departs from these conventions. Whereas opening credits music typically sets a decisive tone for a film, the slow fade-in is more indecisive and ambiguous. Similarly, song lyrics typically prompt audiences to interpret them as somehow foreshadowing or setting a tone for the film as a whole, but these lyrics are of little help in this regard. As a lush spinning-out of the popular topos of an exotic nighttime rendezvous, the lyrics of "Deep Night" willfully deny literalistic connection to the images—unless, of course, the eponymous "Deep Night" is that of the past itself.

In 1967, Vallée—one of the most popular American entertainers of the thirties and forties—was still a broadly familiar performer and cultural personality and could hardly have been described as obscure. But although "Deep Night" had been a hit for Vallée in 1929, the song would nevertheless probably *not* have been considered among the most iconic of old pop standards, nor would it have been particularly tied to a familiar cultural iconography of the thirties.[19] In this way, we might imagine it connoting to audiences a sense of the past that was something *other* than an iconic marker of period. Rather, we might imagine this dreamlike, slightly less well-known song playing like a discovery from your parents' records collection, or from a personal memory of communal radio listening.[20] Beyond simply "fitting" the period, "Deep Night" suggests a mode of expression that will return throughout Bonnie and Clyde—a sensation of "overhearing" the past, of the past as an unmediated actuality, standing outside the categorizations that consign it to meaning.

Period music appears frequently at later points in the film, although, in such instances, its spatial placement characterizes it far more clearly as diegetic source music. Source music naturally tends to become a pointed concern in the historical film, as filmmakers seek to use it to substantiate the period setting. While in the New Hollywood era, filmmakers such as Peter Bogdanovich put considerable energy into researching the temporal specificity of source music, most treated this element of the soundtrack more cursorily or with broadly iconic (even clichéd) gestures. This could have the effect, as Fredric Jameson has argued, of creating a flattened-out, nostalgic image of "period" signifiers that consequently limits our capacity for meaningful critical engagement.[21] In the film music literature, the discussion of such "obvious" source music cues has tended to rest upon a restricted range of interpretive options that might be summed up by the oversimplifying conclusion that music simply "sets the scene."

Bonnie and Clyde's strongest example of such foregrounded period music is its use of "We're in the Money," by stalwart Warner Brothers songsmiths Harry Warren and Al Dubin (0:28:05). With clips from the musical Golddiggers of 1933, the film uses Ginger Rogers's Depression-busting insouciance to create an explicitly ironic counterpoint to the Barrow gang's desperation as they hide in a movie theater after killing a bank teller in a holdup.[22] "We're in the Money" thus registers as a calculated effect—an authorial trace that could hardly have been accidental. A sudden hard cut from the chaos of the robbery to Rodgers singing the title lines makes the textual irony particularly clear. Beyond the lyrics, the music and sound design are also sources of ironic juxtaposition, both in the bubbling energy of Rogers's performance and in the "canned," tinny resonance of the scene's representation of theatrical sound. These ironic gestures erect an audible barrier and pointed contrast between the Barrow Gang's grim circumstances and the world of escapist Hollywood fantasy.

Although all the film's source cues clearly function as period music, not all of them work in this way—and some are considerably closer to "Deep Night" than to "We're in the Money." Some lack iconic recognizability or are mixed into the soundtrack at a low level to suggest an overheard, indeterminate environment. These "backgrounded" cues frequently waft from radios as the gang rests from the road or amuses themselves during stretches of tedium. In another such example, an instrumental recording of "The Shadow Waltz" (also Warren and Dubin) is heard as the gang hangs around, teasing C. W. about his new tattoo (1:14:23). For some listeners, a small strand of intertextual connectivity might be drawn from the fact that "The Shadow Waltz" and "We're in the Money" were both featured in Golddiggers of 1933.

But this connection is neither dwelt upon nor brought to the forefront of our attention—rather, it hovers below the surface.[23]

Ultimately, however, it is these "backgrounded," ambiguous uses of diegetic music, rather than the forceful irony of "We're in the Money," that give the film its distinctive character. We might consider an image articulated by Benton and Newman in an interview from the summer of 1968. Alluding to actor George Raft's famous portrayal of a coin-flipping hoodlum in *Scarface* (1932), the writers reflect upon the importance of *Bonnie and Clyde*'s low-key moments—such as when the gang is hiding from the law, settling into a fragile, skewed version of traditional domesticity—pondering "all those scenes that were in the George Raft movies but were never in them, which is when George Raft went back to the house and listened to the radio."[24] Likewise, period source music often sits both low in the mix and low in our consciousness—the musical equivalent of imagining those off-screen moments when the world created by cinema departs from our attention— the temporal ellipses characteristic of narrative film's editorial excision of the banal minutia of living. From a dramatic perspective, the implications of this environmental wallpaper might seem minimal, but it is this very minimal quality that encourages us to view *Bonnie and Clyde* around the edges of the drama, encouraging us to engage with the unassuming details that suggest a distinctively imagined world.

Sound Design and the Machine

Taken as a whole, *Bonnie and Clyde*'s sound design generally preserves the traditional aural hierarchies of classical Hollywood cinema, privileging above all else what Michel Chion has categorized as narrative-driving "theatrical speech."[25] In isolated set pieces, however, vocal speech becomes decentered and supplanted in importance. These interludes tend to convey a sensibility distinctly oriented toward the expression of temporal ephemerality and physical presence. Mechanical sound becomes one such aural trope in the film. Later, we will consider the human voice as another. *Bonnie and Clyde*'s mechanical sounds, like its use of source music, is alternately backgrounded or foregrounded, subtly connotative or physically assaultive. Studies of *Bonnie and Clyde* have frequently singled out the film's opening scene for its unconventional visual editing. The opening credits dissolve onto an extreme close-up of Bonnie's lips, initially denying us a secure establishing shot (0:02:13). Naked and bored, she applies makeup and paces the room like a caged animal. Jump cuts and excised frames create an erratic, nervy feel, resonant with Bonnie's evident frustration. Throughout the film, similar edgy, "rule-breaking" visuals helped to position *Bonnie and Clyde* as a herald of New Hollywood style. But what do we hear? We hear a chirping bird, revealed by a medium shot to be emanating from a cage within the room. We also hear a repetitive off-screen noise, low-pitched and only faintly audible, like a mechanical heartbeat. Even as the editing of the visual image is fragmented, challenging our sense of conventional editing as a transparent representation of temporal experience, the rhythm of this dull pulsation never changes, becoming a sort of inflexible "aural cage," in which the distraught image flutters like a trapped bird.

When Bonnie eventually rushes outside to join Clyde, their dialogue shifts our attention away from the sound, dramatically neutralizing it, at the same time as the exterior shot's visual background (panning to follow the character) reveals that Bonnie's house is next to an industrial plant (0:05:22). This pattern of withholding and revealing the identity of an omnipresent mechanized sound allows us to read the noise as what Michel Chion has dubbed the "acousmachine." The acousmachine extends Chion's concept of the *acousmêtre*, or "sound-being." But whereas the *acousmêtre* is a cinematic voice that resists visualization and, as such, is understood to be the site of uncanny power (a particularly familiar example being the voice of Mrs. Bates in *Psycho*), the acousmachine is not a human voice, but rather a mechanical sound of ambiguous origin whose lack of onscreen explanation generates a sense of tension, creating the impression that it exercises a controlling power over the visual field.[26] And yet, at the same time, what we are hearing is also "just" *a noise*—a verisimilar detail of the world Bonnie inhabits. By grounding and "caging" the image, the thumping noise also grants it a sense of realistic temporality that the image itself lacks, but this temporality is understood as mechanical—a stultifying container for Bonnie's dissatisfaction. The acousmachine is thus a gesture of both aural stylization *and* immersive realism. The thumping noise "frames" the past through an unconventional gesture, while, at the same time, actualizing it through a realistic use of ambient sound. Notably, it accomplishes this feat not with foregrounded aural spectacle, but rather with a small detail possessing an understated, ephemerally *overheard* quality that—in marked contrast to the experimental visuals of the same scene—does not actively draw our attention.

The juxtaposition between mechanical and natural sounds plays a key role throughout *Bonnie and Clyde*. Foregrounded wind effects particularly mark dramatic scenes such as Bonnie's anxious escape from the gang to visit her mother (1:07:56), the family reunion that follows (1:10:03), and the couple's culminating love scene (1:39:30). These effects convey the implied importance of the film's exterior landscapes. Whatever relationship this may or may not bear to historical reality, the physical world of Bonnie and Clyde is one in which these wide-open spaces provide both a rationale (boredom, social disenfranchisement, existential isolation) and an advantageous position (disconnection from the forces of civilized order) for engaging in anarchic criminality. At the same time, harshly juxtaposed to the film's murmuring radios, throbbing factories, and evocative winds, the mechanical sounds of *Bonnie and Clyde* can be also brutally loud—particularly the sounds of gunfire—reminding us that the soundtrack itself is a dynamic entity, capable not just of interiorized contrasts, but also of increasing and decreasing in overall amplitude. By Penn's own recollection, producer and star Warren Beatty was an important agent here, with his "hand on the levels" during press screenings.[27] It seems that the filmmakers wanted, essentially, to wound their audience with sound, to position the sound of gunfire as a force of brute physical impact. While Penn's gritty aesthetic priorities and Beatty's desire to shock and awe audiences left an evident mark on post-production editing and perhaps even exhibition practice, however, these aesthetic values were already anticipated as early as the pre-shooting script. The script's description of the battle with the police in Joplin, for example, specifically reads "the audience should be assaulted" by the sound of gunfire. When a posse later quasi-ritualistically shoots up the gang's car to prevent their escape, it is "a noise so loud as to be an almost impossible sound."[28] The desired goal, it seems, was not "realistic" loudness, but rather a hyper-real, "impossible" intensity.

In all of these examples of mechanistic and mechanical representation, however varied they are in decibels and expressive character, sound contributes to a central tension between stylization and realism, a tension that lies at the heart of how *Bonnie and Clyde* evokes a sensibility of the past. Despite the fact that all the sounds in *Bonnie and Clyde* are duly encoded on celluloid—artifacts of mechanical reproduction—we may nevertheless read into the paradoxical "there-ness" of *Bonnie and Clyde*'s machine sounds a broader discourse of sound as a privileged medium of both corporeal immediacy and fugitive transience, one that is present not just in the affective gestures that reach out from the screen to assault us, but also in those that imaginatively lure us *into* the screen.

Bluegrass and the Sixties Pop Score

Bluegrass first enters the film with its characters' headlong plunge into criminality, underscoring Bonnie and Clyde's first robbery with the riotous energy of "Foggy Mountain Breakdown." For an era in which music was rarely commented upon in film criticism, the film's distinctive music attracted an unusual amount of mainstream critical attention, both positive and negative. In the film's reception, the use of "Foggy Mountain Breakdown" as compiled music has tended to overshadow the original underscoring composed by Charles Strouse and performed by a small studio ensemble led by banjo player Doug Dillard.[29] In its totality, however, *Bonnie and Clyde*'s underscore is a fascinating and innovative example of the sixties pop score. The expressive dynamics of this score, I will argue, represent another critical venue for the film's engagement with the idea of the past.

As we saw in greater detail in the Introduction, filmmakers in the sixties increasingly composed original scores employing styles familiar to audiences from popular music, and, in the later sixties, increasingly employed compiled popular music as underscoring. *Bonnie and Clyde* represents a mixture of both traditions. Despite a critical backlash against the pop score—and especially the pop *compilation* score—voiced by some established composers, many of the expressive functions of the classical score were simply translated to a new stylistic language, invested with new rhythmic, timbral, and formal properties, as well as newly discovered (and readily exploited) audience accessibility and marketability.[30] A closer look at Strouse's score reveals some comparable influence of the classical Hollywood film score. All of Strouse's underscoring in the finished film engages securely traditional formal and expressive tropes such as "transition music," "chase music," or "love music." The same may be said for the compiled uses of "Foggy Mountain Breakdown" on the soundtrack. Taken as such, the film's music largely fulfills expected classical functions.

But at the same time, the placement of this music and its relative invariability over time also call attention to the music's more modern, distanced relationship to the action. Strouse's score thus operates according to traditional expectations, but also challenges them from the inside with an element of mechanical alienation. To a degree, this "cooler," more distanced relationship to dramatic action might be said to be broadly characteristic of the pop score as a whole, especially in a decade when its departures from a classical sound were still in the process of being naturalized. The familiarity of popular music, its ear-catching use of melodic hooks, its self-contained formal structures (in the case of popular songs or tunes), and its tendency to resonate with audiences' extra-filmic cultural affiliations (as Jeff Smith and Anahid Kassabian have both shown) can also work against its classical invisibility and seamless audiovisual integration.[31] In an edgy, provocative film such as *Bonnie and Clyde*, these tendencies might be amplified even further.

In making this claim for the music of *Bonnie and Clyde*, I am drawing, in part, upon what is frequently termed "anempathy" (or, confusingly, "counterpoint"): music that works *against* the visual field, often in an expressive register analogous to dramatic irony. But Strouse's music isn't *truly* anempathetic—in fact, it frequently draws upon a sense of empathetic presence, of *there-ness* that aligns us subjectively with the propulsive energy of the film's shootouts and car chases, or, in its softer moments, aligns us with the protagonists' emotional bond and the profound sadness of their deaths. Musically, this subjective alignment is analogous to the expressive work done by the film's sound, whether in the form of gunfire or melancholy winds. But the visceral affective energies specific to *Bonnie and Clyde*, critically, locate this expressive work not just in the representational language of narrative or characterization, but in the phenomenological language of experience. They also, at key points, seem to *turn against themselves*, to seamlessly veer between empathy and mechanical distanciation, as way of expressing a breakdown, an objectifying loss of control.

Clyde and Bonnie have just met. Excited by his prison background, she cajoles him into robbing a store and they escape together in a stolen car. As we hear "Foggy Mountain Breakdown," the film's first non-diegetic cue, the music clearly conveys excitement in the speed and exhilarating dexterity of Earle Scruggs's virtuosic picking as Bonnie launches herself at Clyde, only to discover his sexual impotence (0:08:20). Later in the film, two bluegrass-infused cues by Strouse clearly attempt to absorb Flatt and Scruggs's influence into newly composed material. The first is a pentatonic riff, which we shall here call "Theme A," first heard at (0:13:15). This theme functions within a set of narrative associations comparable to "Foggy Mountain Breakdown," in fact seeming to "take over" for Flatt and Scruggs, perhaps because more varied music seemed expressively desirable. In this scene, Clyde has just convinced Bonnie to ride with him by appealing to her desire to escape small-town living. Again, they steal a car, and again the music both marks a scene transition and empathetically expresses a thrill in flouting the law. This music draws us, as experients, into the film, while, at the same time, it's mechanical repetition begins to bring its externalizing nature into the foreground.

Even without extramusical considerations, however, we can still find subtle elements of objectifying alienation in the film's non-diegetic music, due to the mechanical, propulsive repetition within individual cues, and in the limited use of musical development across the multiple cues making up the film's musical structure. A second Strouse cue is first heard after Clyde's first bank robbery comically backfires when he inadvertently targets a bank that has recently failed. This cue, which we'll call "Theme B," is more laid back, a shuffling tuba bass and bent "blue" notes helping to give it a more bumptious, comic quality (0:19:40). After this point, however, with two very brief exceptions (the closing credits and a brief love theme), alternations of A, B, and "Foggy Mountain Breakdown" represent the entirety of the film's non-diegetic scoring—and this scoring takes up a strikingly *small* amount of screen time: roughly 13 minutes of a 110-minute film. By the late sixties, such minimal use of underscoring was becoming increasingly common, often—as Julie Hubbert has argued—with the intention of emphasizing a quality of realism by restraining the use of music in places filmgoers were most conditioned to expect it.[32] Examining the film's remaining bluegrass cues, we discover a continuation of the expressive and narrative associations that are established early on. The exhilarating Theme A returns after a grocery clerk attacks Clyde during a robbery (0:20:59). The comic Theme B returns as Clyde and Bonnie add members to their motley gang—the hapless mechanic C. W. Moss (0:24:17), as well as Clyde's blustery brother Buck and his priggish wife Blanche (0:39:09). "Foggy Mountain Breakdown" also returns for the film's most extended and exhilarating car chase, intercut with press interviews representing the Barrow gang's high point of complicity in their own media stardom (0:56:28).

This last scene—the longest cue in the film—requires additional comment. In a film inspired by the French New Wave, the audiovisual work in this scene represents *Bonnie and Clyde* at its closest to the radical style of Jean-Luc Godard. Throughout this chase, the collage-like soundtrack cuts between shots of the fast-paced action (accompanied by "Foggy Mountain Breakdown") with cuts (unexpected, out of sync with the musical phrases) back to the bank they have just robbed. In the cut-away shots, which lack any music, a preening cop recounts his death-defying experience (0:57:29), a farmer whom Clyde let keep his money dryly offers to bring "a whole mess 'a flowers to their funeral" (0:57:57), and the bank managers pose for a photograph ("*click!*"), proudly pointing to the bullet hole Clyde has left in their wall (0:58:18). As was stylistically typical in Godard's films of the early to mid-sixties, abrupt cuts to and away from non-diegetic music functionally jolt us into an alienated awareness of music as a normative force of emotional manipulation. These cuts, in addition, occur between different *non-musical* aural tempos—moving between panicked shouts, revving engines, and staccato gunfire to the plodding, comic theatricality of the cop and the farmer's folksy effusions. This sequence breaks us out of the uninterrupted, participatory thrill of the chase, and pulls us, instead, into a reflection on the complicity of "straight" culture in creating desirable celebrity-outlaws—and the discomforting awareness (which Bonnie and Clyde don't yet share) that this trajectory inevitably ends in death. Contrary to what we might imagine as a typically Godardian style, however, these "gaps" remain open no longer than they need to in order to make their point. As the scene progress, bits of bluegrass crowd in on the cutaway shots, gradually drawing them back to the energy of the chase and tying the sequence's moments of disjuncture into a synthesized, empathetic whole.

This sense of interruption (of "breaking down" the breakdown, so to speak) may be read across the staggered appearances of Strouse's bluegrass cues. Throughout the film, there are key moments where the rigidity of a musical pattern is brought to our attention and highlighted by the very fact of its rupture. After a disastrous bank robbery in which Clyde brutally murders a teller, for example, bluegrass scoring is conspicuous by its absence, dramatically undercutting any expectation for an exhilarating chase (0:27:20). The point here is not that Strouse's score, or even the film's use of it, represents a form of authentic "subversion." As has been pointed out, it is marked as much (or more) by its classically expressive synchronization with the film's narrative and visual qualities. But, at the same time, between the aesthetic cracks, it is possible to locate other, more alienating qualities in *Bonnie and Clyde*'s non-diegetic music. These "framing" qualities externalize us as audiovisual experients, pushing us outside of the film's temporality. This externalizing tendency infuses a sense of objective reality into the past of *Bonnie and Clyde*—by pushing us out, the past becomes viewable as a *thing*—not just a "story" but a *world* whose presence doesn't depend on us to exist. As much other technical considerations, such as the use of squibs to create realistic eruptions of blood, this sense of *thing-ness* functions as an aural "reality effect" accounting for the visceral discomfort of the film's shocking and controversial violence.³³ After all, perhaps the clearest possible example demonstrating a categorical overlap of a human being with a *thing*, or *object*, is the example of a corpse. These two experiences of the film world—subjectively empathetic and objectively detached—are not wholly separable, but rather dovetail disconcertingly with one another. Caught up in the experience of the breakdown, we might suddenly grasp an objectified sense of participating in a death drive. We might realize that we are hearing corpse music.

As the gang's fortune begins to turn and Bonnie, in particular, begins to foresee their inevitable violent end, new motivic material is belatedly introduced into the film. A lyrical love theme first appears when Bonnie and Clyde share an emotionally intimate moment in which she begs to see her family (1:09:33). This odd departure from the musical style we've come to expect emphasizes the tenderness that has developed in their relationship, which began as escapist kicks and develops into real love. And yet, in Strouse's score as a whole, repetition still far exceeds variation. When the bloodied gang, minus Blanche and Buck, who have been respectively captured and killed, steal a car and get back on the road, the bluegrass themes A and B limp back into action, but the music's previous associations with good-natured joviality now seem ironic, mechanical, and distanced (1:27:40). Similarly repetitious is the final occurrence of "Foggy Mountain Breakdown": after Bonnie's poetry is published in the newspaper, the libidinal thrill of carving his name into history—"You've made me someone they're gonna remember!"—liberates Clyde from his impotence and the couple has sex for the first time (1:40:10). As the camera pans up and away, we see the newspaper blow across the field, as Flatt and Scruggs fade into the soundtrack one final time. In its repetition, "Foggy Mountain Breakdown" now seems to link the thrill of criminality with the thrill of sex, and to tie together the pairs' celebrity image with the self-conscious creation of history. Thus, at first, nothing seems much out of order—despite the lack of a car chase, the sexual subject matter is, of course, appropriately exhilarating. But there is something anticlimactic, even ironic, in the way the camera focuses on that newspaper, of which Clyde is so proud, as it blows across the field, a paper-thin reminder of the ephemerality of things. The listener becomes even more disoriented by a sudden cut to an inaudible discussion in which we see C. W.'s father betraying the gang to Frank Hamer, the Texas Ranger who, after being humiliated by the Barrow

Gang, now orchestrates their final ambush. The effect is to further destabilize the meaning of the cue. Suddenly cut loose from its dominant expressive function, it acquires a decentered quality, foregrounding its nature as a prerecorded pop tune. This sense of mechanical repetition is only emphasized further, of course, by the fact that "Foggy Mountain Breakdown" is the same recording every time we hear it.[34]

One complaint sometimes levied against the compiled pop score was its lack of potential for dramatic development and the connotation of complex emotions.[35] Even abandoning this dated (and condescending) claim, however, we must admit that while the pop score could be richly expressive, the large-scale rhythm of its expressivity fundamentally differs from that of the classical score. This was not necessarily bound to be the case with *Bonnie and Clyde*, however, as is demonstrated by comparing the score of the finished film with the material that was evidently left out of it. Additional portions of Strouse's score are extant on the film's soundtrack album, released by the music industry arm of the film's distributor, the recently conglomerated Warner Bros. Seven Arts.[36] It seems likely, given the contents of this album as well as identical musical material that appeared in the film's theatrical trailers, that considerably more music was composed and recorded than was eventually used in the finished film.[37] A closer examination of this music reveals that much of Strouse's unused material was far less oriented toward bluegrass, and more oriented toward a variety of popular-leaning modern classical styles, including Copland-esque musical Americana, angular, jazzy dissonances à la Leonard Bernstein, and symphonic pop in the popular mode of Henry Mancini. If we assume (as is reasonable, given the economics of film production) that this soundtrack album was "filled out" to LP length with unused cues from the scoring sessions (rather than with additional material composed and recorded specifically for the album), then two larger points arise.[38] First, nearly all the modernistic, jazz-influenced, or symphonic material was left on the cutting-room floor, with the noteworthy exception of a melancholy love theme, to which we will return later. Second, the bluegrass ensemble—despite the overall brevity of the score—is maximized, spinning as much music as possible out of extremely condensed resources. *Bonnie and Clyde*'s score was thus a classical-pop hybrid that, it seems likely, became even more solidified as a pop score in the editing room. The mechanistic elements of *Bonnie and Clyde*'s score were not present due to lack of material, but rather by design.

What do we make of films that negotiate the modern aesthetics of the pop score in the diegetic terrain of the past? Rather simply being anachronistic, misplaced marketing gimmicks aimed at a youth audience—a common response among critics—perhaps such scores offer us a vantage point from which to rethink the shifting film music aesthetics of the sixties, less in terms of "composition" vs. "compilation," and more as the emergence of new ways of positioning the listening subject by holding in mutual tension the qualities of internalizing absorption and externalizing alienation from the world of the film. In the context of historical fiction, then, we might adapt this schema to describe an intersection of two temporal tropes, two distinct ways of experiencing the past, that are likewise held in tension. On the one hand, we have an ideal of subjective, empathetic involvement, in which music draws us into the past as an experiential present. On the other hand, however, the disjunctures, or "breakdowns," embedded into this unifying experience create a "reality effect" characterized by our perception of an objectified past held at an unbridgeable distance. And yet *both* of these modes convey the past in terms of its inassimilable reality, its *presence*—the former as a mythic, participatory experience, the latter as a past whose radical *otherness* lies in its imagined materiality.

Sound Design: Voices and Silences

The interaction of aural presentness and pastness in *Bonnie and Clyde*'s expressive use of non-musical sound may also be viewed through both the marked presence and absence of the human voice. As with the trope of mechanized sound, voices might be backgrounded or foregrounded, characterized either by a subtle sense of tangible, ephemeral presence or by a violent broaching of representational borders. Midway through the film, the gang holds a family reunion in an abandoned quarry. Visually, the sequence has a dream-like feel, created by the slightly slowed motion and by the lens filter used by cinematographer Burnett Guffrey. This is also a moment of musical disorientation. In the preceding scene, an emotional interlude between Clyde and Bonnie, we have first encountered the love theme, the film's only use of orchestral, rather than bluegrass, scoring (1:09.40). This romantic yet oddly curtailed cue dissolves quickly into a seemingly disconnected fragment of non-diegetic bluegrass (1:09:56), itself quickly evaporating into the ever-present wind effects that mark many of *Bonnie and Clyde*'s exterior scenes (1:10:04).

As it turns out, the music evaporates when it is most needed. The scene opens with an audiovisual montage, a stylistic gesture that traditionally compresses actions assumed to be discontinuous in time and space into a singular formal unit, typically smoothing over the discontinuous edges with music that continues across the cuts between shots. Here, by contrast, this work is done by the human voice. Voices bridge impossibly juxtaposed shots, impossible because the voice of a speaker in one shot bridges into the next shot, in which the same speaker has moved—as we hear, for example, when the voice of Bonnie's sister bridges a shot of a private conversation between the two women with a shot of the same sister in a larger group (1:10:10). We get the sense that time in this sequence is stitched together from faded images, akin to the family album around which the characters gather. Pushing the metaphor still further, it seems as if time is itself fraying at the seams, bleeding over its edges in prescient omens, as when a boy rolls down a dune, plays dead, and a clouded look crosses Bonnie's face at this foreshadowing of the final shootout (1:10:40).

This stylized, dreamlike sense of temporality relies upon the decentering of narrative speech, creating instead what Chion has called "emanation speech." Unlike "theatrical speech," emanation speech does not allow the voice its customary priority in advancing narrative action. In emanation speech, by contrast, speech is "one expression among others in the sensory world," comparable, Chion argues, to the actor's physical profile.[39] The prosaic, yet ritualized speech actions in this scene—saying grace, sharing family albums—are edited in a way that makes them seem to float above the surface of the action, tying the images together, but doing so with slender threads seemingly worn thin by the wind. These voices are fragile and don't say much to move things forward, in part because the montage has dissolved their linear causality. This de-theatricalizing mode of speech, with its anti-dramatic naturalism, further enhances the effect of unmediated observation—of overhearing the past. Penn would later recollect that, in moving from theater to film, he had been impressed by how "what people say in a scene is often the least important of its many aspects," indicating that unconventional approaches to speech in his films may be traceable to a newly expanded awareness of the possibilities of cinema.[40]

Penn's comment about the decentering of speech also raises the question of scenes that are deliberately "silent," not in the sense of lacking any sound, but created by the pointed absence of traditional scoring where we might have a strong expectation for its presence. We might draw a connection between the marked *lack* of music in the reunion scene and other pointedly unscored scenes in the film—such as Clyde and Bonnie's two awkward, abortive attempts at lovemaking. The first functions as a sort of aural detumescence, just after the first exhilarating statement of "Foggy Mountain Breakdown" winds down and the couple escape from their first holdup (0:08:47). Flush with the thrill of breaking the law, Bonnie jumps Clyde only to discover, in his words, that he "ain't no loverboy." The second, after Bonnie insists on staying with Clyde now that he is wanted for murder, results in even more awkwardly prolonged efforts and ultimate letdown (0:30:45). While the choice not to use the film's love theme in this second example might seem to make dramatic sense, emphasizing the abortive nature of the encounter and reinforcing dysfunctional sexuality as a motif in the film, it is difficult to avoid the sense that we are hearing not just an absence, but rather absence *used as a presence*. The quietness is no less penetrating than the gunfire at the final, climactic shootout. Every rustle of fabric, every nuance of background sound, every awkward gasp or grunt the characters make becomes foregrounded by music's absence; one can easily imagine a film viewer accustomed to traditional Hollywood musical practices spending the entire scene wondering when the music was going to start. The soundtrack feels deliberately *evacuated*, creating an extended reality effect—a symphony of body noise that grounds us, perhaps uncomfortably, in a corporealized present.[41]

An instructive comparison may be made, here, to a particular selection on the soundtrack album. Titled "I Ain't No Rich Man," this track follows form with the rest of the album by framing the music with dialogue excerpts from the movie. In this case, the music is framed by dialogue such that anyone who had seen the film would associated it with this second abortive sexual encounter, creating a sort of alternate, imaginary soundtrack that might well have represented Strouse's intentions for the scene at an earlier stage of post-production. "I Ain't No Rich Man" offers us the love theme at full, rhapsodic length—far longer than it appears, later, in the finished film, punctuated by gently dissonant wind and string choruses in gently rocking contrary motion—a musical motive which was used in one of the film's theatrical trailers, but appeared nowhere in the finished film.[42] The cue resembles the accessible mid-century modernism of Aaron Copland and Samuel Barber, a style that had long since been unidentifiable with the cutting edge of concert music but was actually no longer a particularly edgy gesture in film music, either. Composers such as Copland himself, as well as Leonard Rosenmann and David Raksin, had absorbed comparable techniques into a larger

Hollywood vocabulary in the fifties.[43] What *was* considered modern in film music style in 1967, however, was the pointedly minimal use of non-diegetic music. In comparison with the *Bonnie and Clyde* album, then, it seems as if the soundtrack of the film was not just made more popular by the selection of one musical type over another, but also by a process of subtraction, creating a space for the expressive *lack* of music.

Another marked use of voice in the film is found in the character of Frank Hamer. Although he clearly can speak, Hamer is a nearly mute character.[44] When he is captured by the gang, Hamer says nothing, the only sound he produces being to spit furiously in Bonnie's face as she is photographed play-kissing him (0:54:05), a pointed mark of establishment disgust toward the gang's aberrant sexuality.[45] Hamer's only lines occur after Clyde's sister-in-law Blanche has been blinded and captured in the shootout that killed her husband Buck. Sneaking into the cell unheard, Hamer manipulates Blanche's recently acquired disability, terrifying her by announcing himself suddenly, inches from her ear (1:35:00). Feigning sympathy through the persona of an unseen interlocutor, Hamer tricks Blanche into giving him a lead, and, in one of the film's most poignant shots, he silently slips out, leaving her to continue defending her dead husband's integrity to an empty room.

In *Bonnie and Clyde*'s sound design, the machine and the human voice form a conceptual spectrum. These two polarities resonate with the film's larger dialectic of stylism and realism, through the objectifying artifice of the machine and the voice, traditionally understood to be a marker of tangibly human presence. In exploring this dialectic, we might extend our discussion of representing the past through sound to an even broader set of metaphors. The machine *is history*: denatured repeatability and the translation of the ephemeral moment into an artifact. By contrast, the image of the voice suggests pastness, something that, once uttered, dissolves into air and is lost outside of human memory.[46] But, like the larger aesthetic dialectic onto which it may be mapped, these categories of inorganic and organic sound in *Bonnie and Clyde* are not truly polarities, but are, in fact, interconnected on a deeper level. The recording of Rudy Vallée speaks not just to the distanciation of its mechanized repeatability, but also conjures up its role in creating the aural fabric of everyday life. Recordings may document history—they may, so to speak, "set a scene"—but they can also speak to the rituals of irretrievable past experiences. The machine can become human. But the human can also become machine. As a near-silent character, speaking almost entirely to a character that has been blinded, Hamer is doubly disembodied—less a human being than a basic, mechanized drive, a distilled emblem of society's need to eradicate disturbances such as the Barrow gang. In turn, by vocally filling the emptiness with what we suspect might become her perpetual creed of exculpation, Blanche herself becomes something like a machine: the human voice as a broken-down, abandoned phonograph, unspooling her sounds into the empty air—an unnoticed footnote hovering on the margins of history.

Hearing, Feeling, and Being History

In his book *The Old, Weird America*—a study of Bob Dylan's "basement tapes" and their relationship to American folk mythos—music critic Greil Marcus attempts to convey the emotional tenor of the summer of 1967, a time particularly instrumental to the iconicity of the late sixties as a period of intense social conflict. Marcus draws upon the ending of *Bonnie and Clyde*, released that August, as an aural artifact, characterizing both "a season of loud noises" and conversely, a sense of disconcerting quietude—like being in the eye of a passing tornado:

> On the screen hundreds of rounds smashed into metal and bone. In the theater, you could hear every one of them, and with the sounds bouncing off the datelines of the newspaper you carried in your head you could hear every echo: Newark, Detroit, Saigon, Hanoi. . . . In the theater, Bonnie and Clyde stopped on a country road. Just before the police opened fire you heard birds singing, then like Clyde you heard them flutter off in fright. The day was so bright you could almost hear the sunlight. With the execution over, the police emerged from the bushes, their faces set; the silence was so complete, it was as if what you saw had made you deaf. That was the end of the movie.[47]

Marcus shows here how cinema audiences might experience sound as actuality as well as representation. The loud gunfire that forces him to rehearse a late-sixties horror show of domestic and foreign violence seems to physically assault the bodies of both characters and audience alike. The movie, of course, did not literally draw tommy-guns, riddle Marcus's body with bullets, and leave it dead by the side of the road, but it did the next best thing—hitting his sensorium with physical waves of sound, leaving its mark on both his consciousness and his battered eardrums.

This passage also shows the role that sound can play in the historical imagination. *The Old, Weird America* is not specifically a book about film, but it *is* about imagining and experiencing the past through sound. Sound inscribes into a historical moment a sense of present tense actuality by capturing fugitive, ephemeral perceptual details. It is one thing to represent history's loud, triumphal, or terrifying sounds—history's noise, so to speak. History, in a figurative sense, *is* noise—the noise of significant events and beings leaving their trace on a moving scroll. History (especially popular history) is akin to an electrocardiogram of social discourse: if something didn't make (or wasn't *allowed* to make) at least some noise, we simply wouldn't remember it. It is another thing, however, to represent history's quietude, or even its silences, as well as to convey an apprehension of a subjective state of being that registers and navigates the spaces in between the noise and the silence—to represent, so to speak, history's *hearing*—the physical ear of the past.

This notion of an "ear of the past" is a fanciful one, as is the notion that *Bonnie and Clyde* somehow transcended representation to communicate as an embodied actuality. That the film was received as *allegorical* of its cultural climate is inarguable, as the discourse of nearly every critic and interpreter of the film since its premiere clearly demonstrates. But to go beyond allegory to make a claim for a fictionalized artwork as an actuality may seem counter-historical, or even irrational. To be clear, I am not making a claim for *Bonnie and Clyde*'s mystical transubstantiation—or, at least, I am not making this claim in a critically naïve fashion. Nor am I claiming, necessarily, that even the most starry-eyed countercultural experient would not have recognized that *Bonnie and Clyde*, at least on one level, was *just a movie*, that is to say, that it was a *representation* rather than an *actuality*. But we are not discussing just "one level" of reality, here—we are discussing *Bonnie and Clyde* as a representation deeply intertwined with historically situated methods of engaging belief and fantasy—methods in which magical thinking should not necessarily be theorized away. More than any other film we will examine in this study, *Bonnie and Clyde* was not just directed at or broadly sympathetic with the counterculture, but was rather entirely "adopted" by it. Not only were its antiheroes appreciated allegorically, but there was also a sense in which the counterculture adopted the image of *Bonnie and Clyde* as a sort of ritualized costume, an artifice through which to act out one's life. One focal point of this cultural phenomenon was the film's unique sensibility of the past, including, potentially, its approach to sound and music. For the counterculture, *Bonnie and Clyde* projected a paradoxical sensibility of the *presentness of the past* as an actuality that superseded representation.[48] These paradoxical qualities are, perhaps, appropriately substantiated by film sound itself: a paradoxical medium, suggestive of and enacting itself through ephemeral experience, but also a repeatable, highly constructed and recorded artifact.

Bonnie and Clyde was deliberately conceived as a product of its own time, in which the thirties and sixties mirrored one another as periods of disillusionment and rebellious anger directed at established authority. Arthur Penn went so far as to note on multiple occasions the similarity between a shot in which a piece of Clyde's scalp is visibly blown away from his head to the Zapruder footage of the Kennedy assassination, and to proudly reflect on his perception that the film had been well received in Black militant circles.[49] The film's status as a watershed work was not the result of a slow accumulation of canonical status over time, but was instead foisted on it almost immediately upon release.[50] For all the ways in which *Bonnie and Clyde* was legitimately "of the moment," however, the film's reception by a growing American counterculture demonstrates not just an ideological *use* of the past, but also a radical overlapping of past and present—an idea that was, itself, deeply embedded in the countercultural imagination.

The *Bonnie and Clyde* fad was far-reaching, encompassing clothes, TV commercials, and music.[51] In addition, it arguably initiated a cycle of films over the next several years, all featuring violent, Depression-era outlaws, contemporary political allegory, and pop Americana soundtracks, including *Bloody Mama* (1970), *A Bullet for Pretty Boy* (1970), *Boxcar Bertha* (1972), and *Dillinger* (1973). While a desire to exploit *Bonnie and Clyde*'s popularity was doubtlessly an important factor, such fads still represented more than simply the commercial co-optation of a countercultural moment. In his book *The Dream Life*, critic J. Hoberman has analyzed the ways in which the American public in the sixties and seventies constructed and related to an essentially cinematic imaginal self-image, using *Bonnie and Clyde* as a key example. As Hoberman also points out, the film's reception was a generational testing ground, dividing the old American Left of social progressivism from the New Left of anti-establishment radicalization.[52] In the words of Peter Collier in his review for the leftist journal *Ramparts*, *Bonnie and Clyde* was "a happening."[53]

This fluidly defined "magic word" of the era originally described an approach to avant-garde performance art, in which events occurred not as representations but as actualities, a conceptual "frame-breaking" exercise serving to expand or liberate the consciousness of the participant.[54] In its broader popular usage, however, the term gradually became applicable to any cultural construct even vaguely connected to a celebration of the Now. Although it may seem contradictory, or even impossible, for a film to be a Happening in the word's original, avant-garde sense, the application of the term to *Bonnie and Clyde* was nevertheless more than just a vague outpouring of countercultural excitations. Much as fashion articulates our aesthetic preferences in real life, as a sort of everyday performance art, *Bonnie and Clyde* was a representation, but was also a moment in which American history, political partisanship, Hollywood storytelling, and lived experience all overlapped. *Bonnie and Clyde*'s leftist "partisans"—to use Hoberman's term—viewed the film as embodying a previously unarticulated aspect of their lived experience, and responded by living out their own fantasy of the experience that was *Bonnie and Clyde*.[55]

Collier's *Ramparts* review certainly doesn't represent a mainstream critical response to the film. Nor, for that matter, does Collier himself necessarily posit his own conclusion as a good thing. Rather, his position reflects another, more critically skeptical impulse particular to the New Left's adoption of *Bonnie and Clyde*. Collier uses the term "Happening" critically—for Collier, *Bonnie and Clyde* is like an archetypical middle-class white kid appropriating the gestures of Black Power; the film, in essence, hasn't paid its dues. One wonders if, under the dogmatic presumptions of such critique, it ever actually could, or what it might look like if it *did*, but, at the same time, Collier still *gets it*. He recognizes that the role of *Bonnie and Clyde* in the public consciousness has the capacity to transcend mere representation, going so far as to compare the *Bonnie and Clyde* fad to the early sixties Davy Crockett craze, another example of contemporary Americans living vicariously through an image of the past. But for Collier, ultimately, writing from the perspective of New Left activism, "if it is true that *Bonnie and Clyde* belongs to 'us,' perhaps we should be all the more careful about what it says."[56]

Clearly, the film's popularity, overlapping with the co-optation of the authentic avant-garde practice of the Happening, could be—from a leftist intellectual perspective—cause for concern. But the concept of the Happening also appears in negative terms among the film's numerous apolitical or conservative critics. *Bonnie and Clyde* immediately became a lightning rod for debates over the nature and ethics of film violence. Beginning with influential *New York Times* film critic Bosley Crowther's denunciation of the film as "a cheap piece of bald-faced slapstick comedy that treats the hideous depredations of that sleazy, moronic pair as though they were as full of fun and frolic as the jazz-age cut-ups in *Thoroughly Modern Millie*," critical battle-positions began to be drawn with greater or lesser subtlety.[57] Toward the less subtle end of the spectrum, Page Cook, writing for *Films in Review*, lamented that the film presents "murder and mayhem as mere 'happenings.'"[58] By contrast, *The Antioch Review*'s Jerry Richard—although he doesn't use the term "happening" specifically—engages with closely related ideas, using *Bonnie and Clyde* as a platform from which to mount a thoughtful critique of the "against interpretation" paradigm initially associated with critic Susan Sontag and, increasingly, with the experience-oriented ideology of the counterculture.[59]

Although positive appraisals of the film, with few exceptions, generally overlooked the soundtrack, negative reviews were more likely to discuss the film's use of bluegrass, usually as an element of a discomforting (and for these critics, aesthetically and ethically flawed) mixture of comedy, tragedy, and violence. While the music itself was not regarded as a source of moral panic or as a pernicious influence (as in the conservative response to rock and roll in films of the fifties), critics noted and responded to the uneasy relationship between the music's connotations of innocent Americana and the film's graphic violence and moral ambiguity.[60] One reviewer noted with ethical bafflement that crime and violence were accompanied by "a soundtrack which is built-in for laughs: music which seems to be right out of 'The Beverly Hillbillies.'"[61] The choice of example here was no coincidence: in 1963, "The Ballad of Jed Clampett" had been Flatt and Scruggs's first crossover hit. Through the lens of cultural phenomena like *The Beverly Hillbillies* (or the television show *Hee-Haw*), bluegrass had clearly become readable as inherently comic music. On a nastier note, Page Cook—one of the very few critics of the era to consistently focus on film music—derided Charles Strouse with scare quotes, as having "'composed' the music," adding that the fact that Strouse "would be willing to provide smarty-pant, Keystone Kop guitar tinkles by Flatt and Scruggs for this film's chase sequences will long be the index of *his* artistic creativity."[62]

While for most listeners, bluegrass as a topic might suggest a detemporalized sense of mythic Americana, other listeners—particularly those knowledgeable about this genre and its specific roots in post–World War II American culture—might read the music's presence as fascinatingly, perhaps even productivley blurry in its historical associations. Or perhaps not: no critic of the film, whether positive or negative in their appraisal, seemed to notice that for all its overtones of comedy, Americana, or both, bluegrass itself was anachronistic to *any* depiction of the thirties. In fact, bluegrass evolved as a distinctive genre from earlier forms of string band and country western music in the mid-forties, led by pioneers such as Bill Monroe, whose western swing ensemble had also launched the career of Lester Flatt and Earl Scruggs. The recording of "Foggy Mountain Breakdown" used in a film set roughly thirty-five years in the past was, in fact, less than twenty years old, dating from just before the group's upward move from Mercury to Columbia in the early fifties.[63] Following the success of their radio variety show in 1953, and with the sponsorship of Martha White Flour, Flatt and Scruggs became regulars at the Grand Ole Opry, at that time the single most important venue for country performers.

In the sixties, as Neil V. Rosenberg has shown, the cultural associations of bluegrass grew increasingly complex, even seemingly paradoxical. Early in the decade, bluegrass—and Flatt and Scruggs in particular—began to draw an extended audience both from modern jazz and from the folk music revival.[64] Simply put, bluegrass became hip. This was, however, a contested hipness, complemented by its association with an image of regressive Americana embodied by the success of *The Beverly Hillbillies*, along with Flatt and Scruggs, who had recorded the theme song and periodically appeared in the series in cameo roles. Following the popularity of *Bonnie and Clyde* and, the following year, of *Deliverance* (1968), bluegrass solidified as a signifier of the rural, the uncivilized, and the anarchic—whether this image was conceived as liberating, as in the former film, or as an uncontrollable threat, as in the latter. As the reception of bluegrass continued to mutate in the late sixties, dovetailing into an emerging West Coast country rock movement (in which *Bonnie and Clyde*'s session banjo player Doug Dillard would play a small, but noteworthy role), the cultish popularity of the film even led Flatt and Scruggs, shortly before breaking up, to experiment with adapting their own image, abandoning the Grand Old Opry look that graced the cover of their 1957 album *Foggy Mountain Jamboree* (Figure 1.2), and dressing up as slick thirties gangsters on the cover of their 1968 tie-in album *The Story of Bonnie and Clyde* (Figure 1.3).

The act of constructing an imaginary past, investing it with a peculiar kind of self-conscious, magical belief, and then occupying it as an extension of one's lived actuality—this was part of a broader countercultural ideology that transcended this particular film. The era offered its countercultural participants numerous ways to play Cowboys and Indians, among them

Figure 1.2 Cover of Lester Flatt and Earl Scruggs, *Foggy Mountain Jamboree* (1957).
Columbia Legacy Series. Sony BMG Entertainment, 2005. Compact disc.

Bob Dylan's Western-drenched turn in his 1968 country album *John Wesley Harding*, and, eventually, his extension of this persona to both film scoring and acting, with Sam Peckinpah's *Pat Garrett and Billy the Kid* (1973). For those willing to travel out into the desert (and many were), there was the Red Dog Saloon, a psychedelic Nevada hangout modeled on the set of *Gunsmoke*.[65] By donning Fay Dunaway's beret, or by musing on the film's implications for Black Power, *Bonnie and Clyde*'s partisans were similarly articulating an overlapping of past and present, not just as allegory, but as an embodied, radically presentist form of experience—that is, as a Happening.

To be clear, however: this response to *Bonnie and Clyde* isn't *just* a function of the film's appropriation within a small and highly specific reception

Figure 1.3 Cover of Lester Flatt and Earl Scruggs, *The Story of Bonnie and Clyde* (1968).
Columbia CS 9649. 33 1/3 rpm record.

community. The audiovisual aesthetics of the film to some degree allow for and even facilitate this aesthetic response, even if, for most people, the model of allegory was and continues to be an adequate explanation for the film's role within the cultural imaginary. If, however, the idea of *Bonnie and Clyde* as an actuality seems farfetched, a far more common framing of the film—that of myth—might also allow insight into the relationship of authorship, allegory, and experiential actuality. Mythic time exists outside of (or *other than*) the nature of everyday time and thus may be the perfect medium for collapsing past and present experiences into a single felt entity. In an essay comparing Penn to director Terrence Malick, film scholar John Orr argues that both directors tend toward showing "the movement of history *into* myth in the arena of spectacle," allowing us essentially to see both sides—that is, to experience the mythic but to witness its creation from the perspective of critical distance.[66] Orr further argues that Penn's "intimate psychodramas" have a dramatic intensity that distinguishes them from the objectively observational, emotionally distanced work of Malick.

Although I would not entirely contradict Orr's distinction, I would expand upon it, arguing that while the quality he identifies in *Bonnie and Clyde* does indeed stem from an intensity of dramatic affect, it *also* stems from a sense of distanced observation (perhaps more akin to the work of Terrence Malick than Orr seems to recognize) and that sound and music play out these interconnected dimensions of the film. Focusing on the film's extremes of noise and emotional outburst, Orr misses its quietude. It is only through a holistic accounting of both of these dimensions that the film's approach to the experiential past emerges. Orr, tellingly, also proceeds from a definition of myth that, in the following chapter, I will attempt to complicate and expand. For Orr, myth and history are complicit rather than in conflict; myth is the result of historical reality becoming frozen into archetypal patterns that preclude critical engagement. On the other hand, history, as I have been conceptualizing it in distinction to experiential actuality, *already* accomplishes this end. By contrast, understood as a dimension of human experience existing outside of time, myth eradicates the distinction between the visceral and the distanced—showing them to be two intertwined ways of connecting the experient to the world of the imagined past. The experiential "reality effect" of *Bonnie and Clyde* is thus not about historical accuracy, nor is it—despite the film's self-conscious attention to the construction of media celebrity— only about myth as an obfuscating falsehood that conceals a historical truth. *Bonnie and Clyde* is mythic, and thus unreal. But it is also a self-consciously visceral myth, a myth with flesh that may be slammed and punctured by bullets; or a myth that might waste its time in a run-down motel in the middle of nowhere, listening to whatever happens to be on the radio.

The film's play of time, memory, and experience were noted early on, in a 1973 essay by John Cawelti, who observed about the opening credits sequence that

> the sense of a mythical past, as opposed to a purely historical representation, involves a paradoxical feeling that the events and characters represented are not limited to a specific past moment. Rather, they exist outside of our ordinary experience of time, in an ahistorical past that can be felt as continually present, as part of our own lives.[67]

If this is the case then the film has the cruelest possible ending, one that absorbs the audience into a spectacle of meaningless obliteration. I refer here not just to the famed final shootout, but also to the ending that follows. It is important to remember that, as a film auditor, Greil Marcus was struck not just by bullets, which punctured flesh and caused an involuntary reflux of violent images from the public imaginary. Marcus also experienced a silence, "as if what you saw had made you deaf." Just as, in the opening credits, the photographic "click" of memory had culled the film into existence, overpowering quietude now seems to suck the image entirely out of existence with a direct cut-to-black. This stylized visual gesture may be read as another reality effect, "realizing" the image through its seemingly arbitrary obliteration, as if the camera just happened to run out of film, or to experience a mechanical breakdown. Suddenly, in mid-action, the image is simply gone. Only after we have been given time to absorb the blackness and the only *true* silence we've heard since the opening credits, are we offered the solace of a tender bluegrass elegy (1:50:03). This cue features a gently winding melody, intertwining solo guitar and banjo, over a soft arpeggiated accompaniment, a pointed contrast to Benton and Newman's pre-shooting script, in which the shocking climax is followed by a turn toward musical irony, bringing back the "wild country breakdown music" as the scene cuts to black.[68]

But given the ambiguous role of music in *Bonnie and Clyde*, what do we make of this cue? Although the banjo and guitar instrumentation recalls the bluegrass topic we have encountered many times, we have never heard *this* music, and as such it lacks any clear, concrete association, its only "message" being its ambiguous pathos. As the film ends, we are left uncomfortably poised between older and newer aesthetics of sound and music, as well as poised between the ways in which their use can both represent the present and embody the past. For the revolutionary culture that accepted Bonnie and Clyde as two of their own, as a past tense manifestation of their embodied present, this may have been exactly the right note to strike.

2
The Revisionist Western and the Mythic Past

Defining Mythic Film Music

If we were to choose a single word to conceptually organize as much of the popular and critical discourse on the genre of the film Western as possible, that word might be easily be "myth." Since at least the fifties, beginning with the work of critics such as Robert Warshow and André Bazin, interpreters have effectively drawn on myth as both a critical and aesthetic category in order to locate the Western as a privileged site of both Hollywood classicism and ideology, a testing ground for what made American film seem particularly American. More recently, film scholar Jim Kitses, preferring to view "American history" as the genre's essential subject, has pointed to the inconsistency with which myth has been defined in this discourse. But it is, to some degree, this very tendency of myth toward heterodox definition and use that makes it such a persistent figure, helping to make the film Western genre doggedly resilient over time, flourishing across multiple decades of changing tastes, and cycles of ideological revisionism and counter-revisionism.[1]

The focus of this chapter will be on two revisionist Westerns: *Butch Cassidy and the Sundance Kid* (1969) and *McCabe and Mrs. Miller* (1971). In comparing these two films, both representative of a vital New Hollywood genre, we shall approach myth through a framework similar to that which entered the discussion of *Bonnie and Clyde* at the end of the previous chapter, which is to say a view of myth less as a narrative construct with ideological import, and more as a spatiotemporal mode of audiovisual expression. Through this lens, myth becomes an *experiential* category, in addition to an archetypal narrative present in the text. The experiencing of filmic myth, in this way, becomes an extension of the larger topic of this study, namely the use of the New Hollywood soundtrack to reimagine the experiential past.

As discursive narratives, myths leave little room for falsifiable, rational counterargument, hence the commonplace popular dichotomy of (false) myth and (true) history, as well as the equally commonplace academic dichotomy of (uncritical) myth and (critical) history. The latter, in particular, has led to myth's vexed role in the contemporary culture of academic humanism. In being understood to occupy a numinous time beyond, or somehow *other than* the contentious material polyvocality of historical time, myths seem problematically self-contained, eluding critical encounter with anything outside their self-defined borders. Myths thus risk rendering the non-normative Others of the cultures that create them invisible, potentially even making their marginalization or exploitation seem naturalized or inevitable. For this reason, the basic understanding of myth running through the work of modernist thinkers as diverse as J. G. Frazer and Mircea Eliade—that is to say, a "religionist" understanding of myth as irreducible to reality ("reality," in this instance, definable as material reality, together with the dynamics of power inherent to culture)—has become open to suspicions of primitivism, anti-modern nostalgia, and association with politically regressive ideologies.[2]

Within the structuralist tradition associated with anthropologist Claude Levi-Strauss, by contrast, the emphasis is less on an essentializing understanding of what myths *are*, and more on a functional understanding of what they *do*: myth is understood as a technique for reconciling the deeply held conceptual binaries that lie at the root of any culturally legible form of meaning. Myths, in this sense, solve problems for us—not merely with euhemeristic explanations for historical or natural phenomenon (i.e., "Why does the sun seem to move across the sky?"), but as a conceptual apparatus that helps navigate the most complex dimensions of human experience (i.e., "How do seasonal cycles correlate to our understanding of procreation and death?"). Film scholar Rick Altman has argued that a similarly mythological problem-solving function is central to the idea of film genre. For Altman, one level of generic articulation is "semantic," a sort of toolkit of surface-level signifiers, while on a deeper, "syntactic" level, genres offer mechanisms for reconciling narrative binaries akin to those examined by structuralist mythography.[3] Defining the film Western along these lines, for example, we would identify its semantic signifiers as being set in the mid- to late nineteenth century, positioning a positive representative of law and order against an anarchic or despotic "bad guy." There are horses, six-shooters, and exoticized Indians. On a deeper, syntactic level, however, the genre explores the complexities and contradictions of human cultural values as they encounter an unknown wilderness, providing a mechanism of utopian closure—a way, so to speak, for us to have our wild, untamable frontier *and* to eat it from domesticated, civilized tableware.

The fluid distinction between a semantic surface and syntactic depth allows genres to adopt to shifting perspectives by potentially pushing one parameter to the breaking point while maintaining the recognizability of the other. This potential becomes particularly pointed in the revisionist New Hollywood Western, where traditional narratives of the inevitable advance and triumph of white civilization were increasingly recognized as politically objectionable, while at the same time a mythos of the frontier continued to offer a sense of utopian magic for countercultural communities. The revisionist Western thus exposes the deep-seated contradictions built into such powerful words as "frontier," "progress," and, perhaps most of all, "freedom." This critical ideological move has been emphasized in most accounts of the revisionist Western in the New Hollywood era. But in addition to a critical "anti-myth," revisionist Westerns also possessed a strong tendency to engender counter-myths, renavigating and rearticulating the same underlying problems in forms that remain, despite their subversive intention, not anti-mythic, but rather *differently* mythic.

In the film musical, according to Altman, these binaries are navigated and resolved through the performance of songs. But even in non-musical films, music arguably plays a key role in evoking the mythic, often by manipulating our experience of time and duration. In general, critical studies of myth and film music have explored: (1) the temporality in which we experience music within the film (i.e., as rhythmic expressivity); (2) the temporality of music's *placement* within the film (that is, the significance of music's presence or absence); and (3) the expressive use of music to imply readings that foreground the concept of time. Royal S. Brown, in particular, has examined the relationship between film music and myth by contrasting diachronic and synchronic temporal elements. Diachronic, or experiential time exists for the characters and, to an extent, for the audience (around the edges of conventions such as continuity editing). Synchronic time, on the other hand, operates with respect to a synoptic perspective of a film as a whole, and is generated by the interconnected use of communicative patterns such as the style topic, the leitmotif, or other extra-filmic associations. For Brown, it is this synchronic dimension of music, with its "element of the paradigmatic" that is the stuff of myth, transforming aspects of the filmic experience such as characters, places, or ideas, into things that we might call "timeless" in the sense of "iconic," "epic," or otherwise "bigger than life."[4]

By contrast, James Buhler has drawn upon the thought of Theodor Adorno to explore the dialectical nature of musical myth in a close reading of *Star Wars* (1977). The contrast between Brown's and Buhler's approaches is instructive. For Buhler, the filmic leitmotif, despite the "demythesized" quality posited by Adorno (resulting from its displacement from Wagnerian aesthetics) nevertheless retains an analogously mythic function in film. In Buhler's reading, the Hollywood leitmotif becomes something more than Adorno's redundant, aesthetically degraded "calling card." Rather, Buhler argues, "the demythifying impulse of film music leads not away from myth but back toward it. This is the riddle of the leitmotif, which entwines myth and signification in a knot almost impossible to solve."[5] Whereas in Brown's reading, mythic temporality is a specific *effect* (as in the sense of myth as being "larger than life"), mythic temporality is more intrinsic to Buhler's reading as a broader expressive *register*, in which a variety of meanings, sometimes contradictory ones, might circulate. Myth thus becomes, rather than an experience, a *way* of experiencing.[6]

The post–World War II period of profound cultural shifts and waning studio control had engendered a palate of musical myths that functioned as a departure point for the Westerns of the New Hollywood era. At the same time, however, traditional musical topics still maintained a strong communicative power within the popular imagination. By the early sixties, a musical body of (following Altman) "semantic" mythic tropes were already at play in the soundtrack of the Hollywood Western. These had been drawn from older musical topics of exotic primitivism in depictions of Native Americans, as well as from the Americana of accessible mid-century modernists such as Aaron Copland. Folk music also represented an important source, particularly in the films of John Ford.[7] As the sixties wore on, however, this picture was complicated by the complex position of Mexico within the American imagination. With its historical resistance to European colonial domination, its nineteenth-century conflicts with the United States, and its own messy revolution in the early twentieth century, by the late sixties Mexico (and Latin America more broadly) could easily function as an allegorical Vietnam. But it could also represent a final stronghold of utopianism exoticism—a lawless, deregulated zone to which romantic outlaw heroes could flee to escape the soullessness of modernity.

Nevertheless, when it came to the representation of both Native Americans and Mexico, the musical topics of ethnic otherness in the late sixties were, in a broad sense, little different from what they had been in the thirties and forties. Shifting representations of Native Americans would eventually mitigate, to some degree, the musical primitivism with which they had traditionally been represented, drawing upon either musical modernism or foregrounded ethnographic specificity.[8] However, despite shifting narrative and imagistic portrayals of Latin America, these musical tropes remained comparably stable. This was true even of revisionist Westerns, whether they sounded more modernist, as in Jerry Fielding's score for *The Wild Bunch* (1969), or more pop-oriented, as in Bob Dylan's score and songs for *Pat Garrett and Billy the Kid* (1975). If anything, these two films show us that the sounds of Sam Peckinpah's revisionist hacienda weren't significantly different from those of John Huston's *Treasure of the Sierra Madre* (1948)—we hear in both of these scores the same exotic, mariachi-inflected guitar strumming and melodious trumpets playing folksy triple-meter melodies in euphonious parallel intervals.

Can we, then, identify a musical signature specific to the New Hollywood Western's mythic revisionism? How could filmmakers extend their concern with counter-mythic expression into sound? One possibility might be to deform existing tropes, maintaining their recognizability but rendering them hypertrophied and grotesque to the point where the mythic West is deconstructed through self-consciously exaggeration. We hear this, perhaps, at places in Fielding's score for *The Wild Bunch*. As Mervyn Cooke has argued, Fielding articulates the counter-mythic brutality of Peckinpah's world by dramatically contrasting dissonant sonorities with more familiar, often diegetic sources of consonance, encompassing diverse elements (brutally violent marches, dissonant travesties of Protestant hymnody, and strung-out hedonism in its Mexican exotica) to convey a deeply conflicted poetics of masculine reverie.[9] In this way, we might describe Fielding's score as a "revisionist-modernist" approach to the genre.

Another solution might be for music to playfully dissolve temporality into a big, wet puddle—what we might term a "revisionist-psychedelic" approach to musical myth. This was, perhaps, easier to achieve in a film in which the visual signifiers of pastness were already extremely blurry. George Englund's "electric Western" *Zachariah* (1971), for example, is a woozy, loose adaptation of Herman Hesse's *Siddhartha* that drifts deliriously through an ambiguously late-nineteenth-century setting where gunslingers are rock stars (and vice versa) and electric guitars and drum sets inexplicably dot a pastoral landscape. Psychedelic rock band Country Joe and the Fish and post-Bop jazz drummer Elvin Jones play characters whose on-screen musical performances knowingly embrace the anachronism of their respective musical idioms. In this way, both semantic and syntactical dimensions of myth are subjected to radical reworking, with the alienating effect of the music going well beyond the "expanded vocabulary" of Hollywood's musical modernism. In a film such as this, mythic temporality becomes all-pervasive, attempting to exist simultaneously in mythic time and the contemporary moment. But it does so by foregrounding unresolved heterogeneity rather than attempting to create any meaningful mediation between timeless myth and contemporaneous immediacy. As a result, *Zacharia* maintains surface-level semantic signifiers (horses! six-shooters!) while its deeper syntactic signifiers dissolve into fascinating incoherency that is ultimately disconnected from the film's musical personality.

A third possibility—that, in effect, negotiates elements of these first two—would be to imagine a mythic musical revisionism that, as in *Zachariah*, projects the mythic experience through anachronistic dissonance, eluding the presumption of universalism associated with classical scoring with a turn toward recognizable contemporary pop. Unlike the psychedelic free-for-all of *Zachariah*, however, this third mode would adopt a more stable balance of revisionist and traditional genre elements, in which recognizable mythic tropes were modernized but not distorted beyond recognition. Instead, mythic temporality would be the site of productive transformation and fusion. Music, in this model, would mythicize while letting us *perceive* a process of "mythicization," opening up an experience of timelessness by actively engaging specific temporal contrasts and ambiguities. It would thus participate in a broader New Hollywood tradition by thematizing its own sense of pastness through the non-traditional sounds of the pop score. This type of score would open up to our perception a self-conscious conflict between mythic and historical temporality in which we might simultaneously perceive elements of both. We might call this process "revisionist re-mythicization."

Several of the approaches to film music and myth discussed in this brief survey privilege the classical, leitmotivic, neo-Romantic score. The third term we've arrived at here—"revisionist re-mythicization"—can, by contrast, be understood to privilege the pop score. As we have already seen, a normative bias against the expressive value of popular music in film was particularly tangible in the New Hollywood era. Such criticism, with respect to the Western, tended to problematize pop music as an agent of anachronism. With regard to Burt Bacharach's score for *Butch Cassidy and the Sundance Kid*, critics also focused upon another facet of popular music in film—the use of music almost entirely in self-contained "music video" sequences, which was read as a sign of inorganic artifice and, particularly in the case of the non-diegetic song "Raindrops Keep Falling on My Head," as tainted by the crassness of commercialism. *Time*'s review, for example, complained of a score that

> abruptly annihilates the nostalgia with a scat-singing sound track by Burt Bacharach at his most cacophonous. Coupled with a mod love song, "Raindrops Keep Falling on My Head"—wedged in while Newman does stunts on a bicycle—the score makes the film as absurd and anachronistic as the celebrated Smothers Brothers cowboy who played the kerosene-powered guitar.[10]

Other critics were less imaginative in their imagery but emphasized the same basic point. Writing for *Film Quarterly*, Dennis Hunt listed Bacharach's "jazzy" score as one of several "chic touches" tailoring the film "to the tastes of the Pepsi generation."[11]

McCabe and Mrs. Miller (1971) met with some similar reservations. In *Film Quarterly*, Jackson Burgess's otherwise extremely appreciative review files his "one complaint" with the score:

> When a director wants a folk ballad in the background, why shouldn't he find a nice Irish, Appalachian, or Western ballad? *McCabe* features a dismal, fake ballad by Leonard Cohen—one of those concoctions of extravagant and incoherent metaphor, à la Dylan, which passes in childish circles for heavy stuff. What's wrong with "Dried Apples" or "The Frozen Girl"? Cohen's pretentiousness is totally out of key with this film.[12]

Clearly, critics could identify the use of contemporary pop music in both films as an aesthetic fault predicated upon its commercial appeal, the perceived artistic quality of the selected music, and its anachronistic lack of "fit" with the film.

While contemporary critics, in general, have created more a nuanced toolkit of interpretive strategies, these strategies still tend to share a goal of "pattern recognition"—of connecting narrative dots to show how pop music "fits" the film, often in order to validate auteurist readings. It is, however, just as much the *divergence from* patterns—the ambiguities and discontinuities of audiovisual interaction—that are enhanced by the tendency of the pop score to embrace the discrete, self-contained musical structures offered by song forms. This tendency is maximized in *Butch Cassidy and the Sundance Kid*, for example, in which nearly all of the music is placed within self-contained musical "numbers." Likewise, while the dramatic "fit" of the preexisting compiled songs in *McCabe and Mrs. Miller* is highly relevant, the songs also simultaneously pull *against* this "fit," imposing formal and lyrical structures whose seams, however cleverly edited, remain tangible and relevant.

The New Hollywood was frequently a site for the absorption and mainstreaming of European art film style. The audiovisual aesthetics I am tracing might also be described as vaguely "European," at least in their most proximate models. Discussing the music of Nino Rota, for example, Richard Dyer has identified a tendency he terms a "side by side" aesthetic—a form of audiovisual interaction in which music "carries on alongside the narrative, broadly in tune with it but not underscoring every minute action, gesture, or shift of emotion *à la* Steiner."[13] Dyer extends the basic premise of this model in several interpretive directions, showing how it might suit the expression of particular atmospheres, narratives, characters, or even worldviews, all of which foreground a paradoxical sensibility of ironic attachment. The two films examined in this chapter manifest a quality akin to Rota's use of the waltz or theme-and-variations forms, in which the use of contemporary pop idioms in the New Hollywood Western creates a perceptible simultaneity of independent audiovisual forms. But whereas Dyer ultimately views this relationship as mirroring an audience's balancing of absorptive identification with independent subjecthood, I will attempt to locate a comparable aesthetic within the network of ways in which New Hollywood films explored the mythic past. In this way, Dyer's concept of a "side by side" aesthetic might be understood to imaginatively suspend the experient between (or perhaps outside of) distinct temporal sensibilities, evoking the imagined experiential quality of myth.

Ghosts of Silent Film Music

Were anyone familiar with *Butch Cassidy and the Sundance Kid* to encounter a forty-eight-page, staple-bound book of piano-vocal music, published by Charles Hansen Music to promote the film, they might have noticed something strange. The medium (promotional sheet-music collections) wasn't itself that unusual, particularly for a film banking on music to be part of its commercial appeal. But this book also contains a summary of the film that gets a significant detail of the plot very pointedly wrong. It is sometime around 1908, and our eponymous outlaw antiheroes and their girlfriend, Etta Place, have fled to Bolivia to escape the menacing corporatist threat of a "super-posse," which a railroad baron has hired to exterminate them. The summary continues:

> realizing that Butch and her lover [Sundance] are nothing but bandits and not wishing to see their end, Etta decides to return to the States. On their last night together, Butch, the Kid and Etta go to the movies, where they view actors playing Butch Cassidy and his bunch. As "Sundance" dies in the film, Etta's face is full of sadness.[14]

Although present in William Goldman's published screenplay, and shot during production, this scene was eventually cut in post-production and doesn't exist in the finished film.[15] Promotional materials, such as this music book, were sometimes created from information available before the assembly of a final cut, and presumably the writer of this summary simply managed to miss the boat, with the error making it into print. The scene has since become available on DVD, however, albeit without an extant dialogue track.[16] The music elements in this scene can still be heard, however, and they seem to have adopted fairly standard tropes for representing diegetic silent film music: an out-of-tune piano hammering away at melodramatic "chase" and "danger" topics. In the finished film, the footage from this "film-within-a-film" instead appears as a prologue accompanying the opening credits. It is also truncated from its presentation in the cut scene—most importantly, we do not actually see the actor-versions of "Butch" and "Sundance" die. Also, whereas in the Bolivian screening the fictionalized misdeeds of the film-within-a-film's outlaws prompt the audience to hisses, the opening credit sequence is carefully cut to maintain a morally ambivalent tone. Nevertheless, the tone of postmortem eulogy (heavily objected to by the still-living outlaws) remains the same. The footage thus becomes a sort of elegiac gesture, preceding the film's playfully evasive textual epigraph: "Most of what follows is true..." (0:02:50).

These opening credits are the first of several references in the film to early moving-picture media. At multiple points, the film attempts to evoke the mythical origins of cinema in a movie set during the era in which film was first becoming a form of popular mass entertainment. In the famous bicycle scene, a tracking shot follows Butch and Etta's ride from the far side of a gapped fence, the slots letting the morning light through and creating a cinematographic effect reminiscent of the zoetrope, an early animation device (0:28:00). Later, we will see a "silent" photographic montage depicting the modern marvels of turn-of-the-century New York City that is gradually sped up to create a persistence-of-vision effect (1:08:30). Along with the birth of cinema came the birth of the film Western, some of whose earliest exemplars were cast with real cowboys. The historical Butch and Sundance, whose exploits as train robbers peaked in the late 1890s and led to their presumptive deaths in 1908, are thus uniquely "late" Western outlaws. Their lives and deaths, rather than simply symbolizing the "death of the West," actually *overlapped* historically with the subgeneric space J. Hoberman has identified as the "twilight Western."[17] Moved to the margins of the film, the silent film sequence seems to engage even more directly the emergence of Western mythology via cinema. Its gestures speak not to its diegetic audience, but rather directly to *us*. There are, however, several gestures that blur this division between "them" and "us," between "inside" and "outside" the work. One is the mode of visual presentation: the footage appears at screen left, at a slight diagonal angle away from the foreground, seemingly indicating its projection within an undefined cinematic space (Figure 2.1). This "in-betweenness" is further articulated through sound and music. Throughout the opening footage, the sound of a projector provides a sort of structural drone against which the action, and eventually music, are articulated. This noise becomes the primal, originating sound out of which the filmic artifice grows.

Any audience we might assume to be "present" for this screening, however, is silent. Perhaps there is no audience at all; perhaps the theater is empty. We are encouraged to imagine a sort of *mise-en-abyme*—a mechanical reproduction of actors acting out a myth that was once the story of two "real" historical beings, whom *we, in turn* will see acted out by well-known celebrity actor-personas in our *own* recreation. But while the film-within-a-film is played silent, *our* film will have music. This music starts and stops several

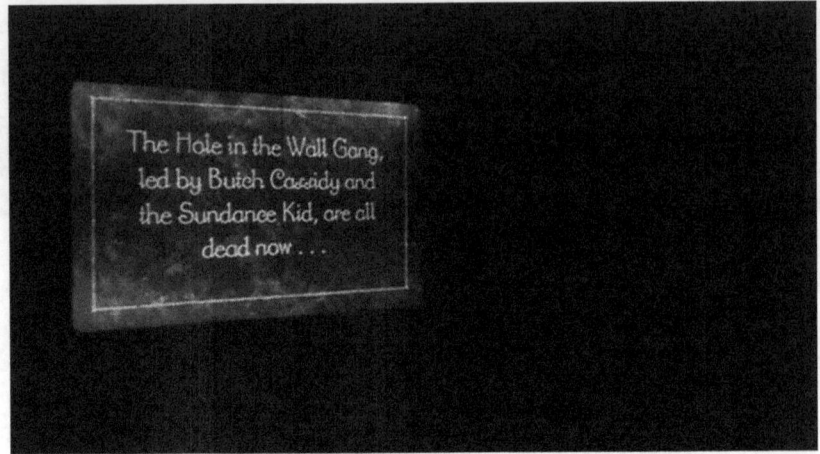

Figure 2.1 Opening credits sequence of *Butch Cassidy and Sundance Kid* (1968) at (0:00:34).
Screen capture from Warner Bros. Home Video, 2002. DVD.

times, as if gradually and only with difficulty building up the momentum to continue (0:00:54). The gaps in the musical statements make the presence of projector noise in the soundtrack and the silence of the film-within-a-film all the more unavoidably tangible. As a whole, the film we're about to see is sparsely scored—its soundtrack album only runs to slightly under a half-hour, barely validating its LP format even with several alternate versions and cut cues. The waltz melody gradually traced out in the prologue cue appears, but only in the more continuous forms taken up later in the film. Despite the album's commercial maximizing of material, then, this abstract, deliberately clunky cue from the film's prologue *still* does not appear on the album, its unsuitability for a listening format testifying to its deliberately awkward quality.

The sound is filtered, distorted, making it difficult initially to latch onto a specific instrument. It was likely produced with an electric piano (the first entrance) and a tack piano (entering second).[18] Whatever it *is*, what it *suggests* as it grows back to life seems more certain: it is a ghost of silent film music. Like the visual field, the music is oriented between ambiguous layers of diegetic and extra-diegetic experience, neither entirely "ours," nor entirely "of the film." Instead, it navigates a liminal expressive space of its own by adopting a stylized (but nonetheless recognizable) popular image of silent film. As a ghost, it lingers—rather like a myth—in an ambiguous non-time, a temporality in which we are drawn into the mythic construct while being at the same time confronted with its artificiality.

What does silent film music *mean* in *Butch Cassidy and the Sundance Kid*? The revival of interest in silent film in the late sixties, particularly as associated with historians and cultural advocates such as Kevin Brownlow and Rudy Behlmer, was an effort to rescue silent film music from popular associations of ineptness or primitivism, associations that were arguably deeply tied up in the sonic association we are hearing: the clunky, tinkly honky-tonk piano.[19] In this era, modern silent film preservationists were attempting to move beyond the dominant image of the solo (and usually amusingly out of tune) piano to explore alternate, historically accurate options, including theater organs, small chamber groups, and the full orchestra scores of contemporary composers such as Carl Davis. Paramount in the interests of this loosely defined movement was to renew public knowledge of silent film on its own terms, along with the grandly majestic musical experiences that could accompany it. Stacked up against the goals of the silent film revival was the image of "primitive," honky-tonk silent film music, understood as a metonym for the supposedly amusing kitschy primitiveness of the medium as a whole.

But if the "primitive" nature of silent film music was a myth of sixties film culture, it was also something more than just the product of ignorance, or a smug sense of superiority fostered by technological teleology. It could also be perceived as a sort of cosmological origin story for the medium. In this sense, the myth may have served as an assurance of the superiority of the present, but also as a moving reminder of the popular cinema's supposedly lowbrow, pre-artistic origins. These polarities were held in a productive tension, yet were perhaps imagined to generate a "mythic" utopian resolution of an irreconcilable binary opposition: silent film could be populist art, consummately *of the people* in its unsophisticated guilelessness, but it could also, as self-conscious *artistry*, challenge and provoke new understandings and sensibilities, opening up new thresholds of understanding. This, perhaps, is the utopian binary present in all primitivism—simultaneously familiar and strange, rough-edged, yet highly complex. The music of *Butch and Sundance*'s opening prologue audibly projects this primordialism through its self-conscious traces of mechanical mediation and through its distorted musical timbres, inspired, perhaps by the so-called honky-tonk piano revival of the fifties and early sixties, in which tack pianos, virtuosic tempos, and an exaggerated "period look" were important elements.[20]

Musical distortion is thus not simply the butt of an evolutionary joke. The prevailing aesthetic tone in the opening credits is instead of melancholy, distance, and absence. The musical score reframes the subgeneric concerns of the twilight Western within a self-consciously modernist frame. Throughout the film, similarly archaic signifiers are placed in tension with signifiers of contemporaneity. The film goes out of its way to present its characters as analogues of the contemporaneous "younger generation" *and* to present them as emblematic of a dying past, free-spirited rebels and outlaws, stuck in a world increasingly dominated by murderous, technocratic super-posses. This world is antithetical to the outlaws' ideals of freedom and resistance, leaving them dreaming of escape to the exotic vistas of distant, untarnished lands. But this is an escape that, deep down, is understood to be naive and impossible.

Tin Pan Echoes: Historicism, Pastiche, and the Brill Building

One has to suspect that a desire for a rich musical negotiation of past and present may have, perhaps latently, motivated the choice of *Butch Cassidy and the Sundance Kid*'s composer. Burt Bacharach was associated with the hip yet sophisticated sensibility of mid-sixties adult contemporary pop, as well as with the Brill Building and its stylistic associations: sophisticated, culturally syncretic song-craft, recorded with polished sound production.[21] The Brill Building was thus, in several respects, Tin Pan Alley's direct descendant. Despite the fact that he did, in fact, work for a time out of an office in the Brill Building, Bacharach is a peripheral presence in the literature on this conjunction of business model and songwriting style. This is probably due to his relative independence from several of the more prominent channels of the popular song industry that have helped define this moment in popular music style.[22]

In addition, Bacharach's period of breakout success largely occurred in the post–British Invasion era that often serves as historiographic marker for the waning of Brill Building pop as a central force in American popular culture. In the shifting cultural terrain of the late sixties, the Brill Building seemed increasingly to fade from the map of cultural urgency. Thus, by 1969, when *Butch Cassidy and the Sundance Kid* was released, Bacharach was simultaneously experiencing the most successful and productive years of his career—while at the same time, shifts in popular taste were occurring that would eventually, in the early seventies, lead to his becoming viewed as a musical and cultural anachronism.[23]

In his essay "The Return of Burt Bacharach," critic Geoffrey O'Brien examines the later Bacharach revival of the nineties, arguing that the aesthetic of cultural sampling characterizing so-called "lounge music" was, in fact, anticipated by Bacharach's music *in the sixties*, which was already synthesizing broadly diverse traditions into finely crafted pop artifacts.[24] This effect was amplified, according to O'Brien, by the listening habits of many fans of adult contemporary pop—habits which, if not exactly "postmodern," were nevertheless heterogeneous in ways that have been habitually overlooked or undervalued by countercultural rock criticism.[25] Bacharach's nineties lounge revival also placed him (somewhat clumsily) next to the broader moment of musical exotica in mode of Martin Denny, Les Baxter, or the mid-sixties bossa nova fad. There is, indeed, some degree of geographic exoticism in *Butch Cassidy and the Sundance Kid*, as when the theme from the opening credits is transformed into a breezy jazz samba. But the film's more prominent exoticism, by far, is temporal rather than geographical, drawing the listener into a variety of complex, sometimes conflicted ways of mythicizing the past. In this way, Bacharach's *Butch Cassidy and the Sundance Kid* score participated in a broader current of nostalgic revivalism that was a minor, yet tangible vector in American popular music of the late sixties and early seventies. Several singer-songwriters, such as Harry Nilsson and Randy Newman, drew upon older, pre-jazz and pre-rock vernaculars. This influence extended along multiple cultural vectors, as demonstrated by the overlapping of these American vernacular styles with English Music Hall style in several songs by the Kinks or the Beatles. Further outlets would emerge in the early seventies, with a revived interest in ragtime manifesting in the historically informed recordings of Joshua Rifkin, as well as in the popularity of the 1973 film *The Sting*, scored with Marvin Hamlisch's arrangements of music by Scott Joplin.

These forms of archaic musical Americana are most strikingly deployed in a montage of still photography that compresses the outlaws' stopover in New York City before setting sail for Bolivia (1:06:30). While the film makes entirely clear the trio's antipathetic relationship to the perils of modernity, their relationship to its pleasures—whether in the form of city life and leisure, photography, motion pictures, or (famously) bicycles—is one of ambivalence. This, importantly, is the only scene in which modernity is a source of wonder, rather than an existential threat. The ebullient music suggests early jazz, ragtime, and Tin Pan Alley style of American vernacular music. We hear a tuba bassline articulating the first and third beats of the measure, syncopation, predominant wind band instrumentation, and an altered march-and-trio form that breaks, at one point, into a double-time galop topic reminiscent of circus music. The cue accompanying the montage is thus not just a historical reconstruction, but rather a self-conscious pastiche, in which several canny touches prevent us from taking the score "too straight." Unexpected rhythmic and phrasal asymmetries occur, ostinatos cram against one another in odd ways, and angular little repetitions give the melody an occasionally lopsided, out-of-synch feel, something like a dauntless, but rhythmically imperiled marching band that occasionally must drop a beat or two in order to stay coordinated.

As in the opening prologue, the mediation of the image in the travel montage impacts how we read the audiovisual whole. The scene offers a string of doctored historical photographs, with our trio inserted into locations in turn-of-the-century New York. While this technique was, in part, an exigency of production (they weren't able to film on the set from *Hello, Dolly!*) the results play upon the aesthetic resonances of the photographic image as an indexical glimpse of reality superseding representation. Historical photography thus conveys not just images, but potentially also what Roland Barthes, in his book *Camera Lucida*, called the "punctum," a moment of semantic excess and indexical resonance that provokes an encounter with contingency, the photograph as a brush with the inexhaustible reality of what once was.[26] The photograph is a moment that captures and preserves time, yet serves as an inevitable reminder of its passing. The seams are further exposed by the overlap of historical photography and the extra-filmic personas of these actors. In a "star system," for example, Robert Redford and Paul Newman are perceived simultaneously *as character* and as their (discursively textual) selves. Bacharach's musical pastiche of modern and archaic gestures thus resonates with its visual parallel—Redford, Newman, and Katherine Ross splashing in the surf at Coney Island, side by side with children who were actually *there*.

There was, of course, nothing particularly new or unusual, by 1969, about montage techniques bringing music to the structural foreground while compressing narrative time into a series of iconic images. The use of stock historical photography was also common. Although I cannot think of an earlier example of modern actors being inserted into historical photography in quite this way, the techniques for doing so were standard, well-established procedures of optical printing and matte photography. What *is* unique, however, is the expressive resonance of this scene as a navigation of mythic history. Its use of still images makes the *silence* of those images all the more apparent, and allows the music to "speak," in its mythically ambiguous way, for all the sounds that are implied, and yet repressed by the medium—the bustle of the city, the synchronized hits as Etta knocks down tin birds in a shooting gallery, and, most of all, the crazed moment on the tilt-a-whirl where the frozen photographic past seems to pile up upon itself, pushed to the verge of coming to life as a moving picture.

Bacharach and the Baroque

Not all of the score's historical gestures map, like silent film music, onto the period in which the film is set. This is most evident in the film's longest musical set piece, a montage compressing the outlaws' successful careers as bank robbers in Bolivia (1:17:30). Following awkward beginnings in which they don't know enough Spanish to successfully navigate this task, it is here that their naïve dreams briefly seem capable of becoming reality. At the end of the sequence, however, the gang realizes that their success has led to visibility, bringing the American posse again onto their trail. The montage thus depicts the apex of their ambitions, while also dovetailing with an awareness of the reality that their lifestyle cannot be prolonged indefinitely. Following this turning point, the outlaws experiment unsuccessfully with legal professions, ultimately taking up robbery again, at which point Etta leaves them and returns to the United States.

The large-scale ABAB form of the cue alternates fast A sections, accompanying chases, with contrasting, slower-paced B sections. The B themes, with their melancholy turn to minor and smooth vocal lyricism, are particularly reminiscent of the melodicism of Ennio Morricone's mid-sixties Italian Western scores—in particular those scores' frequent use of the fluid, luxuriant vocalize of session singer Edda dell'Orso (1:18:30). The action scored by these B sections, however, does not (as we might expect) establish a straightforward binary of action and repose. At first the cue simply seems oddly set against a robbery in which Sundance and Etta trap the bank manager by posing as husband and wife. The melancholy affect of this contrasting B material, however, is "grown into" structurally as the cue progresses, gradually becoming more explicit as it accompanies a celebratory dinner that suddenly ends as the trio catches a glimpse of the posse arriving in Bolivia.[27] At this point, an alternate reading of the sequence might click into place, in which the structural alternation mirrors not so much the immediate visual context, but rather the interrupted circularity of the outlaws' lifestyles—an alternation that, like the cycle of robbery, high living, and more robbery, becomes both mechanized and melancholy.

Looking in greater detail at this sequence, we again discover ambiguous temporal associations. The cue may be read as a fast jazz waltz with a complex, angular melody, but also suggests an engagement with mid-sixties Baroque pop. A connection might be found in the music of the Swingle Singers, whose successful 1963 LP *Jazz Sébastien Bach*, with its pure-toned scat singing and contrapuntal vocal arrangements, was a likely model for Bacharach's cue.[28] In any case, the cue diverges from either of the possibilities William Goldman suggests in the screenplay—"loud, rhythmic ... Spanish" music or "a simple, Quaker-type tune extolling the virtues of work."[29] Issues of Bach à la Swingle aside, however, and unlike the artificial harpsichord effect on the Beatles' "In My Life," or the organ of Procul Harum's "A Whiter Shade of Pale," the Baroque quality of this cue lurks less in instrumental signifiers and more in its formal and stylistic gestures. The most obvious such gestures are on the surface—the vocal writing, while it doesn't manifest the polyphonic rigor of a Bach invention, nevertheless conveys something of that sound, with a busy, layered arrangement suggesting fugal entrances. In the B section, an unexpected major cadence against shifting inner voices suggests a Picardy third (1:19:45). Breaking down the form further, we might even see the alternating structure itself as a loose analogue to Baroque formal devices that privilege cyclical alternation over linear development—such as the alternation of concertino and ripieno sections within ritornello form. In the interior of the B section, a fragmentary keyboard interlude in a new tempo periodically intrudes between vocal phrases, functioning akin to a miniature ritornello (1:18:55).

What do these Bolivian Bacharachian Baroquisms amount to? How do they inflect the diegetic territory of turn-of-the-century Latin America, or a meta-diegetic context of the late-sixties New Hollywood? Perhaps they project an expressive sensibility of complexity as play—a golden, ornamental game, cut off from the "real world" in the trio's temporary, South-of-the-Border bubble. We might even, at this point, imagine a happier ending, a real Old Hollywood myth, in which this circularity of adventure and repose never *has* to end, implicitly continuing beyond the triumphalist gesture of closing credits—but that would be a different, and a far less sad film. In this sense, it is particularly vital that the cue abruptly terminates without harmonic resolution after Butch and Sundance glimpse the leader of the American posse (1:22:59), knowingly breaking its established, self-sustaining mechanical circle of breakneck adventure and romantic, melancholy repose. By positioning us between these ambiguous temporal associations (Bacharach and the Baroque), the film allows us to feel, for a little while, suspended in this mythic timelessness with the characters, albeit with the knowledge that it can't last. For us, experiencing the film, the past *itself* becomes what Butch and Sundance expect from their encounter with "Bolivia"—a melancholy topos in which old myths are subverted and new myths established, a place in which timelessness pervades, but is only allowable at the expense of its self-conscious status as a comfortable illusion.

While there was no single defined "meaning" for sixties Baroque pop, this style overlapped in significant ways with the cultures of psychedelia. But while there may be little in the musical *sound* of this film that seems particularly attuned to psychedelia, we might nevertheless consider how *Butch Cassidy and the Sundance Kid* might suggest the psychotropic displacement and fantastic realities of psychedelia by other, more subtly temporal and mythic means. As Michael Long has argued, psychedelic pop of this era frequently utilized a sense of aural spatiality to evoke imaginal, as well as physical distances. For example, the "distances" present in Long's reading of Procul Harum's Baroque pop classic "A Whiter Shade of Pale" are psychedelic by virtue of their mapping of aural spatiality onto historical distance. By extending this reading into the song's use in *The Big Chill* (1983), Long demonstrates that such metaphors can acquire additional layers of meaning through their spatialized cinematic deployment.[30] In the scene Long analyzes, the dynamic levels at which diegetic sound is mixed are complexly multidimensional, articulating physical space, but also possessing suggestive overtones of interpersonal and psychological distance.

Each of the four robberies compressed into *Butch Cassidy and the Sundance Kid*'s Bolivian robbery montage is presented with a minimum of diegetic sound, allowing music to dominate the soundtrack. At first this effect might seem to make the montage, in comparison with Long's reading of psychedelic pop, rather *one-dimensional*—not "spatialized" at all, but rather possessing a flat aural signature akin to the prototypical music video, in which, lacking any diegetic placement, sound simply floats *over the surface* of the image. But it is not in the realistic space of the diegesis that these montages create their distinct meaning. Rather than equating physical and imaginal distances, as in *The Big Chill*, the Bolivian robbery montage playfully manipulates the temporal registers *themselves*. In doing so, it creates analogous effects of *conceptual-temporal* distance, in which temporalized frameworks (silent film music, the Baroque era, the Old West, the hip, psychedelic present of Baroque pop) overlap and reinforce one another as revisionist re-mythicizing.

Strangers in the Landscape

The opening credits of *McCabe and Mrs. Miller*, set to Leonard Cohen's "The Stranger Song," immediately offers us a very different type of West: the soggy, muddy Pacific Northwest woods, rather than the arid, mythic landscape of John Ford's Monument Valley. The music, also, already seems somehow unexpected. Despite its acoustic simplicity, its lyrics project a surreal phantasmagoria of images. And yet, at the same time, as the camera follows a man on a horse—a man we will eventually discover is named John McCabe—we are self-consciously staging one of the most familiar semantic tropes of the classical Western: *a stranger rides into town*—a mysterious, potentially dangerous stranger. We know he's a stranger because the song tells us—it would be surprising if, say, we were to discover that McCabe was simply a native of the town who was returning home. From the beginning, then, music helps to articulate the mythic tropes that make this film "a Western," and not just a story about some people living in a dirty Northwestern mining town in the late nineteenth century.

In several ways, "The Stranger Song," both here and in its subsequent uses, works analogously to the most traditional functions of classical film music. The song's lyrics frequently fit the film in ways that were (in all likelihood deliberately) brought out by the visual editing—not just by eponymously marking McCabe as the archetypal "stranger riding into town," but in smaller, looser synch points, as well. For example, lyrics referring to "curling like smoke above his shoulder" and "some Joseph looking for a manger" accompany McCabe lighting a cigarette before he crosses the bridge to Sheehan's saloon and peering in the door, clearly seeking shelter from the inhospitable weather (0:04:00 and 0:04:37).[31] These lyrics also map onto the way in which we will come to understand McCabe, who, we are about to discover, is a man with a shady (and, it turns out, largely fictionalized) past, looking to settle down, raise a business, and make his place in the world through capitalist entrepreneurship.

The film begins with a number of slow-paced establishing gestures: a tracking shot of the landscape gradually "finds" McCabe, following him at a distance. At this point, the "stranger" trope is the only tangible narrative connection between the song and the images we are seeing. In the flow of the sequence, the numerous other connections between the song lyrics and film narrative necessarily await retrospective consideration. The cultural imaginary evoked by the film and the Western dream world of the lyrics is thus *itself* like "some Joseph looking for a manger": an ambiguously resonant set of associations seeking, but never completely finding its grounding in the visual field. The image of the "dealer," that Western character trope of the free-living gambler, will find its place as McCabe wins the townspeople over by fronting them drinks and striking up a poker game (0:08:00). The emphasis on fatalism ("reaching for the sky just to surrender," waiting for the "high and wild" card dealt from a "rusted" golden arm) anticipates McCabe's symbolic rise and fall to come. After establishing a successful brothel and developing the town of Presbyterian Church into a growing community, McCabe ultimately falls victim to the brutal advance of a mining corporation, who send assassins to kill him after he botches their attempt to buy out his business. The romantic emphasis characterizing the "you" of the song's address ("you caused his will to weaken with your love and warmth and shelter") might anticipate the character of Mrs. Miller—the cynical, enterprising Madam who partners with McCabe and with whom he falls into (mostly) unrequited love.

But none of this has happened yet. In this sense, it is the song that creates an imaginal register and narrative anticipation that are eventually answered by the film, rather than a song that is mapped onto the narrative of a preexisting film. This distance between a rich set of aural images and their ambiguous visualization—a visualization that, if you will, is still "holding its cards"—functions as particular type of aesthetic effect. Although "The Stranger" does contains obvious, surface-level synch points, its broader narrative correspondences, as they are experienced, lie in the song's sense of ambiguous lyrical indirection, offering the possibility of transparent signification while simultaneously burying it in a haze of psychedelic archaisms. Cohen's lyrics feel something like "mythemes," the fundamental building blocks of Western mythography, in this case only slightly poeticized, and retaining the traces of their rough, not-yet-entirely-differentiated quality. Like a template for the patterns of genre fiction, we might imagine any number of stories that could be spun out of them.[32]

The song is also considerably edited from its original form—that is, as it appeared on the album *Songs of Leonard Cohen* (1967). After the first three verses, a lengthy instrumental passage, absent from the album, is cut into the song on the film soundtrack, in which melody is played by a solo guitar with only slight melodic elaboration (0:01:45). This occurs as McCabe arrives in town, and we move from extreme long to medium-long shots—the mysterious mythic figure moving through a landscape becomes simply *a guy*, clumsily attempting to hitch his horse in lousy weather. The guitar solo gives the filmmakers flexibility to manipulate the length of the cue in order to fit the length of the scene, of course, but it also eliminates the lyrics just in time for us to focus our attention on the film's first close-up, in which we see that McCabe is clearly dirty, tired, and is muttering to himself discontentedly (in what will become an amusing ongoing character trait). The lack of lyrics also frees our attention to notice that this dirty, tired, muttering man is played by Warren Beatty, allowing Beatty's hyper-attractive star persona to resonate in pointed contrast to the gritty setting.

The lyrics then re-enter the soundtrack as McCabe crosses the bridge leading to Sheehan's saloon, where he will begin to insinuate himself into the life of Presbyterian Church. In doing so, the music editing returns us to the original fourth and fifth verse, but then skips verses six through eight and ends, as the song on the record does, with a repetition of the second verse and "some Joseph looking for a manger." This omission of three verses probably served to better match the overall length of the cue to the scene, and to maintain two specific visual synch points: the road "curling like smoke" and "some Joseph looking for a manger." These editing patterns, as Gayle Sherwood Magee has shown, demonstrate the creatively adaptive process inherent to using preexisting songs as film music.[33] Beyond the pragmatics of timing and music editing, however, these missing verses, had they been present, might have complicated the song's "story," with its use of potentially confusing lines like "it is you, my love, you who are the stranger"—an intriguing transferal of identity between the ambiguous "characters" that populate Cohen's lyric. Such lines might have made the song lyric too *specific*, negatively affecting its capacity to serve as ambiguous, yet somehow harmonious title music for this particular film. Ultimately, the sequence's music editing serves both a pragmatic goal of transforming a preexisting song into synchronized film music, and an aesthetic goal of balancing textual ambiguity and specificity.

This sense of balance allows mythic tropes, such as "the stranger riding into town," "the dealer," or even the broader Western trope of "civilization vs. wilderness" to emerge, but to seem neither overdetermined nor *too seamless* with the larger film text, which does, after all, foreground a popular song that was only a few years old.

But how old does this song actually sound? And is its expressivity marked by a specifically "countercultural" datedness, or by some other, more mythic temporal signature? "The Stranger Song" consists of two phrases that repeat tirelessly, tracing a larger descending vocal arc broken by a medial phrasal cadence. Compared to the well-crafted blend of memorable hooks characterizing the American Songbook tradition of Burt Bacharach, Cohen's melody is barely even a melody—it's a repeated descending scale ornamented with as many rising neighbor tones as are needed to fit the text. It's less of a *song*, and more of a template, or a recitation formula. With its stripped down melodic construction that flexibly adapts to a strophic text, "The Stranger Song" sounds not just like folk music, but something like a kind of rough homologue to the medieval troubadour or trouvère song, a gesture relevant to Cohen's connection to the late-sixties remnants of the post–World War II American folk revival, with its evocation of the troubadour as a Romantic image, as well as Cohen's own poetic and literary interests in medievalism.[34] The troubadour—or, rather, his representation through the Romantic imagination not only as a poet-musician, but also as a sort of eternal "stranger" in the affairs of love and transcendence—hovers in the margins of Cohen's song. The song itself sounds built upon the mythemes of an anonymous chanson that might have been part of dozens of other textual worlds, floating among a web of imagined manuscript variants. "The Stranger Song" thus seems to play both *with* and *against* the film. Its mythic aura suggests a timeless past by floating over the image, drawing us into its ambiguously archaic qualities, while at the same time leading us to immerse ourselves in the film's everyday world.

The Folk-Fantastic Imaginary

Is Leonard Cohen's music in *McCabe and Mrs. Miller* "psychedelic"? Not really—at least not in the sense that the term is typically used in reference to music that evokes the altered perceptual states associated with psychotropic drugs by creatively distorting sound. The film *does* have its somewhat druggy moments—it is revealed, eventually, that Mrs. Miller secretively hides an opium addiction—but the film's pipe dreams are framed with a larger critique of the social forces that lead us to desire escape through the use of narcotics. There is very little sense of aural distortion or experimentation in the Leonard Cohen songs that are used as the film's underscore. Nevertheless, traces of psychedelia remain in Cohen's disjointed, poetic lyrics, which are full of inscrutable and colorful shifts of metaphor and image. And while it may not sound much like Jimi Hendrix, a playfully imaginative aural sensibility is, to some degree, evident in portions of the songs "Winter Lady" and "Sisters of Mercy," which feature a distorted, bell-like jangling reminiscent of a toy piano, a percussive, mechanical cranking sound, and an electronic humming effect, effects unique on a soundtrack otherwise confining itself entirely to acoustic music (0:19:30, 0:21:04, and 0:26:20). Beyond trippy lyrics and occasionally trippy sounds, however, the psychedelic implications I will pursue here manifest in the cracks of the film's audiovisual sensibility, as well as through the significance of Leonard Cohen's presence itself.

In *Beautiful Monsters*, Michael Long considers the implications of "the past" (via the register of classical music) as a figure in "fantastic" rock. In this latter category, Long draws in particular upon psychedelia and progressive rock of the late sixties and early seventies as representative of imagistic styles of listening in which a "zone of uncanny in-betweenness was given an aural dimension."[35] Psychedelia thus thrived not just in the manipulation of spatial signatures associated with sound experimentation, but also within the *temporal*-spatial signatures that emerge when these contemporaneously coded sounds overlapped with borrowings from the "musical museum" of the classical, and in relation to audiovisual spatialization in both the real space of the theater and the imaginal space of the film world.[36]

Although its aural techniques are far less obvious in their sense of spatialized play, and although music's functional role as a multimedia component means that imaginative listening is always already restricted (or, more positively, *focused*) by the visual field, a similar dynamics of the fantastic nonetheless comes through in the expressive effect of Cohen's songs in *McCabe*. In much of Cohen's music from the late sixties, a dense array of highly ambiguous and often surreal images contrasts with a characteristic "sound" that is more reminiscent of the sixties' folk revival. The understated, even monotonous tone of Cohen's vocal delivery, as well as the use of simple, schematic song forms, serves to depersonalize the music, even while the lyrics themselves explode with dazzling imagery. When used as film music, this essential contrast *within* the songs is mirrored and doubled by the songs' interaction with a second, visual medium. This ongoing tension locates *McCabe and Mrs. Miller* in an extra-temporal, which is to say mythic, register. Just as Long suggests that the Baroquisms of the Doors or Procul Harum could map the temporal distances of history onto the imagined spatiality of psychedelic music, this temporally ambiguous conceptual space becomes linked, in Altman's Western, to the experience of myth.

This relationship between sound, image, and narrative within this experiential mode might be characterized as a "folk-fantastic imaginary." Interpreters of film music naturally tend to map music onto film in a way that produces as seamless (and thus logically convincing) a set of meanings as is possible, and I am not, by any means, opposed to such interpretive tendencies as a whole. Nevertheless, as a corollary to this act of pattern recognition, we might also focus upon, rather than letting slip through the cracks, ambiguous or perceptually mis-synchronized elements that almost inevitably emerge through the union of film and preexisting music. For example: Mrs. Miller, knowing full well that the assassins will kill McCabe the next day, has sex with him and leaves him sleeping. We learn little of Mrs. Miller's background over the course of the film, but we know that whatever she has endured has left her extremely fatalistic. Rather than defend her business partner and sometimes lover, she flees to a local opium den to wait out the violence. As Gayle Sherwood Magee has pointed out, Cohen's "Winter Lady" serves as a sort of theme for Mrs. Miller herself.[37] But, as is often the case with preexisting music with lyrics in film, the deeper we go, the more the connections start to fragment and become less literal, more abstract, and, ultimately, simply seem to be *about something else*, something we cannot see but can perhaps feel—an articulation of mood reliant upon ambiguity. In a broader sense, the images in the lyrics of "Winter Lady" easily map easily onto the relationship between the film's eponymous protagonists: fond, yet emotionally remote and inevitably temporary. The speaker is identified as a "soldier," who must fight for the lady, an image that seems more indirect when interpreted literally, but which could be understood as an expression of McCabe's masculine vanity. The identification of a "child of snow" could apply to Mrs. Miller's life-damaged emotional frigidity, or it could simply apply to the prevalence of wintery imagery throughout the film. But while this reading would clearly map the speaker onto McCabe, the two other personae in the lyric, the Traveling Lady ("you") and the Child of Snow ("she") would then *both* be identified as Mrs. Miller, which makes the third verse, in which they are compared and contrasted on the basis of their hair, rather puzzling.[38]

As film music, "Winter Lady" thus continually weaves between synch points of lesser and greater literality or abstraction. The instrumental melody first enters the soundtrack under dialogue (1:36:50).[39] McCabe has realized that he can no longer bargain his way out of his situation, and that the assassins will try to kill him. The scene represents the closest the pair gets to genuine intimacy. But as the lyrics enter the soundtrack at "Well, I lived with a child of snow . . . ," we cut to Mrs. Miller leaving in the middle of the night, during the beginnings of the snowfall that will continue throughout the climactic gunfight the following morning (1:37:18). Snow imagery aside, the lyric strophe at first seems to be an odd fit to a shot emphasizing the emotional subjectivity of the female character, rather than that of the male "soldier" who is presumptively speaking the lyric. Nor does the following verse, the puzzling one, with its dreams and hair woven by smoke and gold, find a credible interpretive niche. But this suspension is only temporary: shortly thereafter arrives a synch-point "reveal," the lyrical correspondence that we might easily imagine the music editing of the entire shot having been constructed to emphasize: "And why are you so quiet now / Standing there in the doorway? / You chose your journey long before / You came upon this highway." Once the parallel to Mrs. Miller's moment of reflection is obvious, it is impossible that we will not read this "doorway" as the symbolic threshold of her decision to leave McCabe to his fate.

In general, the preexisting lyrics offer the film many correspondences—some likely deliberate, some perhaps coincidental—but these correspondences are constantly in flux between literal and non-literal frames of reference. The point of this analysis is not to pursue such moments to the point of absurdity, but rather to probe this type of loose quasi-synchronization for its unique interpretive and experiential value, embracing both their simultaneity and distinction from the image. The amount of surprisingly close lyrical synch-points in this film is, indeed, striking. In fact, the use of musical themes for characters and ideas actually serves to counterbalance (to a degree) the pessimistic, anti-Romantic realism of the film with a warmth that is otherwise largely avoided. Ultimately, however, the music-image-narrative relationships in *McCabe and Mrs. Miller* are along the lines of what Richard Dyer has termed "side-by-side," and their relaxed, fuzzy points of synchronization merge its "folk-fantastic" music to produce an audiovisual aesthetic of suspended temporality. *McCabe and Mrs. Miller*, I would argue, *makes use of* these floating semi-abstractions to produce a mythic, timeless aura—conveying the sense of a film that is both dreamily poetic and grittily material.

Sound Design and the Worlding of the Past

McCabe and Mrs. Miller was dogged, from its premiere, by issues regarding the clarity of its soundtrack, and these have continued to be the basis of much commentary by both the filmmakers and critics.[40] The film's sound has been described as flat, murky, even unintelligible, and varying opinions and positions have circulated regarding the extent of the problem, whether it was deliberate or accidental, and who was to be blamed or credited. Seen in the larger context of Altman's career, however, the sound work in *McCabe and Mrs. Miller* clearly fits within his developing preoccupations with overlapping dialogue and complex soundscapes that require the audience to listen actively, a type of immersive aural modernism that might be described as de-hierarchized and even ideologically progressive. But in the context of this specific film, it is also possible to read this characteristic use of sound as conveying a grittily un-varnished, realistic West through an aesthetic sensibility of presence. That this "real" is located in the inevitably distanced past connects *McCabe and Mrs. Miller* to the worlds of films such as *Bonnie and Clyde*.

But although it ostensibly cultivates a "realistic" contrast with the "mythic" style of the classical Western, Altman's sound aesthetics also bend back around the curve, becoming their own type of myth—a re-mythicization. Altman's intense sense of rootedness in temporal actuality ultimately becomes a *way out of time*—both for the characters (such as Mrs. Miller, who ultimately survives only by withdrawing into an opiate haze) and for us, lingering in the world of a film that, for all its de-mythicizing, cynical ugliness and political edge, possesses and offers a great deal of sensory beauty.[41] This worldly beauty, a kind of stoned mysticism of the real, is continually intertwined with its own rougher, de-glamorized aspects, foregrounding the role of sensuous experience in conveying a mythic experience of the past.

Altman's characteristic overlapping dialogue is frequently used to undercut a sense of Western mythos. An example of this occurs at the beginning of the film, when local saloon proprietor Sheehan first recognizes McCabe's name (or so he thinks) as that of a known gunfighter. Being a gossipy meddler, Sheehan excitedly attempts to spread this news among his customers but is not taken seriously. The dialogue mix, in this case, literally "acts out" and actualizes the anti-mythic dynamic of the scene, with Sheehan's concern over this "gunfighter" visitor evaporating into a haze of sardonic backtalk and disinterested digression (0:11:20). The fact that this "stranger" might be *the* "Pudgy McCabe" who "killed Bill Roundtree" is not presented with the authority of foregrounded narrative speech but is rather undercut with drunken uncertainty as to who Bill Roundtree even was. (Wasn't he the mayor of Wyoming?)

Sound design is also used to position diegetic music within filmic space. While, in Altman's idiosyncratic style, such gestures are often deeply ironic, they also borrow an old trick from John Ford Westerns in their linkage of diegetic music-making to the cultivation of the domestic sphere—the social spaces of characters, the physical spaces they occupy, and the ways in which these two interact. This is particularly noticeable in the film's use of fiddle music. An anonymous fiddler, played by actor and session musician Brantley F. Kearns, serves as a sort of musical factotum throughout the film, playing the saloon, weddings, and funerals. His music occasionally crosses over into a non-diegetic register, used to finesse transitions (0:15:20) and structurally "frame" several scenes, but it can also be heard and read as a sort of aural glue, a symbolic form of social cohesion, while his distinctly "all-purpose" functionality serves as a wry comment on the smallness of Presbyterian Church. Also, while serving as a symbol of social cohesion, sometimes the fiddler's work offers a decidedly more salty or subversive commentary, as when an awkward silence accompanying the priggish Reverend's intrusion into the saloon is coyly broken by the fiddler toying with the risqué music hall number "Ta-ra-ra Boom-de-ay" (0:09:48).

McCabe himself is explored as a sounding object, not just producing Chion's category of "theatrical," or narrative-driving speech, but also abundantly producing the alternative category of emanation speech.[42] McCabe regularly mutters to himself—strange little tics of exteriorized frustration and discomfort, complaining about his business, impatience with his associates, and his relationship with Mrs. Miller—but McCabe's actual *words* are, first, always somewhat obscured by the two-dimensional flatness of the sound design, and second, largely irrelevant in their semantic redundancy. Instead of linguistic information, they register largely as *sound*, as a form of body noise comparable to the burps, grunts, and farts that McCabe *also* produces with regularity throughout the film. In this way, body sound is used to subversively undercut McCabe's relationship to the clean-cut ethos of larger-than-life masculine heroism characteristic of the genre. It is difficult to imagine such a profusion of earthy corporeal signatures emanating from John Wayne, let alone from Randolph Scott.

Taken together, such subversive, ironic, or otherwise "realist" gestures of the soundtrack, in terms of dialogue, diegetic music, and body sounds, might be read as undercutting a mythic sensibility. But through sound, the film does more than simply subvert Western myth—it also reinscribes the mythic on a different level—that of de-temporalized experience of a "time outside of time." It is here that the film's characteristic foregrounding of natural, environmental sounds becomes critical, as in the regular use of prominent wind effects. Such sounds are positioned *against* the sounds of society, thus creating a sense of the fragility of human presence in the world. This temporalized "world" of the past, by extension, is in constant danger of obliteration through cultural change, human decay, and the immensity of forgetting.

This "forgetting," in the sense of being buried by or lost to history, is most prominent in the climactic fight scene. As McCabe fends off and kills his assassins before dying of his wounds, a snowstorm slowly blankets the town while the townspeople are preoccupied with putting out a fire in the church. While the people celebrate containing the fire, a growing snowbank slowly covers the dying McCabe (1:56:40). The windy, muted sound here is not merely verisimilar, but also poetically evocative. In one sense, it aurally actualizes the anti-mythic smallness of McCabe's death: like the tiny Icarus in the corner of Brueghel's famed painting, what might have been a classically grand drama is rendered as a minor detail in the inevitable unfolding of the modern world.[43] And yet we perceive McCabe's death through a kind of dual-focus lens—on one level, the climax of the film is simply the story of a small-time stooge who underestimates the destructiveness of mercenary capitalism. On another it grants McCabe a kind of undeniable moment of mythic significance, undercutting the binary "either/or" logic of myth and anti-myth with an aesthetic offering a "both/and" approach to this conjunction.

Conclusions

This embrace of ambiguous and imaginative temporal contradictions was, I have argued in the present chapter, part of a larger revisionist solution to the cultural problem of mythologizing the past in the New Hollywood Western, a solution with implications for the use of both original and compiled pop music, as well as for the expressive use of sound. These mythic signatures might even unite films—such as *Butch Cassidy and the Sundance Kid* and *McCabe and Mrs. Miller*—that have traditionally been viewed more in terms of their differences than similarities. Despite their distinct musical voices, however, the pop styles of Burt Bacharach and Leonard Cohen both balance contemporary and archaic connotations to mythic effect. As it is used in *McCabe and Mrs. Miller*, Cohen's music manifests in decidedly oblique styles of synchronization, privileged by the unique poetics of the compiled pop score in the early seventies. Bacharach's pop scoring productively suggests similarly mythic modes of expressivity by balancing stylistic tropes that are contemporary, yet tinged with highly eclectic forms of archaism.

The distinct stylistic voice of this score is highly self-conscious of its contemporaneity. We should not, however, generalize this self-consciousness as broadly characteristic of pop scoring as a whole. Such an understanding would merely categorize "pop" as an *essentially* contemporary gesture, perhaps in contrast to the ostensible "universalism" of classical Hollywood scoring, and would thus simply reproduce in an approving key the myopic disapproval of contemporaneous critics of the pop score without fundamentally altering their underlying understanding. On the contrary, a specifically *multi-temporal* form of self-consciousness operates in Bacharach's music, drawing the past into an ongoing multifaceted dialogue with anachronism, contemporaneity, and historical consciousness. In *Butch Cassidy and the Sundance Kid*, the film's non-diegetic musical discourse functions less through productive contrast and more through complementarity.

The deeper myth that animates the revisionist counter-myths of *Butch Cassidy and the Sundance Kid* may be that while utopian nostalgia may ultimately be unfulfillable, it still has its bittersweet charms, whose self-conscious pose of melancholy might belie simplistic labels of cultural regression. From a number of valuable, even necessary critical perspectives, the notion that this film represents a failure of subversion might carry weight, especially as it facilitates useful critiques of the film's less-than-canny cultural and gender politics, critiques I would not contest. The critical act of defining what is "at stake," culturally, in a work such as *Butch Cassidy and the Sundance Kid* can, however, also generate a predictable, almost reflexive ideological rebuttal of the film, centered on the fact that Butch and Sundance, unlike Bonnie and Clyde, never truly deal with the reality of their violence, and never need to kill until they are either temporarily on the side of authority (gunning down Bolivian banditos while working for a mining company) or pushed to self-defense (gunning down the disproportionate forces of the police and army after they relapse into thievery). These dynamics seemed to make questionable points for all the wrong reasons. For critics of the film, it was the playfully boyish *niceness* of Butch and Sundance that rang false in the context of 1969—this, and the fact that they kept their lady reassuringly on the sidelines and imperialistically "invaded" other countries to rob from geographic Others.

Among the gestures that, from this perspective, might seem particularly facile is the final photographic freeze-frame of Butch and Sundance just before they are killed by the Bolivian army (1:49:08). Unlike *Bonnie and Clyde*, which, in Pauline Kael's turn of phrase, "put the sting back into death" by showing *its* attractive lovers having holes blown in them, *this* ambiguously romantic duo is allowed to remain jokey and oblivious to the end, comfortingly crouched in the soft, sepia-toned myth of American male heroism. But considering where we've been, I believe we can also begin to rethink this ending in more nuanced terms. Once again, the film offers us a meditation upon the indexical resonance of historical photography, building upon the frozen images and the sepia coloration that have been tropes of "pastness" throughout the film. The audiovisual split also allows the outlaws to die, but only *on the soundtrack*, with gunfire extending several seconds past the freeze-frame, finally dying into silence before the waltz melody returns. But this closing waltz, as in the opening, or the Baroque-pop interlude, ends on an incomplete, harmonically open sonority, as if the reality of its conjured-up past is already evaporating before our ears (1:50:15). The duo *is* captured in a glorious moment, but this "capture" is imbued with the same melancholy distance that, comic dialogue aside, has marked the film from its opening moments. Butch and Sundance may only die on the soundtrack, but is this necessarily an evasion? By what terms might this death be understood as any less (or any more) "real"?

Describing *McCabe and Mrs. Miller* as a representative of an American cinema of poetic, historical reverie, John Orr described the film as having "recounted the American West as an immediate past, a living dream"—an essential and productive contradiction.[44] The nature of the film's treatment of the past was also noticed by contemporaneous reviewer Jackson Burgess, writing for *Film Quarterly*. Although Burgess viewed Cohen's music as a distracting pretension, he also enthused, first, that "the whores, for once, look like whores, and not like Goldwyn Girls," and second, that the film articulated a turn in filmic self-consciousness that was distinct from that of the film spoof.[45] Burgess continued, emphasizing an aesthetic of tangible actuality, not just of this particular film, but also as a broader Hollywood trend:

> Things dominate these pictures to the extent that *mise-en-scène* gives them their peculiar quality at least as much as story or character: Michael Pollard's baggy underdrawers in *Bonnie [and Clyde]*, the bicycle in *Butch [Cassidy and the Sundance Kid]*, that ratty tent that the Sundowners live in, the watch-chains and derby hats of the posse in *The Gunfighter*.[46]

Later in the review, Burgess extends this idea specifically to *McCabe and Mrs. Miller*:

> Every image is an homage to the "it-ness" of life, to the feel and look and use and enjoyment of physical existence: rarely has the weather and the progress of the seasons been more meticulously attended to in a film *without* investing it with some symbolic or sentimental importance, and the same matter-of-fact respect is accorded to *things* such as underwear, furniture, and hats.[47]

Pauline Kael, similarly, praised *McCabe* for its "delicate, elliptical" style, a "vision of the past" which allows that past to play out with a kind of affect-less sense of affect, a "picture [that] seems to move in its own, quiet time."[48] As she continues, Kael remains preoccupied with the movie's fascinating surfaces and textures, her criticism becoming more associative, even cinephiliac, opening up to encompass the film's soundscape:

> The gaslight, the subdued, restful color, and Mrs. Miller's golden opium glow, Leonard Cohen's lovely, fragile, ambiguous songs, and the drifting snow all make the movie hazy and evanescent. Everything is in motion, and yet there is a stillness about the film, as if every element in it were conspiring to tell the same incredibly sad story: that the characters are lost in their separate dreams.[49]

As viewers, we are never fully allowed to lose sight of the revisionist cultural deconstruction at stake in Altman's film, but we are also encouraged to immerse ourselves in the details of this sad, but beautiful song. This temporal sensibility is invested with the tangible minutia of the world, yet still readable through the broadly symbolic registers of genre. The unresolved dissonance locates the film in a paradoxically self-conscious atemporality.

The tragic revisionism of the film would be less escapable if it actually concluded with McCabe dead in a snowbank. But we return once more to Mrs. Miller—following her exit, she retires to the town's opium den to wait out the storm. The trope of "waiting out the storm," in the model of *The Decameron* and *The Canterbury Tales*, often provides the opportunity to share dreams—stories, narratives, even myths—but here, perhaps the emphasis is on the opportunity for dreaming itself—for using the imagination to pursue those moments of estrangement from the world that, sometimes, are what make reality survivable. This is where *McCabe and Mrs. Miller*'s drug subtext becomes interpretively valuable. The small, tactile details of phenomenal perception are magnified by Mrs. Miller's opium use, but they also extend a thread running through the plot, as yet another way in which the film is concerned with the tangible textures of experience. Earlier in the film, advising a new prostitute, Mrs. Miller suggests dealing with the potential trauma of her profession by meditatively de-centering her mind from the sexual act itself—to "just look at the wall, count the roses in the wallpaper" (1:12:30). As McCabe dies, Mrs. Miller (clearly stoned) seems to be adopting this advice herself, staring at a ceramic bowl as she slowly turns it in the hazy light (1:59:44). As the credits roll, accompanied by "Winter Lady," the camera takes us into her perception, with an extreme close-up of the bowl as it turns, every crack line and color spot becoming a figure on the map of some fantasized country (Figure 2.2).

Paralleling this visual experience, we might imagine the worlding effect of the film's soundtrack as a similar appeal to tactility, to the past as an imagined

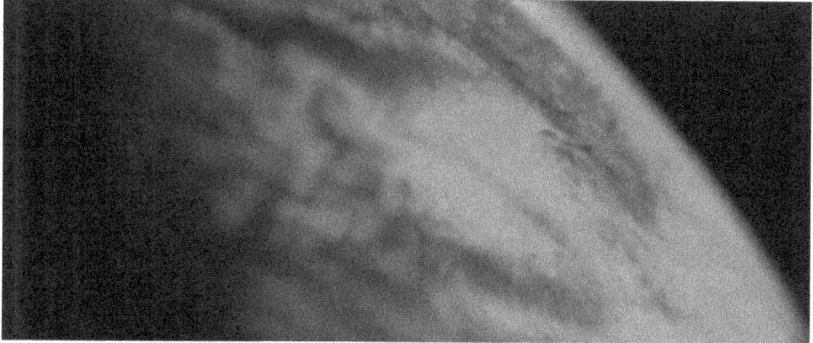

Figure 2.2 Final image in *McCabe and Mrs. Miller* (1971) at (1:59:44).
Screen capture from Warner Bros. Home Video, 2002. DVD.

reality we could imagine reaching out and touching, feeling the wind run over our fingers and the snow crunching under our feet.[50] Myth, in this way, becomes less a body of narrativized cultural gestures, and more an experience of creatively imagining the past through musical sound—sounds that neither entirely universalize nor entirely alienate us from the experience of the past. In the case of *Butch Cassidy and the Sundance Kid*, we are indeed hearing a "contemporary pop" score, but there is, I would argue, room to be far more sophisticated in our reading of what, exactly, this means in practice. Bacharach's score *is* identifiably contemporary, but paradoxically, it may be by functioning as a grab bag of historical gestures that Bacharach's score is perhaps most clearly a product of the late sixties. At the time of its release, this score was divisive. While it was criticized for its supposedly glib and obtrusive pop anachronisms, its sense of contemporaneity was also clearly part of the film's novelty and popular appeal, resulting in Bacharach receiving Oscars for both score and song. I would argue, however, that the image of the film's score as a gesture toward contemporaneity alone simplifies its temporal suggestiveness. Whether we use the term "myth," "counter-myth," or "revisionist myth," in listening to *Butch Cassidy and the Sundance Kid*, mythic expressivity seems to suggest itself—but not in the more familiar registers of Western musicality, namely Coplandesque Americana or John Ford's folk songs. Rather, Bacharach's score freely blurs the contemporary and the archaic, simulating what we might imagine it would feel like to experience multiple temporalities at once, perhaps from the position of a mythic "time outside of time."

Similarly, with its pointedly anti-capitalist sensibilities, *McCabe and Mrs. Miller* might easily be read as a materialist critique of escapism, but it is vital also to note that in such scenes as this final epilogue, this critique is so thoroughly nested in Altman's overriding cynicism that its small, druggy comforts appear to be taken gratefully, at their meager value, while simultaneously drawing us into its world of conspicuous sensory beauty. To lose oneself in this beauty is to be, essentially, outside of time—to not just *read* a myth, but to *experience* it, or—paraphrasing Richard Dyer's well-known formulation regarding utopia in the film musical, to give us a sense of what a mythic reality might *feel like*.[51] Leonard Cohen's music, with its affective parallelism and suggestive ambiguities, draws us into and encourages us to explore this world, losing ourselves in stream of visual, lyrical-textual, and aural images—an experience that, on multiple levels, conveys a sensibility of mythic timelessness.

3
The Mythic Elements of *Chinatown*

Neoclassicism and Elemental Images

From a consideration of myth and sound in the revisionist Western, we move now to a different image for the exploration of an American mythic temporality: an image of California framed by the genre of film noir—specifically Los Angeles and its environs in Southern California—in *Chinatown* (1974). *Chinatown* is frequently categorized as a neoclassical film, although this term can only be used with some qualification. Like the term "New Hollywood" itself, the term "neoclassicism" has been associated with the emergent blockbuster model of filmmaking in the late seventies, complicating its application to films from earlier in the decade. And yet *Chinatown* is, in many ways, extraordinarily "neoclassical," particularly in its unification of thematic and symbolic complexity with a restrained elegance of formal execution that renders its content perceptible with a seeming lack of ostentatious stylism. *Chinatown*'s narrative plotting is methodical and highly linear—there's barely a wasted word in Robert Towne's script, with practically every detail elegantly establishing or developing some logical, yet highly effective eventual payoff. Beyond the tightness of its plot, as numerous interpreters have noted, an intricate network of thematic images holds the film together. These images are not obscure, however, nor do they require much hermeneutic "detective work" to "uncover." Rather, they are laid out with a force that, were it not so elegantly executed, could easily seem blunt. Without requiring any special plea for hermeneutic openness or the death of the author on the part of its interpreters, *Chinatown* presents a generously tangible banquet of carefully interconnected details, like the pieces of an intricate, yet ultimately solvable puzzle.

A more substantial summary of *Chinatown*'s plot will serve, then, not just to introduce the story and characters, but also to enter into dialogue with this system of imagistic resonances. Jake Gittes is a private investigator making a living in Los Angeles in the late thirties, most frequently by surveilling and photographing unfaithful spouses. He is hired along these lines by a woman claiming to be Evelyn Mulwray, wife of Hollis Mulwray, the head engineer of Los Angeles's Department of Water and Power. Jake and his operatives follow Hollis, but initially can't comprehend his actions. Rather than pursuing an amorous affair, Mulwray seems to be concerned with opposing the construction of a new dam, similar to a previous project that collapsed and caused numerous deaths. Hollis also seems to be privately investigating secretive water dumping from LA's water supply in the midst of a drought. Eventually, however, they photograph him meeting a young woman. When these pictures unexpectedly appear in a newspaper exposé, Jake realizes that he had been hired by an actor impersonating Evelyn Mulwray, and the real Evelyn now threatens legal action on her husband's behalf. Jake suspects that he has unwittingly participated in a plot to discredit Mulwray because of his opposition to the dam. He pursues a meeting with Hollis, but the engineer is discovered drowned in a freshwater reservoir (although saltwater in his lungs suggests foul play). When Evelyn quickly drops the lawsuit, Jake is suspicious and investigates further, discovering a large number of fraudulent rural realestate sales connected to powerful industrialist Noah Cross, Hollis's former partner and Evelyn's father.

After Evelyn rescues Jake from a violent encounter, they have sex and he tells her of his experiences years earlier as a police detective in Chinatown, where linguistic barriers and the density of corruption created an atmosphere of pessimistic apathy, and where his attempts to help a woman inadvertently had led to her death. When Evelyn receives a phone call and leaves, Jake follows her and (he believes) sees her holding Hollis's girlfriend prisoner. When he confronts Evelyn, she convinces him not to go to the police by telling him that the woman, Catherine, is her younger sister. When the investigating detectives (Jake's former partners) connect him to the actor hired to impersonate Evelyn, who has been discovered murdered, they suspect that Jake has discovered Evelyn's guilt and that he is blackmailing her. Returning to Evelyn's house, Jake discovers that a misunderstood phrase spoken earlier by the Mulwrays' Chinese gardener actually indicated that their backyard pond is filled with salt water. Closer inspection reveals a cracked pair of glasses at the bottom. Assuming these to have belonged to Hollis, Jake concludes that he was drowned in the Mulwrays' backyard. Newly convinced that Evelyn murdered her husband, Jake contacts the police and returns to the house where Catherine is being hidden. Confronting Evelyn, however, he discovers that Catherine is actually Evelyn's daughter by Noah Cross, and that the glasses belong to him.

Jake decides to help Evelyn and Catherine evade the police and makes plans for them to hide at their maid's apartment in Chinatown, and eventually to flee the city. Confronting Cross, Jake discovers that the industrialist has been illegally buying land in order to horde the water supply and force the city to develop property under his control, and that he murdered Hollis both to remove him as an obstacle both to this plan and to his ability to lay claim to Catherine. Cross and his henchman force Jake to take them to Evelyn in Chinatown, where they also find the police, who have tailed Jake's operatives. As Evelyn attempts to flee with Catherine, the police shoot after the car, killing her. Catherine is left to the implied sexual predations of her father, and Jake is left without any evidence, having inadvertently repeated his personal history by causing another innocent person's death.

Chinatown's "neoclassicism" initially appears to offer up the narrative pleasures of the classical Hollywood detective film on a silver platter, with little of the deconstructive genre play that often characterized New Hollywood revisionism. But this impression is deceptive, as in actuality, *Chinatown*'s neoclassical logic flawlessly sustains itself *only in order to go horribly wrong*. Put another way, the film's finely tuned narrative system generates seamlessness and closure not as pleasure, but rather as an unimaginably grim final turn in which political corruption and sexual violence triumph, seemingly fated like some primal myth to perpetuate themselves cyclically and possibly forever. *Chinatown* is a deeply pessimistic film, even for an epoch of American filmmaking in which pessimism had become attractive to several politically motivated and artistically aspirational filmmakers.[1] In his study of narratological incoherency in the New Hollywood, Todd Berliner identifies *Chinatown* as a "genre bender" rather than a "genre breaker." A "bender," in Berliner's terminology, is a film that "commits its violations without advertisement, subtly reworking traditional scenarios without calling much attention to genre deviance." While "genre breakers" make their abrogation of genre norms into surface-level textual rhetoric, genre benders function "like a booby trap, [catching] spectators off guard and generating unnerving effects."[2]

To add to the irony of *Chinatown*'s deceptive neoclassical sensibility, we realize upon reflection that this pitch-dark final twist is *itself* adumbrated in the film's tightly controlled dialogue and its system of symbolic images. The film seems to flawlessly embody, but actually subtly perverts the archetypal private investigator's search for knowledge and the way this search typically serves as an engine of classical plot development and resolution. As film scholar John Belton has pointed out, *Chinatown* explicitly foregrounds this central paradox, that "through the acquisition of knowledge the limitations of knowledge are discovered."[3] The film's investigators (primarily Jake, but also the detectives, and even Hollis Mulwray himself) all *believe* that they understand an evolving situation, but in fact misperceive and misapprehend it, with disastrous results.[4] *Chinatown*'s ability to unnerve, I would argue, comes not only from the conventions it subverts, or bends, but also from the strength of its imagery, which acquires an affective vehemence that instantiates its pessimistic worldview within the very material substance of its film world. This world is so methodically inevitable in its manifestation, and yet so deeply poisoned, that pessimism and apathy are understood to be the only viable responses to it. Several critics have noted the ways in which a central image of two eyes, one healthy, one damaged, emphasizes *visual* perception as misapprehensive: broken spectacles, Evelyn's kicked-out taillight, the "flaw" that Jake notices in Evelyn's iris just before their love scene, even the bloody hole of Evelyn's eye socket after she is shot by the police.[5] Another vital dynamic axis of the film's imagery, however—one that has frequently been noted but infrequently explored in depth—is the polarity of wetness and dryness. Unlike the representation of vision or other forms of sense perception, images of wetness and dryness link the film's thematic concerns with the substance of its soundtrack.

Wet and dry can, of course, be understood in metonymic relationship to other images in the film: ocean and desert, irrigation and drought, even life and death. But the deeper, mythic resonances of these images betray their more ambiguous dimensions. The ocean is life, but also chaos, primal and uncontainable. The desert is aridity, extinction, and cruelty manifested as an incontestable mode of being, but it is also connected to the archetype of earth, emerging from the chaos of ocean, and foundational to civilization; the desert is earth reduced to nothing more than its bare material substance, stripped of its ability to be built upon or to sustain life. If the film's classical linearity effectively *betrays* us with its manipulation of genre and narrative tropes, putting them in the service of its devastating conclusion, then these elemental images, I would argue, are what remain indissoluble and mythically unassailable. Whatever they "are"—and whether or not they can be believed without ethical risk—they do not lie and they do not mislead. Understanding their affective function in *Chinatown*, I will argue, thus requires that we entertain, at least temporarily, an essentialist reading of the elements and their role. They are not merely cultural representations, nor are they simple forms of false consciousness that can be hermeneutically "exposed" and ethically superseded. They have been there all along, staring us in the face. *Chinatown*, in this sense, posits its elemental imagery as both mythic and as an objectively (and brutally inescapable) material reality.

In a speech given in Los Angeles's City Hall advocating for the building of the new dam, a city planner "classically" lays out the polarities of the film's material imagination. He says:

> Gentleman, today you can walk out that door, turn right, hop a streetcar, and within twenty-five minutes end smack in the Pacific Ocean. Now you can swim in it and you can fish in it, but you can't drink it, and you can't irrigate an orange grove with it. Now remember: we live next door to the ocean, but we also live at the edge of a desert. Los Angeles is a desert community. Beneath the buildings and our streets is a desert. And without water, the dust will rise up and cover us as though we never existed![6] (0:05:45)

Los Angeles in the imaginary of *Chinatown* is thus symbolically caught between the desert and the ocean, between arid, knife-point material certainty and primordial mythic chaos. The material imaginary of the desert, in the film's reception, has become the preferred focus and implied "mode" for critics exploring the film's representations of political power and corruption, a key theme within the aesthetics and politics of seventies paranoia. But an "oceanic" imaginary might be even more germane to how *Chinatown* depicts human action as a futile gesticulation ending inevitably in paralysis, as the ultimate inability to know how our actions will affect the world and whether they will carry or betray the weight of our intentions. In a larger sense, these two polarities are, so to speak, the *yin* and *yang* of paranoia—the arid wasteland of corruption and the oceanic futility of resistance to co-optation.

It is with these archetypal elemental images in mind, I would argue, that we might approach *Chinatown*'s representation of the temporal past, the historical late thirties, through a mythic sensibility that becomes tangible on the film's soundtrack. Unlike the Westerns in the previous chapter, however, *Chinatown* does not employ myth in order to offer the past as a time *outside* of time, a ruefully impossible idyll of the imagination that might help negotiate (or at least delay) the perceived terrors of modernity—a mythic, timeless past to which Butch and Sundance might escape, or that Mrs. Miller can access through a melancholy aesthetics of sensory intoxication. Rather, in *Chinatown*, myth perpetuates its *own* terror, a terror predicated on the mythic *circularity* of time, rather than its atemporal displacement. Time in *Chinatown* is time-present because at any and every point, it is always already the same time. In *Chinatown*'s paranoid mode of being, everything has already happened and will happen again, and always for the worse. At its ending, *Chinatown* simply takes us back to the beginning, with Gittes helplessly doing "as little as possible" (2:07:46).[7] The impossibly of preventing past tragedies from repeating is a key idea in the film. It underlies Hollis Mulwray's power struggle with the city planners over the dam, Noah Cross's incestuous desire—first for his daughter, and then for his daughter's daughter—and of course it ultimately defines Jake's investigation, which inadvertently dooms Evelyn just as it doomed that *other* woman he couldn't save in Chinatown.

Chinatown's Soundtrack and the Mythic-Paranoid Past

Given the film's emphasis on surveillance and misperception, much critical attention has been understandably paid to the role of visuality. But we should not ignore what these imagistic resonances *sound* like. Music and sound play a critical role in *Chinatown*'s deceptively neoclassical paradigm. Mirroring the futurist primitivism of his earlier score for *Planet of the Apes* (1968), composer Jerry Goldsmith employs sounds whose unconventional timbres and atonal tendencies suggest the classical avant-garde, functioning as a "presentist" gesture that effaces historical framing with an sense of immediacy. In this way, the "modernism" of Goldsmith's score functions analogously to the role of bluegrass in *Bonnie and Clyde*. As film scholar Michael Eaton put it, Goldsmith's score thus "avoids the pratfalls of the period score," locating the film's tale of corruption allegorically to the era of Vietnam and Watergate while negating the self-conscious or nostalgic quality associated with genre pastiche.[8]

At the same, however, Goldsmith's prominent, jazz-inflected main theme advances the film's neoclassicist formalism by balancing modernism's "present" sense of pastness (suggesting an allegorical "nowness" of the late thirties) against the strong cultural associations of jazz as a generic marker of film noir.[9] In this way, the score's nods toward jazz represent the historical past through a generic image of the *cinematic* past, ultimately creating not just a "presentness," but also a "pastness" of the past as it is distanced and estranged through the cultural memory of older media. Ironically, then, techniques associated with the avant-garde (such as tone clusters and the use of prepared piano), which are associated with tension and omnipresent corruption, actually ground us in a frame of familiarity, a frame both sensually tangible and (for viewers immersed in the paranoid politics of the early seventies) accessible via presentist allegory. By turn, it is the more culturally "familiar" and nostalgic music of period jazz that estranges us and creates a sense of temporal distance. Although the ensuing analysis will demonstrate some of the ways in which these musical polarities of jazz and the avant-grade are complexly intertwined, our larger focus will be upon the irreducible tension between them, and the ways in which—alongside the score's elemental dimension—this tension cultivates what we might call a sense of "mythic paranoia." Beyond the extra-filmic associations generated by the score's stylistic scope, I will also argue that imaginatively charged, elemental images of earth and water are key to this aesthetic of mythic paranoia, emerging from Goldsmith's use of alternately dry and liquescent timbres.[10]

Chinatown is most immediately readable as a noir-styled mystery, but is nevertheless also a uniquely "historical" entry in the (generally contemporary-set) cycle of seventies paranoia thrillers, such as *Klute* (1971), *The Conversation* (1974), and *The Parallax View* (1974). As Dana Polan has noted, however, *Chinatown* differs from the typical seventies paranoia film not merely in being set in the past, but also in that the murder mystery opens up to reveal a different, far more mythic story—one about patriarchal will, sexual domination, and the origin of civilization.[11] In other films of this cycle, paranoia posits the oppressive and totalized corruption of worldly sociocultural power through money, patriarchy, and political machinations, all things that, however omnipresent, threatening, or difficult to evade, are nevertheless comprehensibly *legible*. In *Chinatown*, however, the legible historicity of political corruption gives way to paranoia as a kind of ineffable mystery, a profoundly negative sublime. Whether by liberal emendation or the prospect of radical utopian transformation, political corruption is *fixable*. *Chinatown*'s initial mystery plot (who killed Hollis Mulwray and why?) seems at first to be about political corruption, but its deeper, and far more mythic mystery is one in which amoral power and sexual depravity are manifestations of a primal chaos inextricably interwoven into the root of civilization itself. Another way to express this distinction is to understand paranoia as a phenomenon with both sacred and secular dimensions. This "sacred" dimension (which Polan rightly characterizes as "a-historical") occasionally lurks below the surface of other seventies conspiracy thrillers, particularly in the distinctly Catholic overtones of Francis Ford Coppola's *The*

Conversation (1974). Only in *Chinatown*, however, is paranoia so blatantly understood as a register of the atemporal and mythic.

For Polan, the absorption of the film's conspiracy plot into its concern with Noah Cross's sexual depravity engages a dynamic of history and myth, with the innately historical frame of the detective story in tension with the primal, mythic ahistoricity of the paranoia thriller.[12] The detective is in essence a "historian," attempting to establish a meaningful connection between the past (the crime) and the present (the investigation), but whereas the traditional fin-de-siècle armchair detectives of Edgar Allen Poe and Arthur Conan Doyle deal with the past in terms of pure cognition,

> in the hard-boiled noir tradition, the story from the past—the story of crimes already committed—interferes and interweaves with the story in and of the present, the story of the investigation and the labor of the detective in the here and now. The past reaches out to engulf the detective, to enable him in its spell.[13]

In this way, Polan argues, "the expansiveness of *Chinatown* is temporal and even historical as well as spatial. As Gittes circulates through the space of the city, he moves not only forward, but also backward into history: the political history of corruption that is endemic to Los Angeles."[14] Expanding on this idea, we might consider the cultural imaginary of the thirties, *reaching out and engulfing* the seventies, not merely as allegory (as in the "Vietnam Western," which answered an ideological imperative to use the past to *address*, or perhaps even *change* the present), but as an altogether more disturbing moral argument about the perennialism of evil. In *Chinatown*'s soundtrack, the polarity of ocean and desert, of wet and dry sounds, thus delimits the edges of a vortex at the bottom of which lurks something worse than mere corruption.

Scrapings and Inundations: Non-Musical Sound Design

These elemental dynamics are present not only in Jerry Goldsmith's score, but in the sensibility of the film's sound design as a whole. *Chinatown*'s system of images is echoed in its use of wet and dry sound effects, which are woven deeply into the film's imaginary. To some degree, *Chinatown*'s sound design, as explored by film scholar Robert Miklitsch, is an extension of Robert

Towne's seamless plotting and director Roman Polanski's visual language of neoclassical realism—intricately constructed, every moment speaking to the film's larger sense of unity, yet seemingly unobstructed by any trace of ostentatious stylization. The soundtrack's "realism," according to Miklitsch, also provides "clues" for Jake to solve, albeit frequently incorrectly. Miklitsch thus views sound as an extension of the film's larger concern with Jake's "radically subjective vision," adding:

> to be a private eye is also, in some sense, to be a private ear. Thus, Jake's ears prick up when he hears certain "enigmatic" sounds: a servant wiping down the Mulwrays' car with a chamois cloth, Hollis Mulwray's name being scratched off his office door.[15]

For Miklitsch, *Chinatown*'s sound is

> as elaborate as its period-perfect Art Deco design, producing a veritable tapestry of colorful sound effects—in particular, those having to do with water, gunshots and car horns—that embellish the deeply entangled themes of sexuality and political economy. Whether it is the waves, accented by gull cries, crashing at Mulwray's feet as he stands contemplating the nature of things at Point Fermin Park or the tap dripping like a metronome in Ida Sessions' house, the sound of water insinuates that in the often morally arid world of *Chinatown*, water is one, if elusive piece of the puzzle.[16]

Wet and dry sound effects thus participate in the film's larger elemental economy. But Miklitsch's evocative readings only go so far in interpreting how these sounds actually accomplish this work. Rather than just a metaphorical extension of a preexisting thematic meaning into a characteristic sound, it is actually, I would argue, the timbral dynamics that actualize these elemental presences as part of the film world. In other words, in addition to just another register in which the film might locate its idealized "concepts," the immediacy of sound lends itself not just toward *expressing* but also toward affectively *being* these meanings—meanings which often come into being through dynamic tensions.

For example, consider the effect of the scene in which Jake discovers the body of Ida Sessions (the actress hired to impersonated Evelyn), in which, as Miklitsch noted, a dripping water faucet is audible throughout the scene (1:39:28). In addition to the obvious work this sound cue does, building suspense by generating aural discomfort, its effect is realized most profoundly in the *contrast* between the metronomic tapping and the fluidity of the force articulating it: water acquires solidity and force by becoming dry and percussive, and by doing this, it articulates the work of time in the presence of an object (Ida's corpse) to which this time is no longer experientially meaningful except as an axis of decay. This object has been "waiting" for Jake, unhearing, in the presence of this repetitive, subtly annoying sound, for an indeterminate amount of time. Reinforcing this image, the aural dripping water is conceptually "rhymed" across the audiovisual divide, with the long shot of Ida's body, next to which a carton of ice cream silently and patiently liquifies and melts into fluid. Later, a ticking clock more than once takes on this dry, percussive role, as it does throughout the entire scene in which Noah Cross's incest is revealed, a scene that Goldsmith's music (perhaps wisely) doesn't even *try* to wrestle with or emotionally mobilize through music (1:48:35). Rather, this motif of the patiently dry ticking manifests the awfulness of everyday space and time, in which the most horrible of things are revealed (and, in fact, happen) quite naturally, as *part of* the world, rather than as expressive enhancements of it. And, Jake's only truly "successful" investigation in the film is arguably into the dry scraping noises that annoy him while he waits at the Department of Water and Power: Jake discovers workers casually erasing dead Hollis's name from his office door (0:53:44). Dryness is thus the sound of inevitability, certainty of knowledge, and the casual banality of death.

Sound in *Chinatown* can, as Miklitsch and Polan have in varying ways suggested, simply represent the work of Jake's conscious perspective, extending the film's visual-spatial atmosphere of claustrophobia to the ears. Jake is in every scene, and almost never out of frame. The camera frequently hovers just behind his shoulder. Jake's sensorium opens up to the views and sounds of a broader world, but just as he cannot escape the inevitability of destroying Evelyn, he is likewise confined to the limits of his own physical being in his own space and time. The claustrophobia in *Chinatown* isn't an externalized space in which the capacity for movement is limited, but is, rather, a metaphorical, or perhaps imaginal, space.[17] But if dry sounds are affective markers of claustrophobic fatalism, then wet sounds do not offer any liberation. Instead, wet sounds tend in general to be chaotic, sudden, and uncontainable. In addition to the ambient water sounds Miklitsch describes, there is also the striking use of rushing water. Water is thus a clue, but it is one that arrives so suddenly it almost drowns Jake twice, when he becomes caught in torrents of runoff.

This "elemental" reading of sound deviates from the way in which studies of the seventies paranoia thriller have tended to treat sound, namely through an examination of surveillance and its aural signatures, which potentially undermine the consistency and logic of visual perception—this is what Helen Hanson, for example, has called the "unsoundness of sound," pointing to films such as *The Conversation* or, later, *Blow Out* (1980), that use sound to emphasize a sense of misperception and ambiguity analogously to that which *Chinatown* enacts through vision alone, thus "contributing to the prevailing filmic mood of anxiety that forms a continuum across classic and neo-noir."[18] Curiously, however, while *Chinatown* is undoubtedly a paranoia film, it is one in which surveillance has no aural signature. The film's emphasis is not merely on vision, but on *pure* vision, or vision *understood to exist in the absence of sound*, thus forcing us to consider the implications of sound's exclusion.[19] The film abounds with visual surveillance from the very first shot in which Jake shows his client photographs of his wife having sex with another man, but it is the lack of corresponding *aural* data that often becomes the source of misapprehensions: Jake voyeuristically photographs Mulwray with his daughter Catherine but does not hear the conversation that might clarify their platonic relationship (0:15:55); Jake's racist mishearing of the Mulwray's Chinese gardener ("Sure, bad for the *glass*," Jake grins) leads him initially to overlook a vital clue (0:27:30); unable to hear the conversation between Catherine and Evelyn, Jake assumes that the distressed girl is being held prisoner (1:31:30).

Jerry Goldsmith and *Chinatown*'s Neoclassicism

If there is no signature for audio surveillance in *Chinatown*, what, then, would be the aural parallel of the film's signature image of epistemological failure: two eyes or lenses, one transparent, the other smashed or opaque? Like the water in the Mulwrays' saltwater pool, which permits a distorted glimpse of an (ultimately false) clue, Goldsmith's liquescent music shimmers, letting us hear *through* the aural spaces left by its resonances. On the other hand, the dry hits of the woodblock, such as when Jake peers through Catherine's window and falsely confirms his misogynistic theory of Evelyn's guilt, oppressively direct our thinking, leaving no room for doubt. Aridity offers us certainty, a singular, *over-defined meaning*, which often proves inadequate or false. Water, on the other hand, paralyzes us with excessive perception, too many meanings, and no way of knowing which is true or which may be effectively acted upon. By diving into the film's aqueous imaginary, Jake inadvertently assures the triumph of Earth in the form of the corrupt (and biblically named) Noah, the bringer-of-civilization whose sexual abuse and patriarchal dominance are understood to be coextensive. The film's profound pessimism thus lies in the fact that wet sound offers not a liberating alternative to desiccation, but rather an obliterating depth in which constant motion is no less paralyzing than the deathly stillness of the desert.

If sound design actively instantiates the film's paranoia through its juxtaposition of elemental images, Jerry Goldsmith's celebrated score equally participates in this work. In several ways, however, Goldsmith's score is as neoclassical as the film's other dimensions. Its seamless updating of classical Hollywood formulas feels fresh and modern while remaining dramatically familiar, following traditional tropes wherein, for example, aggressive sounds and harmonic dissonance remain indicative of threats and implied danger, and the film's instrumental jazz ballad becomes readable, at least to some degree, as a "love theme." Music also tends to classically mitigate formal gaps, bridging and linking together dialogue scenes.[20] The pacing and expressive work of musical cues classically guides our perception (there are even a few unqualified "stingers") and empathetically absorb us into Jake's perspective just as much as those famous "behind the ear" shots. Thus, although atonal gestures certainly extend the harmonic and timbral range of the classical Hollywood score, and Goldsmith follows the more "modern" approach of a using a single memorably melodic motive rather than a dramatic "gallery" of leitmotivic characterizations, the *Chinatown* score nevertheless maintains much of the logic of formal seamlessness and empathetic directness that characterized the classical Hollywood film score. This savvy balancing act of modern and traditional approaches, in fact, is what made Goldsmith one of the most successful and prominent Hollywood composers of the era, one who could adapt to the times, while also continuing a recognizably traditional stylistic idiom. For this reason, Goldsmith is the most "traditional" film composer examined in this study, one whose work fits congenially into both definitional senses of the term "New Hollywood"—the "auteur renaissance" and the "neoclassical blockbuster."[21]

Chinatown's production history offers several industrial considerations relevant to an understanding of its soundtrack. In journalist Charles

Higham's profile in the *New York Times* in 1975, Goldsmith bucked the impulse toward reading *Chinatown*'s music through the lens of *auteur* theory, emphasizing (as he would repeat twenty-five years later in a separate interview) Roman Polanski's perceived disinterest in the film's music, identifying instead producer Robert Evans as his principal creative overseer.[22] Goldsmith also took the opportunity to compare his work on the film to that of composer Philip Lambro. Goldsmith had come onto the production quite late, hired to replace Lambro's score after it had tested poorly with preview audiences. Goldsmith's late participation might seem to preclude reading the film in terms of unified sound design, given that the production of the film offered no place where music and effects could have been creatively in mutual dialogue. In fact, the opposite may be the case, with Goldsmith, by his own description, pressed for time and using the film's unusually finalized effects track as a source of compositional ideas. Although his examples are limited in scope (and may easily be argued to function primarily as self-promotion), Goldsmith had this to offer:

> It was an interesting situation because the picture had been dubbed and previewed. All the sound effects were as they were going to be. All they had to do was go back and put the music in. So I got the sound effects and I always remember that scene with this fly buzzing around Jack Nicholson. You got this arid feeling and I kept that in mind and I actually wrote around the sound of that fly.[23]

In this way, Goldsmith's music and *Chinatown*'s expressive sound design quite plausibly articulate a larger, seamlessly neoclassical whole.

But as with the rest of the film, understanding the music's neoclassical attributes should ideally form a point of departure rather than of arrival—an entry into the experience of the film's actual audiovisual qualities and their significance. Echoing Michael Eaton's approval of the way in which Goldsmith avoids pastiche, Miklitsch argues that Goldsmith's score "works precisely because it works against itself, playing a certain avant-garde dissonance off its more conventional melodic and harmonic passages."[24] Miklitsch is referring here to the division between Goldsmith's theme for the film, first heard in the main title sequence, which we initially hear played by a solo trumpet in a clearly tonal, jazz-inflected idiom, and the score's passages of modernistic sounds verging on atonality. This division has prompted many interpretive readings oriented toward narrative and character.[25] In the remainder of this chapter, however, I will extend the film's concern with elemental images into a reading of timbre in Goldsmith's score and its mythic implications for the representation of the past. My conceptual model for this approach is the elemental philosophy of Gaston Bachelard (1884–1962).

Gaston Bachelard and Elemental Film Music

In a series of books on the material imagination, Bachelard argued that the traditional theory of the four elements as they are understood in pre-Socratic and other pre-modern Western traditions, however much their applicability has been superseded in scientific thought, nevertheless remain the foundational materials of the human imaginative faculty. These elements are most tangibly engaged and actualized through our experience of art. Bachelard explored in depth the material images that would define *Chinatown*: water and earth, divided into an array of distinct, and sometimes mutually contradictory "complexes" reminiscent of, but departing in critical ways from psychoanalytic traditions.[26] As a philosopher of science and epistemology who also wrote extensive phenomenological explorations of the aesthetic and poetic functions of the human imagination, Bachelard has had relatively minimal influence on the contemporary academic humanities, particularly outside of Francophone scholarship, although there have been recent signs of renewed interest in his thought.[27] In traditions of the humanities deriving from the social sciences, such as anthropology, history, media studies, or cultural studies, there is little place for Bachelard, who professed in his work on poetics a general disinterest in biographical or sociocultural contexts for literary analysis. Bachelard's place has been likewise minimized in traditions descending from continental philosophy and critical theory, albeit in ways that require much more qualification. Although Bachelard's critique of scientific epistemology was influential on the discourse theory of Michel Foucault, as well as on early structuralism more broadly, this influence has been minimized over time due to the difficulty (if not impossibility) of accommodating into his thought any dimension of ideological critique. Nevertheless, the humanities have seen a growing recent interest in Bachelardian thought, particularly as it is engaged with phenomenology, ecocriticism, and imaginal and aesthetic philosophies of affect.[28]

Bachelard's writing on the poetics of the imagination often reads like literary criticism of a highly impressionistic, subjective style, and yet it actually pursues a distinct project—understanding how poetic images (literature offering Bachelard's primary example) and the human imagination reciprocally engage and, in effect, co-create one another. To accomplish this, Bachelard engages a rhapsodic, or even Romantic style of interpretation, albeit also one of precise and rationally articulated rigor. His methodology, however, is irreducibly unfalsifiable. Bachelard's work on the poetic image manages this difficulty by sidestepping any subject/object split, claiming that poetic images, however else they might be understood as representations, are most actively *real* as mutually co-creative resonances that *reverberate* with our experience of being.[29] They thus represent a humanism engaged in an existential, co-creative exchange with the non-human world. According to Mary McAllester Jones:

> If humanism necessarily implies idealism, if it argues that man is allpowerful, autonomous, the origin of all experience, then of course Bachelard's humanism would be an embarrassing legacy. Humanism need not though rest on idealism. I wish to show that Bachelard's humanism does not, that it rests on a conception of man decentered, transcended by something beyond his control, yet paradoxically neither denied nor destroyed by this transcendent "other," but rather nourished and sustained by it.[30]

It is beyond the scope of the present study to introduce Bachelard's thought in depth. I focus instead on the specific potential for Bachelard's approach to elemental images, particularly images of water and earth, to inform a reading of the film soundtrack. These elemental timbres, I argue, make *Chinatown* distinctly mythic in its framing of the historical past.

Any use of Bachelard's thought and methodology for the primary purpose of aesthetic criticism must also acknowledge its *distance* from Bachelard's thought, however apt its application might seem to a given context. First and foremost, my primary interest, unlike Bachelard, is less in the phenomenological exploration of the imagination as a subject *in and of itself*, and more oriented toward how this understanding of active imagination enables the interpretation of an aesthetic work. Second, by way of distinguishing his work from literary criticism, Bachelard was also open about his lack of intellectual investment in art's cultural and historical context. I do not intend to follow this logic, at least not as thoroughly as Bachelard does. Although the present chapter is perhaps less attentive to integrating cultural history than others in this book, this history nevertheless forms an implied background—one that,

I hope to show in the following, possesses striking ethical implications. With his knowledge of science, Bachelard understood rationalism, like subjective and objective positionality, to have been fundamentally undermined by radical transformations of theoretical physics in the first quarter of the twentieth century.[31] Thus, while the truest "subject" of his thought might be the human imagination (rather than, say, the *oeuvre* of Stephane Mallarmé) Bachelard did not separate the imagination and the work of art by a binary distinction, but rather understood them as being mutually and co-creatively imbricated. Even if Bachelard himself was not interested in making his work *about* literature, it thus still retains the potential to offer significant insight into aesthetic meaning and experience.

Scholarship has sometimes been uncomfortable with Bachelard's generally positive, even redemptive understanding of the role of poetry in human experience.[32] While I do not, in general, share this discomfort, there is nevertheless a undeniable tension in adopting Bachelardian thought to interpret *Chinatown*, a bleakly pessimistic and deeply paranoid film in which elemental images of water and earth are associated with paralysis and terror—a film bereft of any final imaginative rejuvenation or reparative sense of well-being.[33] It is thus strange, given the sense of possibility that I feel Bachelard's thought does, in fact, hold for the exploration of aesthetic experience, that this foray into adopting it immediately strips out his optimistic, affirmative images, replacing them with chaos, hostility, and sexual and economic exploitation. My reading, necessarily devoted to my own "resonances" with the soundtrack of *Chinatown*, will nevertheless attempt also to maintain a self-reflexive stance *outside of*, or perhaps *alongside* these impressions. I will try to acknowledge the ethical imperative on the part of contemporary film viewers to engage with *Chinatown*'s mythic paranoia *on the mythic level at which it is communicating*, while also maintaining a subjective locus that questions mythic paranoia's very specific and troubling ethical limitations. While the "philosophy of well-being" with which Bachelard has been associated feels, frankly, perverse in application to *Chinatown*, I nevertheless think it works—allowing for an investment in the experiential reality of the elemental imagination, while also sharpening the need to conceptualize the limits of mythic paranoia as a way of thinking about the past, the present, and their relationship through the medium of cinema. To do so, however, is not to effect a heroic binary operation in which we oppose dangerously retrograde myth with the rationalized "daylight" force of critique. Rather, it is a kind of opening, allowing us explore these myths in a way that gives empathetic, yet critical voice to their irreducible paradoxes and disturbing potential truths.

What, then, does Bachelard's thought offer us in terms of understanding *Chinatown* and its soundtrack as navigations of a mythic past? For one, his thought provides a departure point into a hermeneutics that is rooted in aural materiality and the affective weight of elemental images, thus offering conceptual extensions of, and perhaps even alternatives to a dominantly narratological tradition of film music analysis. While traditional expressive ends of story, character, and locale will inevitably be of pragmatic importance to filmmakers and cognitive importance to audiences, I would argue that by focusing less on what a particular timbre or melody *means*, and more on how it unfolds along the connotative pathways by which it directly impacts and resonates with our imagination, we might do justice not only to the poetic world of the film and its inevitably situated readers, but also to the strange co-creative energies that tie them together. Music, like sound itself, possesses not only metaphorical and representational properties, but also a secondary, interrelated ontology as a structure of feeling that is deeply intertwined with our ways of imagining and experiencing the world. The use of sound, in other words, doesn't just "refer" to the presence of water and aridity as diegetic objects, or even as narrative themes—it also instantiates their affective effects, resonating with a mythic imaginary as a field of meaning that directly inflects our perspective toward the perceived distance and presence of the past.

This approach to *Chinatown*'s mythic past also engages the aesthetics of timbre, which has remained underrepresented in the literature of film music.[34] Whereas most readings of the film have emphasized Goldsmith's blend of traditionalism with modernist techniques, or have explored the score's narrative logic through the deployment of melodic motives, an examination of timbre arguably offers greater insight into phenomenal or imaginative experience itself. Using concepts of "strong" and "weak" theory, as explored by Eve Kossofsky Sedgwick, among others, we might note that timbre, more so than other musical parameters, engages these categories. Thick textual descriptions of timbre can come across as merely impressionistic, yet they also possess the virtue of weak theory in evading prescriptively rationalist parameters. By contrast, strong theoretical approaches to timbre, such as wave-form analysis, can seem entirely abstracted from the mysterious and irreducible aesthetic affect of a sounding object. This shows us how a close interpretive attention to timbre might also speak to the phenomenal reality of mythic presence. More than any other musical parameter, timbre seems to *happen to us* as we encounter music experientially. Timbral analysis (at least in its thickly descriptive form) constitutes something closer to "weak theory," complementing the "stronger" knowledge of denotative analysis rooted in more objectively stable structures of melody or harmony. Bachelard's thought, in turn, arguably interlaces elements of weak and strong theory to creative and productive ends, an approach Sedgwick advocated in her touchstone article on "paranoid" and "reparative" styles of reading.[35] Bachelard is invested not only in reading myths (his "complexes," which adopt both traditional Greco-Roman myths and modern literary images) but also, by engaging with the "direct ontology" of the material imagination, in *re-writing* myths, often in order to find in them a more constructive or liberating role for the imagination. This effort, Bachelard's own "revisionist mythology," was motivated by his desire to depart from what he understood as the prescriptive interpretations associated with the consummately strong theory of psychoanalysis.[36]

Chinatown's Elemental Soundtrack

My reading of "wet" and "dry" images in *Chinatown*'s soundtrack departs in several ways from Bachelard. While *Earth and Reveries of Will* (1943) develops ideas that are perhaps most resonant with the role played by Noah Cross in the film's imaginary, there is in Bachelard's writing no exact parallel to the desert, or dryness, as we are employing this category. This is likely because Bachelard generally understands the element of earth not through "dryness," but through its moisture and malleability. Nevertheless, there are implications for how Bachelard reads earth as being imbued into the process of work, will, and agency—of bending matter to one's desires: for Bachelard, these are sources of a fundamentally precognitive pleasure, deeply interwoven into our sense of being and our experience of the world. For Noah Cross, however—who bends to his desire the rule of law, the incest taboo, and the economic future of Los Angeles—the pleasure of work and making is understood to be fundamentally corrupt.[37] Reading Noah Cross, we discover a figure balanced between the film's central images. A bringer of life-water, Cross also embodies the paralysis of the desert and the inevitability of death and corruption: he offers water, but does so with the desert looming threateningly behind his back. The fear of the desert thus grants him power within the social world of human beings, and his water is imbued with a sense of moral complicity inherent in civilization itself. The domesticated water that drips from the tap in Ida Sessions's kitchen and the torrent of runoff water that almost drowns Jake function as diverse, yet interlinked, aural reminders of water's power to sustain, but also to obliterate life.

We needn't be chained to Bachelard's complexes. The present reading isn't necessarily about finding one-to-one correspondences, but rather in a broader application of the elements as the vectors of imaginative dynamism that Bachelard understood them to be.[38] Our interpretation of *Chinatown* is thus more broadly "Bachelardian" in spirit. In this spirit, moving through several of the most striking musical cues in the film, we find that a complex interpenetration of wet and dry mythic images construct our aesthetic experience within a tightening grip of paranoid inevitability. One factor within this dynamic is the evocation of pastness and presentness conveyed by modernist and jazz styles. While musical styles are, of course, conveyed by multiple factors working in complex, often slippery conjunction, and while essentializing bonds between styles and instruments (which can, of course, be performed in many styles) inevitably risk reduction, we can nevertheless locate two principal instruments whose material presence functions in association with the score's elemental stylistic dynamics—the solo trumpet with jazz, and the piano with modernism.

The solo trumpet, in *Chinatown*'s score, is reliably—if not exclusively—paired with Goldsmith's haunting, and jazz-inflected central melodic theme, first articulated in the opening credits. We might read this period jazz sensibility as articulating Jake's character: an imperfect yet chivalric figure making his way through the ethical and physical threats of the modern world, reminiscent of Raymond Chandler's recurring protagonist, Philip Marlowe. In this way, the theme immediately brings both stylistic and temporal implications into the foreground—the trumpet work in the score, performed by studio veteran Euan Rasey, blends a phrasal and timbral fluidity with an identifiably "showbiz" brightness of tone—a sound we might associate with older (pre-bop, pre-cool) players such as Bunny Berrigan, whose popular 1937 recording of "I Can't Get Started" also appears on the soundtrack. Rasey's sound also recalls one player more proximate to the *noir* tradition, namely Harry James, whose sound (in many ways implausibly) characterized Kirk Douglas's alcoholic descent through the spheres of the modern cityscape in *Young Man with a Horn* (1950), from the company of its decadent socialites to the naked city realism of its grimy, desperate gutters.[39] In this way, Goldsmith's score also taps into cultural associations of the solo jazz trumpet with alienated masculinity.[40]

In addition to the musically "composed" imprint of jazz harmonies, instrumentation, and melodic gestures, the unique resonance and physicality of the instrument itself play a key role in the score's material dynamic imagination, with the elemental suggestiveness and timbral scope of the trumpet also imbricated in its affective meanings.[41] The trumpet is a thing of forged earth (metal) and yet, through the interfacing medium of the performer, it is also a thing of air and water. The trumpet is a physically hard instrument imbued with and speaking through the varyingly relaxed and propulsive forces of breath. It is a sound with both hard edges and moist internal softness. The opening theme of the film, which becomes Goldsmith's mono-thematic musical resource, first emerges in the main title credits through liquescent glissando shimmers seemingly played on the inside of the piano, and high, whistling string harmonics, the latter of which articulate, as through a watery blur, the rising major second that will also memorably define the melody of the theme (0:00:03). As Rasey's solo begins, we thus already sense that behind the discrete, memorable melody lies a sphere of resonant liquescent depths, a wash of sound (0:00:22). We've been given cause to doubt the transparency and authenticity of this melody: its evocation of the past is undercut by its modernist framing within oceanic depths and airy whistles—as if Bunny Berrigan had somehow gotten lost in Henry Cowell's "Tides of Manaunaun."[42]

The theme is in two slow, eight-bar phrases, with melodically mirrored first halves and bridge-like second halves, thus suggesting an ABAC form. A single chorus-like statement is followed by a two-measure coda that returns to the opening rising gesture that initiated A, creating some sense of melodic return, even as the ensemble quickly dies away under Rasey, compromising its closure with a larger sense of incompleteness as the cue ends (0:01:38). Two points of juncture between solo and ensemble are particularly noteworthy for their stylistic and temporal implications. Closing the first large phrase, a bridge-like section features a descending sequence of rising seconds (which Rasey gives a modestly, yet deliciously padded sense of Berrigan-like rhythmic play), which leads into a return to A, slightly augmented with ruminative ornamental turns on the melody's initial sustained pitch (0:00:53). Taken together, this moment presents the specifically *vocal, breathy* quality of the trumpet's delivery by pointing outside of the instrument, and toward a style of jazz ballad singing in which performative variation often consists of relatively small deviations from the notated melody, rather than melodically free improvisation over changes. The trumpet thus emphasizes itself not as a machine built for speed and agility, but as a substitute for the human voice—Rasey *croons* his solo. Second, in C, when the strings take over and articulate the melody in high register and close voicings, it's Old Hollywood all the way—an old arranger's trick of varying a chorus-based structure by swapping solo and ensemble voices halfway through the bridge (0:01:23). Juxtaposing strange sounds with familiar stylistic models (Berrigan, James, jazz ballad singing and arranging), the film immediately presents a tension between Hollywoods Old and New, pasts mythic and pasts present.

The film's second major cue begins to draw the elemental sound-images established by the main title into more pointed juxtaposition. The cue marks a hard cut from the city planning meeting at which Hollis rejects the new dam. The meeting gives way to chaos as a desperate farmer stages a protest by releasing his sheep in city hall. From this sonically thick moment, audiovisual space suddenly and abruptly opens up and empties out (0:08:07). We cut to Jake following Mulwray from a considerable distance as he investigates a dried-up riverbed. With this second major cue, we begin to explore the piano itself as a Bachelardian image. The piano functions here as a liminal instrument, whose exterior conceals the disconnect between the hard, percussive attack of modernist objectivity and the soft, Romantic subjectivity of the solo character piece, polarities which are resonant with surface and depth, dry and moist images. As the cue begins, we hear a percussive, rearticulation of a single note played on the keyboard—perhaps translating the buzzing fly on the effects track that had caught Goldsmith's attention. But, after the tactile *ping* of its initial sound, the energy of the piano figure is gradually *dissolved* by the slowing of its unmetered articulation, like a hard pebble that falls, dissolving into its own aqueous resonance (0:08:12). The sound-image of the piano, in this way, tends toward liquescence, or perhaps *liquefaction*— an unmetered spilling over borders. With these notes suspended over resonant depths of gong percussion, sustained strings, and upward sweeps on the interior piano strings, we perhaps sense the riverbed as a wet location alienated from its proper purpose.

The extended performance mode of playing a piano directly on the strings similarly draws, as does the solo trumpet, upon embodied images. Reaching into the piano to play it, you reach *down* to the instrument's depths, claim them, and bring them up to the listenable surface; you turn the piano inside out. But your plunder drawn from the depths, your hard pinch and release as you pluck the strings, or the dry rubbing across their surface, can only dissolve upon reaching the surface, into blurred pools of resonance. As Hollis speaks with a Latino boy on a horse, their conversation inaudible to Jake, the piano gesture stretches, expands, and sequences downward, wanders a bit before slowing to a stop—the pebble, again, like a conceptual rough spot that engages Jake's inquisitive curiosity (0:08:45). As the cue concludes, these gestures (strum, hit, dissolve) alternate with muted octaves on the harp, hinting at intervallic elements of the main title theme—a rising major second, followed by a rising fifth that turns, arpeggiating, downward (0:09:10). Elemental sensations are drawn together and given coherence by the syncretic presence of the central theme.

As Jake's investigation proceeds and he and his operatives spy on Hollis and Catherine, wet and dry images continue to intertwine and mingle. Beginning with a near-repetition of the previous cue's sequenced piano dissolves, the cue transitions between locations, as Jake first photographs Hollis and Catherine rowing in Echo Park, and then spies on them having lunch at the hotel where Catherine has been hidden from Noah Cross (0:14:50). As this apparently "wet" scene (both in terms of the location and the salacious relationship the detectives mistakenly presume), we hear a recurrence of music that previously characterized the dry riverbed. Music thus forms a link between a "dry" scene and a "wet" scene. The rowing scene "repurposes" the liquescent cue, making it suggestive of the tangible, iridescent beauty of the location, rather than desiccated absence. It also suggests Bachelard's thoughts on the placidity, but also superficiality, of clear transparent water. For Bachelard, this type of water image suggests the free play of light and narcissistic reflection, but can also portend hidden depths of material resonance.[43] In this new context, Goldsmith's dappled musical gestures now sound positively Ravelian, but reinscribed as pastoral prettiness; we might also perhaps sense their capacity to deceive, intuiting the presence of darker, oceanic depths beneath the clear surface.

As the scene transitions, Jake follows the pair to the hotel where we hear the first instance of what will become an important timbral gesture throughout the remainder of the film—a kind of "busy signal" created by muted bells struck in a metronomically regular rhythm, a striking contrast with the freely unmetered dissolves we've become familiar with on the piano and harp (0:15:34). This sound, too, is a complex of the film's diverse timbral polarities: we hear a sound that *should* ring, that *should* possess ambience but which forcibly doesn't, sounding dully and monotonously under string lines that spiral upward, aggregating into a chord that grows increasingly dissonant. Underneath this progression, we hear for the first time a subtle element of Latin percussion—a güiro sets up a tightly controlled rhythmic ostinato.

The güiro, frequently paired in the score with woodblocks, seems to draw our attention to an element of the Latin exotic, but this is far more complicated than it might initially appear. Exoticism is not what it seems in *Chinatown*. While the most common example is the complex thematics of East Asian association suggested by the film's title, the role of a Latin exotic is similarly duplicitous, like the diegetic mariachi music that seeps into the background as Noah Cross meets Jake for lunch at the recreational club that he owns (1:03:48). As Cross assures Jake, the mariachis are an exotic trapping, entertaining key donors to the local sheriff's re-election campaign. The mariachis are not presented as uninflected "local color"—instead, everything in Cross's world can be co-opted, assimilated into a cynical politics of show business whose only ultimate end is Cross's accumulation of power. Thus, hints toward a Latin topic in Goldsmith's score never really *deliver* as non-ironic ethnic or cultural reference points, reinforcing their more abstract role as sonorities whose timbral quality within the score (dry scrapings) is coextensive to their affective purpose.[44]

One additional recurring timbral-melodic gesture that Goldsmith keeps in play is a sequence of low piano "hits," usually in mechanically repetitive, occasionally contrapuntal, yet melodically unpredictable patterns. This Bartokian gesture is prone to sudden starts and stops, and an atonal (or at least freely chromatic) harmonic scope. These aggressive piano hits lurk throughout the film, frequently arising in moments of narrative threat, or when Jake is acting upon his cynically suspicious nature. The muted, thudding, dry quality of these sounds associates them with both the threatening brutality of the desert and the barren and corrosive force of Jake's cynical (and often false) assumptions. First introduced at the end of a brief cue in which Jake snoops around Mulwray's office (0:22:36), they are developed more fully as Jake returns to the dried-up riverbed after Mulwray's murder (0:38:40), when Jake suspiciously exits the love scene, kicking out Evelyn's taillight so he can follow her car (1:28:56), and when Jake arrives at Ida Sessions's house to find her murdered (1:38:35).

The piano "hits" also appear prominently in two scenes in which Jake is threatened by Cross's thugs, but in these instances, the sound quality depends not on artificially altering the sound of the piano, and rather upon timbral effects created by register, dynamics, and the tactility of the performer's attack.

In these instances, we hear a sound that increasingly blurs the boundary between wet and dry sound—the short, forceful attack leaves us both with the dry *slap* of hammer against string, the quick, biting *tang* of sympathetic resonance from the immediate percussive attack, and the broader, more fluid resonance of the vibrating piano string. As Jake confronts assailants at the nursing home that serves as a front for Cross's fraudulent land purchases, the eruption of physical violence is synchronized to a forceful iteration so extreme in register and forceful attack that the "grain" of the piano sound becomes as important to cue's affective charge as its coiling chromatic runs (1:19:43). The brutality of these gestures is thus a brutality of both dryness and oceanic resonance, an attack of the desert, like the sting of a scorpion, dissolving into a wash of ambience, like breakers on the shoreline.

Flowing Certainties: Love and Paranoia

As Jake flees the nursing home and is rescued by Evelyn, the brutal fight cue dissolves into the recognizable main theme, plausibly reinscribed for the first time as a love theme, cutting across the scene transition and taken up without break by the harp as Evelyn and Jake regroup at the Mulwray house (1:20:11). As the cue ends, Jake begins to open up to Evelyn about his troubled past. She can't open up about hers, of course. Whereas his is simply traumatized, hers is defined by an unspeakable taboo—even in the later scene where she discloses her father's rape, Evelyn speaks largely in euphemisms and connotation. The developing scene plays in a subtle, but unmissable way upon the film's thematic array of images. Jake requests peroxide to tend to his nostril, slit open by Cross's thugs in an earlier scene. As he exposes his damaged nose (perhaps an olfactory iteration of the film's central thematic image of epistemological doubt: two perceptual apertures, one functional and the other damaged), Evelyn reveals her analogous physical atypicality, as Jake gazes into her eyes, and realizes that one of her two irises has a discoloration, or "flaw."

The ensuing love scene cleverly uses temporally marked jazz idioms to create a brief moment in which Jake and Evelyn, we might say, are "flowing" into one another. As Jake notices the flaw in Evelyn's iris, the love scene's musical cue begins with the score's only use of the electric piano—an instrument associated with contemporary, rather than traditional or "period" jazz. The electric keyboard is present only as an introductory gesture, playing a short, sinking series of chromatic submediants, giving a sense of unexpected transformation and softening as Evelyn and Jake embrace and kiss. The instrumentation briefly and efficiently provides a noticeably "seventies" frame to the sound (1:23:02). Rasey's solo on the main melody floats overtop, somewhat unmoored from the accompaniment, repeated chords and a descending scale fragment on an acoustic piano. Thus, when the film achieves a sense of emotional immediacy and authenticity, it does so by combing and comingling musical gestures of past and present. The mythic presence of "the modern" and its musical style, however, are nowhere in sight, and a different and distinct sense of contemporaneity created by an unexpected move toward jazz fusion, playing here as non-ironic and sincere, but extremely short-lived—this is the only cue in the film to strike this balance of elements, suggesting perhaps a momentary engagement with more positive Bachelardian associations—Jake and Evelyn's sexuality as an impulsive "giving in," articulated through images of aqueous flow.

If Jake and Evelyn experience these surface pleasures of water, however, they cannot avoid the smothering depths for long, nor can they avoid retreating back into the desiccated wastelands of their individual traumas. After a characteristically classical ellipsis jumps ahead to the couple's post-coital chit-chat, the melody shifts first, mid-phrase, into the high register strings as a transitional gesture (1:23:55). The electric piano, with its immediacy and sonic warmth, briefly notes the scene transition and is henceforth banished from the score. The melody sinks deeper into lower strings as the conversation moves to Jake's past. The sound of a ticking clock also becomes audible, anticipating the use of this gesture of frozen-yet-moving time: dead Ida Sessions's sink and Evelyn's incest revelation also noticeably feature dripping or ticking sounds. Gradually, as Jake reveals how his experiences as a district attorney's officer in Chinatown have colored his cynical worldview, the melody moves into the solo piano, but continues to sink in register. Jake's revelation that he left the job after his actions brought about the death of a woman he was trying to save corresponds to an arrival point: extremely low piano notes in an extremely soft dynamic, articulating the theme's initial rising second in a watery, echoic haze of low string tremolos (1:25:26). This register of the piano possesses an implicitly percussive, subsonic quality, as if the discrete pitch is only a shadow of the piano string's thudding tangibility, the thickly overtone-laden cloud of resonance that is the real substance of the note. The discrete pitches seem to become tangible through vanishing echoes of themselves. The cue ends, fading out under the ringing phone that will call Evelyn away. Mirroring Bachelard's preoccupation with the dichotomy of surface waters and depth, we might imagine a descent that occurs on a number of levels, of which the most obvious emotional darkening of the scene's tone follows the reveal of Jake's background as part of a larger narrative movement, a "coming down" from their sexual encounter into paranoid reality. It is also, however, a descent into a musical register in which wet and dry images seem somehow to merge—the "bottoming out" of this cue could be imagined as a drowning, or as a paralytic entombment in earth; the distinction, perhaps, becomes pointedly negligible. It also traces another vector, a temporal one, that links together Jake's lived, experienced past with the historical past represented by the film world, as implicitly viewed from a later era of cinematic spectatorship.

As the film proceeds, Goldsmith begins to orchestrate a subtly shifting series of recurrences in which these timbral elements continually circulate. And yet these recurrences seem to have less to do with narrative development than they do with constructing the elemental dimensions of a film world, a specific *type* of world in which certain types of things—horrible things, mythic things, inevitable things—will always cyclically recur. *Chinatown* is often understood as a monothematic score, and the theme introduced in main title credits is, indeed, the only *melodically* recognizable and traditionally phrasal recurring element. But despite its monothematic nature, the score also employs an arsenal of recognizable timbral families (strums and prickly rubs over open strings, punctuated attacks and ringing resonances, muffled and muddy sounds) that are constantly in dialogue with its highly recognizable central melody, conveying the imaginative substance of this past world as being paralyzed, timeless—hopelessly trapped between opposing elemental forces.

After their reverie is interrupted by the ringing phone, Evelyn is clearly panicked and makes unconvincing excuses for suddenly needing to leave. His curiosity aroused, Jake secretly follows, and discovers her keeping Catherine—whom he assumes to have been Hollis's lover—in what he assumes to be captivity. As Jake follows her car, the main theme reasserts itself in a faster tempo, conveying Jake's newfound suspicions and concerns (1:29:25). But beyond the thematic-narrative dimension, remarkably, the "busy tone" muted bell, the percussive low piano hit, and the dry güiro percussion all return as well, forming synchronized accompaniment figures woven around the solo trumpet melody, a striking feat of cumulative musical cohesion. This rough combination of elements will later recur, in varied form, in another cue in which Jake again pursues Evelyn, returning to this house newly sure of Evelyn's guilt after finding the spectacles in the Mulwray's saltwater pond (1:47:15). In both scenes, this thick proliferation of recognizable elements creates a sense of Jake enmeshed in a swirl of clues, associations, and potential meanings—they are cues that show Jake in hot pursuit of the truth, but these truths will prove to be false, overwhelmed by the blind contingency of data.

In both of these cues, the theme vanishes upon Jake's arrival. In the second scene, the cue ends entirely to make room for the potent aural vacancy that characterizes the scene in which Evelyn and Noah Cross's incestuous relationship is revealed. But in the first, as Jake spies through the window, observing (but not hearing) Evelyn and Catherine's confrontation, the musical soundtrack dissolves into various ostinati and athematic riffs on these evocative sounds (1:29:28). We hear *col legno* snapping of bows against strings. Sweeping harp and nervy glissandos played directly on the piano strings, and a gesture consisting of three quick woodblock hits, take over the texture (1:30:00). The sounds, as it were, recede from the middle ground of the theme, leaving a kind of gap between wet and dry sounds that is occupied by a unique sound occurring nowhere else in the film. We hear, as Jake peers through the window from outside, a sound like distorted human voices (1:30:50). This curious sound challenges the ontological distinction between sound and music in a way that appears nowhere else in *Chinatown*'s soundtrack—the sound is rhythmically distinct from the musical texture, but aurally distinct from the *actual* diegetic sounds of muffled, indecipherable speech that we understand to be diegetically audible to Jake.[45]

This sound is, in one simple word, muddy. Mud, a mixture of earth and water, is a crucial idea in Bachelard's theorization of the material imagination. The dynamic imagination of mud (and, by extension, clay) is fundamental to Bachelard's view of art as an artisanal act of making, a form of creation in which our imaginative will intermingles with the agency, knowledge, and sense work that are unique to our hands *themselves*, as well as to the resistance or complicity of the non-human medium we are manipulating.[46] The image of mud here destabilizes the ontological division of sound and music, as well as the division between dry (legible, intelligible) and wet (blurry, slippery) sound. Elsewhere in the film, the timbres of ocean and desert can at least be conceptually distinguished, however much they interpenetrate within the musical texture, or even within a single instrumental sound (the paradoxically percussive ringing of the piano, for example). But this distorted effect binds together intelligible and unintelligible speech into same sound. As the scene ends, we hear the main title theme, that mediator of the film's elements, seem to give up, reduced to pure abstraction—a group of three, then four identical pitches—essentially the rhythm groupings of the theme, with no melodic profile—plucked on the inside of the piano, ending the scene (1:31:25).

In general, the polarity of water and earth drawn out in the present chapter is specific to broader images of ocean and desert, the physical and geographical, as well as imaginative polarities of the film world. In the center of the mutual tension between these elements, however, is a kind of imaginal vortex, a blank space standing for an awareness of the primal horror that myth is capable of abetting. Mud is, as it were, the exception—we hear muddy sound at the point that might represent Jake's most significant moment of cynical misperception. But mud is also associated, in a more abstract way, with the figures of Noah Cross, civilization, and perhaps human life itself—the Stones of Deucalion, cast by "Noah" himself.[47] If Cross, in a perverse way, *is* civilization, then civilization is his mud, his act of willful making and sculpting. "Hollis was always fascinated by tide pools," Cross muses, standing next to the pond in which he murdered his son-in-law, continuing, "he used to say, 'That's where life begins'" (2:01:38). This mud, however—a demonstration of both the depths of Cross's depravity and its inescapable imbrication into the sculpting of civilization—is unlike the muddy sounds of Jake's misperception. Instead, it is marked by a musical absence that might stand in for that very vortex. There is a pointed lack of music in the scene in which Evelyn reveals the incestuous dimension of her father's patriarchy, or the scene in which, confronted with Hollis's murder, Cross blandly acknowledges that his goal is not the accumulation of monetary wealth, but power as its own end—his reward is to create the future, to create civilization. These gaps, perhaps, speak of this type of mud through a kind of abjection—we might imagine the musical soundtrack recoiling from this vortex, retreating to a place where aestheticized horror is still possible.

Chinatown's Chinatown: Hitting the Bottom

The main title theme is used a bit more freely, more liberally—even unimaginatively—in the last quarter of the film. We hear it in as Jake returns home, having suspiciously rejected Evelyn's overtures to continue their relationship after discovering that she has been hiding Catherine (1:35:25), as transition music as he drives to Ida Sessions's house (1:37:43), lurking in the low strings as the Mulwray's gardener fishes the spectacles from the pond (1:46:50), and as a beautifully pure statement on the solo piano as Jake is finally introduced to Catherine, cementing his decision to help them escape from Los Angeles (1:53:33). It is as if, exhausted by the interplay of theme and elemental images, the score retreats to a less provocative, more predictable place in our attention. Or, alternately, it is as if (with the pieces of the puzzle together and Hollis Mulwray's murderer revealed) the score's conceptual tensions recede, its investigative work done. After Evelyn's death, the film ends with a final statement of the main theme, largely identical to the opening credits (2:08:30). In terms of narrative, this return to the beginning might create a sense of formal closure, or a sad reflection on the lost possibility for Jake and Evelyn's relationship. Most depressingly, this final melodic return might express the circularity of mythic temporality, a reprise that denies that we might ever have gotten anywhere different or better. But before this point of closure, one penultimate cue does some more interesting work within the film's elemental imaginary.

As Cross and his henchmen turn the tables on Jake and head to Chinatown, where Evelyn and Catherine are hiding with their butler, the film briefly enters a state of visual abstraction, with two shots of illuminated neon signs at night, the first reading "Hong Kong," and accompanied by hanging paper lanterns (2:03:44). Following the film's larger logic of minimizing the exotic, this is the only scene actually set in Chinatown. We hear the pounding percussive resonance of the piano hits, playing the same twisting, Bartokian lines that earlier appeared in the fight scene at the nursing home. This time, however, the energy of the cue is strangely altered by its slower tempo and the enormous, metrically suspended gap between the first two musical phrases. After the camera position moves to the interior of the Jake's car, *sixteen seconds* of diegetic sound with no dialogue elapse before the gesture returns for a second, equally forceful phrase (2:04:09). The moment is a startling and disorienting deformation of traditional expectations for filmic rhythm.[48] The line repeats once more, this time on a heavily muted prepared piano, accompanied by a single low pitch on the solo trumpet, blown with a strangled, air-less timbre that seems not to stop, but instead to sputter out (2:04:27). Rasey's solo trumpet, up to this point, has been indelibly associated with the main theme and its role as a mediator of the score's elemental images, and this transformation of its sound so late in the film is highly uncharacteristic. But there is no need for mediation anymore. We're at the center of the vortex, having arrived in Chinatown. Chinatown is the terminal locus of the film's logic—both moving forward, to its inevitably grim narrative conclusion, and backward, to the oppressive resonance of the past. Through carefully dispersed bits of dialogue and backstories, the film has consistently and conscientiously prepared us for this moment of unsought return. We even see this in how Jake carries himself as a character. Earlier in the film he is prone to condescending anti-Chinese racism, yet when Jake angrily confronts the Mulwrays' butler toward the end of the film, he impulsively yells a few words of Chinese (1:47:42). As Jake gets closer to Chinatown, physically and psychologically, old knowledge returns to the surface, and old experiences repeat themselves.

What is Chinatown? Among other things, we should acknowledge that Chinatown is a colloquial term for a geographic area of Los Angeles in which large East Asian communities resided in the late thirties—and still reside—living lives as complex and irreducibly multifaceted as those of the (almost entirely) white characters of the film *Chinatown*, whose only contact with Asian Americans is through their employment as domestic servants. And yet I think a critique of the relationship between the geographical, factual Chinatown and the film's mythic imaginary in terms of racist erasure would be shortsighted and largely uninteresting. The mythic Chinatown of *Chinatown* is uninterested in complex ethnic and cultural reality, but it is also (perhaps to its credit) almost entirely uninterested in exploiting the image of the factual Chinatown for exotic ends. As screenwriter Robert Towne related, this caused some friction in preproduction, with producer Robert Evans concerned that the title's abstract meaning would confuse audiences.[49]

Chinatown's Chinatown is a locus defined by permanent stasis, the terminus of paranoia and its resulting ethos of paralysis. This Chinatown is mythic because it supersedes historical temporality, presenting an image of elemental density that cannot be logically deconstructed, rationalized, or argued away. It speaks not just to things that have happened in the past, but to things that have always already happened, and which will inevitably always happen again. Rooted in images of elemental materiality, this Chinatown is mythically paranoid with a vengeance, and any critical effort to reduce it to social reality would simply spin its wheels as Chinatown looks on and laughs. Chinatown is the (ostensible) mythic truth that, at a depth of the human experience preceding culture and perhaps even preceding cognition, we are deeply and eternally fucked, because the seminal gesture that creates civilization out of chaos is the very same gesture that imbues it with perennial corruption.

This vision of the world clearly resonated with director Roman Polanski, and its relationship to his artistic proclivities and persona, as well as to his personal circumstances, decisions, and actions in the years both before and since he directed *Chinatown*, bears some concluding discussion here. Polanski's horrific childhood experiences during the Holocaust and the murder of his pregnant wife and several close friends by the Charles Manson cult are, of course, well documented, as are the circumstances surrounding his flight from the United States in 1978 after sexually assaulting a thirteen-year-old girl, a crime which, on the occasions where he has been willing to discuss it in recent years, he clearly remains able to delude himself into understanding as a misconstrued instance of consensual sex.[50] Although the number of people willing to accept such a rationalization at face value thankfully seems to be in decline, the painful realities of inequity and abuse that such attitudes enable are, of course, far from extinct. Although the multiple authorship inherent to film often makes unraveling the threads of intentionality difficult, there is no disagreement among anyone involved in *Chinatown* that the brutal pessimism of Evelyn's death and Catherine's capture resulted from Roman Polanski's intervention during filming. And while Polanski has always been unwilling to entertain interpretive connections between his life and his films, his collaborators have not: in a 1994 interview, Robert Towne speculated upon the ways in which Polanski's fatalistic alteration of his screenplay had likely been colored by the murder of his wife three years earlier: "That's life. Beautiful blondes die in Los Angeles. Sharon had."[51] We should note, however, how easily one might, adopting the same cynical disaffection, hypothetically manipulate this rhetoric in a different, and deeply troubling, direction: "That's life. Young girls get raped in Los Angeles. Roman Polanski raped one."

Chinatown itself implicitly accepts the fatalistic and deeply pessimistic notion of mythic paranoia embodied by its Chinatown. Perhaps it shouldn't— but then again, perhaps it isn't this simple. Perhaps to critique mythic paranoia from the outside, as if its acceptance were simply a matter of rational choice, is to limit ourselves to the confines of a critique unsuited to engaging with the edges and limits of rationality that are so vital to the phenomenal experience of art. These affective realities—whatever they *are*— represent more than simply the transparent falsehoods of power which might be exposed and thus vanquished through discourse. It is perhaps these realities that have made myth such a perennial tool for imagining and navigating the complex relationship between the past and the present. In any case, the history of *this* film, its meanings, and its creators places ethical issues at stake that are uniquely pointed among the films considered in this book. Ultimately, *Chinatown*'s elemental imaginary allows us to explore the role that myth plays in understanding the past through the cinematic soundtrack. By allowing the conceptual space for myth to be both imagined and, following Bachelard, for it to be understood as mutually interwoven with our imagining selves, like *Chinatown*'s Chinatown the mythic past becomes something that is *both* "in here" and "out there," a sensibility in which timelessness can, as in our reading of the revisionist Western, be understood experientially, if only as an act of the imagination. But with *Chinatown*, it is also urgently important to recognize that it can be *experienced-around*, and thus negotiated rather than simply exposed and rejected, and that this perspective might afford us both an empathetic sense of caution and a sense of possibility—a sense that *Chinatown*'s Chinatown, however powerful, however real, is just one story among many.

In a psychoanalytic reading from the early nineties, John Belton discusses *Chinatown* as a film in which the Real has "broken through the cracks" of postmodern, reified culture. For Belton, this possibility is facilitated by the film medium's unique representational system that "exceeds language and other Symbolic systems" and puts us "into contact," or a direct apprehension of the irrational.[52] However, Belton's argument, essentially that *Chinatown* exposes and productively deconstructs the rationalism of the classical detective story, remains as de-pathologizing and, essentially, curative as any psychoanalyst or gumshoe might want. If the Real is the function of the imaginal that marks the limited ability of rationality to reify irrational experience, then its apprehension, according to Belton, might offer a "cure" for the reification that associated with the detective story, which functions as a larger system of control in which knowledge, narrative, and (frequently patriarchal) power are knotted together. But the Real, we might very easily argue, only does this at the expense of any "cure" that might be directed toward the film's own pessimistic and undeniably politically retrograde worldview. Perhaps, with these dueling and incompatible cures at play, both ironically emerging from an implicitly shared location within academic-political progressivism, we might simply drop the term "cure" and use the more familiar one: critique.

The ethical questions raised by *Chinatown*, then, are perhaps relatable to an academic tradition that has sought to contextualize and critically understand the worldview of academic critique itself, and the ways in which this worldview's self-definitional assumptions might be challenged or expanded. From this perspective, a hermeneutics of suspicion can easily become complicit *with paranoia*, albeit in an ostensibly secularized form.[53] In pointing this out, my intent is not, as Rita Felski has cautioned against, to critique the mode of critique for not being sufficiently critical—this would, in fact, be an exercise in the very essence of paranoia.[54] But critical language that exposes the substance of mythic experience as false consciousness, subject to confrontational, objectifying dissection, can only operate on the presumption of being separable from the object of its critique. If this is the case, it is arguable that by critiquing the worldview of *Chinatown* as reactionary nihilism, we simply dig ourselves deeper into Chinatown. Perhaps one way out of this impasse would be a sense of openness toward (yet simultaneous distance from) the experience of myth. To perceive the limitations of mythic paranoia as a way of understanding the past, then, we must also empathetically perceive its significance as aesthetic experience, *working through* its truth value using critical language as a tool of experiential affordance that opens us to the affective reality of the material imagination—and with it, to the potential affordances that Gaston Bachelard understood it to hold. In this way, a more vital, living, and imaginatively reciprocal relationship to the presence of the past might become accessible to critical dialogue.

The timbral immediacy and material immanence of New Hollywood representations of the past, which are as much a thing of the imaginal world as they are representations of screen and soundtrack, allow us to understand myth as a form of reality, and to thus recuperate its sense of possibilities and utopian alternatives, its affordances for escape into aestheticized sensory immersion, as well as the danger that might accompany its terrifying and cynical visions of modernity.[55] But this reality is always incomplete, and thus ethically insufficient, in that both melancholy pleasures and paranoid terrors open up engagement with a field of affective meaning at the expense of foreclosing the possibility for meaningful action. To hold both of these realities—that of myth as irreducible temporal otherness, and that of our critical externality to this state of being—in a sustained, productive tension would not only be a valuable exercise in critical pluralism, but might represent a path toward a more richly imaginative and meaningful engagement with the aesthetic and ethical complexities of cinematic art.

4
Radio, Memory, and the Past in the Nostalgia Film

In the first scene of *The Last Picture Show* (1971), the camera slowly pans left across a movie theater and a dusty, desolate line of buildings to reveal working-class teen Sonny struggling to get his truck started (0:00:26).[1] The engine seems to be fighting against the prominent wind effects that dominate the soundtrack. Since the opening credits consisted of simply the film's title shown in silence against a black screen, an expectation for traditional establishing music is delayed until a cut to inside Sonny's truck offers us Hank Williams on the radio. The setting is late autumn, 1951. The song, "Why Don't You Love Me," had charted the previous summer, in 1950. Sonny takes a moment to adjust the frequency, tuning out the static before successfully turning over the engine, winning a temporary aural victory over the wind (0:01:05).

Up to this point, however, the music has been marked by its fragility and ephemerality, by the marked fuzziness of the diegetic radio signal. This filtering effect makes the music seem to speak all the more to its hardscrabble environment. Like Sonny and his truck, the music seems to be struggling to establish itself, to *carve itself out a space* against the obliterating force of the wind. This cue thus fills the unexpectedly blank space left by the lack of traditionally expository non-diegetic music under the opening credits, but only in a deferred way, in which its spatialized sound quality and technological mediation are as vital to its meaning as any musical or culturally associative content. While the tune, decades old in 1971, certainly establishes a historical period and cultural milieu, its aural mediation also speaks to an unsentimental, yet vulnerable sense of the "now" of this "then"—*this* moment, *this* radio signal: we have "tuned in" to the "frequency" of the past, a frequency that is implied to hover at the edge of inaudibility.

In the final scene of George Lucas's 1973 *American Graffiti*, middle-class teenager Curt, following a long night of soul-searching and comic misadventure, leaves his small California town to go to college on the East Coast.

The Presence of the Past. Daniel Bishop, Oxford University Press. © Oxford University Press 2021.
DOI: 10.1093/oso/9780190932688.003.0005

The setting is late summer, 1962, and the song—the Spaniels' "Goodnite, Sweetheart, Goodnite"—had charted the better part of a decade earlier in 1954. Although it is synched primarily to Curt's airport farewells, the song enters slightly earlier, overlapping from the previous scene, where it is introduced diegetically on the radio after Curt, in a phone booth at sunup, loses contact with the mysterious, anonymous blonde woman he has been futilely pursuing throughout the previous night (1:47:23).[2] Despite its clear diegetic establishment on the radio, the song also functions as sneaky transitional editing, compressing a presumed temporal gap into the structural perimeters of a single song. The way in which the song is mixed in the airport scene, however—at first relatively high in the levels, then dipping under dialogue—is a far more characteristic mixing practice for non-diegetic underscoring. At the same time, however, the scene takes pains to locate the music within its diegetic world. A persistent low-key distortion is audible at the airport, suggesting that we are still hearing source music from the car radios, and before takeoff, a shot of the plane door (clearly and unnecessarily marked "Radar Equipped") perhaps serves as some kind of explanation as to how Curt, once on the plane, can continue to listen to the radio show he and his friends have been listening to all night (1:47:23).[3]

Settling into his seat after takeoff, Curt listens to a final fragment of "Goodnite, Sweetheart, Goodnite." The aural distortion is greater than ever—not in the form of static, as in the opening of *The Last Picture Show*, but as a muddied, submerged quality that is *distanced* rather than *disfigured*. As the radio fades to nothing and Curt muses on a final distant glimpse of the mysterious woman's white T-Bird cruising the highway, the drifting away of the music under the sound of the plane seems to reflect the loss of connection to the physical space associated with Curt's adolescence. In an uncertain, potent final moment, a set of superimposed yearbook photos of Curt and his friends describe the roles they will play (or not play) in the turmoil of a sixties to come (1:49:03).

Two scenes, two uses of spatialized sound to temporalize a representation of the historical past, and two ways of manipulating conventions of diegetic music—these scenes bookend two key New Hollywood films made a few years apart in the early seventies. Critical commonplaces of this era have centered discussions of these films on industrial factors (such as the youth of their two directors and the relative artistic freedom of their independent productions); stylistic factors (such as the artsy, self-consciously austere "Old Hollywood" look of *The Last Picture Show*, or *American Graffiti*'s pulpy, yet dreamlike evocation of fifties teenager films), and cultural factors, in particular their nostalgic depictions of the American past. The soundtracks of these two films, however, also have much to tell us regarding New Hollywood and American popular culture in the early seventies. The present chapter will focus, in particular, on intersections between sound, music, and nostalgia, as they are cinematically explored through the medium of radio.

For musicologist Michael Long, musical nostalgia in film draws upon music's ability to create spatialized images in the mind of the listener and to affectively convey a sense of temporal, as well as physical, distance. In this way, a film might transcend a less complex ("stylistic" or "formal") use of nostalgia (accessed simply through the employment of recognizable imagistic or narrative tropes) and achieve a deeper employment of nostalgia *as an aesthetic*—that is to say, as a complex body of ideas related to the formation of expressive meaning or artistic value. Long distinguishes this latter, more aesthetically engaged manifestation as "chronotopic" nostalgia. Understood as an aesthetic, nostalgia becomes more than an index of "period" markers, and more than a projection of (often implicitly regressive) ideological values shared, by implication, with the film audience. Rather, an aesthetic of nostalgia both creates and engages its experient in a meditation not just on a specific (and usually commodified) past, but on the nature of temporal distance itself.[4]

Interpretations of *The Last Picture Show* and *American Graffiti* have generally treated music within two broader categories: first, historicizing the creation of the soundtracks through an industrial or aesthetic lens; second, interpreting the music and lyrics of the compiled songs in relationship to either the films' narratives or to broader ideological contexts. Of the two films, it is noteworthy that nearly all critical discussions of *American Graffiti* recognize the centrality of music in the film, whether as an industrial precedent, a narrative device, or as an attempt to cultivate nostalgia.[5] Such discussions often, and appropriately, home in on practical concerns, such as the perceived value of a commercial soundtrack album, or the relatively small budgets—both factors that did indeed shape the film's musical sensibilities.[6] Supplementing industrial-historical readings, Jeff Smith has also offered a valuable perspective on how the traditional functions of classical Hollywood film music were variously maintained, adapted, and altered by *American Graffiti*'s compiled pop score. While music, in general, has been far less dominant as a factor in the reception and critical study of *The Last Picture Show*, scholars such as David Brackett have examined this film's music through an ideological lens, demonstrating how its dialogical employment of country and pop articulates issues of cultural authenticity and identity.[7]

Though all of these perspectives yield valuable understanding and insights, their limitation has been a tendency to focus upon the unit of "the song itself"—whether in the form of its extra-musical associations, its lyrics, or its relationship to film narrative. This methodology risks fixing the popular song as a sort of ideal object that might be discussed apart from how it *actually sounds* in the film. Particularly lost in this strategy is the role of music in constructing a sense of spatiality *within* the film—a dynamic constantly in dialogue with the idealistic construction of "the song itself," creating distinct and expressively vital meanings.[8] One such meaning, the present chapter will argue, is a sense of what we might call "temporal resonance." Through such temporal resonance, I would argue, listening to fictional representation of the past can become imbued with a sense of the physicality of sound, an aesthetically loaded image of sound as a medium that necessarily exists in and moves through space and time.

The time was ripe for this aesthetic in American cinema of the early seventies, as a larger stylistic preoccupation with gritty realism came to leave its mark on the soundtrack. By the early seventies, the American filmgoer had experienced a dramatically increasing number of film soundtracks that strongly foregrounded compiled popular music. There was also, overall, a larger trend toward using significantly less music than had been common in films of the studio era. A number of prominent films even abandoned the use of underscoring entirely, whether original or compiled, relying entirely upon diegetic music, and both *The Last Picture Show* and *American Graffiti* follow this model. As we have seen in other contexts, from the perspective of many established film composers these practices were cause for serious concern, frequently articulated in tandem with a critique of the commercialization (and hence the aesthetic devaluation) of their own artistic practice. As Julie Hubbert has convincingly argued, however, one of these trends—the prevalence of soundtracks that privileged source music to the near or total exclusion of underscoring—may not have been the result of commercialization alone, but also of a particular aesthetic value: a desire to challenge the illusionistic Hollywood practices with which classical scoring was associated, and to create instead an effect of unvarnished, authentic reality.[9]

This certainly holds true for *The Last Picture Show* and *American Graffiti*, both of which feature prominently within Hubbert's analysis. Each film, in its own way, achieves a kind of realism by foregrounding the diegetic media—car stereos, jukeboxes, record players, or live performance—that explain music's audible presence. But I would go one step further and argue that, in these two films, the exclusive use of diegetic music goes beyond articulating aesthetic *realism* to also suggest the importance of an aesthetic *imaginary*—a conceptual space constituting collective identities, memories, dreams, and fantasies. What sets these two films apart from others in Hubbert's discussion is not only that they are both period pieces that attempt to cultivate viewers' nostalgia, but rather that both films are self-consciously *about* nostalgia. In both films, nostalgia is explicitly thematized. It exists in the framing of "the past" by the film itself, but it is also gestured toward by the lives and desires of characters who, in differing ways, long to recover a lost past.

The cultural phenomenon of nostalgia is traditionally associated both with a melancholy longing for a lost past and the characterization of this past as a better, simpler time than the present. As an aesthetic phenomenon, however, nostalgia is also a particularly useful framework for exploring the spatialized use of sound in filmic depictions of the past. In the long history since its seventeenth-century origins as a diagnosed physiological condition akin to homesickness, nostalgia has frequently, perhaps inherently, tended to cross the wires of time and space—with nostalgia for one's homeland, for example, melding intuitively with nostalgia for one's childhood. In both *Last Picture Show* and *American Graffiti*, cultural memory and a sense of pastness are evoked by the spatiality of musical cues, by their deployment within the physical diegetic world of the film. In other words, in both films, the image of sound moving through space becomes a metaphorical marker for the effects of time.

This being said, however, the two films employ sound, space, and nostalgia in strikingly distinct ways, with considerable differences in style, form, and sensibility, which brief narrative summaries might begin to help establish. Set in late summer of 1962, *American Graffiti* is director George Lucas's ode to the nightlife of the American teenager. Over the course of a single night, four boys, two of them debating whether or not to leave for college, cross paths multiple times. The two recent graduates essentially trade attitudes over the course of the film: thoughtful, hesitant, and nostalgic Curt is ultimately the one who leaves town, while brash, adventurous Steve decides to postpone college and stay with his girlfriend, Laurie. Their friend John, an older blue-collar hot-rodder, sees his drag racing legacy challenged by a mysterious newcomer. Meanwhile, nerdy schlemiel Terry "the Toad" manages, in a picaresque series of misadventures, to get lucky with a girl. As the closing intertitles inform us, Curt will eventually become a writer living in Canada (easily read as a detail aligning his future with the antiwar movement); Terry will die in Vietnam; John will die in an auto accident; and Steve will marry Laurie and sell insurance.

In the sound world of *American Graffiti*, music emerges almost entirely from a single source broadcasting to multiple receptors, encountered by its audience over a single night—a radio show heard on multiple overlapping car speakers. Musical sound is thus identified with a collective imagined space, inhabited by its teenaged characters and linked through the medium of radio—a medium that manifests itself in the film as a sort of mystical, reparative presence. The film's chronologically diffuse approach to its musical selections conveys a timeless quality, formally structured around the radio show in a way that emphasizes its personalized and non-repetitious format. The show, hosted by real-life deejay Wolfman Jack (Bob Smith), playing himself onscreen, creates a near-continuous simultaneity as the characters' interweaving paths play themselves out. The radio broadcast constantly moves between different spaces at varying levels of audibility. Songs and the Wolfman's on-air antics both structure key scenes and provide transitions between them. On one level, the musicalizing of the spatialized diegetic world creates a sense of a communal consciousness, while, on another, it creates a melancholy sense of distance and estrangement from this shared collective through the passage of time.

Set between the fall of 1951 and the spring of 1953, *The Last Picture Show* traces the paths of three teenagers in a rural Texas town: a love triangle connecting blue-collar buddies Sonny and Duane and wealthy Jacy. Like *American Graffiti*'s teens, these three also pinball between the comforting, yet suffocating stasis of small-town life and the desire to leave and move toward an uncertain future. As their high school experience—characterized far more by tedium than by *American Graffiti*'s wry affection—draws to an end and seems to fade, like their dilapidated town itself, into nothingness, these younger characters inevitably recapitulate the unhappiness and sexual frustrations of their parents' generation—a generation yearning, in turn, for its *own* lost youth. Unlike *American Graffiti*, in which Curt actively engages his nostalgia, encouraging his friends to go to the Sock Hop "to remember the good times," the golden age longed for in *The Last Picture Show* exists less in the experiences of the young characters, who flirt far less with nostalgia, and more as mediated through the recollections of their elders.

In *The Last Picture Show*, spatialized musical sources convey two distinct, yet interrelated sensibilities of nostalgic pastness—sensibilities of *fragility* and *entrapment*. Particularly in scenes foregrounding the mobility of car radios, the weakness of a musical signal can suggest a loss of connection, both *within* the diegetic world of the past and *between* this past and the present of the film audience. The ephemerality of source music can be read, in this way, as a kind of presence of loss and absence, in contrast with *American Graffiti*'s sense of plenitude. *The Last Picture Show*'s exclusive use of source music and its repetitive, chronologically and stylistically narrow range of the selections suggests a paralytic entrapment within the experiential moment of the past. In a film full of characters who seem stuck in time and space, music expresses pastness less as a *manifestation* of an imaginal collective, and more as a sort of mundane wallpaper that can, only with effort, be set aside for more focused reflection. In two paralleled instances, discussed in the following, these reflections take the form of soliloquies in which characters recollect the past against a nearly silent background, as if this mythic, lost past could only be articulated in isolation from the mundanity of music.

Generational Nostalgia and Film Authorship

In the early seventies, "nostalgia" had yet to become identified as a unique genre of film—if, indeed, it would ever truly become one, which is debatable. Unlike other genres, "nostalgia" itself does not possess secure iconic tropes. Nostalgia is always nostalgia *for* something, and thus as time passes and the object of nostalgia shifts, nostalgia, instead of a toolkit for creating identifiably marketable types of films, becomes more of a broader discursive attitude. In the New Hollywood Western, by comparison, commonplace tropes of genre often predisposed filmmakers to adopt sensibilities and attitudes toward the historical past—whether critically deconstructive, conservative, or a mixture of both. But the toolkit of genre certainly did not make this predisposition obligatory. A Western could be about the past or it could employ the past merely as its setting. Nostalgia, on the other hand, is by definition *always* about the past. In the seventies, nostalgia would thus become a sort of cross-genre discourse, explored through more a variety of stable and traditional genres.[10]

The particularity of *The Last Picture Show* and *American Graffiti* also lies in their being set in a past that lay within the generational memory of many up-and-coming filmmakers, as well as younger audiences, who could actively recall adolescence in the fifties and early sixties as juxtaposed with their contemporary realities. In both films (but especially *American Graffiti*) this generationally shared past is staged as a sort of prelude, an anticipation of a shared cultural "now" represented by the social revolutions of the later sixties. This is not to overstate the autobiographical nature of either film. *American Graffiti*, to a certain extent, had acknowledged autobiographical overtones, drawing upon director and co-writer George Lucas's own teenage years. Despite *The Last Picture Show*'s partially autobiographical roots in author Larry McMurtry's novel, however, director and co-writer Peter Bogdanovich would instead call attention to his personal *disconnection* from the setting of the film, pointing out that he—the consummately urbane New York cinephile—had made a movie celebrated for its depiction of rural Texas.[11] Nevertheless, both films implicitly rely upon a sensibility of generational memory for their affective value.

Bogdanovich was relatively unique in the Hollywood industry as a film critic and historian who had transitioned into filmmaking, a career arc befitting the image of an American New Wave that emulated European models (in particular the French New Wave, in which several critics-turned-directors were prominent figures), particularly regarding. Bogdanovich himself, however, distanced himself from this paradigm. Perhaps trying to out-French the French, he tended to express *his* indebtedness less to the work of Truffaut and Godard, and more directly to the *auteurs* of classical Hollywood that the French New Wave in the late fifties and early sixties had admired: Alfred Hitchcock, Howard Hawks, and especially John Ford. Bogdanovich's films of the early seventies are thus paradoxically both of-the-moment *and* self-conscious throwbacks to the Hollywood past, realized most fully in *Nickelodeon* (1976), a slapstick comedy about the early days of silent film. Like Francis Ford Coppola and William Friedkin (his partners in an ill-fated independent production venture called the Director's Company), Bogdanovich was one of the young directorial talents who seemed to be successfully remaking the industry of the early seventies into a place where freedom, commercialism, and artistic experiment could happily coincide. But as his reputation soured by mid-decade with a critical backlash that increasingly identified his work with empty stylistic pastiche, Bogdanovich began to embody a different historiographic cliché of the era—that of a hubristic young filmmaker who challenged the establishment, was spoiled by success, and ultimately was put in his place by failure. George Lucas's

American Graffiti was likewise a "small" and "personal," yet surprisingly lucrative film by a director whose name would, by the end of the decade, be associated with franchise-oriented spectacle, along with all of the baggage of cultural regression, empty pastiche, and political conservatism that would eventually be lumped together under the (overly) broad label of "Reaganite entertainment."[12] This latter condition has become synonymous with the triumph of the "other" New Hollywood—a model of corporate blockbuster retrenchment, which is often credited with co-opting the noble energies of its early-decade "Renaissance" phase. *American Graffiti* was thus a popular and critical success, but one that would become tainted in the suspicious readings of highbrow criticism and academic film studies.

The two directors also handle the historical dimension of music very differently: whereas Bogdanovich is precise, specific, even scholarly, Lucas is magical, associative, and homogenizing. Bogdanovich and his production team did extensive research, combing Billboard charts in order to "date" selections more or less accurately to the period of the film. This technique perhaps makes even more sense if we consider the personal distance between the director and his material. Bogdanovich has never professed to have particularly strong musical sensibilities, and inasmuch as *The Last Picture Show* represents "his" music, these allegiances seem to have been toward the film's use of pop, rather than country music. In this way, the film tends to locate us on the outside of its music, and the nostalgic affect in *The Last Picture Show* comes less through music itself and primarily through spoken recollections. Lucas, on the other hand, uses music broadly, with a classicizing "Oldies" mentality that demonstrates an evolving generational awareness of a distinct era in popular music, a "pre-British-invasion" epoch encompassing the fifties through the early sixties. This understanding placed the filmmakers and audience on the *inside* of its musical experiences. This is tangible in the film's autobiographical overtones, as well as in Lucas's frequently professed interest in the concept of popular mythology. Radio clearly holds a totemic function in *American Graffiti*, and the plot might easily be read as an ensemble-cast spin on the Jungian-Campbellian "Hero's Journey" that would later be hardwired into the *Star Wars* films, in that all the major characters (but Curt most of all) undergo quests and achieve various forms of self-actualization.

While *American Graffiti* doesn't really reference other audiovisual media, *The Last Picture Show* represents the sound of cinema and television as additional facets of generational memory.[13] As film historian Paul Monaco has pointed out, movie theater audiences declined overall across the fifties and sixties, but *movies themselves* (and the production companies that made and distributed them) were doing quite well—largely because they had begun to view television as an ally rather than a competitor, using this newer medium to generate revenue by selling broadcasting rights to older (and in some cases more recent) films. The *real* losers in this transitional era, then, were theatrical exhibitors, with small-town theaters in rural areas suffering worst of all, since—unlike small theaters in urban areas or college towns—they were unlikely to be repurposed as trendy art cinemas.[14] The old movie nostalgia in *The Last Picture Show* is thus as much a nostalgia for a decaying *exhibition* culture as it is for the classical film styles into which it attempts to breathe new life. In direct contrast, Bogdanovich, always the cinephile, treats television as the soundtrack of brainless banality, distinct from the sacralized space of the movie theater with its aura of teenaged mating rituals. In their depictions of media, however, both films draw heavily upon a generationally driven overlap of the interpersonal, cultural memory of media forms and the personal, experiential memory of sharing their physical space.[15]

Compiled Music and Temporality in *The Last Picture Show*

My goal in this chapter is to use the image of radio to supplement traditional readings of these films, which tend to focus on compiled songs, and especially their lyrics, in relationship to narrative development. Nevertheless, it is remains important to summarize some of the patterns established by the practices of music compilation in both films. This is because these patterns do more than simply articulate a narrative—they also cultivate particular temporal resonances, which are amplified and enhanced by the reliance upon radio as a means of diegetic spatialization. Viewing the larger shape of music in *The Last Picture Show*, we can identify a localized, time-bound quality. This effect could easily be understood simply to pertain to period authenticity, but it also creates a sensibility of mundane presence, reflecting the fixity of these often-unhappy characters in their world. The Texans of *The Last Picture Show* often seem "stuck" both in place and in time, and music and sound help to create this effect. By contrast, in *American Graffiti*, the near-continuous, non-repeating stream of music creates a sense of continual flow, of living in the ephemeral moment, an aesthetic sensibility strongly aligned with the film's depictions of teenage culture.

The musical cues in *The Last Picture Show* are drawn, rather strictly, from a narrow and largely accurate historical window. Historical accuracy, however, is not the only type of authenticity at stake—as David Brackett has shown, genre and ideology are closely linked in the film, which maps country western music onto working class authenticity and pop music onto upper-class inauthenticity.[16] This emphasis on authenticity goes hand in hand with the effects of repetition. Specific songs return multiple times, occasionally in different versions, functioning as motivic markers that establish significant (and often ironic) intertextual connections. In the case of Hank Williams and Tony Bennett's recordings of "Cold, Cold Heart," for example, two recordings of a single song are used to call our attention to the disparate social worlds of Sonny and Duane, on the one hand, and privileged, upper-class Jacy Farrow, on the other. We first hear Williams's rendition on the radio early in the film, played in its entirety as Sonny makes himself at home at the pool parlor run by local businessman Sam the Lion (0:02:40). Sonny affectionately goofs around with Billy (Sam's mute, mentally disabled ward) and dutifully accepts Sam's good-natured ribbing on his poor football skills. What stands out, as the song plays in this scene, is not the lyrics' characteristic tale of unhappy romance but, as Brackett has shown, more generic cultural associations and aural signifiers—such as Williams's plaintive voice—that suggest a hardscrabble masculinity capable of deep affection and respect.[17] By contrast, at (0:20:24), we cut into Tony Bennett's "Cold, Cold Heart" as Jacy's mother, Lois, enters her bedroom and they discuss her relationship with Duane. Lois, unhappily married to Jacy's father, sees Duane as akin to her husband—a dead end who will prevent her daughter from ever leaving town. Perhaps the lyrics of "Cold, Cold Heart" are more germane to this conversation, laced as they are with romantic cynicism, but this hardly seems the most pressing point. The recording itself, with its slick orchestral arrangements and Tony Bennett's smooth, polished croon, provides a perfect aural equivalent to this urbane world of affluent teenaged femininity—with the room's delicate furnishings and its ample stock of glossy magazines and high school memorabilia. At the same time, it also reminds us of the previous "Cold, Cold Heart," emphasizing the distance between the Tony Bennett and Hank Williams versions of the song, and thus heightening the distinctions between the film's two very different social worlds.

In crafting such associations, the filmmakers stuck to a fairly strict temporal specificity. The two versions of "Cold, Cold Heart" were both released within the period represented by the film—both, in fact, were even charting around the same time. This historical accuracy is still somewhat generalizing: in a story extending from 1951 to 1953, the musical selections all date from 1950 to 1952, with only two outlier selections released earlier, in 1948 and 1949.[18] Music isn't always dated with precision to the exact time frame of a given scene, but in a genre (and, more broadly, an industry) not traditionally known for its commitment to historical factuality, this degree of musical research seems to acquire the weight of a deliberate gesture, even if its level of precision may not always have been recognized by an audience. While films and posters acquired for the film's eponymous movie theater were generally a year or more backdated from the time frame of the story, it seems to have been assumed that the film's radio stations would be playing only current (or relatively recent) music—and *replaying* it, too.[19]

Sometimes, this repetition forms tangible dramatic connections—as with the two recordings of "Cold, Cold Heart"—but more frequently, it can convey an accidental quality, as if to challenge its own dramatic functionality with a sense of random contingency, foregrounding the way in which the same music can accompany dramatically disjunct purposes. For example, Frankie Lane's perky orientalist ditty "Rose, Rose I Love You" (1951) first drifts onto the soundtrack as a group of teenagers depart from the movie theater and go their separate ways into the night. This is a strange, affecting moment, in which the "song itself" seems to be less important than the effect of the car radios as overlapping sound sources that foreground the nocturnal ambience that surrounds them (0:11:05). Later, the same song returns in a very different capacity. Playing on a small, portable record player, it breaks the tension as Jacy—having ritualistically stripped on a diving board as an initiation into a skinny-dipping party—plunges into the pool, leading the other swimmers to cheer and do the same (0:40:30). In the first example, set against the backdrop of the nighttime silence, the song becomes a melancholy marker of spatiotemporal distance. In the latter, it represents a return to the structuring and sanctioning norms of social music.[20] The song's placement thus draws upon two distinct sensibilities, both of which might be read as ironic, or at the least, as signifying at an oblique angle to the "song itself." The shared usage of the song thus suggests a pervasiveness of pop as the aleatoric wallpaper of experience, opening up the potential for distance between the pop song (a manufactured object created to appeal to the broadest possible audience) and the far more complex and contingent worlds of the characters listening to it.

My reading, here, would seem to complement Brackett's—a reading in which pop music serves (in contrast with country music) as a signifier of inauthenticity. Along these lines, a single pop song's ability to shift between multiple expressive functions might reinforce our viewing it as a commodity, rather than as a unique work of art. However, country music is, in fact, approached with much the same interpretively fluid aesthetic strategy as pop. For example, the forlorn plaint of Hank Williams's "Lovesick Blues" (1949) underscores two extremely distinct scenes. In the first, Sonny has been banished from Sam's diner, pool hall, and movie theater (essentially, from Anarene social life as a whole) for participating in Billy's cruel sexual hazing. The song plays on Sonny's truck radio as he cruises Anarene's main drag by night, seeing his friends through the windows, but barred from joining them (0:50:07). As the location shifts to a hill outside of town and the music shifts to a different Williams song ("The Wild Side of Life"), Sonny parks his truck and looks down over the lights of Anarene in the distance. It is a brief, but beautifully executed scene that captures Sonny's loneliness and guilt, as well as the sheer smallness of his world and the ease with which its common joys can be withheld or lost.

But when "Lovesick Blues" recurs later, it is attached to a comic scene in which Sonny and Duane grimly weather the ravages of hangovers as they drive back from a spontaneous trip to Mexico (1:03:45). Are we supposed to hear a more proximate signification, perhaps a pun on the word "sick"? Are we even supposed to remember that we've already heard this song, or should it blend into a larger, generalized "Hank-Williams-ness," a sensibility of tough luck and paying one's dues, whether it be by owning up to adolescent cruelty or by enduring the aftereffects of binge drinking? This latter, more tropological interpretation is closer to Brackett's, in that the connecting thread between these two scenes is readable in their association of country music with authenticity. A more straightforward possibility also exists: the filmmakers might simply have decided that the scene felt like it needed a musical element and made a choice that intuitively "felt appropriate," without thinking too much about the implications of the specific selection. But while these interpretations are all valid, neither the ethos of authenticity nor the pragmatics of industrial accident offers a full account for the role of musical repetition in *The Last Picture Show*. Some larger strategy of aesthetic framing seems to be suggested.

The recurrence and transformation of musical motives has long been a cornerstone of film music analysis. The study of film music has tended naturally toward discussions of what music *actively* does—the patterns it establishes through its unique characteristics, whether in the form of an affective gesture signifying a character's sadness or a choice of style topic possessing certain cultural associations. Contrary instances, what Claudia Gorbman (following Michel Chion) has termed "anempathetic," have been identified as functioning in an ironic or otherwise emotionally destabilizing way.[21] It is easy to see both of these patterns at play at in *The Last Picture Show*, and yet an equally important aspect of the film's musical affect is the way in which music *isn't* valued, in which its meanings and ironies don't seem to register for the characters, but merely become a passively accepted *part of their environment*. In such moments, music's strength as an expressive gesture paradoxically derives from the ways in which it pointedly *doesn't express*. This is akin to what Giorgio Biancorosso has called "mundane music"—music that might be easily under-interpreted as unimportant or even as lazily chosen and applied, but which actually serves a critical function in the film's aural world-making.[22] In addition to effecting narrative development, then, the musical repetitions of *The Last Picture Show* may also be read as suggestive of boredom, or of the song as a commodified product rather than a vital, living experience. In *The Last Picture Show*, music frequently stages its own expressive failure: well-researched for historical specificity, focused on the particular (rather than the universal), this music dredges up experiences, but ultimately seems to point only to their falseness, or their absence, receding from our attention into the flattened-out register of aural wallpaper.

Whether in longer or shorter loops, in *The Last Picture Show*, the same music tends eventually to repeat. These cycles can be seasonal—or even annual, as with the Anarene school anthem, whose repetition at a football game toward the end of the film pointedly compresses Sonny's turbulent post-graduation year into the potent mix of banality and profundity. The earth keeps moving around the sun, and Hank Williams and Tony Bennett keep playing on the radio. *The Last Picture Show*'s repetitious soundtrack allows us hear radio *as a medium for broadcasting records*. Music is not portrayed, like it is in *American Graffiti*, as the mysterious, intangible product of the ether itself, but as a desacralized commercial agency that facilitates the circulation of mechanized, repeatable artifacts.

Compiled Music and Temporality in *American Graffiti*

Broadcasting records is, of course, what Wolfman Jack does, too. But *American Graffiti* seems determined to perpetually de-emphasize and deflect this banal reality in favor of something more mythic. There is *no* musical repetition in *American Graffiti*. Almost by definition, this means that the compiled score creates no "motives," only fleeting, transitory associations. The near-constant flow of music never lets us forget that this is a story that takes place over the course of a single night, creating an emphasis on the simultaneity of events and inevitable, propulsive forward movement—especially noteworthy in a film so devoted to the act of looking back on the past. Rather than the record that is the physical object at the root of the radio's airplay, *American Graffiti* guides us toward understanding radio as a medium of fantastic ephemerality—the imagistic signal, rather than the realistic source.

The music in *American Graffiti* also covers a much wider date range, from 1953 to 1962—and even, in the case of two Beach Boys selections, extending two years *after* the film is set.[23] It also represents a considerably wider subgeneric variety of popular music: R&B, surf rock, doo wop, and rock and roll all make appearances. This type of radio play prompts numerous historical questions. Would kids in 1962 still have been interested in the Spaniels' 1954 recording of "Goodnite, Sweetheart, Goodnite"? Would a historical Wolfman Jack show have sounded anything like this?[24] The extent to which radio play in *American Graffiti* reflects, or fails to reflect, what might have been *actually* heard on the air at this historical moment, however, is less important than the ways in which the career and tastes of Wolfman Jack help to ground the film in a historical perspective. Jeff Smith, for example, has speculated that the Wolfman's actual shows in the early sixties were probably more driven by hard-edged R&B and blues than by the anything resembling the broad panorama of "classic rock" that appears in the film, and Bob Smith's autobiography, while it doesn't discuss specific musical choices for *American Graffiti*, generally reinforces this reading. The technological and commercial aspects of amplitude modulation (AM) broadcasting in the early sixties offer additional relevant historical contextualization. The trend of so-called border blasting plays a role in the Wolfman's mythology, in real life as well as in the screenplay. Across the Mexican border, stations beyond FCC regulation and armed with powerful transmitters could broadcast signals that under ideal conditions were receivable across the entire continental United States. Atmospheric conditions and the physical nature of AM signals also generally made this kind of listening only available by night, a happy scientific coincidence with the mythic image of night as the topos of romance and adventure belonging to *American Graffiti*'s young characters.[25]

Also relevant in assessing *American Graffiti*'s representation of historical radio-play is the gradual shift toward the Top 40 format. By the early sixties, this chart-driven format offered a homogenized style of listening that was very different from the chronologically and stylistically freewheeling selections Wolfman plays in the film. Ironically, given *American Graffiti*'s mythologizing of its iconic deejay, Susan Douglas has argued, in her history of radio listening, that by the early sixties the freedom of the deejay as an exploratory tastemaker and a socially rebellious persona was already on the wane, following the Payola scandals of the mid-fifties and the increasing commercial emphasis on Top 40 play by the end of the previous decade.[26] By contrast, music journalist Ken Barnes has identified this transitional period less as a waning, and more as a final, excessive flourish:

> The late fifties and early sixties became a volatile Top 40 battleground, as stations staged the most outrageous contests, the wildest stunts, hired the most manic DJs, and ran wide-open playlists, hoping to uncover the newest irresistible smash. (The "40" in Top 40 was a guideline rather than a strict playlist limit; stations in the early sixties often played seventy, eighty or more records, to the detriment of effective music rotation.) The era was the stuff of legend.[27]

In the tension between the contrasting pictures offered by Douglas and Barnes, however, we are led to imagine airplay in the early sixties through images that are very hospitable to nostalgic reflection: as a sort of a "beginning of the end," in which the irrepressible figure of the deejay is experiencing a "twilight era," or, perhaps, a "decadent phase." The musical flow of airplay in *American Graffiti*, along with its cultural affinities and expressive temporality, are thus *themselves* exercises in nostalgia—fantasies of what radio might have meant, or perhaps might have *felt like* to listeners of the previous decade, listeners whose memories of this era would inevitably exist in tension with their awareness of the changes in the decade that had passed.

By contrast, even though *The Last Picture Show* is set well prior to the dominance of Top 40 homogenization, this film's music is already looking the other way, completely ignoring rock and roll—or, rather, ignoring the dominantly African American musical genres of the early fifties that anticipated it, in favor of genres that would speak to the film's localized (and predominantly white) sense of rural Texas authenticity. By drawing upon discreet, well-established commercial genres and by tapping into a sense of period through a close reading of Billboard charts, Bogdanovich implicitly folded the commercialized business of airplay into the structure of the film. But if the repetitive, mundane accuracy of *The Last Picture Show*'s music registers as an effect of realism by conveying how drearily time is experienced in the world of the film, then the ephemeral, ahistorical fantasy of radio in *American Graffiti* represents, by contrast, a kind of imaginal escape from the demands of mundane experience. If the airplay in *American Graffiti* is unrealistic in the historically material sense, Wolfman Jack nevertheless functions as a historicizing presence, a sort of metadiegetic curator whose presence homogenizes the stylistic and chronological diversity of the film's music by locating it implicitly within the tastes of a single character—one who was also, of course, a "real" persona both inside and outside the film. With his iconic status as a real-life figure of the rock and roll era, Bob Smith's persona served to position the film's music against the grain of Top 40 format, locating it instead within the broader imaginal space of "early rock and roll," or, increasingly, in the space of "classic rock."[28]

As music critic Simon Reynolds has shown, by 1973 "early rock and roll," or "rock revivalism," was already a strongly articulated cultural phenomenon, representing a strange mix of museum, avant-garde laboratory, and nostalgic memorialization.[29] In Reynolds's narrative, the very moment in which rock began to adapt itself to the cultural territory of high art, a contrary aesthetic urge began to manifest, nostalgically celebrating an imagined cultural innocence and pursuing early rock styles, either as a return of the primitive or elevated as an object of ironic, celebratory camp. In this broader sense, we might see *Grease*, Sha Na Na, John Lennon's psychotherapeutic primal blues screaming, or the proto-punk fifties-camp of the New York Dolls as diverse parts of a shared larger picture. The nexus of "classic rock," then, could offer far more than the ahistorical and reified commercial radio format. It could also play into a subtle and complex aesthetics of historicism.

Radio Nostalgia as Time Regained

While the nostalgic elements of *The Last Picture Show* were not nearly as prominent in its reception, *American Graffiti* was quickly recognized as a key text in an emerging "nostalgia boom" within American culture of the early seventies. This discrepancy was perhaps due to the generally lighter tone of the later film—nostalgia has often tended to be reductively understood as a politically regressive sense of goodwill toward a historical legacy that should properly warrant suspicious critical contestation. Thus, while the unhappy denizens of *Last Picture Show*'s Anarene fit comfortably into a commonplace liberal narrative that tended to characterize the fifties as a decade defined by stringent conformism and sexual repression, *American Graffiti*'s dwelling upon on the joys and anguishes of a bunch of generally well-adjusted, generically middle-class, and uniformly white suburban kids was easy to read as a betrayal of an intellectual obligation to critique the past—or more specifically, to bring criticism to bear upon mainstream popular culture and its hegemonies.[30]

Nostalgia's sense of yearning for an implicitly "better," "simpler," or "more innocent" time can (and s*hould*) grate against our imperative to respect the past as the complex and frequently fraught reality that it actually *was*, and to do justice to the legacies of oppression, erasure, and resistance that have marked it. But nostalgia's temporal and aesthetic sensibilities also offer more than a simple pretext for contestatory criticism. There is also the need to understand nostalgic art as an affective experiential and imagistic reservoir of complex joy and sadness, and to understand how nostalgia's profundity often goes hand in hand with its limited value as a way of understanding reality and social experience. What I am advocating, then, is a critical approach to nostalgia predicated on a "both/and," rather than "either/or" perspective toward its effects and workings. A deeper reading of nostalgia's aesthetic function in the soundscapes of these two films leads to a richer understanding of the compiled pop score as capable of a complex range of affective gestures. In return, hopefully, such a study can add much-needed complexity to the notion of nostalgia itself. This reappraisal, ideally, would not just distinguish the bad, politically regressive nostalgia from the somewhat redeemable nostalgia of the historically dispossessed (as in Svetlana Boym's analysis of diasporic nostalgia), but would attempt to empathetically value the ways in which, through ideas about sound, space, and time, we think about the past.[31]

Viewing *American Graffiti* in this way requires a restructuring, if not necessarily a relinquishing, of our critical faculties around an act of the subjective imagination—an ability to accept and creatively engage with the overlapping of reality and illusion within the aesthetic object. Along similar lines, Giorgio Biancorosso has discussed the role of perception and the imaginative agency of the listener in a phenomenology of film music. For example, diegetic music is creatively and actively (if not always attentively) imagined to be *within* the world of the film, despite the fact that we simultaneously "know" perfectly well that it is *actually* coming through the theater's speakers.[32] Likewise, attending to *American Graffiti*'s nuanced construction of nostalgia in sound and space may require the imaginal willingness to entertain a utopian view of nostalgia's recuperative function, while attempting to maintain enough critical distance to regard this reading, however attractive it may or may not be, as a cultural construction with its own origins and, potentially, ethical lacunae. How does nostalgia, in *American Graffiti*, serve what we might call a "redemptive" function—and what is it, exactly, that is being "redeemed"? The answer, in short, is our imagined essential selves, as they might be recuperated from the inevitable losses of space and time—our selves as a sort of still image recoverable within the "moving picture" of adolescence. The spatialized mediality of radio thus becomes critical to this reading, in particular as it leads us to understand the role of Wolfman Jack as a curatorial agency, a central point from which the signal radiates. As a medium, radio facilitates simultaneous listening in separate or shared spaces, but it also cultivates a sense of listening together in an *imaginary* space—a participation mystique in which teenaged identity might be understood as a vibrant, yet melancholy collective fantasy, or perhaps an "imagined community," as historian Benedict Anderson has characterized the image of the nation.[33] This community doesn't merely share an interest in music. Rather, I would argue that its very architecture is constructed in sound.

Significant shots in *American Graffiti* are given over to the spectacle of teenagers cruising the strip in period cars. These shots don't actively advance narrative action, but simply step back and perceive, offering poignant moments, following along as the radio signal seemingly bounces mercurially from car to car, filling the air with a larger collective field of individually amplified sources. As the example that opened this chapter shows, however, the film's singular reliance on source music is created with tangible tricks, challenging the borders of the ostensible "realism" we might associate with source music. Close viewing of these cruising scenes shows us that Lucas (and sound designer Walter Murch) weren't after precisely realistic synchronization. Rather, a general distortion of the sound envelope and an inconsistent bobbing of levels creates a larger sense of spatiality. There is nothing so specific, for example, as panning effects mapped onto the visualized motion of individual cars.[34] Only when we move into closer shots—usually accompanying dialogue—does the radio sound become more specifically localized within the frame. Ultimately, then, the fantasy of radio's omnipresence is both completed and created in the perception of the audience.

These magical fantasies of radio space are challenged only once within the film, and then in order to be ambiguously reaffirmed. When Curt goes to the radio station, with the intent of reaching the mysterious woman through an on-air dedication, his progress into the station is matched by transitions between several aurally distinct sound filters. As he advances into the Wolfman's lair, these perceptible changes create a sense of stripping away the layers of magic that surround the medium. First, Curt hears the radio in his car, and then he hears it filtered through the on-air speakers in the interior of the station, and finally it is stripped of its spatialized distortion, playing as a record inside the sound booth itself (1:35:50). Ultimately, this progression visually reveals Bob Smith spinning the record on his studio turntable. But Smith then deflects Curt's identification of him as the Wolfman by playing a pre-recorded tape, fooling Curt into believing that the shows are pre-recorded, rather than broadcast live. This gesture engages a mythic narrative of distinction between recorded and "live" (broadcast) sound in order to perpetuate the mystery of the Wolfman within further (perhaps infinite) layers of mediation. The Wolfman's adolescent mythology clearly requires that the object of desire remain always beyond our grasp, unmarked by participation in reality. Only as Curt leaves does he get a brief, accidental glimpse of Smith continuing to speak on-air as the Wolfman, and he accepts this unification of Wolfman's voice and body in rueful silence (1:40:20). The perpetuation of "the Wolfman" as an etheric aural myth, consumed in the ephemeral moment by his teenaged audience, is only possible at the expense of his tacet demythification for a newly mature Curt, a revelation of artifice that assures us that the Wolfman is just an ordinary person.

Common to many critiques of nostalgia is the idea that it represents "memory with the pain removed,"[35] ironically contravening the word's own etymological roots (*algia*, Greek for longing, aching, or pain).[36] But the playful humor and warm affection that many critics noted in *American Graffiti*'s cultural memorialization have their own, less obvious, reserves of pain—the inevitable pain of losing connection to this imagined community, as well as the pain of our own historical foresight. From the perspective of filmgoers who had undergone the social turmoil of America in the late sixties and early seventies, the presumptive loss of the supposed cultural innocence represented in *American Graffiti* (whether or not that innocence had ever been demonstrably "real," as opposed to the lacunae of age and privilege) could represent an open wound. The way in which sound and music articulate this pain is one of the principal differences between *American Graffiti* and *The Last Picture Show*. In *American Graffiti*, the radio medium intensifies and channels a sense of nostalgic loss, but it also offers a sort of magical balm for its effects.[37]

The ubiquitous spatialization of sound in *American Graffiti* paradoxically foregrounds *the distance that sound must travel*, an image that often, as in the film's ending, "stands in" for the melancholy distances of time. And yet, as Bob Smith pointedly tells Curt in the sound booth, "the Wolfman is everywhere." As he says this, the pre-recorded voice is distorted with a spacey echo-effect—whether deliberate or not, a lovely coincidence well in keeping with the film's magical logic of sound mediation (1:38:10). If the Wolfman is "everywhere," he might also by analogy exist "every-when"—or, at least, both in the film's depicted *then* and its projected *now*—existing *then* as a character, and in the perceived *now* of the film's spectator. Bridging a fictional story of the early sixties and the cultural moment of early rock revivalism in the early seventies, the Wolfman physically embodies the era onscreen while also acting as a sort of musical curator, his persona appearing to "score" the film in diegetic real time by sympathetically matching music to the action taking place at the other end of the signal. It is the Wolfman who magically *knows* to play Chuck Berry when it's time for rebellious hijinks, or to play the Platters when it's time to make love.

Sometimes, these semantic connections can be more literal, dependent not just on the affective associations of a musical style, but on the linguistic text of the song itself. This technique can occasionally be quite funny. *The Last Picture Show* does this in its more humorous scenes, such as when Duane and Jacy's attempt to lose their virginity ends with Duane's detumescent failure, played against Eddie Fischer's syrupy 1951 ballad "Wish You Were Here" (1:10:40). In *American Graffiti*, we find similar patterns, occasionally verging on the cartoonish, as when geeky Terry is discovered by the hoodlums from whom he is attempting to steal back his car—an awkward moment precisely timed to the vocalized "Hellllo Baaaaby!" that opens the Big Bopper's 1958 hit "Chantilly Lace" (1:31:09). We could go further, teasing out more connections according to the same logic: thoughtful Curt ponders the authenticity of his life decisions underscored by "The Great Pretender";

when John's car-to-car flirting backfires with his accidental pickup of thirteen-year-old Carol, the turn of events is set to a transition from "Why Do Fools Fall in Love" to "That'll Be the Day." While this might seem at first like a well-worn (even clichéd) style of matching compiled song to narrative, it is by focusing on the agency of the Wolfman as a meta-diegetic curator that it becomes something far more interesting. In *The Last Picture Show*, the voice of a deejay is mostly absent, and, when present, it is not the active force it represents in *American Graffiti*.[38] In *American Graffiti*, however, this authorship constantly hovers below the surface of the film, regularly brought to our attention via the Wolfman's on-air voice. Understanding musical authorship in this way transcends the extra-filmic, factual knowledge that these coincidences are, of course, created by the filmmakers. Within the logic of the film world, they also register as something akin to acausal synchronicities—phenomena whose combination of phenomenal significance and (diegetically) impossible causality gestures toward a fundamentally strange relationship between mental and physical worlds.

Throughout the film, the kids share with each other different versions of the Wolfman's mythic story, some of which (that he broadcasts from a station in Mexico) are indirectly close to the factual truth, while others (that he broadcasts from an airplane, allowing him to stay one step ahead of the FCC) are pointedly fantastic. The Wolfman is what the kids could be if they could escape everyday life into a world composed entirely of the sensations associated with their favorite songs—a world similar, in many ways, to that which *American Graffiti* might have offered the nostalgic viewer of 1973. In the midst of this potent techno-utopian exoticism, it is all the more telling that these uniformly white kids ascribe to the Wolfman an exotic (and, of course, factually inaccurate) black identity.[39] He is their shaman, or—as he is (somewhat less problematically) described in the published screenplay— their "best friend, confidant, and guardian angel."[40] Through the figure of the Wolfman, the one-way act of listening to the radio is thus fantastically reconceived as a sort of imaginary dialogue, recuperating and impossibly collapsing distances of space and time.

American Graffiti's appeal to its audience's cultural and autobiographical memory was cannily played out in advertising taglines implying a form of direct address, prominently featuring the phrase "Where were you in '62?" A trailer for the film likewise depicts a yearbook opened to caricatures of the cast, which come to life in a series of vignettes.[41] This yearbook, the film seems to say, might just as easily be yours. And yet, I would argue, there is more to this gesture than effective ad copy. The yearbook, in this sense, becomes a sort of ritualistic object—like the radio, it is a talisman for recalling (or perhaps *conjuring*) the past. Even more explicitly, the use of radio to magically recover the past is hinted at by the film's opening, both in the published screenplay and the finished film. The screenplay calls for the film to open with an abstract visualization of a radio dial, filling the entire screen, and gradually tuning through the spectrum and landing on Bill Haley and the Comet's "Rock around the Clock."[42] In the finished film, this effect is created on the soundtrack alone, accompanying first the Universal logo and then a black screen. But although slightly more ambiguous, the effect remains basically the same: the radio becomes a memory box, an instrument for mnemonic divination, *creating* the movie itself by dialing up its frequency and conjuring it into being.

Critics of so-called postmodern nostalgia, such as Fredric Jameson, have generally tended to regard nostalgia (or at least nostalgia under the presumptively inevitable cultural conditions of postmodernity) as a liquidation of historical complexity, in favor of a gallery of increasingly empty and inflexible metonymic signifiers.[43] The likes of tailfins, hair gel, and Bill Haley, in such a reading, would be collectively understood to absorb and nullify our ability to critique the past. This reading, however, is strikingly limited by an assumption that nostalgia is definable through coherent signifiers that exist within a representational object, an understanding that fails to engage in any meaningful or complex way how nostalgia affectively *feels* to the viewer—or, rather, it renders such feelings inextricable from the conveyance of a regressive and ideologically comfortable false consciousness. To render the nostalgic subject not as a passive receiver, but as a co-creating author of his or her own aestheticized pain and pleasure would also be to dismantle the stable Archimedean point from which nostalgia's supposedly insidious cultural effects might be deconstructed. It is this aesthetic subject position, however, that *American Graffiti*'s use of radio leaves so pointedly open. Through radio, the film suggests a sense of imagined space inextricably linked to the very notion of the past. The audience is invited to fill this virtual space of sound and signal with its own complexities, its own desires, and our own understanding of temporal loss.[44] Radio, in *American Graffiti*, offers characters and viewers alike an adolescent dream-space that, although lost, might be regained by opening a yearbook, or (happily, for the success of a commercial film) by buying a ticket and going to see a movie. Like most so-called coming of age films, *American Graffiti* also deals with the inevitability of leaving the past behind, as embodied by Curt and his ultimate choice to leave Modesto. But when Curt flies off to college, he still preserves something of this utopian space by guarding the secret of Wolfman Jack's mundane reality, allowing the Wolfman to remain for Curt's peers an ambiguously disembodied, omnipresent pop oracle, saturating the airwaves with his presence and furthering the illusion that the auditor really is (narcissistically, magically) inscribed into the song.

Radio, Nostalgia, and Time's Silences

By contrast, in *The Last Picture Show*, music tends to depict the past as a time-bound reality defined by an unbridgeable distance from the present. In *The Last Picture Show*, music functions as a reality effect that conveys entrapment and temporal loss. As Julie Hubbert has shown, one effect of the minor seventies trend toward diegetic-only scoring was to draw upon and cultivate a sense of actuality, an effect of uninflected presence, of "being-there" that was also key to new forms of non-fiction documentary cinema.[45] Music in *The Last Picture Show* may emerge from class relationships in the narrative; it may follow patterns of authorship and expression in the manner of traditional classical Hollywood film music. But as we have already seen, this documentary-like sense of uninflected presence also establishes a quality of contingency and alienation. In addition, music's spatialized quality within the film helps to create this sense of presence—a presence that is distinctly temporalized as an oppressive state of entrapment within which the characters' lives are interwoven.

For this reason, although music in *The Last Picture Show*, as in *American Graffiti*, certainly sets an emotional tone and conveys elements of narrative and characterization, it projects no sense of mystical communion with the radio signal. The sources of music in *The Last Picture Show* are also more diverse, encompassing not only radio but jukeboxes and record players, eliminating any sense of radio's specialness and undercutting the transcendent agency of the deejay with the agency of this world's far more mundane inhabitants. At its best, diegetic music seems to offer characters a fragile island, like the radio in Sonny's car or the jukebox in Genevieve's café, which underscores Sonny's rapport with Sam and Genevieve as surrogate parents. But the convivial jukebox is also given a negative parallel in the record player that the film's spoiled rich kids use to underscore their sexual rituals, which are self-consciously understood less as acts of erotic fulfillment than as brazen practice for the adult rituals of social climbing. When characters listen to music, no benevolent Wolfman is present to make sure that the music is just right for the moment. In *The Last Picture Show*, music doesn't offer even the illusion of imaginary freedom. Instead, it glues us into the past, just as its characters are unhappily glued into their world. As we heard in its opening scene, *The Last Picture Show*'s use of radio carefully balances music and obliterating noise. The fragility of the signal often seems to suggest its ephemerality and its potential extinction. Whereas in *American Graffiti* the spatialized signal cultivates a faith in music's essential omnipresence, retrospectively solidifying the past as a moment in cultural memory, the emphasis in *The Last Picture Show* is on mediation as noise, as a threat to the emotional coherence of the signal, able, perhaps, to extinguish it through wind or through pervasive stillness.

In a scene in which the movie theater's teenaged audience go their separate ways for the evening, there is a moment briefly comparable to *American Graffiti*'s use of spatialized car radios. But the contrast is also vital: the radios play different songs—located along the central musical-narrative axis of pop vs. country western—one plays "Rose, Rose I Love You," the other plays a fragment of Hank Williams's "Why Don't You Love Me" (0:10:45). The cues are also framed differently, allowing the musical elements on the soundtrack to break into a palpable, preexisting stillness, and then gradually die away into the wind, creating a sense of music as a finite interval rounded by a far greater void. Bogdanovich's choice of framing the scene in a series of sustained long shots offers a visual corollary to this image, preventing us from becoming enveloped in the musical worlds of the teenagers, and instead maintaining our focus on the small figures performing their routine chores at the cinema, activity that continues before and into the stillness after the cars leave (Figure 4.1). In such scenes we sense that the *emptiness* of marked aural absence can be just as spatialized a force as that of musical presences.

American Graffiti's imaginary collective, created by radio broadcast, similarly implies the existence of a sort of "outer edge"—an awareness of something beyond the comfortable, familiar world in which music draws together and solidifies time and space. When music is absent in *Graffiti*, it tends to be located in the contemplative stillness that emerges from car-sex or car-death. Car-sex is mostly romantic or comic: when Terry's car is stolen—in one of the film's few self-aware nods to its nearly omnipresent

Figure 4.1 Exterior shot of Sam the Lion's movie theater, (0:11:25).
Screen capture from *The Last Picture Show* (1971). Criterion Collection. Under license from Sony Pictures Home Entertainment, 2010. DVD.

music—it is the *absence* of the radio (which Terry had left playing while sojourning in the woods with Debbie) that suddenly forces home the realization (1:06:13). The flip side of car-sex is, inevitably, car-death. Death marks many of the images lying in the silence beyond this "outer edge" of the signal: the melancholy of leaving childhood places, times, and people, as well as actual, physical death. We have already encountered the final moment of atmospheric silence as Curt flies away, pondering his future as the town (and the radio signal) disappear beneath him, replaced with yearbook photos indicating that two of the major characters (John and Terry) will be, respectively, dead and missing in action within the next year. In another scene, when John and his young friend Carol pay a visit to an auto junkyard, it is clear that, as the town's undefeated hot-rodder, John views this place as a window into his possible future, a future that will be verified by his obituary in the film's credits (0:50:44). This is also the first insistently *quiet* scene in a film in which music is a near-constant presence. Lucas and Murch emphasize this shift in tone with a move away from the omnipresent musical sphere of radio space, instead using natural environmental night sounds. The space of the signal is revealed to be finite, and beyond it lie disturbing adult realities.[46]

But if, in *American Graffiti*, emptiness and silence are depicted as threats lurking around the edges of a warm, shared collectivity, *The Last Picture*

Show's music and sound depict this shared generational collectivity as illusory all the way down. Perhaps this is because, rather than suggest the challenging but conquerable threat of adult realities, or even the simple fact of death, *The Last Picture Show*'s "outer edge"—the conceptual territory beyond the reach of musical space—tends to draw upon a pointedly anti-romantic, anti-sentimental aesthetic of gritty realism. Several of the film's most uncomfortable scenes have no music, an "anti-Hollywood" sensibility in line with broader New Hollywood tendencies of the era. This pointed lack, particularly striking in several scenes of awkward and humiliating sexual encounters, or scenes of sudden, unexpected violence, render the film more painful for lacking the sense of emotional significance and empathy that music can offer. There are moments in *The Last Picture Show* where the comforts of music are simply, cruelly, and (we must suspect) deliberately absent.[47]

But such scenes, in the final analysis, perhaps form pointed contrasts with a very different use of musical absence, in which, rather than pressing home the bleak reality of the present, the absence of music feels intended to create a sort of sacralized space of solemnity, dignity, or reflection, freed from the mundanity of music in order to facilitate a nostalgic act of memory. This effect is particularly pointed in two key scenes. In the first, Sam takes Sonny fishing, and lapses into a reflection on his youth, when he took an unnamed girl skinny-dipping in a rural reservoir (0:55:50). Later, Jacy's mother Lois reveals to Sonny that she was this girl. Sam has been dead since the movie's midpoint, a death symbolizing a gradual decline leading to the closure of the local movie theater he had owned. By this point, too, Jacy has left Duane for a rich kid, lost the rich kid, and settled for eloping with Sonny, less out of any feeling for him than as a way of provoking her wealthy father. After the young couple has been broken up, Lois commiserates with Sonny, reminiscing about her youthful romance with Sam. As in Sam's earlier, clearly paralleled act of reminiscence, the absence of music and the emphasis on wind effects are striking. Even more noticeable is the abruptness with which music (again, Hank Williams's "Lovesick Blues") cuts back in when Lois returns to the present and starts her car (1:41:10). We suddenly depart from a powerful space of remembrance in which our focus is entirely concentrated on the soliloquy itself and back to the mundanity. If in the opening scene the music of Hank Williams signified an arrival, a "tuning in" to a dying frequency of the past, here it seems to signify a departure, back to the banal world of musical wallpaper.

Sounding the Nostalgic Past in the Early Seventies

The production and reception cultures of *Last Picture Show* and *American Graffiti* were clearly marked by a self-conscious awareness of the significance of the past. In general, *The Last Picture Show* tended to be read in terms of its precocious maturity, whereas *American Graffiti* tended to be read in terms of its precocious youthfulness. Several critics viewed Peter Bogdanovich's austere, classical direction of *The Last Picture Show* as an ideal fusion of New and Old Hollywood currents, with more mainstream or conservative critics attracted to *The Last Picture Show*'s lack of the reflexive stylism of film modernism and the narrative ambiguities that characterized much art-house fare. Here was a film that seemed to be both reverently traditional *and* of the moment.[48] By contrast, *American Graffiti* was widely seen as an important calling card from an arriving filmmaker whose youthful cohort was changing the way the game was played.[49] In the reception of both films, then, we can easily trace the negotiated values of a transitional industrial moment—a moment in which the dynamic interplay of Old and New Hollywood engendered its *own* temporal frame for nostalgic recollection. Despite their differing backgrounds, Bogdanovich and Lucas both professionally exemplified a Hollywood in which historicism was an increasingly important sensibility. Bogdanovich's career beyond directing had variously positioned him as a film historian, curator, and critic with a strong devotion to the classical cinema of directors such as John Ford and Howard Hawks. Lucas, who had pursued academic film study at the University of Southern California, was one of what journalists Michael Pye and Lynda Myles dubbed "the Movie Brats," a group of filmmakers for whom industrial tutelage had been supplemented (or even replaced) by study at academic institutions.[50] In this way, both Lucas and Bogdanovich were representative of a generation of filmmakers for whom the "film past" was important, who were broadly literate in film history and theory, and whose initial training and experience tended to be outside of or parallel to the traditional trade apprenticeships of the old studio system.[51]

But nostalgia also plays a role in contextualizing these films within their broader cultural background. Throughout the seventies, cultural critics regularly commented upon a turn toward nostalgia for the pre-countercultural era. This turn was usually read suspiciously, and was eventually viewed as culminating at decade's end in Reaganite neo-conservatism. Grand historical narratives are at stake here—narratives which have tended to characterize the seventies as a decade of burn-out, confusion, and identity crisis, setting the stage for the political regression of the eighties. Film was recognizable enough as part of this so-called nostalgia boom to warrant mention not only by film critics, but in sociological studies such as Fred Davis's *Yearning for Yesterday* (1979), which includes (brief) discussions of *The Last Picture Show* and *American Graffiti*.[52]

Popular music culture represents another important and temporally marked field of reference for both films. As David Brackett, Greil Marcus, and others have shown, as the sixties progressed into the seventies, some audiences for folk and rock music latched insecurely and ambiguously onto country music, attracted to its images of authenticity and Americana, but alienated by its associations with cultural conservatism.[53] And as rock music itself continued to evolve, it began to display a self-conscious interest in its own past. It was in the early seventies that the "Oldies" format—key to *American Graffiti*'s broad soundscape—began to gain radio traction. Frank Zappa playfully deconstructed doo-wop on his 1968 album *Cruising with Reuben and the Jets*. Retro band Sha Na Na played Woodstock in 1969. *Grease* opened on Broadway in 1972. Finally, in part due to the success of *American Graffiti*, network television saw the premiere of *Happy Days* in 1974.

For all that the two films examined in this chapter were hallmarks of a New Hollywood sensibility, however, their relationship to the broader contexts of early seventies nostalgia contains as many points of divergence as similarity. Sometimes, these divergences coexist within the paratexts of a single film. For example, *The Last Picture Show*'s promotional trailers plays upon far more conventionally nostalgic invocations of simpler times ("Tony Bennett was on the radio. . . . Boys were wearing ducktails . . .") while also mixing in subversive contemporary allegory ("the police action in the far East was Korea . . ."). There seems to have been multiple narratives at stake, here—both a "good old fifties" and a "repressive, conformist fifties," both of which seek to engage audience identification. Ultimately, however, *The Last Picture Show* draws upon nostalgia less *for* the fifties, than *through* the fifties, aching, with Sam the Lion and Lois, for a mythic moment in American consciousness in which the promise of real value, real experiences, and the forging of new frontiers was still understood to be possible.[54] *The Last Picture Show*, thus, in a sense, reworks in the more proximate past what J. Hoberman has called the "twilight Western"—a subgenre in which the old heroes of the frontier, haunted by mortality, wander a fallen world in which they no longer have a place.[55] Bogdanovich acknowledged that a desire to evoke this idea led to his replacing the inauspicious Audie Murphy B-film that closes the cinema in Larry McMurtry's novel with Howard Hawk's magisterial classic *Red River*, so as to more pointedly juxtapose the mythic Hollywood West to the real, dead one outside the walls of the cinema.[56]

American Graffiti, by contrast, spoke directly to nostalgia *for the early sixties* as a moment of innocence prior to the cultural turmoil to come. The suspicion with which this narrative was regarded by more politically progressive critics was articulated early and has, in many ways, has become the pervasive narrative through which the film has been read, leaving alternative readings with a perceived obligation to somehow negotiate nostalgia out of the picture. In his perceptive review for *Film Quarterly*, for example, critic Michael Dempsey declares up front that *American Graffiti* "has more on its mind than nostalgia"—ultimately concluding that the film possesses a covertly *anti-nostalgic* dimension in its self-aware foreshadowing of the troubled relationship between the characters and the adolescent idyll they are leaving, despite "being firmly plugged into the nostalgia boom that plays upon our desires for a sense of roots, for a more comprehensible world, for a half-fearful look back at our own innocence."[57] In this way, Dempsey prioritizes the humanity of the characters, and the way in which the film does not condescend to their adolescent joys, miseries, and complexities. While I agree with such observations, it remains important to point out that they function in what seems, to me, to be a dubious and reductive strategy, namely, *redeeming* the film from the pernicious effects of nostalgia. Redemption *from nostalgia* is still assumed to be necessary, rather than the enrichment or complexification of our understanding of nostalgia itself.

Numerous connections thus link these two films and their use of nostalgia within a larger network of ideas, extending from the industrial and stylistic dynamics of New Hollywood filmmaking to broader cultural phenomena invested in historicizing and aestheticizing America's recent past. By drawing attention to the role of sound, radio, and nostalgia in these two films, we see that the medial characteristics of sound—in particular, broadcast radio sound and its depiction within diegetic space—might be relevant to the construction of distinct, yet relatable nostalgic sensibilities of pastness. Studies of radio listening have frequently emphasized the way in which the medium implicitly draws upon the active agency of the imagination of its human listeners, as well as the role of physical spatiality in listening itself.[58] In many cases, some such studies negotiate their *own* nostalgia when dealing with the dual mediation of listening and memory—whether this memory is personal or cultural.[59] In this spirit, we might supplement Svetlana Boym's polarity of "restorative" (regressive, pragmatic, dangerous) and "reflective" (ruminative, alienated, and melancholic) nostalgia with a distinct middle ground that might be called "magical nostalgia." Magical nostalgia lacks the intellectual pedigree or contestatory authenticity of Boym's characteristic examples of reflective nostalgia, which tend to be engaged with the aesthetics of modernism, self-reflexivity, and diaspora. Nevertheless, magical nostalgia bears a similarly paradoxical, and even utopian foundational gesture—it can only exist in the shade cast by its own impossibility. It cannot be *found*, but it can, perhaps, be *conjured*. These two films represent two starkly contrasting dimensions of New Hollywood nostalgia employed as an act of conjuration, aimed at recapturing—even if only in our imagination—the lost experiences of the past.

5
Badlands and the Music of Temporal Immanence

First, Some Funny Business with Dogs . . .

The opening sequence of Terrence Malick's *Badlands* (1973) quickly and efficiently encapsulates many of the film's larger complexities. The film opens with a formally isolated and fragmentary scene, consisting of a single tracking shot. The brief musical cue, composed by George Tipton in the style of Erik Satie, accompanies a voiceover that begins *in media res*, as a teenaged girl is shown sitting on her bed accompanied by a very large dog.[1] Film scholar Michel Chion has mused upon this shot, and its strangely skewed sense of physical perspective, arguing that in Malick's films, such shots point to an essential strangeness that is innate to the fact of human presence in the world. This strangeness, all too easily overlooked by everyday perception, is cracked open by a glimpse into something akin to a fairy tale world, in which normal rules of perspective inconsistently apply.[2] Is that a very big dog, or a very small girl? Are we witnessing an anthropomorphizing act of play, or, perhaps, can this animal actually talk to her? The girl, whose name is Holly, appears to be telling her dog a story, but we don't hear her diegetic voice. Rather, her visualized speech to the dog roughly parallels, without audiovisual synchronization, the story Holly begins to tell *us* in the voiceover. Even in this very brief scene, then, we are presented with a number of diverse thematic and perceptual strands that tease the edges of audiovisual and narrative coherence (Figure 5.1).

Holly's voiceover articulates several tonal affectations, all of which will become pervasive throughout the film: a starkly unsentimental response to trauma, the awkward mediation of profound experience by melodramatic rhetoric, and a human tendency to invest non-human objects with human meanings and value.

Figure 5.1 Holly and her dog (0:00:32).
Screen capture from Badlands (1973). Criterion Collection, 2013. DVD.

My mother died of pneumonia when I was just a kid. My father had kept their wedding cake in the fridge for ten whole years. After the funeral he gave it to the yard man. He tried to act cheerful, but he could never be consoled by the little stranger he found in his house. Then, one day, hoping to begin a new life away from the scene of all his memories, he moved us from Texas to Fort Dupree, South Dakota.[3] (0:0:36)

The scene then fades to black as Tipton's pseudo-*Gymnopédie* dies away under the sound of ambient morning quietude in a small Midwestern city. Nothing so far, save a long shot we now see of a single car, has decisively located this film in the fifties, and this reserved use of historical signifiers will be maintained throughout the film. Save for cars and very occasional compiled song or pop-cultural references, most everyday things (clothes, houses, storefronts, mannerisms, language) tend to appear largely as they might in a contemporaneous rural Midwestern setting of the early seventies. While nothing is pointedly anachronistic, surprisingly little about the film goes out of its way to self-consciously articulate its historical period, in part because so much of it takes place in a wilderness populated only by the film's outlaw couple. A sense of pastness is perhaps most tangibly present through our awareness of the film's loose historical inspiration for this couple—the 1957 string of murders committed by Charles Starkweather and his teenaged girlfriend Caril Fugate.

The character loosely modeled on Starkweather (as Holly is modeled on Fugate) is Kit Carruthers, Holly's soon-to-be boyfriend, now introduced collecting garbage. Kit's personality is likewise established quickly, through disconcerting humor reciprocated by his pal Cato, whom Kit will, considerably later, shoot and kill. Finding a dead dog along their garbage route, Kit offers Cato a dollar to "eat this collie." Cato replies, "I'm not going to eat him for a dollar. Don't think he's a collie, either. Some kind of dog, though . . ." (0:01:45). The humor of this strangely funny line goes beyond the implicit question of how high the offer would need to be before Cato might consider eating this dead dog. There is also the humorously absurd fixation on breed, as if this taxonomy somehow entered into either the animal's deadness or its edibility. If Holly's dog was anthropomorphized into a human-like subject, the dead dog (see Figure 5.2) is objectified, a thing of pure matter to be collected with the trash.

Holly's dog, however, will eventually assume the role of an object, too, when her father later shoots it as punishment for continuing her forbidden relationship with Kit. The unceremonious dumping of Holly's dog into the river thus closes a circle, converting the animal back into trash. Through these paired opening scenes, then, a set of categorical distinctions is established that will continue to be important—between Object and Being, between a treasured pet and a bit of garbage, and between human linguistic and

Figure 5.2 Kit finds a dead dog (0:01:46).
Screen capture from Badlands (1973). Criterion Collection, 2013. DVD.

conceptual constructs such as "collie" and the ontology of the animal itself. These distinctions will all become the subject of ambiguity and play.

In this chapter, we will explore the category of "play" as it is central to *Badlands*: to its philosophical work, its aesthetic beauty, and its musical approach to representing the past. In *Badlands*, play is far from being a uniformly positive or liberating action. Conceived broadly as the spontaneous manipulation and reworking of material reality, play can also manifest in destructive, violent ways. Not long after meeting Holly, Kit murders her father, removing him as an obstacle to their relationship, and they flee this subdued city together. In their flight, Kit kills (with an increasingly tenuous logic of self-preservation) several bounty hunters and police officers, his pal Cato, and (although this is left uncertain) possibly a friendly young couple who randomly cross his path at the wrong time. Throughout their adventure, Kit and Holly also engage in a kind of homespun style of philosophical play, a self-conscious construction of the world surrounding them, sometimes through Holly's digressive voiceover, sometimes through their engagement with the physical objects that cross their path, and sometimes quite literally, when they build an elaborate treehouse in the forest. The film's considerable challenge to its viewer is to understand its violence, whatever other cultural or ethical meanings it might hold, as also coextensive with this sense of creative play.

After dispensing with the ostensible collie, the film cuts between Holly, practicing baton twirling alone on her front lawn, and Kit deciding to ditch work for the day. We begin to hear a musical work by Gunild Keetman, titled "Gassenhauer," fading into the soundtrack and underscoring the main title sequence as Kit and Holly gradually draw closer together. "Gassenhauer" originated in a large collection of pedagogical compositions broadly known as the *Schulwerk*, composed by Keetman and Carl Orff.[4] Although Kit's "official" job is done, and a series of quick dissolves emphasizes his aimlessness as he wanders away, Kit is not done *working* inasmuch as he is not done *playing*. He finds an abandoned mop and attempts to balance its handle upright on his palm. A continuation of Kit's garbage picking, Kit's play with the mop demonstrates in-the-moment improvisation. This object has become more than an object for him, but instead something into which he is projecting his energies, bringing it to new, repurposed life. But the mop is just as quickly abandoned. In the next shot, Kit instead takes to a can, briefly kicking it down the alley before stomping on it with all his weight and discarding it: violence and play.

As he comes across Holly, who continues to twirl on her front lawn, Kit quickly looks both ways. Does he wonder if anyone else sees her, too? Is he stunned by her, and if so, then by what? Perhaps not by her "adult" qualities, which Holly's voiceover later tells us that Kit professes to admire. Rather, twirling her baton and essentially *playing* in her front yard, Holly looks very much like a little girl. Her twirling forms a "rhyme" to Kit's play with the mop. Kit's attraction seems to be more one of fascination and curiosity, rather than sexual in nature. He seems to see in Holly a potential playmate, but to avoid infantilizing (or sexualizing) connotations, we might say that Kit finds a *philosophical* playmate—someone whose strangely alien, disengaged, yet actively constructive relationship to the world aligns with his own. But unlike Kit, Holly doesn't occasionally kill people when she perceives herself to be threatened.

Despite its high potential for the thrilling melodrama that often characterized the "lovers on the run" sub-genre in the New Hollywood era, *Badlands* is a deliberately evasive, coolly distanced, and strangely *funny* film. Its violence is approached with a dry, matter-of-fact opacity, and utter absence of clear judgment. Rather than human drama or ethical complexities, Malick continually focuses our attention upon tangibly sensuous details of image and sound, obliquely decentering a conventional narrative. The film thus extends its fascination with creative play and worldly objects into the stylistic gestures through which it manifests itself—including, I will argue, through music. By examining how music functions in *Badlands*, I hope to build upon a philosophical literature focused on Malick's films, but also to reconsider this particular film from the perspective of how its soundtrack conveys a sensibility of temporal presence.

The two musical categories we've just encountered—Satie (here, George Tipton's canny emulation of Satie) and the music of Orff and Keetman—mark out the film's broader musical scope.[5] Malick himself set a template for such readings in a pair of interviews published in 1975. In one of these, with Michel Ciment for *Postif*, Malick credits his mentor, director Irvin Kershner, with suggesting the series of recordings documenting the *Schulwerk*, collectively titled *Musica Poetica* (1963–1975).[6] Malick's description of the music, however, is actually rather dry, even banal in its affective cataloguing:

> The piece by Satie created a feeling of melancholia contrasting with the piece by Orff, which is in a major key and uplifting. Satie's music went well with scenes where Holly's walking on the grass, where she's looking at the

rich man's house, or when the plane takes them back to South Dakota at the end. Orff's music accompanies the house fire, the scenes in the forest, and the helicopter's taking off.[7]

If anything more is to be said about this music beyond the fact that some of it is "uplifting" and some of it is "melancholy"—and I would argue that there is *much* more to be said about it—we are left on our own. By contrast, the richest reading of the film's music to date might be found in James Morrison and Thomas Schur's monograph on Malick, particularly in their reading of the soundtrack's eclecticism. While the authors perceive a tension between the "fragmentary, diffuse" elements that make up the film's soundtrack, they also recognize the music works precisely because of these qualities, as a "variegated composite" that can articulate "ironic commentary and intransitive interjection, both mute and breathless."[8] Morrison and Schur note something vital about the film's use of music: it somehow seems both kaleidoscopic and harmonious, heterogeneous and holistic, that it paradoxically seems to articulate nothing and everything at the same time.

Crucially, this heterogeneous dimension is not disruptive, or "Brechtian." Rather than encouraging critical distance by obstructing our immersion in the world of the film, Malick's "alienation effects" instead balance, or perhaps superimpose, sensibilities of both distance and sensuous immersion. This mirrors a dynamic that film scholar Steven Rybin has traced in the engaged, yet inevitably distanced interaction between Malick's characters and their phenomenal worlds. For Rybin, Malick's characters habitually engage a philosophical practice of living that, by extension, reaches outward to affectively engage the audience.[9] In what follows, I will argue that the *musical* heterogeneity of *Badlands*' soundtrack is distinctly meaningful to the film's philosophical import, resonating with compiled classical music's ambiguous role as a sounding object in the film world, even (or perhaps especially) when such musical objects are imbued with the phenomenal presence of the past. Doing so, I will attempt to extend film musicology's engagement with another hybrid discipline, namely film-philosophy, viewing Satie's ironic and mysterious sense of melancholy and the pedagogical philosophy of the *Schulwerk* as woven together into an act of active audiovisual philosophizing.

Like all the films discussed in this book, *Badlands* is to some degree *about* the past, although this relationship is considerably more abstract and nebulous than in any film we have examined thus far. To characterize *Badlands*' relationship to the past, we might theorize an overlapping of a specific genre (historical fiction) with a broader aesthetic disposition that film scholar John Orr has identified with a "Cinema of Poetry."[10] In this cinema, a "double register" develops a tension between subjective and objective perspective, resulting in what Orr calls "free indirect vision." Poetic cinema, for Orr, relies upon this tension, both subjectively warping film style and narrative to mirror characters' interior states, and drawing upon cinema's unique ability to evoke objective presence by manifesting in a perceptual present tense.[11] In the New Hollywood Cinema of Malick, Robert Altman, Martin Scorsese, and David Lynch, Orr identifies a tendency toward "reverie," in which the objective/subjective doubling of free indirect vision might be meaningfully overlapped with a doubling of presence and past. The subjective register engages stylized, distancing effects that—while disorienting for the viewer—are nevertheless integrated into a unified aesthetic experience of the film world or, as some more recent scholars in film philosophy have explored, into the perspectival "mind" of the film itself.[12] The objective register, in turn, relies upon an effect of affectlessness, upon cinema understood as facilitating a direct apprehension of reality. In the context of the historical film, we might experience this double register as a dual experience of a distinction between an "objective" (past-as-experiential-now) and "subjective" (the past-as-distanced-past) sensibility.[13]

As Orr explains, a central feature of the American Cinema of Poetry is the way in which

> its contemplation of the past tries to replace myth not through document but through reverie, the phantasmagoria of the poetic image rooted in historical knowledge. It thus fashions an imagined history out of verisimilitude during a time when the American present was experiencing a civil turbulence possibly as great as anything since the Civil War. But the cinema of Latent Destiny offers no mythic consolation. The new American cinema of reverie is not a cinema of pastiche but something more vital and more immediate. Pasolini had, as noted, suggested that the cinema as form is always in the present tense. The paradox of the past as immediate present is the paradox of film projected as film. The action takes place on screen. Only in a written review does it enter a text as literary past tense. The classic epic of Ford or Griffiths in which the past is another country is duly transformed. The past as reverie is a living dream of the visual imagination, an existential past, not the mythic past recreated by Leone's America epics which willingly enter the realm of hyperreality, never to escape.[14]

How might Malick's sensibility of the past in *Badlands* engage this double register? *Badlands* is set in the fifties, but we are not expected to become immersed in "the fifties." Rather, the film immerses us in a phenomenal world largely "other" than that of historical experience. The experience of the past, like Kit and Holly, becomes "adrift in a sea of objects."[15] The forms and representations of the past that *are* present in *Badlands* (cars, pop culture ephemera, some diegetic music) become absorbed into our larger perception as an unmarked flow of objects existing within the film's phenomenal world, a world that is insistently located in a sensuous present tense. The past, in *Badlands*, is a world understood as an object that contains other objects, a world taken simply as a bare given, an existential fact. The world of the past is not a single object in which we can become lost, halting the flow of time, as in Mrs. Miller's drug experience. Rather, it is a field of objects understood as raw potential, ripe with possible significance, but remaining mute until transformed from their primal state by subjective human investment in their worldliness. The title of one of the Gunild Keetman compositions used in the film perhaps epitomizes this way of being in the past: "Music for a Puppet Play" allows us to imagine Kit and Holly as material objects on a material stage, striving, in the uncanny way in which puppets seem to strive, after an impossible sense of their own autonomous being that is perpetually in tension with their object-hood.

In this way, strangely, given the subject of this book, time and history hardly seem to matter in *Badlands*—or perhaps they matter *by virtue of* their seeming not to matter. Music in *Badlands* doesn't adopt an aesthetic of presence in order to challenge history, enveloping us in a viscerally propulsive moment (as in *Bonnie and Clyde*). Nor does it interweave its experiential sensibility with ahistorical, mythic images of suspended temporality or elemental immanence (as in *Chinatown*). And while *Badlands* pays close attention to recorded sound media, it does not address these technologies to its audience's presumed nostalgia. Instead, the past of *Badlands* is a perpetually moving target, whose affective charge is constantly diverted through the aggregates that make it up, in particular in a sense of tension between sincerity and ironic distance. These gestures paradoxically objectify the past, while simultaneously digging beneath the idea of "the past" to suggest time as a perpetual "time present" that is always already subjective and experiential, embedded into the same world into which the film's characters are embedded.

Even with the two musical selections that open the film (Keetman's "Gassenhauer" and Tipton's pseudo-Satie), we can start to unpack some of these dynamics. If "Gassenhauer," functioning formally as the film's main title sequence, is music that *creates*, then the sound of Satie, in turn, *obscures*; it transforms the purposive play of being (or, perhaps, the play that *creates* being) into a floating, directionless quality of suspension. If "Gassenhauer" embodies (or, perhaps, *enables*) presence, "Satie" mysteriously floats just beyond denotative signification, suggesting an unstable territory of shifting and elusive meanings. This back-and-forth movement, more than just being the affective poles of "uplifting" and "melancholy" music, is actually the dynamic stage on which the film's philosophical inquiry is given aural resonance. Over the course of the film, this dialectic relationship grows increasingly complex, tying itself in knots, posing unanswerable questions, and occasionally expanding its scope to incorporate other musical registers.

Terrence Malick as Collaborator, "Melomane," and Film-Philosopher

As philosophically heady as this line of inquiry might seem, it is nonetheless intertwined with specific industrial and historical questions of film music and authorship germane not only to film culture of the New Hollywood era, but also to our understanding of Terrence Malick as a distinctive auteur filmmaker. Credited composer George Tipton, for one thing, has remained a largely unheralded presence in *Badlands*, one whose work on the film— specifically *because* it is so self-effacing—all the more requires careful consideration. A talented arranger and composer who had been active in the West Coast music industry since the mid-sixties, Tipton had worked with pop recording artists such as Jan and Dean, Jackie DeShannon, the Ventures, José Feliciano, and singer-songwriter Harry Nilsson.[16] For *Badlands*, Tipton's individual authorship is almost entirely subsumed, first, into the musical styles of Orff, Keetman, and Satie, and second, into the stylistic language of Terrence Malick and his characteristic approach to music. At several places, music clearly meant to sound like Orff, Keetman, or Satie is actually composed by Tipton.[17]

By manipulating the film's various compiled musical elements, along with the overseeing the composer, Malick's work bears comparison to contemporaries (such as Robert Altman) who consistently devoted focused attention to musical expression, placing them into the category of auteurist filmmakers that Claudia Gorbman has identified as "melomanes"—that is to say, possessors of "melomania."[18] In Gorbman's formulation, a "melomane" is a filmmaker (usually a director) who exercises expressive authorship over a film through the selection and application of musical elements (whether original or compiled) that are created by someone else. Malick's melomania is thus invested not just in soundtrack mixing or the selection of compiled music, but also in the manipulation of original composition as it relates to compiled music. As James Wierzbicki has shown, this strategy on Malick's part has been remarkably consistent across his career, from *Badlands* up to his most recent films.[19] Essentially, Malick subjects both compiled music and original composition to his singular aesthetic conceptualization, with composers frequently called upon to dissolve their musical personality into that of other desired compiled selections. In this way, Tipton's seemingly willing subsumption into the expressive musical strategies of the film as a whole demonstrates the ambiguous and blurry lines that often define authorship and artistic creation in a collaborative artwork such as cinema. But they also illustrate Malick's tendency toward *objectifying* and *plasticizing* his musical sources, perhaps turning them—Tipton, Satie, Orff, Keetman, and others—into objects of play.

Malick has also become a central subject in the sub-discipline of film-philosophy. Contributing to this centrality is an awareness of Malick's background in academic philosophy prior to taking up filmmaking. But while Malick's academic background was frequently mentioned as a sort of curiosity in profiles surrounding the release of *Badlands,* this larger interpretive tradition, as film scholar John Rhym has shown, also developed both gradually and largely outside of the critical reception culture of seventies cinema. In their own time, *Badlands* and *Days of Heaven* (1978) were far more commonly understood in relation to the New Hollywood as a cultural and political moment, rather than as objects of close philosophical examination.[20] It was considerably later, following the release of the existentially ruminative World War II film *The Thin Red Line* (1998), that scholars began to focus in greater detail upon the nature of Malick's indebtedness to the thought of Martin Heidegger (1889–1976), of whose *Vom Wesen des Grundes* (1929) Malick produced an edited translation in 1969, shortly before leaving professional academia and enrolling in the American Film Institute. Scholarship focused on Malick's connection to Heidegger has tended to

BADLANDS AND THE MUSIC OF TEMPORAL IMMANENCE   167

liken the filmmaker's meditative approach to the world that surrounds and encompasses his characters (but from which they are often achingly alienated) to a Heideggerian view of the human condition as existentially embedded in the phenomenal world.[21] Our central concern with temporality and presence thus has, in Malick's film style, a uniquely privileged subject.

An early exponent of this approach to Malick's work was critic and philosopher Stanley Cavell, whose second edition of *The World Viewed* (1979) took particular note of Malick's *Days of Heaven* (1978) as an exemplar.[22] For Cavell, anticipating elements of John Orr's later Pasolinian reading, *Days of Heaven* exemplified cinema's unique doubling effect, mirroring both our simultaneous entanglement with the world and our subjective alienation from it. On one level, objects in film self-manifest—they may be understood to *participate* in their filmed re-creation within a representative medium. On another level, however, *human* objects, both characters in the world of the film and spectators in extra-diegetic space, share the capacity to recognize this state of being, but to be divorced from it by the same self-consciousness that also permits recognition. Malick's images, then, if we understand them less as "authored and constructed images," and more as "self-manifesting non-human agents," offer those who attempt to engage with them an intuitively grasped insight into irresolvable tensions familiar from a number of traditional dialectal pairings: spirit and matter, human and non-human, subjective and objective, or the networks that enable meanings (a Heideggerian "world") versus the opaque, unfathomable Real that underlies and perpetually escapes their grasp (Heidegger's "earth").[23]

The "presence of the past" in Malick's historical films thus gestures toward an *objectivity* of the past. This quality is akin to the "overheard" style we've encountered, for example, in *Bonnie and Clyde*'s moments of quiet reverie—a quality that effectively connotes the past as a reality beyond historical mediation. But Malick's pasts are also distinct for the way in which this quality is readable toward more ambitious philosophical ends. This past is perhaps not best understood as the timeless space of myth, but perhaps a post-temporal moment of sublime perception. Objects manifest a presence in Malick's films that is insistently *object-like*, and yet the self-consciousness of such manifestations seems to offer unique capacities for philosophical or even transcendent encounter—or, perhaps, the capacity to reveal that this shattering possibility had been immanent within reality all along, awaiting only the rupturing of ossified styles of perception in order to intuit the presence of "all things shining," as expressed in the voiceover of an American soldier at the end of *The Thin Red Line*.[24] And yet a melancholy aesthetic of failure, and even deadpan humor, frequently seems to underlie these aspirations, at least in Malick's two films from the seventies. One of the few threads connecting the diverse initial reception of these films and their current, more philosophically oriented reception is the perceived importance of irony. For Cavell, the relationship between humans and the self-manifesting world of filmic objects is one in which we desire self-transcendent communion with this world of objects, but this communion, which inevitably takes the form of domination, can only be thwarted by the mute incoherency of non-human nature, such that we are ultimately, ironically *reduced* by the quality of this objective "real" that eludes us—in Cavell's memorable phrase, leaving us "crushed by the fact of beauty left vacant."[25]

Badlands is invested in both landscapes and small, discrete objects. This focus on objects manifests in a sense of intimacy and tactile immediacy, but it also *foregrounds* objects—something about their presentation characterizes them as superseding the realist demands of set-dressing or production design. They command our attention, whether through an accumulated density of individual curios (an ornately furnished rich man's house in which the outlaws hide, Cato's shack filled to the brim with seemingly random items), or through their tellingly cast-off quality (the objects of Kit's garbage-picking, the "junk" Kit discards from Holly's suitcase after she leaves him). More recently, such ideas have opened up a productive space for reading *Badlands*, and the New Hollywood more broadly, through the lens of ecocriticism.[26] Offhand remarks about the film's production might factor in here, as well: various collaborators have discussed how the film made use of "found objects," and "found shots" in its production.[27]

Steven Rybin has argued that Malick's films demonstrate how film might be understood not just to "illustrate" discrete philosophical concepts, but rather that films may be understood to actively *philosophize* in a manner distinct to their nature as aesthetic objects.[28] This imperative has become a broader tenor in the subdiscipline of film-philosophy. Although film-philosophy is a development largely of the past two decades, however, it has roots in older theoretical conversations that focus on film's negotiation of style, perspective, reality, and existential concerns. In addition to the writing of Stanley Cavell in the late seventies, John Orr—writing in the late nineties—as we have seen, placed Malick's seventies work within a tradition that might be said to provocatively overlap with philosophy as much as it distinguishes itself against it—namely, that of poetry. Later, theorist Daniel Frampton would explore the interconnectedness of poetics and film analysis, rooted in film theorist Jean Epstein's concept of *lyrosophy*, or the "singing of knowledge, producing reason and emotion in one fell swoop."[29] For Frampton, Epstein's formulation becomes a path toward interpreting film as its own unique type of "lyrosophical" being. Within the "body" of film, conceived as a lyrosophical being, could film music be understood as a lyrosophical *singing* (both figuratively and, sometimes, literally) of reason and emotion into simultaneous being? If so, then conceiving of it as such would involve entertaining irrational and rational meanings together in harmony (or perhaps in a meaningfully suspended tension), allowing us a kind of intuitive and nuanced, yet still rigorously descriptive engagement to what might otherwise be simply bracketed as "the ineffable." Malick's filmmaking is, if nothing else, committed to a sincere and irreducible engagement with this ineffable, whether understood as a broadly philosophical or—particularly in his more recent films—as a theological task.

Musical Play in the *Schulwerk* and "Gassenhauer"

How, then, might we hear film-philosophical meanings in *Badlands*' use of music by Erik Satie and music from the *Schulwerk*? Discounting, at least for the time being, intertextual connections, and instead regarding these selections simply as affective film music that has plausibly shed any necessary association with its original source, the first thing to note about these two musical modes is their shared distance from Hollywood film music. This is music clearly disengaged from or somehow "other than" the emotionally extroverted vocabulary of neo-Romantic Hollywood. But it is distant, too, from the post-tonal extensions of that language that became topically linked to the frightening, the uncanny, the futuristic, or the psychologically fraught. Both sides of the film's musical binary (*Schulwerk*/Satie), are thus linked by a shared estrangement from expressive expectations. Similarly, although both of these musical "poles" were themselves "of the past" (in terms of their date of composition), the compiled classical music in *Badlands* is noteworthy for having nothing audibly to do with tropes either of the film's setting in the fifties or (at least in the popular imagination) with the respective epochs in which the music was composed. For most viewers, in other words, this music probably does *not* clearly connote Weimar-era or postwar Germany, nor does it connote fin-de-siècle France.

If we look closely at where this music *does come from*, however, we can nevertheless open meaningful hermeneutic doors into its affective work. The repetitive patterns and simple melodies characterizing the music of the *Schulwerk*, and the drifting, exotic chromaticism and modality of Satie create tangible expressive states that are not dependent upon their being plausibly associated with extramusical contexts. We can, however, understand these states as, to some degree, musical materializations of these contexts. Doing so, without necessarily implying intentionality, we can still derive from these contexts a great deal of insight. In particular, a closer look at Orff's pedagogical work (in which Gunild Keetman was a close collaborator) can offer much to a musical reading of *Badlands*. Orff and Keetman theorized their practice an essentialist understanding of authentic being, ideas resonant with the connections that have frequently been traced between the phenomenological existentialism of Martin Heidegger and Malick's films. Orff's vision for the *Schulwerk* suggests a primal vitalism founded upon the figure of the child, who ideally should begin with the most familiar and simplest musical objects and parameters and progress toward more complex ones—an argument in which ontology essentially recapitulates phylogeny, and the musical progression of the child taps into primitive states of music, culture, and being that gradually evolve into higher ones. In this view, children benefit the most from a pedagogical approach that both recognizes and directs these essential creative energies. This body of ideas also valorizes everyday musical "objects" such as folk songs and nursery rhymes, and a simplified, or perhaps "objectified" approach to selecting ideal beginning instruments (the well-known emphasis on mallet percussion), aimed at facilitating what is understood to be an innate, fundamental impulse: *hit something and hear what sound it makes*. The ideal purview of music education, for Orff, also extended beyond music's intrinsic qualities to embrace a totalizing approach to music as a life activity, and for this reason, Orff also favored the combining of musical training with kinesthetic movement and narrative storytelling, a kind of *gesamtkunstwerk* without the central Wagnerian *auteur*.[30]

Orff instructors have long grappled with the potentially troubling aspects of this worldview. The attitude of philosophical essentialism has the potential to read, today, as a universalist disregard for the reality of cultural difference. Orff's blend of Romantic vitalism with a *volksich* sensibility could also potentially be understood to validate troublingly organicist forms of nationalism. But the fundamental pragmatism of applied pedagogy has allowed educators to salvage Orff's thought, finding value in the *Schulwerk* while mitigating its dated assumptions.[31] Orff educator Werner Thomas, as early as 1974, already emphasized the need for a flexible approach to the method's Herderian view of folk culture as *Bildung*, writing that "neither the postilion's horn in the forest nor the merry peasant can be offered to today's children as valid images."[32] Elsewhere in that volume, Keetman advocates a kind of situational realism, suggesting that instructors adopt children's names, the names of local flowers, and so forth as "rhythmic building blocks."[33] In this logic we also find in the *Schulwerk* a method that valorizes improvisation as a form of creative play.[34] Songs function as something like found objects of everyday life, there to be picked up, manipulated, shaped, and otherwise played with, just as Holly and Kit manipulate their own creative tools in the opening sequence. In the absence of a legitimizing educational raison d'être, however, Kit and Holly employ their objects (mop, baton, dead dog) as something closer to the ontological orphans that so clearly fascinate Malick—figures of play whose functional "purpose" is left deliberately and tellingly obscure.

There is little discussion in the *Schulwerk* literature on expression, affect, or on encouraging students to verbally discuss how particular sounds make them feel, at least among its interpreters and practitioners up to the time in which *Badlands* was created. This is perhaps not surprising in an elementary teaching method emphasizing embodied practice rather than critical reflection. But it also points toward a larger sensibility oriented toward a pre-aesthetic moment, in which sound, vision, movement, discovery, play, and hearing are magically unified rather than divided. In *Elementaria*, for example, Keetman emphasizes the importance of the performative, "real time" moment in the *Schulwerk*. Continuing this point, she characterizes the educational value of this moment through the image of mirroring, in which the student's "reaction to optical stimuli means in this case taking up and imitating another's (at first the teacher's) movement."[35] If, in Orff education, we mirror perceptual patterns with embodied movement and sensations, in cinema we mirror perceptual patterns with *imagined* movement and sensations, bridging a gap between the sensuousness of imaginal and embodied, material reality.[36] This role of embodied engagement in the *Schulwerk*, I would argue, leaves traces in what this music *sounds like*, as well as, in turn, how it functions as film music.

This is, in other words, music of creative play—music that, while fixed and non-improvised in its printed and recorded forms, is also predicated upon the value of improvisation, foregrounding the manipulation of musical objects in real time. And, perhaps most importantly, it is also music tied to an aesthetics of existential nostalgia, understood to emanate from an authentic, primal source of being that has been obscured by modernity. This authentic being is understood to be accessible in a unique and innate way to children—consider how Kit and Holly are depicted, albeit ironically, as essentially "child-like"—and its power can be recaptured as a valuable pedagogical tool.[37] Within *Badlands*, however—which is not only a non-pedagogical art work, but one that is almost defiantly non-didactic in its representation of violence—this impulse becomes less focused toward any specifically pragmatic end, and instead functions as affective expressivity.

How, then, does Keetman's "Gassenhauer" establish and create a sense of phenomenal presence? Simply put, through the affective and embodied work of hitting things. As in *Chinatown*, the physical presence of instrumentation and the insistently simple anacrusis-downbeat pair ("ta TA") that forms the melody's core motive become part of the music's tactile charge. "Gassenhauer" is built entirely from aggregated, single-pitch articulations of this motivic pair, mostly played on "hard" instruments—soprano and alto pairs of xylophones, castanet, and tambourine, although even the softer, airier instruments such as soprano recorder and the pulsating membrane of a tympani maintain similarly *percussive* melodic profiles. Grouped into a segment of the *Schulwerk* scores (*Musik für Kinder*) that explores the fourth scale-degree as a harmonic subdominant, the piece consists of a period of two simple eight-bar phrases moving within a simplified harmonic palate of tonic (C), subdominant (F), and dominant (G), followed by an eight-bar extension that repeats the same cadential formula twice. The entire twenty-four-measure formula is repeated eight times, gradually elaborated with the addition of instruments, but with no alteration of the harmonic or phrasal structure.[38]

We might hear in this tactile hardness of attack something of the *Schulwerk*'s origins in interwar German artistic culture, a blend of elemental, vitalist essentialism and tough-minded, pragmatic *neue Sachlichkeit*. Film scholar Jennifer Bleek has argued that the wooden hardness of the mallet instruments, associated with the film's scene of the forest world, contrasts with the quality of Tipton's Satie's arrangements, frequently paired with images of openness, space, and sky.[39] This idea resonates Henrik Gustaffson's study of landscape in the New Hollywood, which emphasizes in *Badlands* a gradual process of "unearthing" over the course of the film.[40] But perhaps both of these poles—hard earth and soft air—are present within "Gassenhauer" itself, with the interaction between them engaging the music's sensibility of creative play. What we hear from the xylophones is not simply a continuously sustained melodic line. This is the product of a perceptual abstraction. Instead, the sound of the xylophones manifest as a dry, tactile *tap*—an instant from which a melody comes to exist as an aural afterimage. This resonance reminds us that sound's natural inclination is toward Gustaffson's trajectory of "unearthing," understood as acoustic decay and fade. Sound is haunted by its tendency to trail off, invisibly, into space. Keeping it there, playing with its tendency to escape—this is part of the game.

Another part is the rhythmic interplay of individual lines against each other. The propulsive quality of the triplet iambs that characterize the first section (mm. 1–24) bounces off the opposing downbeat accent and subdivided triplet dactyl of the next phrase ("TÁ-ka-ta-ka Ta") where the second alto xylophone enters and the harmonically guiding bass pitch shifts to the weak second beat. This type of interplay continues throughout, building accessible complexity through aggregated repetition. In addition to such dynamic ebb and flow of the piece's formal or harmonic structures, the additive quality of instrumentation *dramatizes* the collectivity of game play. This is music that plays as an invitation, a call to join in and add to the texture. Listening to it, perhaps even without intertextual knowledge, we might imagine a closed circle of participants that might always open to include one more, perhaps even to include you. This circle is a form of play as world creation, a musical work that is for its participants as much as for an external audience, that in fact draws the external audience into the circle.

Describing the style of Keetman's compositional voice in a 2004 festschrift, Hermann Regner emphasized its embodied physicality and in-the-moment quality through the metaphor of dance:

> Keetman's music dances. Sometimes it is only a small gesture, a wink, a lift of the hand. Then again turns and jumps, whole sequences that have a beginning, a climax and then come again to stillness. These movement impulses have become music through turns of melody, rhythm, and meter. Of course, such music requires a special interpretation. One cannot play them at sight. One must penetrate them, absorb and internalize their impulses in order to be able to externalize them. But that is the case with all good music.[41]

More than just expressing a broadly "playful" affect through topical elements (simplicity) or through an intertextual awareness of the *Schulwerk* method, "Gassenhauer" enacts, through instrumental embodiment and its formal structuring, the creative work of play. Whether or not Kit and Holly *notice*—whether they are abstractly or self-consciously aware of themselves playing—is a more complicated question. But they are, undoubtedly, in the circle—they *play along*, and the music *plays back*.[42]

Counterpoint: Satie, Melancholy, and Estrangement

Tipton's cue in the opening prologue, discussed earlier, is the first of several times the film engages with the music of Erik Satie. Satie's suite, *Trois morceaux en forme de poire* (1903), specifically the first, third, and sixth movements, becomes a collective voice that intertwines with and plays against the film's other musical registers.[43] Of these three movements, the first and sixth date from considerably earlier than their publication, from the early 1890s, when, with early works such as the *Gymnopédies* and *Gnossiennes*, Satie explored exotic modality and minimalized formal development, creating works of hypnotic calm and stasis that conveyed (whether tongue-in-cheek or sincere) a mystical or otherworldly sensibility. The *Morceaux*, as published in 1903, were thus a compilation, combining revised versions of Satie's earlier works with more up-to-date compositions. In *Badlands*, not only are the more pervasively, bitingly dissonant movements of the suite not used, but even within the selected movements Tipton frequently "arranges away" some of the more disruptive moments. For example, in his arrangements of the third movement, composed in 1903, Tipton omits a recurring musical gesture in which Satie's soft and harmonically sinuous melody is suddenly interrupted by a brusque *fortissimo* cadence in an unrelated key.[44] Similarly, when the first movement appears in *Badlands* (1:05:10), Tipton leaves out the highly dissonant, melodically unrelated opening four measures of the first movement, instead beginning directly with the lyrical principal theme.

This editorial "smoothing out" of the music raises an important preliminary question: who was Terrence Malick's "Erik Satie"? What currents of Satie's reception, if any, may have informed the use of this music in *Badlands*? Again, as with our hermeneutic connections to the *Schulwerk*, the point is less to establish intentionality than to understand a broader field of mutually resonant ideas that connect the music to its affective use in the film. Beyond Malick's (very broad and generalizing) comments on the music offered in his seventies interviews, we have very little information about Malick's choice to use Satie.⁴⁵ Satie's posthumous reception remains a relatively weak spot in his scholarly literature, other than in regard to his influence on *Les Six*, and his eventual appropriation by the post–World War II avant-garde.⁴⁶ Similarly, although Satie's original score for Rene Clair's surrealist film *Entr'acte* (1922) has received considerable attention, there has been no scholarly examination specific to the *compiled* use of Satie's music in later cinema. Although Satie had never gone completely into musical obscurity following his death, it is still necessary to account for his seeming swerve into somewhat greater pop cultural appeal in the mid-to-late sixties. Within the classical world, we might point to individual acts of patronage, such as pianist Aldo Ciccolini's large-scale project of recording Satie's keyboard works between 1966 and 1976. Around the same time, Satie also made some inroads into popular culture, such as the arrangements of the *Gymnopédies* on progressive rock band Blood, Sweat, and Tears' self-titled 1968 album. Somewhere between the austerity of the Cagean avant-garde and the accessibility of Blood, Sweat, and Tears, however, we can perhaps identify a niche for Satie (or at least for his earlier, dreamier music) in an evolving counterculture, and eventually in a New Age mentality.⁴⁷ Within this niche, the use of Satie's music, in particular his *Gymnopédist* period of the 1890s, might enable meditative or other consciousness-altering ends, combined with some degree of countercultural cachet that might be fueled by any knowledge of the frustrations of his career and eccentric persona. It is, perhaps, *this* Satie, poised between a mystique of otherworldly sincerity and an ironic wink (without betraying either) that could appeal to prog rockers, New Agers, and John Cage alike. This image also lent itself well to Malick and Tipton's adaptive choices, which, without completely neutering the music's strangeness, nevertheless left the most aggressively disruptive musical material from the *Morceaux* on the cutting room floor. Satie thus becomes a kind of smooth, opaque surface, whose eccentric harmony and phrasing, upon eliminating his music's disarming extremes or cheeky references, can be encountered without breaking its meditative spell. The opacity of Satie's style in these early works of the 1880s and 1890s, the ironic play and resistance to meaning, is thus not oppositional to sensual, exotic beauty, but rather goes hand in hand with it. This quality, in turn, is amplified as film music that pairs with images mirroring and extending its sense of irony and ambiguity.

Discussing Satie's use of irony, Ann-Marie Hanlon identifies three distinct species at play: verbal, situational, and dramatic. The first two species function, respectively, through text-music relationships and topical or stylistic parody. Verbal irony might involve an ironic stance evident *within* the text of Satie's frequently humorous markings within his scores, whereas situational irony might involve staging a musical moment in which stylistic register is used inappropriately or disruptively. The third type, dramatic irony, which in literature is understood as a discrepancy between the knowledge of a protagonist and that of the audience, is more complex, as it involves text-music relationships in which the music, playing the role of "protagonist," is stylistically "unaware" of the expressive state of being apparent to the audience (or perhaps only to the performer) through textual information.[48] Hanlon doesn't address Satie's actual audiovisual works and collaborations in ballet and film. The irony under discussion exists entirely within the "musical object," even if it challenges those boundaries somewhat with the inclusion of Satie's performance notes as linguistic forms of textuality. In examining this third, richest type of irony, however, Hanlon addresses a particular shading of dramatic irony that is highly relevant to the Satie-Malick relationship, namely Romantic irony. Drawing upon musicologist Julie Brown's study of Bela Bartok, Hanlon argues that the purpose of Romantic irony is not necessarily the creation of the comic, but rather a broader "acknowledgement of a gap between means and ends . . . the gap between the spiritual aspirations of man and his physical limitations . . . a point of dramatic rupture between the material and spiritual realms."[49] Holly's clear sense of the uncanny strangeness of things plays out this mode of irony, giving full Romantic credence to the reality of that which it has been alienated from. A sense of the spiritual lingers in this film, and throughout Malick's work as a whole. It is not necessarily that of a particular religious tradition, but rather a sense of the epiphanic *something* that resides, even if largely unacknowledged, in everyday experience. The "melancholy" affect that Malick attributed to Satie is thus readable as the recognition of this immanent spirituality in the world through a self-consciousness that, in the manner of Romantic irony, both engages and obstructs our capacity for oneness with this epiphanic presence.[50]

Beyond his role as a source of Romantic irony, Satie also becomes a register of the fantastic, as in the opening shot of Holly and her dog. In fairy tales, for example, violence is often a clear force for transparent moral instruction, but to a child encountering these tales from a child's perspective, their violence can seem bizarrely intrusive, randomly dealt out, its putative nature absurd or illogical. The violence of fairy tales is the province of an incomprehensible adult world in which, presumably, it will someday make sense. For people like Holly and Kit, however, this point never arrives. Malick emphasized this in his interview with *Sight and Sound*:

> I wanted the picture to set up like a fairy tale, outside of time, like *Treasure Island*. I hoped this would, among other things, take a little of the sharpness out of the violence but still keep its dreamy quality. Children's books are full of violence. Long John Silver slits the throats of the faithful crew. Kit and Holly even think of themselves as living in a fairy tale. Holly says "sometimes I wish I could fall asleep and be taken off to some magical land, [where] this never happened." But she enough believed there is such a place that she must confess to you she never got there.[51]

Even if Kit and Holly never "got there," perhaps the music of Satie *does* "get there," or at least this music conveys a sensibility that allows us to imagine this moment. If the music of the *Schulwerk*, particularly "Gassenhauer," represents an embodiment of the impulse toward creative play, the presence of Satie frequently offers a dialectical testing of this impulse. Put to the test, we might imagine childlike creation collapsing into reverie, an interiorization of the elemental drive to create things and meanings, rendering it instead as a hermetic loop, a perpetually suspended mode of ambiguity.

In the first significant return of Satie after the pre-credits sequence, Kit and Holly indulge Kit's tendency to memorialize himself through objects, to transform the material world into a marker of his own self-perceived significance. Kit and Holly send up a fire balloon containing a written "vow" that, Holly tells us in voiceover, "he would always stand beside me and let nothing come between us" (0:15:00). This sentimental declaration of love plays oddly, however, with Holly's subsequent intuition that the simplicity of their early courtship is soon to end, and with Tipton's moody chamber arrangement of the sixth movement of *Trois morceaux*, with its winding, digressive melody that drifts between minor and major Lydian modes. In this scene, in particular, a current of violence is suppressed within layers of textual adaptation and development, deepening the ironic effect of Satie in this ambiguous moment. In his oral history of Malick's films, Paul Maher describes an early draft of the script in which this scene contained a shocking act of animal cruelty, which, had it remained, would have been the film's first hint that Kit's eccentricity possesses an amoral and violent dimension. In this early version, rather than Kit's declaration of love going up in the fire balloon, it is a trapped badger, which floats out of sight and is never mentioned again.[52]

In what might be a surviving resonance of this abandoned idea, in a slightly earlier scene Holly recounts her spontaneous decision to toss her sick pet fish into her garden to asphyxiate it (0:12:30) and Kit is shown pondering an incapacitated cow (0:13:00). It is not clear if the cow is sick, dead, or sleeping—the animal lies on its side, frozen, its legs stiffly outstretched in the air. With blankly un-emotive, yet seemingly sincere curiosity, Kit at first ponders the cow from a variety of angles, and then repurposes it as a step stool in a darkly funny act of objectification. This scene, however, is set *not* to Satie, but rather to music by Gunild Keetman, "Musik für ein Puppenspeil." And yet this is a place where the film's two affective "poles" can be understood to blur together. This selection from the *Schulwerk* is tellingly similar to the film's "Satie" sound, featuring harmonically static ostinati, winding melodic figures, and exotic modal inflections, approximating the temporal suspension broadly associated with Southeast Asian percussion ensembles such as the gamelan. At the same time, however, the *harder, brighter* sound of these instruments, highly characteristic of the *Schulwerk*, sharpens this dreamy sensibility, imparting to it something closer to the striking, embodied tactility of "Gassenhauer." Immediately following the fire balloon sequence and the sixth movement of *Trois morceaux*, "Musik für ein Puppenspiel" recurs in a sequence in which Holly's father shoots her dog as punishment for continuing to see Kit (0:15:22).

The elimination of a darker version of the fire balloon sequence might, of course, easily be argued to have been ultimately better for the film's pacing. Obviously, the scene allows a less conflicted space for nostalgic reverie when Kit and Holly are not torturing a badger. But the scene's rueful beauty and its detached melancholy still go hand in hand, and tellingly overlap with similar music in the scenes of violence that surround the fire balloon sequence in the finished film. "We would never live these days again," says Holly, musing on a sense of strangeness inherent in experience itself. Throughout the film, Holly is oddly self-conscious in her verbal awareness of the contingency of human actions and the limits of subjectivity, engaging in fatalistic speculation to inscribe a sense of strangeness into the world: What path has led me here? How might it all have been different? How might things suddenly change, within a single moment of action? The ambiguity that emerges in these reflections is one of human experience understood as intricately and inexplicably networked, and of the uncanny quality of imagined experiences that transcend what Michel Chion has characterized as the "moving box" of the self—the limitations of subjective positionality that we are far more capable of recognizing than transcending.[53]

Another such significant moment is the first return, in an extended version, of the Satie-esque music Tipton composed for the pre-credits sequence, which underscores a key scene after Kit shoots Holly's father. Kit temporarily leaves her alone in the house, allowing her to call the police but assuring her that he would be charged with murder. Home alone, Holly gazes out the window and across the street (0:26:05). Two young boys are silently interacting under a streetlight, a perspective shot intercut with an exterior long shot of the house with Holly, her expression impassive, visible through the attic window. The simplest reading of this scene is as ironic juxtaposition—the boys have an innocence, in their play, that Holly has just lost by being complicit in the murder of her father. But the boys' actions and gestures, here, are *not* simple icons of sentimental innocence. They're not *just* playing—and even if they are, play in a Malick film is rarely a simple thing. They seem to have *something* on their minds, some dramatic, private moment of communicative exchange. One circles a telephone pole behind the curb on which the other is sitting, beckoning the sitting boy twice with a jerky, furtive gesture. Aren't they out a bit late? After a reverse exterior shot of Holly in the window, we see them again from Holly's perspective. The standing boy finds something stuck to the pole which he pulls off. Tromping through a patch of grass, he sits down to show this object to the other boy (Figure 5.3). Rather than a moment of dramatic, or ironic contrast—of experience looking back at innocence—this scene might be more provocatively read as a glimpse into the strangeness that attends the diverging possibilities of other beings and other experiences. The impact of this moment resides in our awareness that Holly *doesn't* know what these boys are up to, any more than they know that they are sitting across from a house in which a murder has just occurred. The use of Tipton's "Satie" cue, here, does not clarify, but rather *amplifies* the scene's ambiguity, granting to these random boys a curiously disproportionate weight and obscure sense of urgency.

As *Badlands* progresses, this ambiguous sense of melancholy reverie becomes increasingly associated with Tipton's arrangements of Satie. The third movement of the *Morceaux* appears in a scene where Kit and Holly hold hostage a wealthy man and his maid. In the previous scene, in his least defensible and most shocking act, Kit had locked in a storm cellar a young couple who randomly cross their paths after he has killed Cato, who—with little cause—he seems to suspect will turn them in. Kit fires several shots blindly

Figure 5.3 Shot of boys outside Holly's house after her father's murder (0:26:40).
Screen capture from *Badlands* (1973). Criterion Collection, 2013. DVD.

through a hole in the door and runs away without confirming or denying the couple's death. This immediate precedent is especially important, as Kit fails to apply the same logic of "leaving no witnesses" to this second couple. This might be explained socially, given Kit's odd respect for authority, which Malick described as that of an "Eisenhower conservative."[54] But it perhaps even more potently foregrounds the *lack* of any consistent logic determining Kit's violence. With the fate of the couple hanging unresolved, the house and its grounds offer Holly and Kit the ground for rumination. It is full of objectified objects, which receive Kit and Holly's (and subsequently our) focused attention. Holly creates and plays a set of pitched glasses from the man's wine glasses. She chooses, with unnecessary fussiness, one of his walking sticks and takes a walk outside, as we hear the third movement of the *Morceaux*. Its sinuously chromatic melody modulates almost continuously, sometimes moving with unprepared suddenness into distantly related keys, creating a sense of aimless wandering. Satie, Malick, and Holly alike are picking up and discarding musical and physical objects with a larger sense of detachment. Holly muses that "the world was like a faraway planet to which I could never return. I thought what a fine place it was, full of things that people could look into and enjoy" (0:56:20).

The ongoing use of Satie's music thus extends its associations with ambiguous detachment and melancholy, beginning also to encompass an *observational* quality, one unusually cognizant of the potential uncanniness of others, whether these objects are human (the boys under the streetlight) or non-human (the belongings of the wealthy man). As Kit and Holly make their way from the human spaces of their treehouse, Cato's ranch, and the rich man's house—all dwellings in varying relationships to the objects within them and the nature that surrounds them, and as they drive into the Badlands, where their only home is the transitory object of their car, this emphasis on observation eventually reflects backward onto itself, with Kit and Holly becoming as much the objectified things observed, as they are the observers. Satie, *in extremis*, creates a strange sense of objecthood, shared by material things and characters alike. This is particularly emphasized in the film's lengthiest cue derived from Satie (1:05:10–1:07:39). Tipton's arrangement of the first movement of the *Morceaux* eliminates Satie's dissonant, mock-dramatic flourishes, skipping directly to a moodily lyrical "Gnossienne" recycled from incidental music to occultist Josèphin Péladan's theater piece Le Fils des étoils (1891). This is Satie in his exotic mode of the early 1890s, with a sinuously ornamented minor-mode melody, with frequent raised fourth-degree and lowered seventh-degree inflections, set against a quietly throbbing, off-beat ostinato in the second piano part. The cue begins with a striking image (reproduced on much of the film's promotional art) of Kit, staring into the empty distance with his back to the camera, his rifle resting across both shoulders and both arms looped over his rifle, making him look like a scarecrow. The camera, however, does not *present* Kit to us like this. Instead, it seems to *discover* him (turning Kit himself into a sort of found object) at the end of a lengthy panning shot of vacant grassland that lasts nearly ten seconds (1:05:12). A reverse shot shows Kit staring into space, his expression inscrutable. Cutaway shots show a mountain in the vast distance, a standing bird, a large lizard, a distant cloud-bank in which lightning briefly flickers, a hawk, and finally Kit himself, in the same position but in a longer shot, as he turns and walks back toward the camera, the moon now hovering over the horizon. Holly begins to speak in voiceover: "We lived in utter loneliness, neither here nor there. . . ." Kit watches things. Things watch Kit. This exchange also implicitly occurs within *our* looking at the film and the things, human and otherwise, that it contains. Does the film, then, *look back at us*, and if so, how might we experience this look? If the strangeness of things speaks through this "Gnossienne," it is in a register of speech that occult historian Tobias Churton has contended is the most obvious namesake for Satie's made-up genre: *gnosis*, or initiatory knowledge that exists, powerful yet rationally inarticulate, only in the moment of its experiential apprehension.[55]

As the cue ends, it continues to play with this strange sense of otherness—following their dialogue, Holly comments on a train that we see, moving silently across the screen in the far distance, which she compares to a caravan in the exotic world of Marco Polo. Again, the emphasis shifts to contingency: other paths, other narratives. Finally, perhaps to shore up a sense of their tangibility as beings, Kit and Holly make yet another time capsule, which they bury in the Badlands. Among the trinkets they bury, the film pointedly shows us that they include her father's stereopticon slides, which in an earlier scene had been the basis of an extended meditation, but which she now abandons with no perceptible hesitation. The gnostic moment of Satie is one of discomforting drift. Our stories might just as easily be other stories, and the things that extend ourselves into the world, validating our presence as beings, continue to persist blindly in our absence. Satie frames these musings as reverie—melancholy and self-reflective, yet distanced and perennially obscure.

Orff and the Polyvocality of the Film World

By contrast, a subcategory of selections from the *Schulwerk* emphasizes sentient presence instead of displacement. But this presence is personified in weird and highly discomforting ways. Three cues in *Badlands* use music composed by Orff for choral voices and instruments. All function as "set pieces"; perceptually foregrounded and aligned with pivotal moments in the plot, all three scenes extend the association between the *Schulwerk* and play as a creatively transformative act. First, after Kit shoots Holly's father, they burn the house down and flee, the camera lingering over the aestheticized destruction of Holly's domestic world (0:29:18); second, as Kit and Holly's camp in the woods is raided by bounty hunters, leading them to murder and flee once again (0:37:30); and finally, as the law closes in and Holly chooses not to accompany Kit as he escapes, instead surrendering herself to the authorities (1:17:20). The texts of these three vocal selections have also been deliberately obscured by the filmmakers.

In film production, non-diegetic vocal music has frequently been viewed as a distinct category that requires particular approaches and framing. In pragmatic terms, sung non-diegetic texts are frequently reserved for moments (such as a song sequence in a "music video" style, or opening and closing credits) where cognitive confusion between diegetic and non-diegetic voices can be effectively minimized. Additionally, a venerable tradition has posited *textless* non-diegetic vocalization as a signifier of the otherworldly or transcendent, such as in the example of the Hollywood historical or biblical epic with its characteristically surging offscreen choirs. The image of the voice, in such examples, serves as a manifestation of human (or otherworldly) presence. In this sense, the non-diegetic voice differs from externalized instruments, in that non-diegetic voices somehow convey more strongly the sense that *someone is there*—that a physical body (albeit an invisible one) necessarily produces this sound. Even beyond the pragmatic concerns of sound editing, however, or a topical association in Western culture of choral voices with religious music, the non-diegetic singing voice can, paradoxically, seem both embodied and disembodied at the same time.

The absence of linguistic signification in textless voices thus leaves an open conceptual space for imagining the transcendent, an effect that also arguably persists in texts where the language is presumed to be largely "foreign" to a film's primary intended audience. The original texts for the Orff compositions used in *Badlands* are in German, serving this purpose, but the words are also *doubly* obscured at certain places. It is difficult to reconstruct exactly how this effect came into existence during production: editor Billy Weber has described a process in which the music in the fire scene was created by recording sung English translations in postproduction, and then mixing these with the original *Musica Poetica* recordings.[56] Weber suggests that the filmmakers did this in order to "cloud" or obscure the language. Interestingly, he attributed this impulse to a desire to avoid connotations linking the German language to Nazism, saying, "we didn't want people thinking we were making a statement with German singing, we didn't want to give it a political statement, or a fascistic statement, or anything like that."[57] Was this concern far-fetched? It is difficult to say in retrospect if more obvious use of German text would have prompted critics to take up this line of interpretation. But if Malick was indeed the prime mover in this decision, we might easily speculate that, in addition to any plausible desire for cultural sensitivity, his background in academic philosophy may have made him equally cautious. Malick had been drawn to Heidegger in an era marked by a growing split between analytical and continental traditions of philosophy, and in which Heidegger's connections to the Nazi party during World War II made discussions of the philosopher a point of sensitivity.[58]

As Holly's house burns, we hear Orff's "Passion," an exercise in the Phrygian mode that convey's something of the score's more Satie-leaning sense of detachment, again indicating the occasional fluidity of these two musical poles. We see a selection of shots, like moving still-lifes, of Holly's home going up in flames—half-eaten food, a dollhouse, her father's dead body in the cellar, her piano, all gradually consumed, as if each shot were juxtaposing the stasis of Holly's comfortably middle-class life with the elemental force now transforming it to ash, like a *vanitas* that moves. Regardless of linguistic familiarity, the text, a strophic poem in a folkish style musing on the sorrow of the Virgin Mary upon the death of Jesus, is only intelligible enough to perhaps discern the *presence* of linguistic text, however buried by distortion. Combined with the evocative images that depict the "deaths" of disparate objects, the voices suggest human presence, but at the same time the cue's cool objectivity (like Holly's detached voice-over, which only peripherally comments upon her father's death) continues to reinforce the characters' fraught relationship to a world in which they are both participants and detached, self-conscious observers—subjects creating meaning by transforming their world into something irretrievably new, in this case by burning down a house.

Non-diegetic vocal presence thus begins to instantiate a film world imbued with, even perhaps defined by, a sense of agential presence abiding in nonhuman nature, inverting—but, importantly, not opposing—the film's emphasis on the playful human relationship to dynamic physical objects. The theoretical category of a "film world" has been explored by several recent film-philosophers. Daniel Frampton and Daniel Yacavone, in particular, have traced the conceptualization of film as a world through other existing theorizations of cinema, updating it to encompass phenomenological and post-phenomenological film theory, as in the work of Vivian Sobchack and Gilles Deleuze. Frampton's discussion of sound and music is minimal, albeit updated to his unique conceptual language.[59] His larger concept of the film world, however, is still useful to our reading of *Badlands*. For Frampton, the film world is the instantiation of a "film mind" (or, in his neologism, a "filmind"): an imagined entity whose empirically theorized existence becomes a conceptual tool that offers insights into a film's agency, narrational style, manipulation of perspective, and expressive affect. Yacavone, by contrast, has critiqued Frampton's "heterocosmic" view, both for its sweeping dismissal of intentionality and its overestimation of film as a self-contained aesthetic object, as opposed to one entangled in complex extra-filmic networks of associative significance and meaning.[60] While Yacavone's view of film worlds speaks much more flexibly to both film authorship and networked worlds (such as those of genre), it leaves little room for the capacity of the film world to *meaningfully seem* as if it were autochthonous, a gesture with potent philosophical and expressive potential.[61] There seems to be room, here, for a view of film worlds in which agency is not problematically anthropomorphized (as in Frampton), but wherein the imaginative resonance of its apparent ontological autonomy, understood as an expressive gesture, is still given voice.

One way in which this might occur is by pluralizing a concept of film mind into something akin to an ecological network of the actors it contains. Rather than a singular film-mind, the sentience of the sound world of *Badlands* in certain scenes feels more plural, akin to an animistic universe in which non-human entities, be they material objects or "supernatural" voices, can nevertheless be understood to possess agency. When, in her monologue describing their forest idyl, Holly talks of the "voices of the forest," we will, before long, clearly hear these emanations voiced non-diegetically through a trio of spectral figures from Act II of *Faust*. In this passage of Goethe's play, four "grey Women" identify themselves as "Mangel," "Schuld," "Sorge," and "Not"—respectively, Damage, Guilt, Worry, and Need. Worry describes how, although her sisters cannot enter the room of a wealthy man, she can still sneak in through the keyhole. Damage, Guild, and Need then depart, singing of the imminent arrival of their brother, Death, who lurks behind the clouds that obscuring stars.[62] This passage of *Faust*, like the philosophy of *Schulwerk*, is perhaps less vital as an intertextual gesture (however evocative of German Romanticism Malick's work may occasionally be), and more vital for the way in which the musical world of Orff's setting, with its evocations of supernatural presence, becomes embedded and affectively tangible in its sound.

Discussing his process in this sequence, Tipton recalled:

There were other sounds in other Orff works, something that sounded like witches or grey-haired ladies. These sounds were vocal sounds but they were not sounds that you could relate to as language. [Malick] said an interesting thing: "I don't know what they are saying, but I want the sound of these voices—a kind of whispering," and so I said, "All right, I will transcribe phonetically the sounds that I hear from this recording of this Orff work. We'll just have the girls and the fellows that we record it with read it and sing it to these syllables, but they won't be English and they won't be German and they won't be anything. No one can sue you for copying someone else's words!"[63]

We have already examined how the larger polarities of the film—creative play and ambiguous reverie as distinct, yet interrelated modes of being in the world—are emphasized by the embodied musical play of "Gassenhauer" and the melancholy reverie of Satie. And we have seen that this mutual tension helps to articulate a film past that reached beyond the nostalgic imaginary of the fifties to engage with the immediacy of temporal experience as an attribute of immanence. But as the film continues, time, this dialectical structure grows increasingly complex. The attributes begin to blur, with cues (such as the meditative suspensions of Orff's "Passion" or Keetman's "Musik für ein Puppenspiel") performing the other pole's more typical functions. Roughly a third of the way through *Badlands*, just after the transformative fire scene, we encounter a complex sequence that embodies these intertwinings, creating a philosophical "knot" that melds these elements while redefining their meanings, moving from a restatement of "Gassenhauer" and climaxing, after several pointed interruptions, with Orff's vocal setting of *Faust*.

The "Gassenhauer"-Faust Knot

As Holly and Kit flee their hometown to hide in the forest, "Gassenhauer" returns for the first time since the opening sequence, this time fading into the non-diegetic soundtrack under a sequence of images of the natural world—an enjambment of wood debris pushed downriver by a current, extreme closeups of leaves, an insect slowly crawling across a branch—these transition into Kit building a treehouse (0:31:20). Holly's voiceover paints an idyllic picture: the pair learn the ways of the woods, developing self-sufficiency, while also lying about and soaking up the ambience. A witty shot captures the interior of their new home, hewn from the raw material of earth, where they hang a Maxfield Parrish print—an ironic gesture of bourgeois aestheticism—and sleep side-by-side with their guns. As the montage develops, this irony deepens, with Keetman's music brightly skipping alongside images of Kit training for guerrilla warfare and extending the sensibility of playful creativity into his building of deadly booby-traps. "Gassenhauer" thus develops many of the same associations initiated by the title credits sequence, and yet, following the film's first murder and the fiery annihilation of Holly's childhood home, the infectiously charming cue is now unavoidably bearing darker undertones.

The formal elements of "Gassenhauer" enumerated earlier—its modular structure, its gradual elaboration through layering, and the work's constant rhythmic ostinato patterning of strong anacrusis-downbeat pairs—these elements also allow an editorial benefit: the cue can be manipulated in the editing room to quickly cadence and stop at nearly any point, potentially conveying abrupt sudden silences without becoming formally incoherent. "Gassenhauer" stops a first time, synchronized to a shot of Holly, carrying heavy bundles of wood (0:33:08). Holly's commentary, in this sudden silence, seems all the more detached in the absence of a musical cue to give it meaningful resonance. Without the suturing of a musical montage, it seems suddenly strange that she makes no transition in her narration between this difficult physical task and a different type of material transformation: "One day I carried thirty pounds of wood a distance of five miles. Another day, while hiding in the forest I covered my eyes with makeup to see how they'd come out." On this line, the sequence's disruptive shifts become more extreme. We cut suddenly from a long shot of Holly's exertions to an extreme closeup of her eyes, caked in eyeliner. The next several cuts continue a pattern of interruptions. Kit and Holly dance to Mickey and Sylvia's recording of "Love Is Strange," their movements unpracticed and oddly jerky (0:33:20). Only a few seconds later, however, the scene abruptly cuts, mid-phrase, to Kit trying unsuccessfully to catch a fish with a homemade net. The aesthetic world of Mickey and Sylvia (along with Kit and Holly's self-conscious attempts at traditional gestures of courtship) is picked up, but just as suddenly abandoned, conveying a sense of disjointed arbitrariness to Kit and Holly's actions, like extraterrestrials attempting to seem human. This device also functionally minimizes pop music's capacity to cultivate an iconic sensibility of historical era. For the first time, the film offers up a gesture of musical "fiftiesness" in Mickey and Sylvia, and yet Malick immediately ruptures and *reframes* this moment. Instead of projecting an aestheticized sense of period, the cue instead ironically emphasizes Kit and Holly's self-conscious *use* of pop music as a tool for self-creation.

After this interruption, in which Kit and Holly quarrel over the lost fish, Holly reflects on their occasional spats, despite which they "mostly get along just fine." This is demonstrated as Holly reads Kit a passage from Thor Heyerdahl's "Kon Tiki" while they relax. "Gassenhauer" slowly returns (0:35:12), closing, with its familiarity, the awkward space left by their attempts at "normal" courtship and quarreling. Holly muses how she "grew to love the forest": "the cooing of the doves and the hum of dragonflies in the air made it seem lonesome, like everybody's dead and gone. When the leaves rustled, it was like the spirits were whispering about all the little things that bothered them." As the montage continues, Holly looks at "some vistas" through her father's stereopticon, and muses,

> it hit me that I was just this little girl, born in Texas, whose father was a sign painter, who had only just so many years to live. It sent a chill down my spine and I thought "where would I be this very moment if Kit had never met me, or killed anybody. This very moment. If my mom had never met my dad. If she had never died. And what's the man I'm gonna marry look like? What's he doing right this minute? Is he thinking about me now, by some coincidence, even though he doesn't know me? Does it show in his face?" For days afterwards I lived in dread. Sometimes I wished I could fall asleep and be taken off to some magical land, but this never happened.

Here, these alternate paths, other beings and other stories, which had formed a running concern of the film, receive their most direct and explicit articulation. As Lloyd Michaels has noted, the stereopticon slides, which soon absorb the entire screen, all seem to date from the turn of the twentieth century, roughly paralleling the birth of cinema, in particular what film scholar Tom Gunning famously termed the "cinema of attractions," in which the reproduction of reality on film was its own source of wonder and amazement.[64] The slides are also randomly ordered, not offering any sequential, or even associative, narrative on their own, and bearing little clear relationship to Holly's musings. But, as in any audiovisual moment, connections are *created* by the act of pairing. The effect is playfully witty when, for example, a shot of a mother and child accompanies "if my mom had never met my dad" or a shot of a soldier kissing a woman in a field accompanies Holly's curiosity about "the man [she's] gonna marry" (who is, implicitly and tellingly, not Kit). The woman in this latter picture is unsmiling, her eyes unfixed and looking into the distance as the man kisses her cheek. And yet these plausible, tangible audiovisual connections slip in among more abstract ones (a shot of the Egyptian sphinx synched to ". . . or killed anyone"), equating the creation of audiovisual meaning as, in a larger sense, unstable and contingent, and locating it within our role as the auditors of Holly's reverie. This reverie is profoundly melancholy, and yet it is underscored with "Gassenhauer"— music we've come to associate with creation, play, and *making*. Like the similar opening credits of *Bonnie and Clyde*, these photographs, with their indexical relationship to the real, tug our attention away from the story itself to its atmosphere of innumerable surface details, a form of representation that draws its particular evocative power from *being*, rather than from *meaning*. Looking into the stereopticon, Holly becomes the external observer of a world that, regardless of her fate, will surely continue without her. Set to "Gassenhauer," then, the scene thus radiates keen paradoxes: joyful fascination and an awareness of mortality, a playful imaginative projection of the self that, so doing, becomes aware of its own limits.

As Holly finishes her monologue, "Gassenhauer" trails off mid-phrase as Kit, still bad at fishing, draws the attention of a passerby by firing his gun into the water. After a cut to black, the next scene begins simultaneously with Orff's *Faust* setting, as a trio of bounty hunters sneak up on the camp (0:37:32). The shared triple meter and similarly percussive instrumentation between the two cues, with a similarly strong emphasis on the anacrusis-downbeat iambic pairings sustains the world-feel of "Gassenhauer," but with a strange turn into the darker imagination of German Romanticism. Tipton has done something rather different here, in terms of distorting the vocals: rather than record over *Musica Poetica* with a textless vocalise, he seems to have re-recorded a new *spoken* text in English that structurally evokes the Three Grey Women, overlapping it with Goethe's German text and music taken, it sounds, from the *Musica Poetica* recording. The additional English text, however, does not plausibly translate the passage of *Faust*, other than in the loosest sense. Critically, rather than identifying themselves as archetypes of human misery (Guilt, Worry, Need), the voices identify themselves as elements of the natural world. The words are difficult to determine by ear: to me, they sound like "I [am?] the Stars and I am the Trees / I [am] the Brook and I [am] the Breeze."[65] When the spoken text begins, it is also oddly coincident with Holly's lips moving as she looks into a mirror and speaks to herself with no diegetic sound, as Kit, seated high in the trees, starts and stares into the distance with a fixed worried expression, like an animal suddenly responding to some humanly imperceptible sound. Seeing the approaching men, Kit crows a signal and as he springs into action the Faust setting is split into two by a brief, rapid passage of original music composed by Tipton (0:38:20).

When the *Faust* setting begins again, the spoken text is even more muddled, all but unintelligible as a result of the re-recording process (0:38:58). Yet, oddly, this is only true of the *spoken* text: the sung choral passages are entirely clear, and obscuring the German language seems to have no longer been a priority. In fact, Jennifer Bleek has identified this as a rather traditionally expressive moment of textual parallelism: as the choir sings the text of the Grey Women who anticipate the arrival of their Brother Death, the bounty hunters move into the camp. The sung text, in fact, ends on the word "Tod," with the closing measures of the cue punctuated by a closeup of one of the bounty hunters audibly cocking his rifle (0:39:35).[66] The music thus falls silent just as the sequence is about to explode into deadly violence.ABt emerges from his foxhole and shoots two of the bounty hunters, and then chases down and shoots the fleeing third.

It would be difficult to classify *Badlands* as a Vietnam film, in the way that the East Asian conflict was clearly present as a subtext in other Hollywood films of this era, such as *The Wild Bunch*. This sequence, with its guerrilla warfare in the forest, perhaps comes closest to a reflection of contemporary cultural concerns, and yet Malick does not differentiate, as many other artists would, the ethical questions raised by violence from the inevitably aesthetic means of expressing it. Instead, the soundtrack of this sequence strikingly aestheticizes this impasse as a whole, an impasse created by the dual impulses suggested respectively by "Gassenhauer" and *Faust*, and their blending, we might say, or Emersonian and Faustian Romanticism. The idyll of "Gassenhauer" and Kit and Holly's creative immersion into their world shift in tone to the *Faust* setting, conveying a supernatural world that has been envoiced, and to which the characters seem preternaturally aware, yet whose message and agency are perpetually obscured.

"Gassenhauer" and the *Faust* setting are thus woven together into an unstable and ambiguous structural knot. As we hear "Gassenhauer," Kit and Holly build a world of play in the forest yet remain alienated from it. They lose fish, toy awkwardly with adolescent symbols of beauty and courtship, and ponder the other worlds that only contingency separates from their own. With the *Faust* setting, however, Kit, Holly, and the bounty hunters they kill seem instead to become absorbed into a collectivity, hunting and killing as part of the same larger agency that spontaneously produces the trees, the brook, and "all the little voices of the forest" who both speak to and through them. And yet the film is far from over, and this animistic envelopment in presence, ironically, merely produces the next narrative turn, again sending them back on the road, and into their alienated and drifting state of being.

Conclusion: The Past and Ethical Possibility

The present chapter has attempted to understand *Badlands* as an opaque world of objects, portentous with possible meanings but definitively yielding none. These objects confront the human impulse to transform them from raw earth into meaningful world through adaptive play, whether physical, verbal, or musical. This argument can also, I believe, be meaningfully extended into the film's troubling ethical territory. Whereas in *Chinatown*, the mechanics of the elemental imagination ultimately not only create a paranoid vision of the past, but validate this worldview by rendering it inescapable. In *Badlands*, however, Kit and Holly's journey hints at infinite possibilities, and although they never "escape" inscription into history, this way of engaging the past has opened up our intuitive capacity to apprehend, if not to quantify or exhaust, such possibilities. The soundtrack of *Badlands* helps to instantiate the film's concern with creative play, and yet it leaves one such impulse (Kit's homicidal tendency) troublingly unquestioned. Most frequently, the film's ethical challenges have been understood through the lens of irony. While I'm certainly not the first to note the deceptively complex nature of this irony, this complexity has rarely been extended to the soundtrack, and has not been explored as a meaningful facet of the film's representation of the past.[67] The irony of *Badlands* emerges from the fact that only *we* philosophize Kit and Holly's increasing liminality to society—a society whose inscription of order and meaning is comparable to that inscribed by the workings of history. Kit and Holly are essentially *embedded* in their world, and they take the fifties with them on the road. They regard their step into the ontological unknown of the Badlands with a mixture of folksy truisms and confidence that the fifties will have them back (whether via Kit's fantasy of finding work in Canada, or, as eventually happens, at the cost of their incarceration and punishment). When this reclamation finally occurs, however, it is neither comforting nor a tragic inevitability—it simply *is*.

In Steven Rybin's film-philosophical reading of Malick's work, characters are understood as actively attempting to create and shape meaning in their worlds, an activity paralleling the position of the audience, who is analogously confronted with a film world that provides intense and subtle sensory experiences while also enabling a philosophically exploratory and highly experiential mode of viewing.[68] In this way, "character" in Malick's films is never a circumscribable dramatic or rhetorical quantity, but a site of active process and evolving potentiality. However, the film world offers a characteristically

Malickean *resistance* to this construction of meaning. Malick's characters attempt to engage a nature that is itself mute, impassive—an objectified nature that does not want to engage with us (if, in fact, it "wants" anything at all). This world offers a potent corollary to the idea of "pastness" as it has variously been treated throughout this study—a shift, often precipitated or augmented by the soundtrack, beyond assumptions of representational realism, engaging instead such alternative registers of meaning as myth, nostalgia, or immediate sensory experience.

For Rybin, this sense of struggle is key to the ethical dimension of Malick's films, in that the force against which Malick's characters struggle is often *history itself*, conceived as a limitation placed upon the actions or thoughts of which a character might be capable. We see this in *Badlands*, in which Holly's narration clearly shows a mind shaped by the narrative expectations (and limitations) of pulp romance, and by the gendered expectations attending her culturally prescriptive role as Kit's girlfriend. We see it, too, in the dynamics of labor, capitalism, and social mobility in *Days of Heaven*. And in *The Thin Red Line*, in which numerous characters, named and unnamed, die in the battle for Guadalcanal, Malick makes it clear that his characters' strivings may be suddenly cut short by history.[69] Malick's cinema is not ideologically or politically didactic, and yet Malick's characters frequently engage, knowingly or unknowingly, in an ethical struggle against history as an agency that would inscribe them with quantifiable, and thus delimiting, meanings.[70] And yet this ethical dimension, what we might understand as the ethics of how the film world behaves with respect to Kit and Holly and how they respond, leaves open the troubling question of how Kit and Holly behave with respect to the film world—most pointedly, with respect to the people Kit murders. Kit and Holly instinctively approach the objects in their world with a childlike fascination and, but in a way that offers little appreciation for the possibility (let alone an ethical imperative) of intersubjectivity with these objects, whether a tin can, a treehouse, a father, or a random passerby—indeed, Kit and Holly seem hardly rooted in their *own* subjectivities, living instead through the fragments of iconic images and the naive championing of self-authentication (Kit's desire to "be someone") that their world of postwar America insistently valorizes.

Philosopher Robert Sinnerbrink's recent monograph on Malick extends this ethical focus further. For Sinnerbrink, *Badlands* is an early example of "negative ethics," or the presentation of ethically charged material that calculatedly refuses to offer judgment, a position capable of evoking confusion, but also "provok[ing] critical reflection or reframing of one's moral ethical assumptions."[71] *Badlands'* "reframing" offers a world of potentialities that Kit and Holly engage with, but ultimately fail to inhabit with ethical self-awareness. They practice what could potentially be a deeply strange, wondrous, but also ethically recuperative practice with regard to the world, but fail to do so mindfully. The film, in this sense, has two "ethics," a negative (or even amoral) sensibility of the film as a narrative or rhetorical text, and a more covert, guardedly optimistic one offered by the film's "world-feeling," borrowing a term from Daniel Yacavone.[72] *Badlands* exists in an amoral world of negative ethics, yet it is also deeply concerned with the creation of meaning and being. It may be hard to consider this "positive" in a moral sense, although, in its awareness of reciprocal transaction with non-human actors, it might potentially be understood as an ecological politics. But more securely, it is "positive" in an ontological sense, a sense of pure wonder at the coming into being of being. With its interwoven aesthetics of melancholy distance and creative play, music not only substantiates this dimension of the film world, but it also leaves open a kind of fundamental porousness through which we can engage with its very present past in a similarly nuanced way.

At the film's conclusion, as Kit and Holly are flown back to South Dakota to stand trial, we hear the film's final use of Satie, the sixth movement of the *Morceaux*, arranged for the bell-like sounds of a solo celesta—another instrument both percussive and airy. Holly's voice-over cursorily explains the outcomes of their trials, Kit's eventual execution, and Holly's eventual marriage to the son of her trial lawyer, all described in the typically offhanded way we've come to expect (1:29:10). The melancholy and distanced sense of restlessness we've come to associate with Satie once more plays out, subsuming the minutia of Holly's blasé description of the future, and drawing our focus instead to the strange beauty of the plane in flight. After brief return of diegetic sound, containing the film's final lines of dialogue (a playful bit where Kit admires a flummoxed state trooper's hat), Holly detaches from the conversation to look out at the clouds as the same cue begins again for a second and final time (1:30:40). This movement of the *Morceaux* calls back to its appearance in an earlier scene, where Kit and Holly sent up a fire balloon and time capsule into the sky. As Kit and Holly themselves now ascend, the world of the film ends in this final state of suspension. The end credits, over a black screen, return us one final time to "Gassenhauer" (1:31:05).

By now, we have become used to hearing "Gassenhauer" as a kind of porous net, a place where play and melancholy can somehow come together and intertwine, where we are given the tools to create and ascribe meanings, but those meanings seem, over time, to slip away into ambiguities. Its earlier returns occurred at moments of transition and creation (building the treehouse), but also at static moments of melancholy and wonder (the stereopticon scene). If we associate "Gassenhauer" with an affect of creative play and playful indeterminacy, its return, implicitly serving as a summative "statement" for the film, has a comparable currency. If the ethics of *Badlands* entails a "both/and" reading of Kit and Holly's unconscionable violence *and* the poetic and philosophical potential of their engagement with the world, then a return to "Gassenhauer" says both everything and nothing.

When the plane takes off, the territory opens up infinitely below them, to paraphrase Stanley Cavell, simultaneously beautiful and vacant.[73] We have, perhaps, grown so accustomed to the film's ironic distancing of Kit and Holly's modes of self-creation that we don't trust this territory. But the territory is still beautiful. We might imagine this ascent as the creation of or entry into the "magical land" that Holly earlier envisioned, a land of contingent possibilities for being that can only last until the plane lands, and which exists only at the expense of our knowledge that Kit and Holly's lives will soon resolve into historically foregone conclusions. If an interweaving of Satie and Orff have affectively defined the film and, now, its ending, then the abandoning of the boundaries of earth into a space bracketed by these two poles, one full of endless light and space, and the other a gulf of extra-textual black leader as the credits roll, seems to plunge us into a world defined by the unmarked space of possibility—at least, until the plane lands, as we know it must.

In several ways, *Badlands* is a less obvious choice of subject in a book about the cinematic soundtrack. Several of Malick's subsequent films, beginning with *Days of Heaven*, engaged the collaboration of more "important" film composers, such as Ennio Morricone, Hans Zimmer, and James Horner. In addition, whereas *Days of Heaven* became a critical *cause celebré* for the creative uses of Dolby stereo, *Badlands*' use of non-musical sound is expressively sensitive, yet undeniably far less technically and aesthetically extraordinary. For a director who would eventually be known for his focus on sound, the non-musical soundtrack of *Badlands*, with the exception of Holly's voiceover, is simply not the site of intense creative work that it would become in Malick's post-Dolby films. The real gap in studies of *Badlands* is the depth and specificity with which the film's music has been explored. Critics of the film have frequently noted the power of its musical moments, but have done so in language that, while sometimes poetically (or even "lyrosophically") evocative, often remains limited by a perception of music as supplementing, but not necessarily actively *creating* the film's philosophical sensibility.

Music and the philosophical concerns of Malick's films are not only intricately co-creative. They also engage several topics far more familiar within film music studies, nuancing the authorial role of the composer, and exploring the aesthetics of classical music in cinema. The present chapter has aimed to expand the conceptual reach of music within film philosophy, and to demonstrate what film philosophy might have to offer film musicology. Music, as Michel Chion has pointed out—with reference to the use of Polynesian music in *The Thin Red Line*—might itself be defined as obscured communication, a form of address "at once compassionate and anonymous."[74] Chion's point might be rendered more specific—describing the way in which *film music*, specifically, functions through associative semantic codes while, at the same time, perpetually exceeding them, a form of communication that gestures toward meaning, but defers this meaning, folding it into what Chion has described as the "moving box" of our subjective engagement: affect, emotion, and the hermeneutic imagination. While it might be over-reaching to apply this construct to "film music" as a whole, this sensibility clearly speaks to the deeply philosophical, ambiguous, and creative role of music in Malick's films.

Although the ways in which the New Hollywood Cinema explored the idea of the past through music and sound were highly varied, encompassing radical aesthetics, myth, the historical imaginary, nostalgia, memory, and philosophy, throughout these diverse frames of reference, the presence of the past itself, and the use of music and sound to convey sensibilities of "pastness," remained important subjects of this cinema. As we have seen throughout this study, movies of this era didn't just look and act new; they *sounded* new as well, recombining new and traditional musical styles in unexpected ways, and using new technological thresholds for aural detail to recast the past as a visceral, living experience, but, at the same time, opening up an awareness of the resistance the past might pose to easy assimilation and prescribed meanings. By attending to the philosophical soundtrack of *Badlands*, we might enrich our experience of a complex, beautiful film, but also our understanding of how this film fits within a broader moment in which representing the experience of presence within an imagined past was a deep and widespread concern.

Notes

Introduction

1. Pauline Kael, Review of *Bonnie and Clyde*, in *Kiss Kiss Bang Bang* (Boston: Little, Brown, 1968), 52.
2. Kael, Review of *Bonnie and Clyde*, 53.
3. Andrew Sarris, "Films in Focus," review of *The Last Picture Show*, *Village Voice*, October 14, 1971. Archived online at: https://www.villagevoice.com/2011/01/06/peter-bogdanovich-entitled-to-gloat-for-the-last-picture-show/. Accessed November 13, 2020.
4. Numerous authors have examined this era in depth. For a characteristic (and in many ways problematic) journalistic account of industrial and biographical history, see Peter Biskind, *Easy Riders, Raging Bulls: How the Sex-Drugs-and-Rock-'n'-Roll Generation Saved Hollywood* (New York: Simon & Schuster, 1999). For a stronger focus on film style and modernism, see Thomas Schatz, *Old Hollywood New Hollywood: Ritual, Art and Industry* (Ann Arbor: UMI Research Press, 1983), especially 217–87. For a more recent view, attending to some of the contradicting and varying ways the term has been used, see Geoff King, *New Hollywood Cinema: An Introduction* (New York: Columbia University Press, 2002). The most comprehensive study of industrial economics, film style, and generic production cycles within the era as a whole remains David Cook, *Lost Illusions: Hollywood in the Shadow of Watergate and Vietnam*, History of the American Cinema, vol. 9 (Berkeley: University of California Press, 2000).
5. Recent literature has made it clear that two important qualifications must be made here. First, the extent to which any Hollywood film of this era represents an actual alternative to dominant narrative and ideological traditions is highly debatable. This line of critique, skeptical of the stylistic distinctiveness and critical agency of the "New Hollywood," has demonstrated the persistence of traditional narrative structures in otherwise unconventional films, as well as offered an imperative to understand the limitations of a predominantly white, male ethos of liberalism as it is exemplified by films and filmmakers of this era that have been canonized. In addition, traditional perspectives on the era can eclipse a larger picture of mainstream cinema that continued alongside "the New Hollywood," elevating the figure of the auteur director at the expense of collaboration. More recent studies have addressed several of these imbalances. Notably, Nicholas Godfrey's recent study explores critical reception, production cycles, and the discourse of canonization. A recent collection of essays edited by Peter Krämer and Yannis Tzioumakis also deftly decenters our understanding of the category with a focus on a variety of collaborative dimensions and industrial

contexts. See Nicholas Godfrey, *The Limits of Auteurism: Case Studies in the Critically Constructed New Hollywood* (New Brunswick, NJ: Rutgers University Press, 2017), and Peter Krämer and Yannis Tzioumakis, eds. *The New Hollywood Renaissance: Revisiting American Cinema's Most Celebrated Era* (New York: Bloomsbury, 2018).

6. Rather than implying any specific association with the antiwar movement, the New Left, or other specific organized group, I use the term "counterculture" throughout this book to describe a broader *zeitgeist* that is understood as the product of any intersection of the era's various cultural tensions with art attempting to challenge or expand perceived cultural, industrial, or aesthetic boundaries. Stylized or "personal" filmmaking is in this sense "countercultural" even if the political impact or credibility of any particular film might be highly debatable.

7. See Tom Symmons, *The New Hollywood Historical Film: 1967–78* (London: Palgrave Macmillan, 2016). Symmons's study brings together the critical focus of the discourse on history on film with an admirably broad reading of the era, drawing from "countercultural" as well as more mainstream cinema, thus addressing some of the concerns raised earlier. Regarding the topic of the historical past, this study differs from the present book in its central focus on the New Hollywood past as "mediat[ing] the concerns of the present" (2). The literature of history on film as a distinct disciplinary paradigm within the larger field of historiography, too large to be comprehensively addressed here, is well summarized by Symmons on pp. 3–9.

8. Stanley Cavell, *The World Viewed: Reflections on the Ontology of Film*, 2nd ed. (Cambridge, MA: Harvard University Press, 1979), 24. For more on Cavell's film philosophy and its relationship to Terrence Malick's *Days of Heaven*, see Chapter 5.

9. Peter Fritzsche, *Stranded in the Present: Modern Time and the Melancholy of History* (Cambridge, MA: Harvard University Press, 2004), 5–8.

10. Theodore Roszak, *The Making of a Counter Culture: Reflections on the Technocratic Society and Its Youthful Opposition* (Garden City, NY: Doubleday, 1969; reprint with a new introduction by the author, Berkeley: University of California Press, 1995), xii–xiii.

11. Roszak, *The Making of a Counter Culture*, 39–40.

12. See J. Hoberman, *The Dream Life: Movies, Media, and the Mythology of the Sixties* (New York: The New Press, 2003), xiv–xvii. Greil Marcus, *The Old, Weird America: The World of Bob Dylan's Basement Tapes* (New York: Picador, 2001).

13. It must be noted, of course, that the "we" I am rhetorically adopting here, in order to map onto the present argument a hypothetical sense of American identity, is a highly exclusionary one. Nevertheless, this admittedly problematic stance serves an important rhetorical and aesthetic function within an evolving cultural imaginary, despite the need to acknowledge its shortcomings. For a valuable critical summary of the trope that America "has no ruins," see Brian McHale, *The Cambridge Introduction to Postmodernism* (Cambridge: Cambridge University Press, 2015), 189–98.

14. Mitchell Morris, *The Persistence of Sentiment: Display and Feeling in Popular Music of the 1970s* (Berkeley: University of California Press, 2013), 11–12.

15. An important examination of this phenomenon is Thomas Elsaesser, "The Pathos of Failure: Notes on the Unmotivated Hero," *Monogram* 6 (1975): 13–19, repr. in *The*

Last Great Picture Show: New Hollywood Cinema in the 1970s, edited by Thomas Elsaesser, Alexander Horwath, and Noel King (Amsterdam: Amsterdam University Press, 2004), 279–92.
16. Roszak, *The Making of a Counter Culture*, xxxiii.
17. Cook, *Lost Illusions*, xvii.
18. Cook, *Lost Illusions*, 4.
19. Andreas Killen, *1973 Nervous Breakdown: Watergate, Warhol, and the Birth of Post-Sixties America* (New York: Bloomsbury, 2006), 6–10. Killen extends this central metaphor in several fascinating directions—reality television, social reintegration of veterans, the public fascination with cults and deprogramming, and the reaction against personal expression in pop art.
20. Morris, *The Persistence of Sentiment*, 12–13.
21. An interesting parallel might be found in shifting strategies regarding the marketing and sale of music recording. Julie Hubbert has recently speculated what, for example, the "megastore" model, and specifically Tower Records' strategy of "deep cataloguing," might offer our understanding of the role of increasingly heterogeneous music in film. See Hubbert, "The Compilation Soundtrack from the 1960s to the Present," in *The Oxford Handbook of Film Music Studies*, ed. David Neumeyer (Oxford: Oxford University Press, 2014), 300–2.
22. Morris, *The Persistence of Sentiment*, 15.
23. Robin Wood, *Hollywood from Vietnam to Reagan* (New York: Columbia University Press, 1986), 12. Wood's emphases on futility, nihilism, crisis, failure, and disintegration were largely taken up in Robert Kolker's study of the era, a key work that has gone through multiple editions. See Robert Kolker, *A Cinema of Loneliness: Penn, Kubrick, Coppola, Scorsese, Spielberg, Altman*, 3rd ed. (Oxford: Oxford University Press, 2000).
24. Wood, *Hollywood from Vietnam to Reagan*, 36.
25. Wood, *Hollywood from Vietnam to Reagan*, 48.
26. Wood, *Hollywood from Vietnam to Reagan*, 68–69.
27. Morris, *The Persistence of Sentiment*, 25.
28. Although this view holds a great deal of undeniable truth, it neither accounts for the variety and richness of these aesthetic experiences, nor provides a compelling reason not to explore them once their limitations have been duly acknowledged. The task of truly diversifying our understanding of a "presence of the past" nevertheless remains vital work in which I hope to participate.
29. Morris, *The Persistence of Sentiment*, 30.
30. For readings of how two historical films outside of New Hollywood canonization carefully manage political optimism, see Tom Symmons's excellent readings of *Sounder* (1973) and *Grease* (1978). Particularly noteworthy is Symmons's study of the less-examined film *Sounder* (1972) and its reception as a work of mainstream cinema complexly engaged with both pastoral nostalgia and racial conflict. Symmons, *The New Hollywood Historical Film*, 57–82 and 174–94.
31. Wood, *Hollywood from Vietnam to Reagan*, 48–49.

32. On this "spectral" aspect of film music, and its ability to cultivate meaning in cinema, see K. J. Donnelly, *The Spectre of Sound: Music in Film and Television* (London: BFI, 2005), especially 20–24 and 36–42.
33. Peter Franklin, *Seeing through Music: Gender and Modernism in Classic Hollywood Film Scores* (Oxford: Oxford University Press, 2014).
34. Paul Monaco, *The Sixties: 1960–1969*, History of the American Cinema, vol. 8 (Berkeley: University of California Press, 2001), 2. Monaco's historical reading somewhat resembles philosopher Gilles Deleuze's notion of the "time image" in cinema, although Deleuze's concept ultimately speaks less to stylistic history and more to his understanding of film's sensory imminence. Like Deleuze, Monaco also theorizes this turn in cinematic style upon historical moments in post–World War II and New Wave art cinemas.
35. These changes were recognized in early histories of the era, written, in many ways, as it was still occurring, thus making the boundaries of a "New Hollywood Cinema" a necessarily flexible construct. In the first edition of Gerald Mast's *A Short History of the Movies*, for example, Mast similarly identifies *Psycho* with the roots of a "New American cinema" (the terminology was even more pliable at the time) whose "self-conscious stylism played upon the emotional power in the visual assaults of the medium itself." Mast, *A Short History of the Movies* (New York: Pegasus, 1971), 416.
36. Monaco, *The Sixties*, 54–55. See also Tino Balio, *The Foreign Film Renaissance on American Screens, 1946–1973* (Madison: University of Wisconsin Press, 2010), especially 227–50 and 279–99.
37. Gerald Mast, *A Short History of the Movies*, 2nd ed. (Indianapolis: Bobs-Merrill, 1976), 483.
38. An important recent re-evaluation of the aesthetics of the French New Wave, with neorealism as an important precursor, may be found in James Tweedie, *The Age of New Waves: Art Cinema and the Staging of Globalization* (Oxford: Oxford University Press, 2013), especially 45–61. Without entirely dismissing the influence of European art cinema on Hollywood in this juncture, Tweedie also offers a concluding overview that is notably reserved in assessing the applicability of the concept of a "New Wave" (as he has specifically linked it to globalized urban youth culture) to an American context. See 303–11.
39. Jay Beck, *Designing Sound: Audiovisual Aesthetics in 1970s American Cinema* (New Brunswick, NJ: Routledge, 2016), 11–17.
40. See Julie Hubbert, "'Whatever Happened to Great Movie Music?': *Cinema Vérité* and Hollywood Film Music of the Early 1970s," *American Music* 21, no. 2 (Summer 2003): 180–213. See also Beck, *Designing Sound*, 29–31.
41. See Chapter 1.
42. Monaco, *The Sixties*, 69.
43. See John Belton, "1950s Magnetic Sound: The Frozen Revolution," in *Sound Theory / Sound Practice*, ed. Rick Altman (New York: Routledge, 1992).
44. While this central idea is explored in a variety of ways throughout Bazin's body of work, perhaps the most representative formulation is in André Bazin, "The Ontology

of the Photographic Image," in *What Is Cinema?*, trans. Hugh Gray (Berkeley, University of California Press, 1967).

45. These biases were toward Italian neorealism and the poetic realism of French filmmakers such as Jean Renoir. For a critique of evolutionary idealism in Bazin specific to sound, see John Belton, "Technology and Aesthetics of Film Sound," in *Film Theory and Criticism*, 4th ed., ed. Gerald Mast, Marshall Cohen, and Leo Braudy (New York: Oxford University Press, 1992), 329–30.

46. Andrew, author of a biography of Bazin, has remained central to renewed theoretical interest in Bazin in recent years, and presents a perhaps unusually sympathetic, though rigorous mid-seventies view of Bazin. See Dudley Andrew, *The Major Film Theories: An Introduction* (London: Oxford University Press, 1976), 134–78.

47. See in particular Dudley Andrew and Hervé Joubert-Laurencin, eds., *Opening Bazin: Postwar Film Theory and Its Afterlife* (New York: Oxford University Press, 2011).

48. Regarding the former, see the introductions and several of the essays contained in David Bordwell and Noël Carroll, eds., *Post-Theory: Restructuring Film Studies* (Madison: University of Wisconsin Press, 1996).

49. A collection of essays broadly representative of this approach and focus may be found in Marijke de Valck and Malte Hagener, *Cinephilia: Movies, Love, and Memory* (Amsterdam: Amsterdam University Press, 2005).

50. Robert B. Ray, *The Avant-Garde Finds Andy Hardy* (Cambridge, MA: Harvard University Press, 1995), 17–23 and 40–73. Ray, for example, has advocated for drawing upon the oblique thinking techniques of surrealist games as a way to force critical thought to engage productively with the unexpectedly contingent, or even accidental.

51. Christian Keathley, *Cinephilia and History, or the Wind in the Trees* (Bloomington: Indiana University Press, 2006).

52. See Greg Taylor, *Artists in the Audience: Cults, Camp, and American Film Criticism* (Princeton, NJ: Princeton University Press, 1999). See also Keathley, *Cinephilia and History*, 22–23. Greg Tylor's historical purview ends with the critical-theoretical retrenchment of the seventies and, broadly speaking, emphasizes the growing division in the sixties between "cult" criticism and the self-conscious modernism in filmmaking which "cult" critics such as Manny Farber typically rejected. See Taylor, *Artists in the Audience*, 98–121.

53. Keathley, *Cinephilia and History*, 59.

54. The latter term is from Michael Pye and Lynda Myles, *The Movie Brats: How the Film Generation Took Over Hollywood* (New York: Holt, Rinehart, and Winston, 1979).

55. James Lastra, *Sound Technology and the American Cinema: Perception, Representation, Modernity* (New York: Columbia University Press, 2000), 167–70.

56. See Beck, *Designing Sound*, 165–70 and 191–207. Note that Beck's discussion, importantly, focuses on Dolby Stereo's limitations and weaknesses, and its eventual role in re-establishing a less adventurous standard of post-classical sound.

57. The essays collected in Elisabeth Weis and John Belton, eds., *Film Sound: Theory and Practice* (New York: Columbia University Press, 1985) represent a good overview. See especially 213–345.

58. See Stephen Handzo, "A Glossary of Film Sound Technology," in *Film Sound*, ed. Weis and Belton, 391–93.
59. See Jeff Smith, "The Auteur Renaissance," in *Sound: Music, Dialogue, Effects*, ed. Kathryn Kalinak (New Brunswick, NJ: Rutgers, 2015), 105–6.
60. For a survey of musical style in this period, see Mervyn Cooke, *A History of Film Music* (New York: Cambridge University Press, 2008), 183–225. See also James Wierzbicki, *Film Music: A History* (New York: Routledge, 2009), 189–208.
61. I refer here to the responses of older, established composers such as Bernard Herrmann, David Raksin, and Elmer Bernstein. Younger composers who were finding success in the new environment, such as Lalo Schifrin, took an understandably more measured tone regarding the aesthetic possibilities of pop scoring, occasionally inspiring more traditionalist voices to take a more measured view of *them*. Schifrin, in particular, tended to be viewed with cautious admiration, with his work simultaneously held as creatively rich, but exemplifying a troublingly fragmenting tradition. See, for example, Mark Evans, *Soundtrack: The Music of the Movies* (New York: Hopkinson and Blake, 1975), 203.
62. Jeff Smith, *The Sounds of Commerce: Marketing Popular Film Music* (New York: Columbia University Press, 1998), 20.
63. See Smith, *The Sounds of Commerce*, 172–85, on *American Graffiti*. The broader issue of cultural affiliation in the compiled score is a major subject of Anahid Kassabian, *Hearing Film: Tracking Identifications in Contemporary Hollywood Film Music* (New York: Routledge, 2001). See especially Kassabian, *Hearing Film*, 51–57, on *American Graffiti*.

Chapter 1

1. Pauline Norton, "Breakdown," *Grove Music Online. Oxford Music Online*. Oxford University Press. http://www.oxfordmusiconline.com/subscriber/article/grove/music/03898. Accessed online November 13, 2020.
2. Bob Dylan, interview with John Cohen and Happy Traum, *Sing Out!* (October/November 1968), repr. in Jonathon Cott, ed., *Bob Dylan: The Essential Interviews* (New York: Simon and Schuster, 2017), 122.
3. Robert Benton and David Newman, *Bonnie and Clyde*, screenplay typescript dated 9/6/66 with isolated later revisions (Hollywood: Script City). Several pages are individually marked as revisions dated 9/30, 10/7, and 10/9. It is likely that these revisions are by screenwriter Robert Towne, who was enlisted by producer and star Warren Beatty to polish the script, in that the revisions involve sections that multiple sources identify as being Towne's contributions. For musical descriptions, see pp. 8, 28, and 134. For an overview of Towne's role, as well as earlier treatments and versions of the script that are now privately held by David Newman, see Matthew Bernstein, "Perfecting the New Gangster: Writing Bonnie and Clyde," *Film Quarterly* 53, no. 4 (Summer 2000).

4. Benton and Newman, *Bonnie and Clyde*, 1. Similarly, Clyde's tussle with a cleaver-wielding butcher he was attempting to rob—the character's first real brush with possible death—is also specified as taking place "in silence," lest some composer get the wrong idea and write dramatic "fight" music.
5. The quotation is the famous, and frequently paraphrased opening line of L. P. Hartley's novel, *The Go-Between*. See L. P. Hartley, *The Go-Between* (1953; repr. New York: New York Review of Books Classics, 2002).
6. See Daniel Belgrad, *The Culture of Spontaneity: Improvisation and the Arts in Post-War America* (Chicago: University of Chicago Press, 1999). See especially 255–60. Belgrad's inquiry tapers off in the early sixties, but is nevertheless instructive regarding how his insights might be extended and, inevitably, transformed in a countercultural milieu of the later part of the decade.
7. I have not been able to attribute any specific creative agency to Francis Stahl, credited simply with "sound." In 1967, this generalized credit was still common. Stahl was likely in charge of production recording, although it is also possible that he may have contributed to post-production Foley, soundtrack editing, or re-recording work. Stahl's other professional credits make little argument for a unique perspective toward sound recording, and his creative presence in the final film was, to some degree, eclipsed by the post-production work of editor Dede Allen.
8. Of course, auteurism—albeit often in a modified, less insistent form—remains a dominant factor in studies of art cinema, and of the New Hollywood in particular, with several key studies (such as Robert Kolker's) organized by director. Also, despite its visualist origins in studies of directorial style, auteurism has continued to impact studies of music and sound.
9. Robert Benton and David Newman, "Lightning in a Bottle," in *Bonnie and Clyde*, ed. Sandra Wake and Nicola Hayden (London: Lorrimer, 1972), 15.
10. Benton and Newman, "Lightning in a Bottle," 14.
11. Newman and Benton, "The New Sentimentality," *Esquire* (July 1964), 28.
12. Distrust of "Old Sentimental" nods to class conflict and disenfranchisement could unite otherwise diverse critics, sometimes even bridging overall positive and negative assessments of the film. Iconoclast Pauline Kael describes a scene set in a squatters' jungle as "too eloquent . . . like a poster" (Kael, review of *Bonnie and Clyde*, 53). Traditionalist Stanley Kauffmann describes a scene in which Clyde helps a farmer shoot cathartic holes in his repossessed house as "economic determinism, which is patently fabricated." Kauffmann, *Figures of Light: Film Criticism and Comment* (New York: Harper and Row, 1971), 20.
13. Newman and Benton, "The New Sentimentality," 26.
14. Benton and Newman, "Lightning in a Bottle," 16–17.
15. Matthew Bernstein's reading is particularly illuminating. See Bernstein, "Model Criminals: Visual Style in Bonnie and Clyde," in *Arthur Penn's "Bonnie and Clyde,"* ed. Lester Friedman (Cambridge: Cambridge University Press, 2000), 116–18.
16. *Bonnie and Clyde*, directed by Arthur Penn, Warners-Seven Arts, 1967. Two-disc special edition. Burbank: Warner Brothers Home Video, 2008. DVD. All timings will refer to this transfer of the film, and are formatted as (hour: minutes: seconds).

17. Carolyn Geduld, "Bonnie and Clyde: Society vs. the Clan," in *Focus on "Bonnie and Clyde,"* ed. John G. Cawelti (Englewood Cliffs, NJ: Prentice-Hall, 1973), 93–98.
18. Lester Friedman has identified the importance of memory and the creation of images as a theme in this sequence. See Friedman, *Bonnie and Clyde*, BFI Film Classics (London: British Film Institute, 2000), 42. See also J. Hoberman, *The Dream Life: Movies, Media, and the Mythology of the Sixties* (New York: The New Press, 2003), 174.
19. This is the version recorded on February 6, 1929 (Victor 21868). See Victor Discography Online, http://victor.library.ucsb.edu/index.php/object/detail/19424/Victor_21868, accessed November 14, 2020. In his autobiography, Vallée reflects on the song's "Slavic, Oriental, mysterious quality," viewing it as suited "for listening" (rather than for buying and playing the sheet music), calling attention to the peculiar, dreamy ambiance of the recording. See Rudy Vallée, *Vagabond Dreams Come True* (New York: E. P. Dutton, 1930), 204, 211–12.
20. The slow fading in of the song would, in this reading, suggest the gradual acquisition of the sound source against some form of resistance, such as time or memory, or perhaps—as in more explicit in the openings of *American Graffiti* and *Last Picture Show*—the symbolic act of tuning in a radio signal. See Chapter 4.
21. Fredric Jameson, *Postmodernism, or The Cultural Logic of Late Capitalism*, in *The Jameson Reader*, ed. Michael Hardt and Kathi Weeks (Oxford: Blackwell, 2004), 203–5. On Bogdanovich's music research, see Chapter 4.
22. On this scene, and *Bonnie and Clyde* in the context of cinematic illusionism in the New Hollywood Cinema, see Richard L. Edwards, "'We Rob Banks': Cinematic Thievery in *Bonnie and Clyde*," in *"Bonnie and Clyde": Critical Insights*, ed. Rebecca Martin (Ipswich, MA: Salem Press, 2016), 111–12.
23. It is also possible, as *Bonnie and Clyde* was financed and distributed by Warner Bros., which had produced the *Golddiggers* franchise, that there was an economic advantage to using this material in the avoidance of copyright permissions. In the absence of detailed archival production records on the film, however, this remains speculative.
24. Stephen Farber, "The Writer in American Films," *Film Quarterly* 21, no. 4 (1968): 12.
25. Michel Chion, *Film, a Sound Art*, trans. Claudia Gorbman (New York: Columbia University Press, 2009), 67.
26. Michel Chion, *The Voice in Cinema*, trans. Claudia Gorbman (New York: Columbia University Press, 1999), 37–43. In Chion's reading, the discomforting force of the acousmachine is its role as a reminder of the mechanization of the cinematic apparatus.
27. Michael Chaiken and Paul Cronin, "A Summing Up," in *Arthur Penn: Interviews*, ed. Michael Chaiken and Paul Cronin (Jackson: University Press of Mississippi, 2008), 208. The interview in question was conducted in 2007 with the editors of the volume.
28. Benton and Newman, *Bonnie and Clyde*, 57, 104.
29. Bill Knopf, "Interview: Doug Dillard," *Banjo Newsletter*, June 1981: 4–6. Dillard and his group were recording artists and session musicians who had also appeared on *The Andy Griffith Show* and would go on to perform on the soundtrack to several films. In this interview, Dillard also recalls playing for a *Bonnie-and-Clyde*-themed Pontiac

commercial, likely made during the *Bonnie and Clyde* fad that followed the film's release. Dillard recalled the other session musicians on the film sessions as including his brother, Rodney Dillard, along with Los Angeles session regulars Tommy Tedesco and Glen Campbell, who was shortly thereafter to break out as a solo artist. Charles Strouse's autobiography briefly discusses his *Bonnie and Clyde* experience, but with frustratingly few details. See Charles Strouse, *Put on a Happy Face: A Broadway Memoir* (New York: Union Square Press, 2008), 173–77. Strouse's papers, at the New York Public Library, are unfortunately confined to the musical theater work for which he is much better known.

30. See Smith, *The Sounds of Commerce*, 7–11.
31. Smith, *The Sounds of Commerce*. See also Kassabian, *Hearing Film*. The literature on the issue of the "invisibility" of underscoring in classical Hollywood style is too large to summarize here.
32. Julie Hubbert, "'Whatever Happened to Great Movie Music?': *Cinéma Vérité* and Hollywood Film Music of the Early 1970s." *American Music* 21, no. 2 (Summer 2003): 180–213. While Hubbert briefly discusses underscoring, the greater focus of her argument is on the use of source music.
33. On squibs as a technology of sensuous materialism, see Amy Rust, *Passionate Detachments: Technologies of Vision and Violence in American Cinema, 1967–1974* (Albany, State University of New York Press, 2017), 71–74. Here, Rust's emphasis is on *The Wild Bunch*, although she acknowledges the important precedent of *Bonnie and Clyde* in their use, and elsewhere, explores the use of multiple camera and multiple film speed shooting in the final gun battle, as a "figure" that presents a moment of temporal omniscience while simultaneously challenging its limits as an "authentic" depiction of reality. See 25–53 on *Bonnie and Clyde*, and 11–16 on the "figure" as a concept intertwining representation and interpretive potential with a sensuous challenge to the limits of representation.
34. The first time it is used, a minor editing loop is noticeably used to provide an extra few seconds of music to match the visual editing of the couple's car coming to a stop (0:08:40). If anything, however, the use of an existing recording makes such deviations, especially the sudden interruptions in the second "Foggy Mountain" cue, even more noticeable.
35. See, for example, David Raksin, "Whatever Became of Movie Music?" *Film Music Notebook* 1, no. 1 (Fall 1974): 24–30, reprinted in *Celluloid Symphonies: Texts and Contexts in Film Music History*, ed. Julie Hubbert (Berkeley: University of California Press, 2011), 372–77. See also Tony Thomas, *Music for the Movies* (South Brunswick, NJ: A. S. Barnes, 1973), 23.
36. *Music Inspired by the Rip-Roarin', Electrifying Sounds of Bonnie and Clyde, Including Excerpts of the Original Dialogue!* (Burbank, CA: Warner Bros. Seven Arts, 1968). W1743. 33 1/3 rpm record.
37. Both trailers are available as features on the DVD cited earlier.
38. See Jeff Smith, *Sounds of Commerce*, 47–56, on the complexities and varied strategies employed as the commercial market for film music migrated from singles to albums. Nevertheless, the economic logic of this hypothesis, even in an uncertain creative

environment, still probably holds. In the sixties, with the turn to pop scoring, and the frequent use of less music in film overall, unused session cues (as well as dialogue tracks, which also appear on the *Bonnie and Clyde* soundtrack cited earlier) could be used to pad a soundtrack to LP length. On the importance of the Warner Bros. / Seven Arts merger, which occurred while *Bonnie and Clyde* was in production, and its stimulating effect on Warners' soundtrack album production, see Smith, *Sounds of Commerce*, 41–42.

39. Chion, *Film, a Sound Art*, 68–69.
40. Quoted in Chaiken and Cronin, *Arthur Penn: Interviews*, xv. Quotation is from an interview conducted onscreen in Robert Hughes's 1970 documentary on the production of Penn's *Little Big Man* (1970).
41. Jay Beck has recently considered this scene in view of Arthur Penn's role as sonic auteur. See Beck, *Designing Sound*, 42. Despite Beck's insightful analysis of the film, his identification of Charles Strouse as a "bluegrass artist" is misleading. At this point in his career, Strouse was probably best known as the composer of the Broadway musical *Bye-Bye Birdie* (1960).
42. It is risky to use the titles and treatment of these cues on the album to imagine an alternate soundtrack for the film, particularly as a way to speculate upon Strouse's possible contrafactual intentions, without more specific evidence. In fact, I have been unable to determine the relationship between the production of the album and the spotting and recording sessions in which Strouse's music was conceived for certain specific scenes. Nevertheless, the consistency with which the music on the album frames dialogue that is proximate in the finished film makes this interpretation inevitable, even if only in the mind of the soundtrack album's listener.
43. See Neil Lerner, "Copland's Music of Wide Open Spaces: Surveying the Pastoral Trope in Hollywood," *Musical Quarterly* 85, no. 3 (August 2001): 477–515.
44. On mute characters, see Chion, *The Voice in Cinema*, 95–100.
45. This was even more pointed in earlier drafts of the script, in which Clyde was bisexual, engaging in a *ménage* with C. W. Moss and Bonnie. Regarding this abandoned dimension of the script, see Mark Harris, *Pictures at a Revolution: Five Movies and the Birth of the New Hollywood* (New York: Penguin Press, 2008), 207–9. See also Bernstein, "Perfecting the New Gangster," 20–22.
46. This essentializing notion of the voice has been questioned by numerous thinkers. It is put forth here not as a simplistic assertion of its truth value, but as a hermeneutic and heuristic tool for understanding the resonance of this particular dynamic in this film.
47. Marcus, *The Old, Weird America*, 140.
48. This line of analysis has been developed, in part, through a discussion of *Bonnie and Clyde* as myth, another conceptual framework in which past and present (as well as narrative and experience) are often deeply intertwined. See John Orr, "Terrence Malick and Arthur Penn: The Western Re-Myth," in *The Cinema of Terrence Malick: Poetic Visions of America*, ed. Hannah Patterson, Directors' Cuts (London: Wallflower, 2007), 63–76. For an earlier example of myth criticism applied to *Bonnie and Clyde*, see John G. Cawelti, "The Artistic Power of *Bonnie and Clyde*," in Cawelti, ed., *Focus on "Bonnie and Clyde,"* 40–84.

49. See Jean-Louis Comolli and André S. Labarthe. "*Bonnie and Clyde*: An Interview with Arthur Penn," *Evergreen Review* 12, no. 55 (June 1968); reprinted in *Focus on "Bonnie and Clyde*," 19. The *Evergreen Review* interview was a translation of an earlier one that had appeared in *Cahiers du Cinéma* the previous December. See also Yvonne Baby, "Violent Times," *Le Monde* (January 26, 1969); reprinted in Chaiken and Cronin, eds., *Arthur Penn: Interviews*, 13.
50. This process, as critics oriented toward the avant-garde or radical politics are always quick to point out, inevitably involved a mainstreaming of radical content—emblematically summed up, perhaps, by Robert Rauschenberg's pop-art rendering of the film for the cover of the December 8, 1967, issue of *Time* Magazine.
51. For a general overview of the Bonnie and Clyde fad, see Friedman, *Bonnie and Clyde*, 21–40. Additional musical examples of the fad include British pop singer Georgie Fame's "The Ballad of Bonnie and Clyde," recorded in a period Music Hall style, as well as Serge Gainsbourg and Brigitte Bardot's recording of Gainsbourg's song "Bonnie and Clyde," whose slick production and coolly sexualized vocals reflect French pop culture's fascination with American outlaws—and mirror Benton and Newman's originating fascination with the French New Wave. See Martin Carter, "*Bonnie and Clyde* in the Charts," in *Bonnie and Clyde: Critical Insights*, ed. Rebecca Martin (Ipswich, MA: Salem Press, 2016), 240–54.
52. For Hoberman's discussion of the film, to which my understanding of it is deeply indebted, see Hoberman, *The Dream Life*, 170–85.
53. Peter Collier, review of *Bonnie and Clyde*, in Cawelti, ed., *Focus on "Bonnie and Clyde*," 27.
54. See Adrian Henri, *Total Art: Events, Happenings, and Performances* (New York: Praeger, 1974). For a more recent perspective on this moment in avant-garde aesthetics, see Belgrad, *The Culture of Spontaneity*, 247–60.
55. Hoberman, *The Dream Life*, 169.
56. Collier, "Review of *Bonnie and Clyde*," 30.
57. Bosley Crowther, "Review of *Bonnie and Clyde*," in Cawelti, ed., *Focus on "Bonnie and Clyde*," 22. Originally published in *New York Times*, August 14, 1967.
58. Page Cook, "Review of *Bonnie and Clyde*," in Cawelti, ed., *Focus on "Bonnie and Clyde*," 24. Originally published in *Films in Review* 18, no. 8 (October 1967): 504–5.
59. Jerry Richard, "Foggy Mountain," *The Antioch Review* 28, no. 3 (October 1, 1968): 388–93.
60. On moral panic and early rock and roll, see James Wierzbicki, *Music in the Age of Anxiety: American Music in the Fifties* (Urbana: University of Illinois Press, 2015) 40–48.
61. Dave Kaufman, *Variety* 217, no. 12 (August 9, 1967): 6.
62. Cook, "Review of *Bonnie and Clyde*," 24. Cook was an active participant in dialogues regarding the pop score, generally inveighing against this tone as a sign of industrial and creative decline.
63. Dillard identifies it as a 1948 recording. See Knopf, "Interview with Doug Dillard," 5. The film's credits acknowledge the credit to Mercury Records, copyright dated 1949.

64. See Neil V. Rosenberg, "Image and Stereotype: Bluegrass Soundtracks," *American Music* 1, no. 3 (Autumn 1983): 3. Also Karen Linn, *That Half-Barbaric Twang: The Banjo in American Popular Culture* (Urbana: University of Illinois Press, 1991), 146–48.
65. Hoberman, *The Dream Life*, 138.
66. Orr, "Terrence Malick and Arthur Penn," 68.
67. Cawelti, "The Artistic Power of *Bonnie and Clyde*," 57.
68. Benton and Newman, *Bonnie and Clyde*, 134.

Chapter 2

1. Jim Kitses, "Introduction: Postmodernism and the Western," in *The Western Reader*, ed. Jim Kitses and Gregg Rickman (New York: Limelight Editions, 1998), 13–21.
2. Along similar lines, Western academia has frequently questioned its own discursive location as a locus from which to study myth, in particular regarding the problematic nature of comparativist studies as opposed to studies rooted in irreducible cultural difference. On this impasse in the field of religious studies, see Kimberley C. Patton and Benjamin C. Ray, eds., *A Magic Still Dwells: Comparative Religion in the Postmodern Age* (Berkeley: University of California Press, 2000).
3. Rick Altman, *The American Film Musical* (Bloomington: Indiana University Press, 1987), 94–102. Altman is careful to distinguish his use of these concepts from the myth theory of Levi-Strauss, on the grounds that in classic structuralism the surface-level semantics are viewed as largely irrelevant in comparison with deeper structural levels of underlying syntax, whereas in the study of popular culture, semantic elements are undeniably central to audience response.
4. Royal S. Brown, *Overtones and Undertones: Reading Film Music* (Berkeley: University of California Press, 1994), 8. See also 8–11 and 27–32, as well as Brown's discussion of *The Sea Hawk* (1942) on 98–118. Note that Brown's uses the terms "diachronic" and "synchronic" minimally (although they do appear in a discussion of Eisensteinian aesthetics, 136–37) and the foregrounding of these terms is my interpellation. More frequently, however, Brown uses the terms "horizontal" and "vertical" in comparable ways.
5. James Buhler, "*Star Wars*, Music, and Myth," in *Music and Cinema*, ed. James Buhler, Caryl Flinn, and David Neumeyer (Hanover, NH: University Press of New England, 2000), 43.
6. Buhler, "*Star Wars*, Music, and Myth," 48.
7. On Ford and film music, see Kathryn Kalinak, *How the West Was Sung: Music in the Westerns of John Ford* (Berkeley: University of California Press, 2007).
8. See Claudia Gorbman, "Scoring the Indian: Music in the Liberal Western," in *Western Music and Its Others*, ed. Georgina Born and David Hesmondhalgh (Berkeley: University of California Press, 2000), 234–53.
9. Cooke, *A History of Film Music*, 198–99.

10. *Time Magazine*, "Double Vision," review of *Butch Cassidy and the Sundance Kid*, August 26, 1969.
11. Dennis Hunt, review of *Butch Cassidy and the Sundance Kid*, *Film Quarterly* 23, no. 2 (Winter, 1969–70): 62.
12. Jackson Burgess, review of *McCabe and Mrs. Miller*, *Film Quarterly* 25, no. 2 (Winter 1971–72): 53.
13. Richard Dyer, "Side by Side: Nino Rota, Music, and Film," in *Beyond the Soundtrack: Representing Music in Cinema*, ed. Daniel Goldmark, Lawrence Kramer, and Richard Leppert (Berkeley: University of California Press, 2007), 251.
14. Hal David, Burt Bacharach, and George Terry, *Original Score Composed and Conducted by Burt Bacharach from the 20th Century Fox Production "Butch Cassidy and the Sundance Kid"* (New York: Charles Hansen Music and Books, 1969), 20.
15. William Goldman, *Four Screenplays* (New York: Applause Books, 1995), 120–24.
16. *Butch Cassidy and the Sundance Kid*, directed by George Roy Hill, 20th Century Fox, 1969. Collector's Edition #28 (20th Century Fox Home Entertainment, 2006), DVD. All timings refer to this video transfer of the film. A reconstruction of the tent scene is also available as a special feature on this release. The reconstruction is credited to Richard Crawford and the Yale University Research Archive.
17. Hoberman, *The Dream Life*, 105–7.
18. A tack piano is a piano prepared with tacks pressed into the hammers, so their striking of the strings creates a jangly timbre reminiscent of a piano whose felt has worn through. Although I've been unable to locate production materials, liner notes by producer Alec Cumming for Rhino Records' ambitiously produced collection of Bacharach's music on CD relate various anecdotal accounts of the film's recording sessions at A&R records in New York, and refer to both instruments. See Cumming, "Let the Music Play: 75 Magic Moments," on *The Look of Love: The Burt Bacharach Collection*, Rhino R2 75339, Rhino Records, 1998. Compact Disc. Liner notes archived online at http://albumlinernotes.com/Look_Of_Love_Disc_3.html. Accessed November 13, 2020.
19. Brownlow's epochal 1968 study of the silent film, despite its comparably limited focus on music, maintains on the whole this defensive tone toward the reputation of silent cinema in the present. See Kevin Brownlow, *The Parade's Gone By . . .* (Berkeley: University of California Press, 1968), 2–3 and 338–41.
20. Most of the literature on this earlier revival is non-academic, produced mainly by collectors and performers, albeit some with considerable historical knowledge. For a particularly comprehensive and well-documented example, see Bill Edwards, "Ragtime and Honky Tonk of the 1950s: An Essay on the First Ragtime Revival." Online at *RagPiano.com: "Perfessor" Bill's Ragtime Resources and Articles*, http://www.perfessorbill.com/ragtime11.shtml. Accessed November 13, 2020.
21. The term "Brill Building" tends to refer to music associated with publishing companies (such as Aldon Music) that were in actuality based in multiple locations, and not just the eponymous building. For a broader overview, see Timothy Scheurer, "The Beatles, the Brill Building, and the Persistence of Tin Pan Alley in the Age of Rock," *Popular Music and Society* 20, no. 4 (Winter 1996): 90–92. See also Ian Inglis, "'Some

Kind of Wonderful': The Creative Legacy of the Brill Building," *American Music* 21, no. 2 (Summer 2003): 215.

22. Bacharach, for example, never worked with Don Kershner at Aldon Music. For an overview of Bacharach's career trajectory in the sixties, see Ken Emerson, *Always Magic in the Air: The Bomp and Brilliance of the Brill Building Era* (New York: Viking, 2005), 166–81 and 238–48.
23. Summing up this trend was the critical failure of the film musical *Lost Horizon* (1973) and the subsequent dissolution of Bacharach's partnership with lyricist Hal David. On Bacharach's age and his earlier struggles to achieve and maintain a young audience, see Emerson, *Always Magic in the Air*, 130–31.
24. Geoffrey O'Brien, *Sonata for Jukebox: An Autobiography of My Ears* (New York: Counterpoint, 2004), 10–14.
25. O'Brien, *Sonata for Jukebox.*, 16–19.
26. Roland Barthes, *Camera Lucida: Reflections on Photography*, trans. Richard Howard (New York: Hill and Wang, 1981), especially 25–27, 76–77.
27. Arguably, the musical shift represents this second robbery as a softer, or more "genteel" affair, but even in those terms, the melancholy quality of the B-theme initially seems oddly synchronized—a disparity that becomes even more obvious when this theme returns at the dinner party.
28. The Swingle Singers, *Jazz Sébastien Bach*, Phillips 840.519 PY1963 (1963) 33 1/3 rpm record. The American release (Phillips PHM 200-097) was retitled "Bach's Greatest Hits" and was released the same year. Later in the decade, 1968 saw the release of a second Bach collection (Philips PHS 600-288), alternately titled *Jazz Sébastien Bach, v. 2*, and *Bach to Bach*.
29. In general, Goldman's published script predicates a great deal about the final film's treatment of music (such as the formal placement as interludes, the contemporary feel, and the use of a texted song), although stylistic determinations appear to have been left to Bacharach himself. See Goldman, *Four Screenplays*, 100. Other musical references written into Goldman's script appear on pp. 44, 90, and 140.
30. Michael Long, *Beautiful Monsters: Imagining the Classic in Musical Media* (Berkeley: University of California Press, 2008), 152–55.
31. *McCabe and Mrs. Miller*, directed by Robert Altman, Warner Bros., 1971 (Warner Bros. Home Video, 2002), DVD.
32. The term "mythemes" is borrowed from Claude Lévi-Strauss. See *Structural Anthropology*, trans. Claire Jacobson and Brooke Grundfest Schoepf (Garden City, NY: Anchor Books, 1967), 206–7. Lévi-Strauss's use of this term, analogous to "phonemes," is far more rigorous than I am applying it here. Rather than a deep-level structural component in the formation of cultural meaning, I'm using the term to suggest an imagistic mode of expression that is suggestively fluid, yet also highly genre-specific.
33. Gayle Sherwood Magee, *Robert Altman's Soundtracks: Film, Music, and Sound from M*A*S*H to A Prairie Home Companion* (Oxford: Oxford University Press, 2014), 61–71.

34. Examples include Cohen's recurring use of the symbolic figure of Joan of Arc, his appropriation (often deeply sardonic) of the tropes of courtly love in songs such as "Leaving Greensleeves" (1974), and his fascination with sainthood and hagiography, most notably in his novel *Beautiful Losers* (1966).
35. Long, *Beautiful Monsters*, 122.
36. Long, *Beautiful Monsters*, 121–39 and 152–55. Theatrical sound was something of an issue in the reception of this film, but not in the sense of literal spatialization in theatrical space, as, for example, in films released in stereophonic sound.
37. Magee, *Robert Altman's Soundtracks*, 68.
38. Robert Self's analysis of the songs displays the risk of overly literalizing Cohen's pronouns, rather than appreciating their value as pointedly ambiguous signifiers. See Self, *Robert Altman's "McCabe and Mrs. Miller": Reframing the American West* (Lawrence: University Press of Kansas), 156–62. This leads him to claim that, at the beginning of the film, "The Stranger" represents Mrs. Miller's perspective on McCabe's character as it would eventually evolve, an interpretation requiring us to retrospectively turn the temporality of the film inside out, viewing the beginning through the lens of how character relationships will evolve by its end.
39. In light of the way in which the supposed muddiness of the dialogue recording became a point of contention in the finished film, it is telling that Cohen's songs reliably follow the basic editing principle of not letting song lyrics and spoken dialogue interfere with one another.
40. Mitchell Zuckoff, *Robert Altman: The Oral Biography* (New York: Alfred A. Knopf, 2009), 228–30, quoted in Sherwood Magee, *Robert Altman's Soundtracks*, 70. See also an interview with editor Lou Lombardo in Patrick McGilligan, *Robert Altman: Jumping Off a Cliff: A Biography of the Great American Director* (New York: St. Martin's Press, 1989), 244, quoted in Ryan Gilbey, *It Don't Worry Me: The Revolutionary American Films of the Seventies* (New York: Faber and Faber, 2003), 129.
41. Robert Self devotes considerable attention to the role of beauty and expressivity in Altman's "art film" style, which he views as dialectically interwoven with the film's blunt realism. See Self, *Robert Altman's "McCabe and Mrs. Miller"*, 164–72.
42. See Chapter 1 on voices and sound design in *Bonnie and Clyde*.
43. See Pieter Breughel the Elder, *Landscape with the Fall of Icarus*, 1560s. Housed in the Royal Museum of Fine Arts of Belgium. The attribution of this painting has been a topic of dispute since the mid-1990s.
44. John Orr, *Contemporary Cinema* (Edinburgh: Edinburgh University Press, 1998), 169. Orr uses the concept of the "cinema of poetry" to examine several American films in relationship to the categories of the past, myth, and an aesthetic of reverie. While Orr's argument moves toward an articulation of past as a reality that is similar to my own, however, he largely employs the category of myth in order to dismiss it by comparison.
45. See Burgess, review of *McCabe and Mrs. Miller*, 52.
46. Burgess, review of *McCabe and Mrs. Miller*, 49.
47. Burgess, review of *McCabe and Mrs. Miller*, 51. Emphasis in original.

48. Pauline Kael, "Pipe Dream," review of *McCabe and Mrs. Miller*, in *Deeper into Movies* (Boston: Little, Brown, 1968), 278. Originally published in *The New Yorker* (October 21, 1967), 147.
49. Kael, "Pipe Dreams," 280.
50. Regarding the role of imagined tactility in the psychedelic listening experience, see Long, *Beautiful Monsters*, 135–36. Long echoes an emphasis here that is also present in recent film theory. For a summary of these trends, see the chapter "Cinema as Skin and Touch" in Thomas Elsaesser and Malte Hagener, *Film Theory: An Introduction through the Senses* (London: Routledge, 2009), 108–28.
51. Richard Dyer, "Entertainment and Utopia," *Movie* 24 (Spring 1977): 2–13, reprinted in *Only Entertainment* (New York: Routledge, 1992), 18. The paraphrased passage: "Entertainment does not, however, present models of utopian worlds.... Rather, the utopianism is contained in the feelings it embodies. It presents, head-on, as it were, what utopia would feel like, rather than how it would be organized."

Chapter 3

1. See Thomas Elsaesser, "The Pathos of Failure: Notes on the Unmotivated Hero," *Monogram* 6 (1975): 13–19, reprinted in *The Last Great Picture Show: New Hollywood Cinema in the 1970s*, ed. Thomas Elsaesser, Alexander Horwath, and Noel King (Amsterdam: Amsterdam University Press, 2004), 279–92. While the narrative linearity and paranoid inevitability of *Chinatown* may seem square with Elsaesser's thesis that radical skepticism in New Hollywood films had permeated down to the bedrock of narrative form, note his brief comment describing the film as "as dismissive of its hero's motives as is Altman in *The Long Goodbye*, except that Polanski's lack of respect for his hero appeases itself in the meticulous craftsmanship of the reconstruction of his moral demise" (285).
2. Todd Berliner, *Hollywood Incoherent: Narration in Seventies Cinema* (Austin: University of Texas Press, 2010), 90–91. The great advantage of Berliner's categorization is to distinguish in a pluralistic way different *approaches* to genre revisionism, rather than assume—as critics often have—that genre "breakers" represent more authentically subversive revisionism, whereas genre "benders" are mere exercises in naive nostalgia or empty pastiche.
3. John Belton, "Language, Oedipus, and *Chinatown*," *MLN* 106, no. 5 (December 1991): 937. This source is explored in greater depth at this chapter's conclusion.
4. Davide Caputo has recently explored this dimension of Polanski's films within a psychological framework. See Caputo, *Polanski and Perception: The Psychology of Seeing and the Cinema of Roman Polanski* (Bristol: Intellect, 2012), especially 182–97.
5. For a particularly rich enumeration of such visual motifs, see Herbert Eagle, "Power and the Visual Semantics of Polanski's Films," in *The Cinema of Roman Polanski: Dark Places of the World*, ed. John Orr and Elżbeta Ostrowska (London: Wallflower, 2006), 48–49. While primarily ocular, this image might be extended to other organs of

perception which, by dint of human physiognomy, are often dual—while the film doesn't really attempt to convey one damaged *ear* in a pair, it does prominently locate Jake's nose (after one of nostrils is slit by Cross's thugs) within the same symbolic logic.
6. *Chinatown*, directed by Roman Polanski, Paramount, 1974. Centennial Collection (Paramount Pictures, 2009), DVD. All timings will be taken from this transfer of the film.
7. This line, which first appears in a recollection of the pervasive cynical apathy that characterized Jake's time as a city detective, recurs after Evelyn's death.
8. Michael Eaton, *Chinatown*, BFI Film Classics (London: BFI, 1997), 12–13.
9. As David Butler has shown, however, the actual role of jazz in films noir of the forties and fifties was more complex, and usually was deployed through diegetic music rather than underscoring, with the exception of a few key films of the fifties. Its prevalence in the underscoring of *neo-Noir*, then, represents an act of cultural "misremembering." See Butler, *Jazz Noir: Listening to Music from "The Phantom Lady" to "The Last Seduction"* (Westport, CT: Praeger, 2002), especially 156 and 166–67.
10. I am certainly not the first to notice the presence of "wet" and "dry" timbral images in *Chinatown*. It is actually a commonplace observation in discussions of the film's score, but it has generally been presented in a broad or peripheral way. For example, William Darby and Jack Du Bois describe the "splashy" piano figures as suggestive of the importance of water in the plot, and read the restrained use of music, overall, as suggestive of "aridity." See William Darby and Jack Du Bois, *American Film Music: Major Composers, Techniques, and Trends: 1915–1990* (Jefferson, NC: McFarland, 1990), 500–6. Other critics to discuss elemental images in the score include Jeff Bond, in his liner notes to the Intrada rerelease of the soundtrack album. See *Music from the Motion Picture "Chinatown,"* Intrada Special Collections 350. Produced by Douglass Fake and Roger Feigelson. Liner notes by Jeff Bond and Douglass Fake. Intrada ISC350 (Oakland: Intrada, 2016), CD.
11. Dana Polan, "*Chinatown*: Politics as Perspective, Perspective as Politics," in *The Cinema of Roman Polanski*, 108–20.
12. Polan, "Politics as Perspective," 115.
13. Polan, "Politics as Perspective," 111–12.
14. Polan, "Politics as Perspective," 111.
15. Robert Miklitsch, "Audio-Noir: Audiovisuality in Neo-Modernist Noir," in *Neo-Noir*, ed. Mark Bould, Katharina Glitre, and Greg Tuck (London: Wallflower, 2009), 33. The effects Miklitsch notes occur, respectively, at (0:25:15) and (0:53:44).
16. Miklitsch, "Audio-Noir," 33. See (0:10:36) and (1:39:28).
17. See Polan, "Politics as Perspective," 117.
18. Helen Hanson, "Paranoia and Nostalgia: Sonic Motifs and Songs in Neo-Noir," in *Neo-Noir*, 44.
19. See Caputo, *Polanski and Perception*, 185 and 187–90. Caputo makes note of this imbalance toward the visual, but derives from this a very different interpretation, in which Jake's epistemological crisis occurs because the investigation "moves from the concrete (actions) to the symbolic (linguistic representation of actions)" and, as a result of this move, visuality alone proves insufficient to establishing knowledge. This

point certainly holds, but it should be also noted that Caputo's discussion of sound only in terms of the symbolic forms of spoken language is quite limiting in a film with such rich sound design.

20. In distinction with classical Hollywood traditions, however, emotionally intense, dialogue-heavy scenes are rarely scored, and the film tends, with only one prominent exception, to refrain from scoring scenes of action or physical violence.
21. For a representative profile of these issues in Goldsmith's career, inclusive of *Chinatown*, see Darby and Du Bois, *American Film Music*, 496–520.
22. Charles Higham, "You May Not Leave the Movie House Singing their Songs, But . . ." *New York Times*, May 5, 1975, p. 119. Reprinted in James Weirzbicki, Nathan Platte, and Colin Roust, eds., *The Routledge Film Music Sourcebook* (New York: Routledge, 2012), 197–200. As the producer of *The Great Gatsby* (1974) and *The Last Tycoon* (1976), Evans was clearly attracted to moody period pieces with a prestige pedigree, reminiscent of "Old Hollywood" glamour, and glossed up with a modestly "artsy" appropriation of European art-house style. In a different version of this study, Evans could easily have represented a key figure in his own right. For the later interview, see Mark Russell and James Young, *Film Music*, Screencraft (Boston: Focal Press, 2000), 62.
23. Russell and Young, *Film Music*, 62.
24. Miklitsch, "Audio-Noir," 34.
25. For example, Miklitsch (34), following Darby and Du Bois (506), thinks that Goldsmith associates Jake with the trumpet, and Evelyn with the harp. More frequent is its generic association as a "love theme" for Jake and Evelyn's relationship (see, for example, Darby and Du Bois, *American Film Music*, 500). By contrast, in a brilliant article that is less about *Chinatown*, per se, than about the theoretical implications of the leitmotif as a semantic act of naming, Giorgio Biancorosso has substantially complicated this picture. See Biancorosso, "Memory and the Leitmotive in Cinema," in *Representations in Western Music*, ed. Joshua S. Walden (Cambridge: Cambridge University Press, 2013), 203–23.
26. It is a bit more complicated: Bachelard wrote two books on Earth, dividing its complexes into images of human agency, or "will," and images of "repose": *Earth and Reveries of Will* (1943) and *Earth and Reveries of Repose* (1948). Also, Bachelard's work on the element of fire can be divided between an earlier book, *The Psychoanalysis of Fire* (1938), and considerably later ones, *The Flame of a Candle* (1961) and the posthumously published *Fragments of a Poetics of Fire* (1988), incomplete at the time of his death in 1962. See bibliography for full references to monographs by Bachelard that are referenced more specifically within this chapter.
27. Examples include Zbigniew Kotowicz, *Gaston Bachelard: A Philosophy of the Surreal* (Edinburgh: Edinburgh University Press, 2016), 92–107. David Macauley has also recently advocated for Bachelard's place in a broader lineage of Continental thought devoted to sensuous imminence. See *Elemental Philosophy: Earth, Air, Fire, and Water as Elemental Ideas*, SUNY Series in Environmental Philosophy and Ethics (Albany: SUNY Press, 2010), especially 293–300. A valuable summary of recently renewed interest in Bachelard can be found in the new introduction to a recently

revised edition of Roche C. Smith, *Gaston Bachelard: Philosopher of Science and Imagination* (originally published Boston: Twayne, 1982), repr. SUNY Series in Contemporary French Thought (Albany: State University of New York Press, 2016), xix–xxix.

28. Examples from film studies include Mark Goodall, who applies Bachelard's poetics of wind to the function of the imaginal in the films of Albert Lamorisse (see "The Three Winds of Albert Lamorisse" *Mise-en-Scène* 3, no. 2 [Winter 2018]: 33–44) and Saige Walton, who draws upon Bachelard's poetics of air to explore the folk horror atmosphere of Robert Eggars's *The VVitch* (2015). See Walton, "Air, Atmosphere, Environment: Film Mood, Folk Horror and *The VVitch*," *Screening the Past* 43 (April 2018): http://www.screeningthepast.com/2018/02/air-atmosphere-environment-film-mood-folk-horror-and-the-vvitch/. Important precedents for engagement with Bachelard in film studies has also emerged from authors working in phenomenology, especially Vivian Sobchack. See "When the Ear Dreams: Dolby Digital and the Imagination of Sound," *Film Quarterly* 58, no. 4 (2005): 2–15. Within musicology and sound studies, Bachelard sightings are even more scarce, with some happy recent exceptions, such as Peter Nelson's study of Bachelardian duration and rhythmic simultaneity, and Chris Tonelli's exploration of aurality and imagined space in early video game music and chiptune. See Nelson, "Cohabiting in Time: Towards an Ecology of Rhythm," *Organised Sound* 16, no. 2 (2011): 109–14, and Tonelli, "The Chiptuning of the World: Game Boys, Imagined Travel, and Musical Meaning," in *The Oxford Handbook of Mobile Music Studies,* vol. 2., ed. Sumanth Gopinath and Jason Stanyek, Oxford Handbooks Online. Online Publication Date: July 2014. doi: 10.1093/oxfordhb/9780199913657.013.016.

29. See Bachelard, *The Poetics of Space*, xxii–xxiv.

30. Mary McAllester Jones, *Gaston Bachelard: Subversive Humanist: Texts and Readings* (Madison: University of Wisconsin Press, 1991), 4.

31. See Kotowicz, *Philosophy of the Surreal*, 13–16; Smith, *Philosopher of Science and Imagination*, 10–12; McAllester Jones, *Subversive Humanist*, 4–6.

32. See McAllester Jones, *Subversive Humanist*, 4, 166–67. John Lechte's profile of Bachelard is characteristically suspicious of "a certain mystical element" in Bachelard that is "a little too Jungian," despite Bachelard's undeniable contributions to later structuralist thought. See Lechte, *Fifty Key Contemporary Thinkers: From Structuralism to Postmodernity* (London: Routledge, 1996), 3–6. In this respect, a sense in which the study of Being is inherently tied up with the integrative pursuit of "well-being," Bachelard's thought indeed bears comparison with that of Carl Jung, a thinker Bachelard claimed to admire, but to have discovered too late for his work to exercise much influence on his own. On Bachelard and Jung, see Smith, *Philsopher of Science and Imagination*, 107–9.

33. In her Bachelardian reading of the element of air as a phenomenon of mood in folk horror, Saige Walton navigates a similar difficulty. See Walton, "Air, Atmosphere, Environment."

34. A valuable exception is a recent article by Miguel Mera on timbre and material hapticity in film music in two Johnny Greenwood scores. Although Mera's focus is

on the experiencing body rather than the dynamic imagination as a subject in itself, there are potentially Bachelardian overtones, for example, in his reading of musical viscosity and the image of oil in *There Will Be Blood*. See "Materializing Film Music," in *The Cambridge Companion to Film Music*, ed. Mervyn Cooke and Fiona Ford (Cambridge: Cambridge University Press, 2016), 157–72.

35. See Eve Kossofsky Sedgwick, "On Paranoid and Reparative Reading, or, You're So Paranoid, You Probably Think This Essay Is about You," in *Touching Feeling: Affect, Pedagogy, Performativity* (Durham, NC: Duke University Press, 2003), 133–36. Sedgwick develops the terms "strong" and "weak theory" primarily from the psychological affect theory of Silvan Tompkins.

36. For example, see Bachelard's reading of the Narcissus myth against the Freudian grain, in which water functions as a sensory reflection that opens up into a sensual extension of the self in an acknowledgment of cosmic beauty. *Water and Dreams*, 20–27.

37. A more apt Bachelardian writing might be found in an earlier work, *Lautréamont* (1939), about the relationship of violence and creation in the proto-surrealist novel *La Chants de Maldoror* (1869), where the metamorphosis of language to create the new is a process of destructive rendering rooted in primal and animalistic instinct and instantaneous violence. Bachelard's desire to explore the positive creative dimension of the imaginary led him away from the topic of violence, despite its shared concern with the creative faculty of the imagination. While Cross's impulsive desire to seize (his progeny, the future) and to nourish Los Angeles by, essentially, sucking it dry might be understood to map, in potentially fascinating ways, onto Bachelard's analysis of the Lautréamontian archetypes of the crab/raptor, or the vampiric octopus, his concern not just with creating, but with *creating the future*, differentiates him from Bachelard's characterization of violence as a primal impulse rooted in durational immediacy. See *Lautrément*, 10–12 (on speed and duration) and 19–26 (on animals and animalism).

38. For example, while there is no exact parallel in Bachelard to *Chinatown*'s images of oceanic violence as semantic excess that can be countered only with paralysis, two images come close—the "Swinburne complex," an agonistic stance of joyous (but also masochistic) physical confrontation with violent water, and the "Xerxes complex," in which this mutual violence is underscored by vengeance and spite, but which (as with Xerxes flogging the Helespont) we might easily read against Bachelard's grain as a gesture of futility and meaninglessness. Bachelard's insistence on reading violent waters in coextensive dialogue with human agency, whether heroic or hateful, clearly gets in the way here. See *Water and Dreams*, 168–71 and 179–83. Another near-parallel might be found in the "Medusa complex" in which the imagination dominated by pessimistic repugnance for matter creates images of mutual paralysis—earth as congealed, rather than dynamic matter. See *Earth and Reveries of Will*, 159–62.

39. On *Young Man with a Horn* as a *noir*-inflected biopic, see Butler, *Jazz Noir*, 71–88.

40. On *Young Man with a Horn* and the trumpet as an archetype of jazz masculinity, see Krin Gabbard, *Jammin' at the Margins: Jazz and the American Cinema* (Chicago: University of Chicago Press, 1996), 67–76 and 138–59. This line of argument resonates with Dana Polan's reading of *Chinatown*, in which the film's move

toward paranoid ineffability overlaps with an incipient "crisis of masculinity" in American film and culture. See Polan, "Politics as Perspective," 119–20.

41. In this way, our inquiry starts to broach into the territory of embodiment that Elizabeth LeGuin has termed "carnal musicology," a relevant mode of expressivity conveyed by the material actuality of instrumental performance. Whereas in LeGuin's work, this expressivity is associated more with the embodied perspective of a performer, here I am extending this to the properties of the instrumental object itself. See Elisabeth Le Guin, *Boccherini's Body: An Essay in Carnal Musicology* (Berkeley: University of California Press, 2006), especially 14–37.

42. It is worth noting that Bachelard also discusses treats liquidity in linguistic and sonic terms (see *Water and Dreams*, 15–16 and 187–95). Here, and in his later emphasis on the aural metaphor of reverberation in *The Poetics of Space*, Bachelard's discussions of sound are promising, but have been less frequently noted, due, perhaps, to his singular focus on literary expression.

43. Bachelard, *Water and Dreams*, 19–20.

44. The combination of muted bell-tone and Latin percussion recurs just prior to this scene, in a transitional sequence as Jake is taken to meet Noah Cross for the first time (1:00:00).

45. According to Jeff Bond's notes on the soundtrack re-release on Intrada, this effect was created by rubbing a rubber ball on the piano strings (Bond, *Music from the Motion Picture "Chinatown,"* 13). While this seems possible, I've not seen this detail corroborated elsewhere. In one interview, Goldsmith seems to be describing this same moment in the cue, but describes it as created by rubbing a ball against a hollow piece of wood (Russell and Young, *Film Music*, 44). In either case, the sound's presence on the soundtrack album also speaks to its conceptualization at the site of music recording rather than sound editing. See the track "The Captive" at (0:01:59) on both the Intrada soundtrack's first disc, which duplicates the content ordering of the 1974 LP release, and the second disc, which reconstructs a complete cue assembly from archival materials.

46. See Bachelard, *Water and Dreams*, 107–8. In this dimension of his writing, Bachelard represents an under-acknowledged predecessor to later phenomenological concerns with embodiment. It is also entirely typical of his work on the elements that associations of the material imagination are not merely frameworks for thinking imaginatively *about* art, culture, or the imagination, but also mutually imbricated in how this imagining actually occurs. A similar dynamic animates Bachelard's understanding of water. While individual art objects, and even individual poets, reward exploration through images of either shallow or deep water, the distinction between shallow and deep water also becomes a model for how the imagination *itself* functions. This duality is central to Bachelard's theoretical sidestepping of the subject–object division: we imagine water, but water is also an image *through which* imagining happens. It is thus, like the image of Chinatown in the film, both "in here" and "out there."

47. In Greek mythology, Deucalion, a son of Prometheus, plays a role analogous to Noah in Genesis. After the flood recedes, Deucalion casts stones which become the human race.

48. On the archival cue assembly produced by Douglass Fake for the Intrada soundtrack album release, the cue does not contain this enormous and uncomfortable gap. The gap seems to have been created by an editorial decision to isolate and repeat the first phrase of Goldsmith's recorded cue in the finished film.
49. Eaton, *Chinatown*, 13–14.
50. For a profile of Polanski that admirably combines empathy for the complexity of his life with ethical clarity regarding the abusive dimension of his actions and character, see Lawrence Weschler, "The Brat's Tale: Roman Polanski," in *Vermeer in Bosnia: Selected Writings* (New York: Vintage Books, 2004), especially 124–31.
51. Biskind, *Easy Riders and Raging Bulls*, 166.
52. Belton, "Language, Oedipus, and *Chinatown*," 949 and 940.
53. The academic humanities have traditionally navigated the topic of paranoia with particular care, for example, empathetically attempting to understand conspiracy theories as strategies of resistance for marginalized groups, while at the same time recognizing their negative cultural effects in radicalized culture and as crude forms of "post-truth" skepticism. Tools for navigating this landscape have most frequently included cultural history (see Peter Knight, *Conspiracy Culture: From the Kennedy Assassination to The X-Files* [London: Routledge, 2000], especially 117–67); and theories of postmodernism (see Saumel Chase Coale, *Paradigms of Paranoia: The Culture of Conspiracy in Contemporary American Fiction* [Tuscaloosa: University of Alabama Press, 2005]). Another unifying focus has been on paranoia as a response to the challenges posed on diverse postwar fronts to the logic of the rational, liberal, individualistic self. See Timothy Melley, *Empire of Conspiracy: The Culture of Paranoia in Postwar America* (Ithaca, NY: Cornell University Press, 2000). These themes overlap in several ways with those of Andreas Killen in his *1973 Nervous Breakdown*, cited in the Introduction. Sedgwick's "Paranoid and Reparative Reading" opened many doors for sophisticated discussions of alternatives to this dominant intellectual style, a critical mode in some ways discomfortingly (and perhaps instructively) similar to the structural worldview of paranoia.
54. Rita Felski, *The Limits of Critique* (Chicago: Chicago University Press: 2015), 9–10 and 35.
55. While ethical engagement in Bachelard's writing is infrequent, recent critics have attempted to explore how the first of these options, a sense of subversive possibility and recuperated intersubjective communication, can be found in Bachelard's thought. See McAllester Jones, *Subversive Humanist*, 168, and Smith, *Philosopher of Science and Imagination*, xxviii.

Chapter 4

1. *The Last Picture Show*, directed by Peter Bogdanovich, Columbia, 1971. CC1965D (Criterion Collection, under license from Sony Pictures Home Entertainment. 2010), DVD. All references are to this transfer of the film.

2. *American Graffiti*, directed by George Lucas, Universal, 1973. High School Reunion Collection 20272 (Universal Pictures Home Entertainment, 2003), DVD. All references are to this transfer of the film.
3. This detail is specifically noted in the published screenplay. See George Lucas, Gloria Katz, and Willard Hyuck, *American Graffiti* (New York: Grove Press, 1973), 172.
4. Michael Long, *Beautiful Monsters: Imagining the Classical in Musical Media* (Berkeley: University of California Press, 2008), 146–55.
5. Detailed readings of music and sound in *American Graffiti* include Jeff Smith, *The Sounds of Commerce: Marketing Popular Film Music* (New York: Columbia University Press, 1998), 172–85; Peter Larsen, *Film Music* (London: Reaktion, 2007), 157–65, Philip Brophy, *100 Modern Soundtracks* (London: BFI, 2004), 20–21, and Michael D. Dwyer, *Back to the Fifties: Nostalgia, Hollywood Film, and Popular Music of the Eighties* (New York: Oxford University Press, 2015), 45–76, especially 64–66 on radio and deejaying.
6. For discussion of the effect of copyright acquisition on the soundtrack of *American Graffiti*, see Marcus Hearn, *The Cinema of George Lucas* (New York: Harry N. Abrams, 2005), 56. See also Jim Smith, *George Lucas* (London: Virgin Books, 2003), 39.
7. David Brackett, "Banjos, Biopics, and Compilation Scores: The Movies Go Country," *American Music* 19, no. 3 (Autumn 2001): 247–90.
8. *The Last Picture Show* was released in monaural sound. Although *American Graffiti* was also released in a four-track stereo mix, it was likely screened far more frequently in prints mixed for playback on monaural equipment. The spatialization I explore throughout this chapter is thus distinct from the spatialization of sound signals in theatrical space made possible by the adoption of stereophonic sound. It is rather an *imagined* sense of spatiality implied to exist within the diegetic world, and in this way acquiring poetic or aesthetic resonance for the viewer.
9. See Julie Hubbert, "'Whatever Happened to Great Movie Music?': *Cinéma Vérité* and Hollywood Film Music of the Early 1970s," *American Music* 21, no. 2 (Summer 2003): 180–213.
10. Other genres intersecting with nostalgia included film noir, such as *The Late Show* (1977); the backstage show business comedy, such as *Hearts of the West* (1975); the musical, such as *That's Entertainment* (1974); and the coming-of-age drama, such as *The Last Picture Show*, *Summer of '42* (1971), and *American Graffiti*.
11. Thomas J. Harris, *Bogdanovich's Picture Shows* (Metuchen, NJ: Scarecrow Press, 1990), 112. See also Alex Simon, "Peter Bogdanovich's Year of the Cat," *Venice Magazine* (April 2002), reprinted in *Peter Bogdanovich: Interviews*, ed. Peter Tonguette, Conversations with Filmmakers (Jackson: University Press of Mississippi, 2015), 151–52.
12. See Dwyer, *Back to the Fifties*, 4–12. Dwyer is refreshingly aware both of the role of neo-conservatism within this discourse, and of the need to extend discussions of fifties nostalgia beyond (frequently reductive) associations with Reaganite politics.
13. The exception to this statement may be the way in which *American Graffiti* broadly emulates narrative tropes familiar from teenager films of the fifties, such as *Rebel Without a Cause* (1955).

14. Paul Monaco, *The Sixties: 1960-1969* (Berkeley: University of California Press, 2001), 41-44.
15. On the relationship between personal and cultural memory and the potential for their overlapping in the form of "prosthetic memory," see Alison Landsberg, "Prosthetic Memory: The Ethics and Politics of Memory in an Age of Mass Culture," in *Memory and Popular Film*, ed. Paul Grainge (Manchester: Manchester University Press, 2003), 144-61.
16. Brackett, "Banjos, Biopics, and Compilation Scores," 255-56.
17. Brackett, "Banjos, Biopics, and Compilation Scores," 256.
18. The Bogdanovich Papers at the Lilly Library contain a considerable amount of preproduction documentation related to the music, clearly showing that accurate dating was a strong and early consideration in preproduction. As early as October 1970, the month in which shooting began, Bogdanovich's production company was acquiring Billboard records and numerous recordings, whittling down the selections based upon dating, aesthetic preference, and issues related to copyright clearance. Bogdanovich mss., 1885-1994. Collection No. LMC1115, Lilly Library at Indiana University, Bloomington.
19. The issue of the dating of film materials, on the other hand, perhaps reflects a savvy awareness of the far more gradual patterns of film distribution in the early fifties. A small town such as Anarene would have been exhibiting films well after their release date.
20. In general, but with occasional exception—such as the jukebox in Genevieve's restaurant—the scenes set among the wealthy characters are more likely to feature media in which the user controls the selection of music. We can always turn a radio off; however, while it is on and tuned to a particular channel, we abdicate control over the flow of the music.
21. *The Last Picture Show* does demonstrate this strategy frequently, never more so than in the film's conclusion, where Sonny and Ruth, his spurned lover, come to terms with the pain of Billy's accidental death and their failed relationship against the aural backdrop of a comedy record, complete with laugh track (1:58:30). On anempathetic music, see Claudia Gorbman, *Unheard Melodies: Narrative Film Music* (London: BFI; Bloomington: Indiana University Press, 1987), 159-61.
22. Giorgio Biancorosso, "Film, Music, and the Redemption of the Mundane," in *Bad Music: The Music We Love to Hate*, ed. Christopher Washburne and Maiken Derno (New York: Routledge, 2004), 190-211.
23. The Beach Boys represent one of the only cases in the film in which characters discuss the near-omnipresent music: younger Carol argues with older John about the group while "Surfin' Safari" plays on the radio. John hates "that surfing shit," and maintains that rock and roll has been "going downhill since Buddy Holly died." This gesture marks the Beach Boys as the music of the future, and John—who, the end credits tell us, will die in 1964—as the remnant of a lost past of early rock authenticity.
24. Bob Smith didn't begin to broadcast as his Wolfman persona until late 1963. See Wolfman Jack and Byron Laursen, *Have Mercy! Confessions of the Original Rock 'N'*

Roll Animal (New York: Warner Books, 1995), 114–19 and 142–44. See also Smith, *The Sounds of Commerce*, 177, and 264 n. 50.

25. On border blasting and AM listening, see Dwyer, *Back to the Fifties*, 65. On the science and imaginal atmospherics of AM listening, see Susan Douglas, *Listening In: Radio and the American Imagination* (New York: Random House, 1999), 37–38.

26. Douglas, *Listening In*, 145–55.

27. Ken Barnes, "Top 40 Radio: A Fragment of the Imagination," in *Facing the Music: Essays on Pop, Rock and Culture*, ed. Simon Frith (London: Mandarin, 1990), 12. Barnes describes a complicated feedback mechanism in the early sixties, in which DJs' desire to *discover* the next big hits of the Top 40 led to extremely varied programming. This would be discouraged both by the "Drake format" in the mid-sixties (emphasizing repetition not just of a literal "Top 40," but of a very small batch of top-ranking hits) and by the eventual fragmentation into niche formatting in the seventies.

28. The irony of this reading, of course, is that "classic rock," thus broadly defined, would become its own radio-ready strategy of homogenization by the end of the decade, a process that the soundtrack of *American Graffiti* and the generational thinking it represented and catered to, arguably helped to accelerate.

29. Simon Reynolds, *Retromania: Pop Culture's Addiction to Its Own Past* (New York: Faber and Faber, 2011), 276–94.

30. This is particularly problematic in cultural histories of the era as a whole, which tend toward broader, less nuanced readings of *American Graffiti* as symptomatic of cultural regression. See, for example Reynolds, *Retromania*, 292–94. See also Andreas Killen, *1973 Nervous Breakdown: Watergate, Warhol, and the Birth of Post-Sixties America* (New York: Bloomsbury, 2006), 178–85.

31. The polarity Boym establishes for this positive/negative act of recuperation is between "restorative" and "reflective" nostalgia. See Svetlana Boym, *The Future of Nostalgia* (New York: Basic Books, 2001), 41–55. This admittedly reduces the complexity of Boym's argument significantly, but does not, I think, misrepresent its larger shape. As her essay on *Jurassic Park* (1993) amply demonstrates (33–39), the richness of Boym's reflective nostalgia seems to be withheld, on her terms, from *any* pop-cultural text. Despite the imaginative power of this remarkable book, this represents a considerable flaw in its scope.

32. Giorgio Biancorosso, "Where Does the Music Come From? Studies in the Aesthetics of Film Music" (Ph.D. dissertation, Princeton, 2002), 53–57. What Biancorosso explores in the language of phenomenology, I am interested in exploring through hermeneutics, as well as what might be best and most simply termed "magic." In all cases, what is at stake is the impressionistic "reality" of subjective images, regardless of whether the phenomena that produce them are in fact objectively or materially "real." Films such as *American Graffiti*, I would argue, thus encourage and instrumentalize a magical engagement with art, reality, and belief.

33. Benedict Anderson, *Imagined Communities: Reflections on the Origin and Spread of Nationalism* (London: Verso, 1983).

34. See, for example (0:10:10), (0:26:15), (0:43:40), and (1:24:50).

35. The original source of this quotation is Herb Caen, a columnist for the *San Francisco Chronicle*, writing during the "nostalgia boom" (April 14, 1975), quoted in Fred Davis, *Yearning For Yesterday: A Sociology of Nostalgia* (New York: Free Press, 1979), 19. The turn of phrase, however, has been thoroughly absorbed and paraphrased by numerous critics. Inverting the image, for example, Fredric Jameson has stated that "history is what hurts" ("On Interpretation: Literature as a Socially Symbolic Act," in *The Jameson Reader*, 56). Thus, Jameson characterizes history as that which is resistant to reification, as a nebulous entity not directly tangible, but perceptible only through a sense of "necessity" that "refuses desire and sets inexorable limits to individual and collective practice." History thus ethically anchors us to reality, dialectically counterbalanced against another perpetually deflected construction, namely that of Utopia. On Jameson's role in the reception history of *American Graffiti*, see Dwyer, *Back to the Fifties*, 52–55.
36. On the word's etymology and translation history, see Boym, *The Future of Nostalgia*, 12–13.
37. This is, I would argue, categorically distinct from what Boym describes as "restorative" nostalgia—a politically regressive attempt to recreate a lost past in the present—which she counterpoints with "reflective" nostalgia, which dwells upon the impossibility of recapturing the past, and the impermanence or the instability of memory and time. While critiques of *American Graffiti* tend to align it, implicitly, with restorative nostalgia, I view it as a substantial misreading that the film articulates a desire to actually *return to* the pre-countercultural early sixties. See Boym, *The Future of Nostalgia*, xviii. Michael Dwyer, in *Back to the Fifties*, also contests this reading.
38. Interestingly, the voice of a radio deejay is periodically present in *The Last Picture Show*, voiced by Bogdanovich himself. The closest this voice comes to fulfilling a function comparable to Wolfman Jack, however, is at one point when he draws the audience's attention specifically to the two different versions of "Cold, Cold Heart," rendering explicit the division between pop and country that will be important throughout the film. With an early background in theater and with his striking skill as a vocal mimic, this is a role that Bogdanovich apparently relishes. He points out on the commentary track from the Criterion Collection DVD of *The Last Picture Show* that he "does the deejaying in all [his] movies" (0:02:30).
39. On racial ventriloquism and deejay performance as a cultural aspect of radio listening in this era, see Douglas, *Listening In*, 222–23 and 240–46.
40. Lucas, Katz, and Huyck, *American Graffiti*, 7.
41. This trailer is available as a feature on the DVD cited previously. For an analysis of *American Graffiti*'s paratextual advertisements as nostalgic addresses to the viewer, see Dwyer, *Back to the Fifties*, 66–71.
42. Lucas, Katz, and Huyck, *American Graffiti*, 4.
43. See Jameson, "Postmodernism, or the Cultural Logic of Late Capitalism," especially 203–5.
44. While we should be attentive to the reality that *American Graffiti* is contextually embedded (i.e., as an object from and for the film culture of 1973), I would argue that we should not allow ourselves to be limited by this reality. *American Graffiti* might

NOTES   223

easily continue to perform this imaginal role, albeit in "prosthetic" form, for the contemporary nostalgic subject despite their spatiotemporal or cultural location. To ignore this possibility is to risk adopting a culturist viewpoint reductively inattentive to the role of the imagination.

45. Hubbert, "Whatever Happened to Great Movie Music."
46. Jeff Smith discusses this "death motif" in connection with its role in popular songs of the period, as well as its associations with a societal loss of innocence following the Kennedy assassination in 1963 and the conflicts of the later sixties. See Smith, *The Sounds of Commerce*, 178–79.
47. In the world of *American Graffiti*, when sexual anxiety and aggression are present, they tend to be emphasized by music, but sometimes with musical irony—as when, for example, Curt witnesses his "cool" teacher, Mr. Wolfe, have a tense, mostly inaudible discussion with a student who is implied to be his lover while the live band from the sock-hop cheerfully seeps into the background. In another scene, the radio continues to play along as Steve attempts to emotionally manipulate Laurie into having sex with him, but—unfortunately—this scene may well have been intended to play as comic or empathetic with Steve's perspective, rather than as coercive.
48. A characteristic review along these lines is Vincent Canby's. See Vincent Canby, "A Lovely 'Last Picture Show,'" *New York Times*, October 17, 1971, https://www.nytimes.com/1971/10/17/archives/a-lovely-last-picture-show-a-lovely-show.html. Interestingly, Andrew Sarris and Pauline Kael, like Canby, both also took advantage of the nearby release of Dennis Hopper's *echt*-modernist cinematic parable *The Last Movie* to compare Hopper's showy self-reflexivity with Bogdanovich's restraint, although Sarris, in particular, was reserved about the effectiveness of this comparison. See Sarris, "Films in Focus," *The Village Voice*, October 14, 1971. Archived online at https://www.villagevoice.com/2011/01/06/peter-bogdanovich-entitled-to-gloat-for-the-last-picture-show/. Accessed November 13, 2020.
49. Stephen Farber discusses the growing divide between critical praise for the film's technical achievements and critical discomfort with its nostalgia for the fifties in Stephen Farber, "George Lucas: The Stinky Kid Hits the Bigtime," originally published in *Film Quarterly* 27.3 (Spring 1974): 2–9, reprinted in *George Lucas: Interviews*, ed. Sally Kline, Conversations with Filmmakers (Jackson: University Press of Mississippi, 1999), 41–42.
50. See Michael Pye and Lynda Myles, *The Movie Brats: How the Film Generation Took Over Hollywood* (New York: Holt, Rinehart, and Winston, 1979).
51. A good summary of the impact of vertical and horizontal industrial models and their impact on New Hollywood sound aesthetics is Whittington, *Sound Design and Science Fiction* (Austin: University of Texas Press, 2007), 32–33.
52. See Davis, *Yearning for Yesterday*, 86–90. Davis notes a trend of nostalgia in cinema, but is generally dismissive of such films, with the exception of *The Last Picture Show*, which he admires for its "antique" look. Davis's rationale for dismissing much of this cinema is interestingly akin to the reason that I am interested in it—a "hypernaturalism" that, for Davis, fails to adequately convey the ideally metaphorical richness of nostalgic experience. While the issue of the "antique look" of *The Last*

Picture Show simplifies matters of film style far more than he seems to recognize, Davis's identification of both naturalism and stylization as factors that inflect nostalgia is nuanced in a way that escaped many film critics at the time.
53. See Brackett, "Banjos, Biopics, and Compilation Scores," especially 254 and 273.
54. Quotes here are taken from an original release trailer and a trailer for a 1974 re-release, both of which may be found on the Criterion Collection DVD cited throughout.
55. This connection is particularly strong, given Bogdanovich's dedication to the work of director John Ford, whose early-to-mid-sixties Westerns (such as *The Man Who Shot Liberty Valance*) are key texts in the "twilight Western" subgenre. Ford also regularly cast a younger Ben Johnson, who, in a referential turn, was cast by Bogdanovich as Sam the Lion. See J. Hoberman, *The Dream Life: Movies, Media, and Mythology of the Sixties* (New York: The New Press, 2003), 105–7.
56. Peter Bogdanovich, commentary track for Criterion Edition DVD (1:48:50).
57. Michael Dempsey, "American Graffiti," *Film Quarterly* 27, no. 1 (Autumn 1973): 58–60. Similar is Lucas's assertion (in Farber, "Stinky Kid Hits the Bigtime") that the film "argues" the perspective of Curt as the path of inevitability, representing the progressive need to leave the fifties behind. More recently David Shumway has attempted to locate the film within a spectrum that distinguishes reactionary nostalgia from its redeemably progressive variants. See David Shumway, "Rock 'n' Roll Soundtracks and the Production of Nostalgia," *Cinema Journal* 38, no. 2 (Winter 1999): 36–51.
58. See Douglas, *Listening In*, 22–34.
59. Douglas briefly addresses the disciplinary tendency toward (and impulsive reaction against) Romantic nostalgia. See ibid., 6–7. By contrast, Gerald Nachman, *Raised on Radio* (New York: Pantheon Books, 1998), is an example of an excellent, historically rigorous survey that nevertheless openly embraces and practices its own nostalgia.

Chapter 5

1. The music, a moderately paced waltz in E-flat minor, alludes in particular to the gestural shape and harmonic piquancy of the sixth movement of Satie's *Trois morceaux en forme du poire*, used extensively later in the film.
2. Chion, *The Thin Red Line*, BFI Modern Classics (London: BFI, 2004), 43–45.
3. All timings refer to *Badlands*, Warner Bros., 1973 CC2244BD (Criterion Collection, 2013), DVD.
4. The most representative published edition documenting the *Schulwerk* is the series *Musik für Kinder* (1950–1954, 5 vols.), with individual volumes referred to and cited in the following. Tipton's source for the *Schulwerk* material was almost certainly the series of sound recordings on the Harmonia Mundi label, collectively entitled *Musica Poetica* (1963–1975).
5. Other, less central musical elements include two prominent selections of compiled period music: "Love is Strange" (1956), performed by Mickey and Sylvia; "A Blossom Fell" (1955), performed by Nat King Cole. Also used in the film is an instrumental

version of the James Taylor song "Migration," credited in *Badlands* as "Migration Theme," and later released on the 1974 album *Walking Man*.
6. Michel Ciment, "Interview with Terrence Malick," *Postif* 170 (June 1975): 30–34, reprinted in Lloyd Michaels, *Terrence Malick* (Urbana: University of Illinois Press, 2009), 110. The *Musica Poetica* recordings were examined from their recently compiled re-release: Carl Orff and Gunild Keetman, *Musica Poetica: The Orff-Schulwerk*, Catalogue No. 88843064192 (RCA Victor Red Seal; Sony Music, 2014), six CDs.
7. Ciment, Interview with Terrence Malick, 111.
8. James Morrison and Thomas Schur, *The Films of Terrence Malick* (Westport, CT: Praeger, 2003), 9–10.
9. Steven Rybin, *Terrence Malick and the Thought of Film* (Lanham, MD: Lexington Books, 2012), xxx–xxxi.
10. John Orr, *Contemporary Cinema* (Edinburgh: Edinburgh University Press, 1998), 5. Orr's use of the concept of a "Cinema of Poetry" is derived and extended from the theoretical writings of filmmaker Pier Paolo Pasolini.
11. Steven Rybin also locates the film medium's inherent, ontological association with pastness as central to the philosophical resonance of Malick's work, which he ties to the nostalgic resonance of film in an increasingly digital age. See Rybin, *Terrence Malick and the Thought of Film*, xvii–xviii.
12. See Daniel Frampton, *Filmosophy* (London: Wallflower, 2006), 73–76.
13. Orr's perspective regarding film reality (or using a later term, a "film world") is not oriented toward the indexical qualities that are key to Bazinian realism, but instead toward Pasolini's adoption of the concept of Heideggerian *Mitsein*, which conveys a quality of "being-with-others" that might be understood as something like an objectivity engendered by the necessity of intersubjective engagement. See Orr, *Contemporary Cinema*, 11–12.
14. Orr, *Contemporary Cinema*, 169. Orr thus differentiates between the Cinema of Poetry and a mythic cinema. His use of the term "myth," however, largely differs from the sense in which the present study has explored it (as an experiential, affective state), understanding it instead as a type of 25narrative.
15. Morrison and Schur use this evocative phrase as the title of a section of their monograph on *Badlands*. See Morrison and Schur, *Films of Terrence Malick*, 8–23, especially 18.
16. Tipton's film and television credits were fewer, but it is worth mentioning some highlights. Tipton did the arrangements of Krystof Komeda's original music for *Rosemary's Baby* (1968), and provided additional underscoring, alongside his own song arrangements, to an animated made-for-television movie based on the Harry Nilsson album *The Point* (1970). Tipton also composed the theme song and underscoring for the popular television series *Soap* (1977–1981).
17. In addition to the pseudo-Satie opening cue discussed previously, an "Orffian" cue early in the film weaves together Tipton's original music with Keetman's "Music for a Puppet Play" (0:10:20 and 0:12:11). Primary documentation of Tipton and Malick's process is not extant, and recollections by various filmmakers are occasionally contradictory regarding the degree to which the final soundtrack was arranged

and re-recorded by Tipton, as opposed to directly using the original *Musica Poetica* recordings. Billy Weber, for example, recalled the *Musica Poetica* recordings being used directly in the film, whereas Tipton's recollections focus more upon the need to "reproduce and rerecord . . . or simply transcribe" Orff's music. See Interview with Billy Weber, on *Badlands*, Criterion DVD, 0:13:00, and Tipton, quoted in Carlo Hinterman and Daniele Villa, eds., *Terrence Malick: Rehearsing the Unexpected* (London: Faber and Faber, 2015), 70–71.

18. Claudia Gorbman, "Auteur Music," in *Beyond the Soundtrack: Representing Music in Cinema*, ed. Daniel Goldmark, Lawrence Kramer, and Richard Leppert (Berkeley: University of California Press, 2007), 149.

19. James Wierzbicki, *Terrence Malick: Sonic Style*, Routledge Focus: Filmmakers and Their Soundtracks (New York: Routledge, 2019), 83–88.

20. John Rhym, "The Paradigmatic Shift in the Critical Reception of Terrence Malick's *Badlands* and the Emergence of a Heideggerian Cinema," *Quarterly Review of Film and Video* 27, no. 4 (2010): 255–66.

21. Morrison and Schur, *Films of Terrence Malick*, 13–15, 97–101. See also Marc Furstenau and Leslie MacAvoy, "Terrence Malick's Heideggerian Cinema: War and the Question of Being in *The Thin Red Line*," in *The Cinema of Terrence Malick: Poetic Visions of America*, 2nd ed., ed. Hannah Patterson (London: Wallflower, 2007), 179–91.

22. See Stanley Cavell, *The World Viewed: Reflections on the Ontology of Film*, 2nd ed. (Cambridge, MA: Harvard University Press, 1979), especially xiv–xvii.

23. On Heidegger's categories of "earth" and "world," see Steven Rybin, "Voicing Meaning: Terrence Malick's Characters," in *Terrence Malick: Film and Philosophy*, ed. Stuart Kendall and Thomas Deane Tucker (London: Continuum, 2011), especially 19–23.

24. Michel Chion has explored this final monologue (or perhaps prayer) and its implication for Malick's approach to language. See Chion, *The Thin Red Line*, 50–53. On Malick and immanence, see John Caruana and Mark Cauchi, "What Is Postsecular Cinema? An Introduction," in *Immanent Frames: Postsecular Cinema between Malick and von Trier*, ed. John Caruana and Mark Cauchi (Albany: State University of New York Press, 2018), 1–28, especially 4–7.

25. Cavell, *The World Viewed*, 2nd ed., xvi.

26. Charles O'Brien, *Transactions with the World: Ecocriticism and the Environmental Sensibility of New Hollywood* (New York: Berghahn, 2016), especially xiii–xiv and 69–71. O'Brien's broader focus on pro-filmic materiality, and its ability to "resist" abstraction into symbolic signification, is particularly relevant here, in that O'Brien thus approaches the film's human *and* non-human objects as potential philosophical agents. His engagement with *Badlands*, however, focuses instead on the intrusive quality of human self-consciousness and violence as points of eco-critical tension discomfortingly lodged within the film's pastoral emphasis on beauty.

27. Among these, production designer Jack Fisk has described the surreal assortment of random objects that litter Cato's cabin and the stereopticon images that Holly looks at in a key scene as chance finds, rather than compositionally crafted details. Quoted in Carlos Hintermann and Daniele Villa, eds., *Rehearsing the Unexpected*, 52–54 and 65.

28. Rybin, *Terrence Malick and the Thought of Film*, xiv–xvi.
29. Frampton, *Filmosophy*, 51. On the relationship between theory, philosophy, and poetics within the methodology of film analysis and interpretation, see also 98–102 and 183–203.
30. See Gunild Keetman, *Elementaria: First Acquaintance with Orff-Schulwerk*, trans. Margaret Murray, introduction by Werner Thomas (London: Schott, 1974), 107.
31. See especially Beth Landis and Polly Carder, *The Eclectic Curriculum in American Music Education: Contributions of Dalcrose, Kodaly, and Orff* (Washington, DC: Music Educators National Conference, 1972), 72, 82, and 105–6.
32. Werner Thomas, Introduction to Keetman, *Elementaria*, 12.
33. Keetman, *Elementaria*, 24–25.
34. On improvisation and completion play see *Elementaria*, 88–93. Also: "working with Schulwerk does not entail the study and performance of melodies and songs with ready-made accompaniments, but rather a continuous *ars inveniendi*, a spontaneous art of discovery with a hundred ways and a thousand possible structures" (Thomas, Introduction to *Elementaria*, 13.
35. Keetman, *Elementaria*, 107–10.
36. An interesting parallel to the present approach to embodiment, music, and philosophy might be found in Vivian Sobchack's reading of existential contingency in Polish director Krzysztof Kieslowski's *Dekalog* (1988). Although Sobchack's approach derives from the predominantly visualist phenomenology of Maurice Merleau-Ponty, she briefly discusses Kieslowski's sound design (102–3) and his metaphysical approach to materiality (91–92) in ways that resonate with the present discussion of Malick. See "The Expanded Gaze in Contracted Space: Happenstance, Hazard, and the Flesh of the World," in *Carnal Thoughts: Embodiment and Moving Image Culture* (Berkeley: University of California Press, 2004), 85–108. On materiality and the haptics of film music, see Miguel Mera, "Materializing Film Music," in *The Cambridge Companion to Film Music* (Cambridge: Cambridge University Press, 2016), 157–72.
37. Billy Weber recalled Malick's motivation for using Orff and Keetman's music as being specifically associated with the fact that it was music "for children" (Criterion interview, 0:12:30)
38. For the published score, see Carl Orff and Gunild Keetman, *Musik für Kinder*, v. 3: "Dur: Dominanten," (Mainz: B. Schott's Söhne, c. 1952), 52–59.
39. Jennifer Bleek, "Terrence Malicks Spielfilmdebüt Badlands und die Musik von Carl Orff: Interferenzen visueller und klanglicher Materialität und ihre signifikative Funktion im Film," *Kieler Beiträge zur Filmmusikforschung* 2 (2008): 32–33 and 39.
40. Henrik Gustafsson, *Out of Site: Landscape and Cultural Reflexivity in New Hollywood Cinema, 1969–1974*, originally published as a dissertation, State University of Stockholm, Department of Cinema Studies, 2007 (Saarbrücken: VDM Verlag Dr. Muller Aktiengesellschaft, 2008), 125.
41. Hermann Regner, "A Wealth of Good, Stimulating, Movement-Inducing Music: Gunild Keetman: *Pieces for Recorder and Drum*—An Attempt at Better Acquaintance," in *Gunild Keetman: Ein Leben für Musik und Bewegung*, ed. Hermann Regnar and Minna Ronnefeld (Mainz: Schott, 2004), 162–77, 176.

42. For further discussion of play as a figure in Malick's films, see Chion, *The Thin Red Line*, 45–48.
43. This ordering of movements requires following the music objectively, rather than taking Satie's notation at face value. The third sequential movement is actually labeled as the first movement, following two prologues ("Manière de commencement" and "Prolongation du même") and the sixth movement is the first of two epilogues ("En plus" and "Redite"). Thus, with Satie's typically absurd humor, a work titled "Three Pieces" actually has seven movements. On the suite's compositional and publication history, see the entry in Robert Orledge's recent catalogue of works, in Caroline Potter, ed., *Erik Satie: Music, Art, and Literature* (Farnham, Surrey: Ashgate, 2013), 270–71.
44. The gesture in question, excised from Tipton's arrangement, appears in the original third movement at mm. 11, 17, and 21. All references to Satie's score in the following are to its reprint in Erik Satie, *Gymnopédies, Gnossiennes, and Other Works for Piano* (New York: Dover, 1989). To the best of my knowledge, production materials for Tipton's arrangements of the suite are not extant.
45. Billy Weber recalled that, in contrast to the *Musica Poetica* recordings, which had been decided upon very early in preproduction, Satie only found a place in the score gradually, after experimenting with several options in the editing room. See Hintermann and Villa, eds., *Rehearsing the Unexpected*, 70.
46. See, for example, Matthew Mendez, "History, Homeopathy, and the Spiritual Impuse in the Post-war Reception of Satie: Cage, Higgins, Beuys," in Potter, ed., *Erik Satie: Music, Art, and Literature*, 183–228.
47. On a rich, still under-explored intersection between Malick, New Age culture, and sound, see Morrison and Schur on Malick's engagement (in the production of *Days of Heaven*) with Syntonic Research Incorporated, producers of ambient and "psychoacoustic" sound recordings. Morrison and Schur, 82–84.
48. Ann-Marie Hanlon, "Satie and the Meaning of the Comic," in Potter, ed., *Erik Satie: Music, Art, and Literature*, 40–42.
49. Julie A. Brown, *Bartok and the Grotesque: Studies in Modernity, the Body, and Contradiction in Music* (Aldershot, UK: Ashgate, 2007), 10; quoted in Hanlon, "Satie and the Meaning of the Comic," 41–42, n. 85.
50. On post-secular spirituality in Malick's films, see several of the essays collected in John Caruana and Mark Cauchi, eds., *Immanent Frames: Postsecular Cinema between Malick and von Trier* (Albany: State University of New York Press, 2018).
51. Beverly Walker, "Malick on *Badlands*," *Sight and Sound* 44, no. 2 (Spring 1975), reprinted in Michaels, *Terrence Malick*, 105.
52. Paul Maher, Jr., *All things Shining: An Oral History of the Films of Terrence Malick*, 4th ed. (self-pub., 2017), 70–71.
53. Chion, *Thin Red Line*, 53–57.
54. Walker, "Malick on *Badlands*," reprinted in Michaels, *Terrence Malick*, 104.
55. My use of the term "gnosis," here, is modeled upon disciplinary currents within religious studies, in which the term is applicable to ineffable experiential insight that supersedes the binary of reason and faith, a category prevalent in numerous esoteric spiritual traditions, and which in this usage extends beyond the diverse, yet

historically specific religious movements of the late classical and early Christian world that the term originally designated. See Jeffrey Kripal, *The Serpent's Kiss: Gnostic Reflections on the Study of Religion* (Chicago: University of Chicago Press, 2007), 4–14. Musicologists, however, may be more familiar with Carolyn Abbate's contrast of "drastic" and "gnostic," in which the term is used with precisely the opposite signification, "gnostic" representing knowledge as rational discourse in contrast to "drastic" embodied insight. Churton's placement of Satie, as well as Claude Debussy, within a *Belle Époque* occult milieu is illuminating, even if his attempt at an empathetically emic occult interpretation of Satie's music, which draws heavily upon numerology, is perhaps less convincing. See Tobias Churton, *Occult Paris: The Lost Magic of the Belle Époque* (Rochester, VT: Inner Traditions, 2016), 327–38. Interestingly, Churton briefly suggests the possibility of using of Satie as "gnostic" film music, in reference to the Hal Ashby film *Being There* (1979).
56. Weber's description indeed seems plausible to my ears, here, as the non-vocal elements of the cue sound identical to the *Musica Poetica* recording, with both elaborating the notated score from *Musik für Kinder* with harp, as well as additional soprano flutes doubling the soprano glockenspiel parts. Inasmuch as a German text can, to some extent, be discerned beneath Tipton's re-recording process, it follows the ordering of verses on the *Musica Poetica* recording. Listening closely to the muddy sound mix, however, it sounds as if, rather than an English translation, Tipton may have actually added a wordless vocalise in unison with the original melody, which is somewhat different from Billy Weber's recollection. For the score, see Orff, *Musik für Kinder*, v. 4, "Moll: Bordun-Stufen" (Mainz: B. Schott's Söhne, 1953), 99.
57. Billy Weber interview, Criterion DVD (0:13:30).
58. See Rhym, *The Paradigmatic Shift*, 261–62. Andreas Tauber, a philosopher familiar with Malick during his time as an academic, has also spoken to Malick's difficult relationship with analytical philosopher Gilbert Ryle and Oxford University's "house style" of "ordinary language philosophy," which Tauber characterized as a "deflationary tool, a method of weaning people away from weighty metaphysical views." Quoted in Maher, ed., *All Things Shining*, 57.
59. Frampton, *Filmosophy*, 120–22.
60. Daniel Yacavone, *Film Worlds: A Philosophical Aesthetics of Cinema* (New York: Columbia University Press, 2015), 11–15.
61. Although he favors the elimination of Frampton's placeholder "being" that thinks and feels the substance of film, Yacavone's application of "global" or "cineaesthetic world-feeling" as a form of symbolic exemplification that extends beyond the local affective gesture perhaps comes closest to the "animistic" turn I'm hypothesizing here. See Yacavone 53–54, 169–71, and 169–201. Also, as Yacavone's theoretical apparatus is far more open to auteurism, this strand of vocal animism in *Badlands* might be understood as what Yacavone calls a "world-marker" (see Yacavone, *Film Worlds*, 149–55), a fluid expressive figure associated with a larger "world" that we might define as "Malickean."

62. Johann Wolfgan von Goethe, *Goethe's* Faust: *The Original German and a New Translation and Introduction by Walter Kaufmann. Part One and Sections of Part Two* (New York: Anchor Books, 1963), 452–55.
63. Hintermann and Villa, eds., *Rehearsing the Unexpected*, 71–72. Tipton's hesitation regarding copyright is curious, as the lyrics, from the original German text of *Faust*, had long been in the public domain, and any copyright concern regarding their musical setting would have been an issue separate from the text. In this light, the end credits of *Badlands* handle copyright rather unusually, acknowledging the *Musica Poetica* recordings by title, but with no actual copyright holder acknowledged for the sound recording, nor for the compositions themselves. This may have been viewed as unnecessary, perhaps if the *Harmonia Mundi* recordings were understood to fall into the cracks of international compliance and, in any case, if they were understood to have been significantly transformed by Tipton.
64. Michaels, *Terrence Malick*, 33.
65. I remain somewhat unsure about the words here. While "am" in the second two lines of the couplet makes the most conceptual sense and parallels the role of Goethe's four women as archetypal embodiments in the original text, the pronunciation sounds a bit more like "send," a substitution that opens up far more interpretive questions than it answers.
66. Bleek, "Terrence Malicks Spielfilmdebüt," 36–37.
67. On postmodern irony and Malick's refusal to condescend to his characters' sincerity and naiveté, see Morrison and Schur, *The Films of Terrence Malick*, 10. See also Michaels, *Terrence Malick*, 4–5 and 38.
68. Rybin, *Terrence Malick and the Thought of Film*, xviii.
69. Rybin, *Terrence Malick and the Thought of Film*, 25–26.
70. In Malick's most recent trilogy of films with autobiographical overtones, all of which are set in the contemporary present, this formulation might be reframed as a broader struggle against the *contemporary world* (and perhaps also a divided or fractured *self*) that similarly inscribes such limitations into its realization.
71. Robert Sinnerbrink, *Terrence Malick: Filmmaker and Philosopher*, Philosophical Filmmakers (London: Bloomsbury, 2019), 15–16.
72. See Yacavone, *Film Worlds*, 137–38 and 196–201.
73. Cavell, *The World Viewed*, xvi. The actual quotation here paraphrased: "Then if in relation to objects capable of such self-manifestation human beings are reduced in significance, or crushed by the fact of beauty left vacant, perhaps this is because in trying to take dominion over the world, or in aestheticizing it (temptations inherent in the making of film, or of any art), they are refusing their participation with it."
74. Chion, *The Thin Red Line*, 30.

Bibliography

Altman, Rick. *The American Film Musical*. Bloomington: Indiana University Press, 1987.
American Graffiti. Directed by George Lucas. Universal, 1973. High School Reunion Collection. Universal Pictures Home Entertainment, 2003. DVD.
Anderson, Benedict. *Imagined Communities: Reflections on the Origin and Spread of Nationalism*. London: Verso, 1983.
Andrew, Dudley. *The Major Film Theories: An Introduction*. London: Oxford University Press, 1976.
Andrew, Dudley, and Hervé Joubert-Laurencin, eds. *Opening Bazin: Postwar Film Theory and Its Afterlife*. New York: Oxford University Press, 2011.
Baby, Yvonne. "Violent Times." In *Arthur Penn: Interviews*, edited by Michael Chaiken and Paul Cronin, 12–14. Originally published in *Le Monde* (January 26, 1969). Jackson: University Press of Mississippi, 2008.
Bachelard, Gaston. *Earth and Reveries of Will: An Essay on the Imagination of Matter* [1943]. Translated by Kenneth Haltman. The Bachelard Translations. The Dallas Institute of Humanities and Culture. Dallas: Dallas Institute Publications, 2002.
Bachelard, Gaston. *Lautréamont* [1939]. Translated by Robert S. Dupree. The Bachelard Translations. The Dallas Institute of Humanities and Culture. Dallas: Dallas Institute Publications, 1986.
Bachelard, Gaston. *The Poetics of Space* [1958]. Translated by Maria Jolas [1964]. Foreword by John R. Stilgoe. Boston: Beacon Press, 1994.
Bachelard, Gaston. *Water and Dreams: An Essay on the Imagination of Matter* [1942]. Translated by Edith R. Farrell. The Dallas Institute of Humanities and Culture. Dallas: Pegasus Foundation, 1983.
Badlands. Directed by Terrence Malick. Warner Bros., 1973. Criterion Collection, 2013. DVD.
Balio, Tino. *The Foreign Film Renaissance on American Screens, 1946–1973*. Madison: University of Wisconsin Press, 2010.
Barnes, Ken. "Top 40 Radio: A Fragment of the Imagination." In *Facing the Music: Essays on Pop, Rock and Culture*, edited by Simon Frith, 8–49. London: Mandarin, 1990.
Barthes, Roland. *Camera Lucida: Reflections on Photography*. Translated by Richard Howard. New York: Hill and Wang, 1981.
Bazin, André. "The Ontology of the Photographic Image." In *What Is Cinema?* Translated by Hugh Gray, 9–16. Berkeley: University of California Press, 1967.
Beck, Jay. *Designing Sound: Audiovisual Aesthetics in 1970s American Cinema*. New Brunswick, NJ: Routledge, 2016.
Belgrad, Daniel. *The Culture of Spontaneity: Improvisation and the Arts in Post-War America*. Chicago: University of Chicago Press, 1999.
Belton, John. "1950s Magnetic Sound: The Frozen Revolution." In *Sound Theory, Sound Practice*, edited by Rick Altman, 154–67. New York: Routledge, 1992.

Belton, John. "Language, Oedipus, and *Chinatown*." *MLN* 106, no. 5 (December 1991): 933–50.

Belton, John. "Technology and Aesthetics of Film Sound." In *Film Theory and Criticism*. 4th ed., edited by Gerald Mast, Marshall Cohen, and Leo Braudy, 323–31. New York: Oxford University Press, 1992.

Benton, Robert, and David Newman. *Bonnie and Clyde*. Typescript dated September 6, 1966, with some pages dated September 20 and October 7, 1966. Hollywood: Script City, n.d.

Benton, Robert, and David Newman. "The New Sentimentality." *Esquire*, July 1964, 25–31.

Benton, Robert, and David Newman. "Lightning in a Bottle." In *Bonnie and Clyde*, edited by Sandra Wake and Nicola Hayden, 13–30. London: Lorrimer, 1972.

Berliner, Todd. *Hollywood Incoherent: Narration in Seventies Cinema*. Austin: University of Texas Press, 2010.

Bernstein, Matthew. "Model Criminals: Visual Style in Bonnie and Clyde." In *Arthur Penn's Bonnie and Clyde*, edited by Lester Friedman, 101–26. Cambridge: Cambridge University Press, 2000.

Bernstein, Matthew. "Perfecting the New Gangster: Writing *Bonnie and Clyde*." *Film Quarterly* 53, no. 4 (Summer 2000): 16–31.

Biancorosso, Giorgio. "Where Does the Music Come From? Studies in the Aesthetics of Film Music." PhD dissertation, Princeton University, 2002.

Biancorosso, Giorgio. "Film, Music, and the Redemption of the Mundane." In *Bad Music: The Music We Love to Hate*, edited by Christopher Washburne and Maiken Derno, 190–211. New York: Routledge, 2004.

Biancorosso, Giorgio. "Memory and the Leitmotif in Cinema." In *Representations in Western Music*, edited by Joshua S. Walden, 203–23. Cambridge: Cambridge University Press, 2013.

Biskind, Peter. *Easy Riders, Raging Bulls: How the Sex-Drugs-and-Rock-'n'-Roll Generation Saved Hollywood*. New York: Simon & Schuster, 1999.

Bleek, Jennifer. "Terrence Malicks Spielfilmdebüt *Badlands* und die Musik von Carl Orff: Interferenzen visueller und klanglicher Materialität und ihre signifikative Funktion im Film." *Kieler Beiträge zur Filmmusikforschung* 2 (2008): 27–41. http://www.filmmusik.uni-kiel.de/kielerbeitraege2/KB2-Bleek.pdf. Accessed November 14, 2020.

Bonnie and Clyde. Directed by Arthur Penn. Warners-Seven Arts, 1967. Two-Disc Special Edition. Burbank: Warner Brothers Home Video, 2008. DVD.

Bordwell, David, and Noël Carroll, eds. *Post-Theory: Restructuring Film Studies*. Madison: University of Wisconsin Press, 1996.

Boym, Svetlana. *The Future of Nostalgia*. New York: Basic Books, 2001.

Brackett, David. "Banjos, Biopics, and Compilation Scores: The Movies Go Country." *American Music* 19, no. 3 (Autumn 2001): 247–90.

Brophy, Philip. *100 Modern Soundtracks*. BFI Screen Guides. London: British Film Institute, 2004.

Brown, Royal S. *Overtones and Undertones: Reading Film Music*. Berkeley: University of California Press, 1994.

Brownlow, Kevin. *The Parade's Gone By . . .* Berkeley: University of California Press, 1968.

Buhler, James. "*Star Wars*, Music, and Myth." In *Music and Cinema*, edited by James Buhler, Caryl Flinn, and David Neumeyer, 33–57. Hanover: University Press of New England, 2000.

Burgess, Jackson. Review of *McCabe and Mrs. Miller*. *Film Quarterly* 25, no. 2 (Winter 1971–1972): 49–53.
Butch Cassidy and the Sundance Kid. Directed by George Roy Hill. 20th Century Fox, 1969. Collector's Edition #28. 20th Century Fox Home Entertainment, 2006. DVD.
Butler, David. *Jazz Noir: Listening to Music from* Phantom Lady *to* The Last Seduction. Westport, CT: Praeger, 2002.
Canby, Vincent. "A Lovely 'Last Picture Show.'" Review of *The Last Picture Show*. *New York Times*, October 17, 1971. https://www.nytimes.com/1971/10/17/archives/a-lovely-last-picture-show-a-lovely-show.html.
Caputo, Davide. *Polanski and Perception: The Psychology of Seeing and the Cinema of Roman Polanski*. Bristol: Intellect, 2012.
Carter, Martin. "*Bonnie and Clyde* in the Charts." In *Bonnie and Clyde: Critical Insights*, edited by Rebecca Martin, 240–54. Ipswitch: Salem Press, 2016.
Caruana, John, and Mark Cauchi, eds. *Immanent Frames: Postsecular Cinema between Malick and von Trier*. Horizons of Cinema, Murray Pommerance, series ed. Albany: State University of New York Press, 2018.
Cavell, Stanley. *The World Viewed: Reflections on the Ontology of Film*, 2nd ed. Cambridge, MA: Harvard University Press, 1979.
Cawelti, John G., ed. *Focus on "Bonnie and Clyde."* Englewood Cliffs, NJ: Prentice-Hall, 1973.
Cawelti, John G. "The Artistic Power of *Bonnie and Clyde*." In *Focus on "Bonnie and Clyde,"* edited by John G. Cawelti, 40–84. Englewood Cliffs, NJ: Prentice Hall, 1973.
Chaiken, Michael, and Paul Cronin, eds. *Arthur Penn: Interviews*. Jackson: University Press of Mississippi, 2008.
Chinatown. Directed by Roman Polanski. Paramount, 1974. Centennial Collection. Paramount Pictures, 2009. DVD.
Chion, Michel. *Film, a Sound Art*. Translated by Claudia Gorbman. New York: Columbia University Press, 2009.
Chion, Michel. *The Thin Red Line*. BFI Modern Classics. London: BFI, 2004.
Chion, Michel. *The Voice in Cinema*. Translated by Claudia Gorbman. New York: Columbia University Press, 1999.
Churton, Tobias. *Occult Paris: The Lost Magic of the Belle Époque*. Rochester, VT: Inner Traditions, 2016.
Ciment, Michel. Interview with Terrence Malick. *Postif* 170 (June 1975): 30–34. Reprinted in Lloyd Michaels. *Terrence Malick*. Contemporary Film Directors. Urbana: University of Illinois Press, 2009.
Coale, Saumel Chase. *Paradigms of Paranoia: The Culture of Conspiracy in Contemporary American Fiction*. Tuscaloosa: University of Alabama Press, 2005.
Collier, Peter. Review of *Bonnie and Clyde*. In *Focus on "Bonnie and Clyde,"* edited by John G. Cawelti, 26–31. Englewood Cliffs, NJ: Prentice-Hall, 1973.
Comolli, Jean-Louis, and André S. Labarthe. "*Bonnie and Clyde*: An Interview with Arthur Penn." In *Focus on "Bonnie and Clyde,"* edited by John G. Cawelti. 15–19. Originally published in *The Evergreen Review* 12, no. 55 (June 1968): 61–63. Englewood Cliffs, NJ: Prentice-Hall, 1973.
Cook, David. *Lost Illusions: American Cinema in the Shadow of Watergate and Vietnam, 1970–1979*. History of the American Cinema. Vol. 9. Berkeley: University of California Press, 2000.

Cook, Page. Review of *Bonnie and Clyde*. Originally published in *Films in Review* 18, no. 8 (October 1967): 504–5. In *Focus on "Bonnie and Clyde,"* edited by John G. Cawelti, 23–24. Englewood Cliffs, NJ: Prentice-Hall, 1973.

Cooke, Mervyn. *A History of Film Music*. New York: Cambridge University Press, 2008.

Crowther, Bosley. Review of *Bonnie and Clyde*. Originally published in *New York Times*, August 14, 1967. In *Focus on "Bonnie and Clyde,"* edited by John G. Cawelti, 22–23. Englewood Cliffs, NJ: Prentice-Hall, 1973.

Cumming, Alec. "Let the Music Play: 75 Magic Moments." *The Look of Love: The Burt Bacharach Collection*. Compact disc. Rhino R2 75339. Rhino Records: 1998. Online at http://albumlinernotes.com/Look_Of_Love_Disc_3.html. Accessed November 13, 2020.

Darby, William, and Jack Du Bois. *American Film Music: Major Composers, Techniques, Trends: 1915–1990*. Jefferson, NC: McFarland, 1990.

David, Hal, Burt Bacharach, and George Terry. *Original Score Composed and Conducted by Burt Bacharach from the 20th Century Fox Production* Butch Cassidy and the Sundance Kid. New York: Charles Hansen Music and Books, 1969.

Davis, Fred. *Yearning for Yesterday: A Sociology of Nostalgia*. New York: Free Press, 1979.

Dempsey, Michael. Review of *American Graffiti*. *Film Quarterly* 27, no. 1 (Autumn 1973): 58–60.

Donnelly, K. J. *The Spectre of Sound: Music in Film and Television*. London: BFI, 2005.

Douglas, Susan J. *Listening In: Radio and the American Imagination*. New York: Random House, 1999.

Dwyer, Michael D. *Back to the Fifties: Nostalgia, Hollywood Film, and Popular Music of the Seventies and Eighties*. New York: Oxford University Press, 2015.

Dyer, Richard. "Entertainment and Utopia." Originally published in *Movie* 24 (Spring 1977): 2–13. In Dyer, *Only Entertainment*, 17–34. New York: Routledge, 1992.

Dyer, Richard. "Side by Side: Nino Rota, Music, and Film." In *Beyond the Soundtrack: Representing Music in Cinema*, edited by Daniel Goldmark, Lawrence Kramer, and Richard Leppert, 246–59. Berkeley: University of California Press, 2007.

Dylan, Bob. Interview with John Cohen and Happy Traum, *Sing Out!* (October/November 1968). Reprinted in Jonathon Cott, ed. *Bob Dylan: The Essential Interviews*, 119–47. New York: Simon and Schuster, 2017.

Eagle, Herbert J. "Power and the Visual Semantics of Polanski's Films." In *The Cinema of Roman Polanski: Dark Places of the World*, edited by John Orr and Elżbieta Ostrowska. 38–50. Directors' Cuts. London: Wallflower, 2006.

Eaton, Michael. *Chinatown*. BFI Film Classics. London: BFI, 1997.

Edwards, Bill. "Ragtime and Honky Tonk of the 1950s: An Essay on the First Ragtime Revival." [2004/2015]. Online at *RagPiano.com: "Perfessor" Bill's Ragtime Resources and Articles*. http://www.perfessorbill.com/ragtime11.shtml. Accessed November 13, 2020.

Edwards, Richard L. "We Rob Banks: Cinematic Thievery in *Bonnie and Clyde*." In *Bonnie and Clyde: Critical Insights*, edited by Rebecca Martin, 97–114. Ipswich: Salem Press, 2016.

Elsaesser, Thomas. "The Pathos of Failure: Notes on the Unmotivated Hero." Originally published in *Monogram* 6 (1975): 13–19. In *The Last Great Picture Show: New Hollywood Cinema in the 1970s*, edited by Thomas Elsaesser, Alexander Horwath, and Noel King, 279–92. Amsterdam: Amsterdam University Press, 2004.

Elsaesser, Thomas, and Malte Hagener. *Film Theory: An Introduction through the Senses*. London: Routledge, 2009.

Emerson, Ken. *Always Magic in the Air: The Bomp and Brilliance of the Brill Building Era*. New York: Viking, 2005.

Evans, Mark. *Soundtrack: The Music of the Movies*. New York: Hopkinson and Blake, 1975.

Farber, Stephen. "George Lucas: The Stinky Kid Hits the Bigtime." In *George Lucas: Interviews*, edited by Sally Kline, 33–44. Conversations with Filmmakers. Jackson: University Press of Mississippi, 1999.

Farber, Stephen. "The Writer in American Films." *Film Quarterly* 21, no. 4 (Summer 1968): 2–13.

Felski, Rita. *The Limits of Critique*. Chicago: University of Chicago Press, 2015.

Frampton, Daniel. *Filmosophy*. London: Wallflower Press, 2006.

Franklin, Peter. *Seeing through Music: Gender and Modernism in Classic Hollywood Film Scores*. Oxford: Oxford University Press, 2014.

Friedman, Lester D. *Bonnie and Clyde*. BFI Film Classics. London: British Film Institute, 2000.

Fritzsche, Peter. *Stranded in the Present: Modern Time and the Melancholy of History*. Cambridge, MA: Harvard University Press, 2004.

Furstenau, Marc, and Leslie MacAvoy. "Terrence Malick's Heideggerian Cinema: War and the Question of Being in *The Thin Red Line*." In *The Cinema of Terrence Malick: Poetic Visions of America*, 2nd ed., edited by Hannah Patterson, 179–91. Directors Cuts. London: Wallflower, 2007.

Gabbard, Krin. *Jammin' at the Margins: Jazz and the American Cinema*. Chicago: University of Chicago Press, 1996.

Geduld, Carolyn. "*Bonnie and Clyde*: Society vs. the Clan." In *Focus on "Bonnie and Clyde,"* edited by John G. Cawelti, 93–98. Englewood Cliffs, NJ: Prentice-Hall, 1973.

Gilbey, Ryan. *It Don't Worry Me: The Revolutionary American Films of the Seventies*. New York: Faber and Faber, 2003.

Godfrey, Nicholas. *The Limits of Auteurism: Case Studies in the Critically Constructed New Hollywood*. New Brunswick, NJ: Rutgers University Press, 2017.

Goethe, Johan Wolfgang von. *Goethe's Faust: The Original German and a New Translation and Introduction by Walter Kaufman. Part One and Sections from Part Two*. New York: Anchor Books, 1963.

Goldman, William. *Four Screenplays*. New York: Applause Books, 1995.

Goodall, Mark. "The Three Winds of Albert Lamorisse." *Mise-en-Scène* 3, no. 2 (Winter 2018): 32–44.

Gorbman, Claudia. "Auteur Music." In *Beyond the Soundtrack: Representing Music in Cinema*, edited by Daniel Goldmark, Lawrence Kramer, and Richard Leppert, 149–62. Berkeley: University of California Press, 2007.

Gorbman, Claudia. "Scoring the Indian: Music in the Liberal Western." In *Western Music and Its Others*, edited by Georgina Born and David Hesmondhalgh, 234–53. Berkeley: University of California Press, 2000.

Gorbman, Claudia. *Unheard Melodies: Narrative Film Music*. London: BFI; Bloomington: Indiana University Press, 1987.

Gustafsson, Henrik. *Out of Site: Landscape and Cultural Reflexivity in New Hollywood Cinema, 1969–1974*. Originally published as a PhD dissertation, State University of Stockholm, Department of Cinema Studies, 2007. Saarbrücken: VDM Verlag Dr. Muller Aktiengesellschaft, 2008.

Handzo, Stephen. "A Glossary of Film Sound Technology." In *Film Sound: Theory and Practice*, edited by Elisabeth Weis and John Belton, 383–426. New York: Columbia University Press, 1985.

Hanlon, Ann-Marie. "Satie and the Meaning of the Comic." In *Erik Satie: Music, Art, and Literature*, edited by Carolyn Potter, 19–48. Surrey, UK: Ashgate, 2011.

Hanson, Helen. "Paranoia and Nostalgia: Sonic Motifs and Songs in Neo-Noir." In *Neo-Noir*, edited by Mark Bould, Katharina Glitre, and Greg Tuck, 44–60. London: Wallflower 2009.

Harris, Mark. *Pictures at a Revolution: Five Movies and the Birth of the New Hollywood*. New York: Penguin Press, 2008.

Harris, Thomas J. *Bogdanovich's Picture Shows*. Metuchen, NJ: Scarecrow Press, 1990.

Hartley, L. P. *The Go-Between*. [1953]. New York: New York Review of Books Classics, 2002.

Hearn, Marcus. *The Cinema of George Lucas*. New York: Harry N. Abrams, 2005.

Henri, Adrian. *Total Art: Events, Happenings, and Performances*. New York: Praeger, 1974.

Higham, Charles. "You May Not Leave the Movie House Singing Their Songs, But...." *New York Times*, May 5, 1975, p. 119. Reprinted in *The Routledge Film Music Sourcebook*, edited by James Weirzbicki, Nathan Platte, and Colin Roust, 197–200. New York: Routledge, 2012.

Hintermann, Carlo, and Daniele Villa, eds. *Terrence Malick: Rehearsing the Unexpected*. London: Faber & Faber, 2015.

Hoberman, J. *The Dream Life: Movies, Media, and the Mythology of the Sixties*. New York: New Press, 2003.

Hubbert, Julie. "'Whatever Happened to Great Movie Music?': *Cinéma Vérité* and Hollywood Film Music of the Early 1970s." *American Music* 21, no. 2 (Summer 2003): 180–213.

Hubbert, Julie. "The Compilation Soundtrack from the 1960s to the Present." In *The Oxford Handbook of Film Music Studies*, edited by David Neumeyer, 291–318. Oxford: Oxford University Press, 2014.

Hunt, Dennis. Review of *Butch Cassidy and the Sundance Kid*. *Film Quarterly* 23, no. 2 (Winter, 1969–1970): 62–63.

Inglis, Ian. "'Some Kind of Wonderful': The Creative Legacy of the Brill Building." *American Music* 21, no. 2 (Summer 2003): 214–35.

Jameson, Frederic. "On Interpretation: Literature as a Socially Symbolic Act." Originally published in *The Political Unconscious* (Ithaca, NY: Cornell University Press, 1981). In *The Jameson Reader*, edited by Michael Hardt and Kathi Weeks, 33–60. Oxford: Blackwell, 2004.

Jameson, Frederic. "Postmodernism, or The Cultural Logic of Late Capitalism." Originally published in *New Left Review* 146 (July–August 1984): 52–92. In *The Jameson Reader*, edited by Michael Hardt and Kathi Weeks, 188–232. Oxford: Blackwell, 2004.

Kael, Pauline. "Pipe Dream." Review of *McCabe and Mrs. Miller*. In Kael, *Deeper into Movies*, 277–85. Originally published in *The New Yorker*, July 3, 1971, 40–44. Boston: Little, Brown, 1973.

Kael, Pauline. "Review of *Bonnie and Clyde*." In Kael, *Kiss Kiss Bang Bang*, 47–63. Originally published in *The New Yorker*, October 21, 1967, 147. Boston: Little, Brown, 1968.

Kalinak, Kathryn. *How the West Was Sung: Music in the Westerns of John Ford*. Berkeley: University of California Press, 2007.

Kassabian, Anahid. *Hearing Film: Tracking Identifications in Contemporary Hollywood Film Music*. New York: Routledge, 2001.

Kauffmann, Stanley. *Figures of Light: Film Criticism and Comment*. New York: Harper and Row, 1971.
Kaufman, Dave. Review of *Bonnie and Clyde*. *Variety* 217, no. 12 (August 9, 1967): 6.
Keathley, Christian. *Cinephilia and History, or the Wind in the Trees*. Bloomington: Indiana University Press, 2006.
Keetman, Gunild. *Elementaria: First Acquaintance with Orff-Schulwerk*. Translated by Margaret Murray. Originally published by Ernst Klett Verlag, 1970. London: Schott, 1974.
Killen, Andreas. *1973 Nervous Breakdown: Watergate, Warhol, and the Birth of Post-Sixties America*. New York: Bloomsbury, 2006.
King, Geoff. *New Hollywood Cinema: An Introduction*. New York: Columbia University Press, 2002.
Kitses, Jim. "Introduction: Postmodernism and the Western." In *The Western Reader*, edited by Jim Kitses and Gregg Rickman, 15–31. New York: Limelight Editions, 1998.
Knight, Peter. *Conspiracy Culture: From the Kennedy Assassination to the X-Files*. London: Routledge, 2000.
Knopf, Bill. "Interview: Doug Dillard." *Banjo Newsletter* (June 1981): 4–6.
Kolker, Robert. *A Cinema of Loneliness: Penn, Kubrick, Coppola, Scorsese, Spielberg, Altman*, 3rd ed. Oxford: Oxford University Press, 2000.
Kotowicz, Zbigniew. *Gaston Bachelard: A Philosophy of the Surreal*. Edinburgh: Edinburgh University Press, 2016.
Krämer, Peter, and Yannis Tzioumakis, eds. *The Hollywood Renaissance: Revisiting American Cinema's Most Celebrated Era*. New York: Bloomsbury, 2018.
Kripal, Jeffrey. *The Serpent's Kiss: Gnostic Reflections on the Study of Religion*. Chicago: University of Chicago Press, 2007.
Landis, Beth, and Polly Carder. T*he Eclectic Curriculum in American Music Education: Contributions of Dalcrose, Kodaly, and Orff*. Washington, DC: Music Educators National Conference, 1972.
Landsberg, Alison. "Prosthetic Memory: The Ethics and Politics of Memory in an Age of Mass Culture." In *Memory and Popular Film*, edited by Paul Grainge, 144–61. Manchester: Manchester University Press, 2003.
Larsen, Peter. *Film Music*. London: Reaktion, 2007.
The Last Picture Show. Directed by Peter Bogdanovich. Columbia, 1971. The Criterion Collection. Under license from Sony Pictures Home Entertainment, 2010. DVD.
Lastra, James. *Sound Technology and the American Cinema: Perception, Representation, Modernity*. New York: Columbia University Press, 2000.
Le Guin, Elisabeth. *Boccherini's Body: An Essay in Carnal Musicology*. Berkeley: University of California Press, 2006.
Lechte, John. "Gaston Bachelard." In Lechte, *Fifty Key Contemporary Thinkers: from Structuralism to Postmodernity*, 3–6. London: Routledge, 1996.
Lerner, Neil. "Copland's Music of Wide Open Spaces: Surveying the Pastoral Trope in Hollywood." *Musical Quarterly* 85, no. 3 (August 2001): 477–515.
Lévi-Strauss, Claude. *Structural Anthropology*. Translated by Claire Jacobson and Brooke Grundfest Schoepf. Garden City, NY: Anchor Books, 1967.
Lin, Karen. *That Half-Barbaric Twang: The Banjo in American Popular Culture*. Urbana: University of Illinois Press, 1991.
Long, Michael. *Beautiful Monsters: Imagining the Classic in Musical Media*. Berkeley: University of California Press, 2008.

Lucas, George, Gloria Katz, and Willard Huyck. *American Graffiti: The Complete Scenario of the Film with 70 Illustrations*. New York: Grove Press, 1973.

Macauley, David. *Elemental Philosophy: Earth, Air, Fire, and Water as Elemental Ideas*. SUNY Series in Environmental Philosophy and Ethics. Albany: State University of New York Press, 2010.

Magee, Gayle Sherwood. *Robert Altman's Soundtracks: Film, Music, and Sound from M*A*S*H to A Prairie Home Companion*. Oxford: Oxford University Press, 2014.

Maher, Paul, Jr., ed. *All Things Shining: An Oral History of the Films of Terrence Malick*, 4th ed. Self-Published by editor/author, 2017.

Marcus, Greil. *The Old, Weird America: The World of Bob Dylan's Basement Tapes*. Originally published as *The Invisible Republic: Bob Dylan's Basement Tapes* [Henry Holt, 1997]. New York: Picador, 2001.

Mast, Gerald. *A Short History of the Movies*. New York: Pegasus, 1971.

Mast, Gerald. *A Short History of the Movies*, 2nd ed. Indianapolis: Bobs-Merrill, 1976.

McAllester Jones, Mary. *Gaston Bachelard, Subversive Humanist*. Madison: University of Wisconsin Press, 1991.

McCabe and Mrs. Miller. Directed by Robert Altman. Warners, 1971. Warner Bros. Home Video, 2002. DVD.

McHale, Brian. *The Cambridge Introduction to Postmodernism*. Cambridge: Cambridge University Press, 2015.

Melley, Timothy. *Empire of Conspiracy: The Culture of Paranoia in Postwar America*. Ithaca, NY: Cornell University Press, 2000.

Mendez, Matthew. "History, Homeopathy, and the Spiritual Impulse in the Post-War Reception of Satie: Cage, Higgins, Beuys." In *Erik Satie: Music, Art, and Literature*, edited by Caroline Potter, 183–228. Surrey, UK: Ashgate, 2011.

Mera, Miguel. "Materializing Film Music." In *The Cambridge Companion to Film Music*, edited by Mervyn Cooke and Fiona Ford, 157–72. Cambridge: Cambridge University Press, 2016.

Michaels, Lloyd. *Terrence Malick*. Contemporary Film Directors, James Naremore, series ed. Urbana: University of Illinois Press, 2009.

Miklitsch, Robert. "Audio-Noir: Audiovisuality in Neo-Modernist Noir." In *Neo-Noir*, edited by Mark Bould, Katharina Glitre, and Greg Tuck, 28–43. London: Wallflower 2009.

Monaco, Paul. *The Sixties: 1960–1969*. Berkeley: University of California Press, 2001.

Morris, Mitchell. *The Persistence of Sentiment: Display and Feeling in Popular Music of the 1970s*. Berkeley: University of California Press, 2013.

Morrison, James, and Thomas Schur. *The Films of Terrence Malick*. Westport, CT: Praeger, 2003.

Music from the Motion Picture "Chinatown." Composed and conducted by Jerry Goldsmith. Intrada Special Collection, vol. 350. Produced by Douglass Fake and Roger Feigelson. Liner notes by Jeff Bond and Douglass Fake. Oakland: Intrada, 2016. ISC350. CD.

Music Inspired by the Rip-Roarin', Electrifying Sounds of "Bonnie and Clyde," Including Excerpts of the Original Dialogue! Burbank: Warner Bros. Seven Arts, [1968]. W1743. 33 1/3 rpm record.

Nachman, Gerald. *Raised on Radio*. New York: Pantheon Books, 1998.

Nelson, Peter. "Cohabiting in Time: Towards an Ecology of Rhythm." *Organised Sound* 16, no. 2 (2011): 109–14.

Norton, Pauline. "Breakdown." *Grove Music Online. Oxford Music Online.* Oxford University Press. Accessed November 13, 2020.
O'Brien, Adam. *Transactions with the World: Ecocriticism and the Environmental Sensibility of New Hollywood.* New York: Berghahn Books, 2016.
O'Brien, Geoffrey. *Sonata for Jukebox: An Autobiography of My Ears.* New York: Counterpoint, 2004.
Orff, Carl, and Gunild Keetman. *Musik für Kinder.* Vol. 3, *Dur: Dominanten.* Mainz: B. Schott's Söhne, c. 1952.
Orff, Carl, and Gunild Keetman. *Musik für Kinder.* Vol. 4, *Moll: Bordun-Stufen.* Mainz: B. Schott's Söhne, 1953.
Orff, Carl, and Gunild Keetman. *Musica Poetica: The Orff-Schulwerk.* Compilation of the *Musica Poetica* series released by Harmonia Mundi. RCA Victor Red Seal. Sony Music, 2014. 8843064192. Six compact discs.
Orr, John. *Contemporary Cinema.* Edinburgh: Edinburgh University Press, 1998.
Orr, John. "Terrence Malick and Arthur Penn: The Western Re-Myth." In *The Cinema of Terrence Malick: Poetic Visions of America*, edited by Hannah Patterson, 63–76. Directors' Cuts. London: Wallflower, 2007.
Patton, Kimberley C., and Benjamin C. Ray, eds. *A Magic Still Dwells: Comparative Religion in the Postmodern Age.* Berkeley: University of California Press, 2000.
Polan, Dana. "*Chinatown*: Politics as Perspective, Perspective as Politics." In *The Cinema of Roman Polanski: Dark Places of the World*, edited by John Orr and Elżbieta Ostrowska. 108–20. Directors Cuts. London: Wallflower, 2006.
Potter, Caroline, ed. *Erik Satie: Music, Art, and Literature.* Surrey, UK: Ashgate, 2013.
Pye, Michael, and Lynda Myles. *The Movie Brats: How the Film Generation Took Over Hollywood.* New York: Holt, Rinehart, and Winston, 1979.
Raksin, David. "Whatever Became of Movie Music?" *Film Music Notebook* 1, no. 1 (Fall 1974): 24–30. Reprinted in *Celluloid Symphonies: Texts and Contexts in Film Music History*, edited by Julie Hubbert, 372–77. Berkeley: University of California Press, 2011.
Ray, Robert B. *The Avant-Garde Finds Andy Hardy.* Cambridge, MA: Harvard University Press, 1995.
Regner, Hermann. "A Wealth of Good, Stimulating, Movement-Inducing Music: Gunild Keetman: Pieces for Recorder and Drum: An Attempt at Better Acquaintance." Originally published in *Orff-Schulwerk Informationen* 47 (1991). Reprinted in *Gunild Keetman: Ein Leben für Musik und Bewegung*, edited by Hermann Regner and Minna Ronnefeld, 162–77. Mainz: Schott, 2004.
Reynolds, Simon. *Retromania: Pop Culture's Addiction to Its Own Past.* New York: Faber and Faber, 2011.
Rhym, John. "The Paradigmatic Shift in the Critical Reception of Terrence Malick's *Badlands* and the Emergence of a Heideggerian Cinema." *Quarterly Review of Film and Video* 27, no. 4 (2010): 255–66. Published online at https://doi.org/10.1080/10509200802350331.
Richard, Jerry. "Foggy Mountain." *The Antioch Review* 28, no. 3 (October 1, 1968): 388–93.
Rosenberg, Neil V. "Image and Stereotype: Bluegrass Soundtracks." *American Music* 1, no. 3 (Autumn 1993): 1–22.
Roszak, Theodore. *The Making of a Counter Culture: Reflections on the Technocratic Society and Its Youthful Opposition.* Originally published Garden City, NY: Doubleday, 1969. Reprint with a new introduction by the author. Berkeley: University of California Press, 1995.

Russell, Mark, and James Young. [Interview with Jerry Goldsmith]. In *Film Music. Screencraft*, 59–69. Boston: Focal Press, 2000.

Rust, Amy. *Passionate Detachments: Technologies of Vision and Violence in American Cinema, 1967–1974*. Horizons of Cinema. Albany: State University of New York Press, 2017.

Rybin, Steven. *Terrence Malick and the Thought of Film*. Lanham, MD: Lexington Books, 2012.

Rybin, Steven. "Voicing Meaning: Terrence Malick's Characters." In *Terrence Malick: Film and Philosophy*, edited by Stuart Kendall and Thomas Deane Tucker, 13–39. London: Continuum, 2011.

Sarris, Andrew. "Films in Focus." Review of *The Last Picture Show*. *Village Voice*, October 14, 1971. Archived online at: https://www.villagevoice.com/2011/01/06/peter-bogdanovich-entitled-to-gloat-for-the-last-picture-show/. Accessed November 13, 2020.

Satie, Erik. *Trois morceaux en forme de poire (à 4 mains) avec one manière de commencement, une prolongation du même & un en plus, suive d'une redite*. Paris: Rouart, Lerolle, 1911. Reprinted in *Gymnopédies, Gnossiennes, and Other Works for Piano*, titles and directions translated by Stanley Appelbaum, 66–95. Mineola, NY: Dover Publications, 1989.

Schatz, Thomas. *Old Hollywood / New Hollywood: Ritual, Art, and Industry*. Ann Arbor: UMI Research Press, 1983.

Scheurer, Timothy E. "The Beatles, the Brill Building, and the Persistence of Tin Pan Alley in the Age of Rock." *Popular Music and Society* 20, no. 4 (Winter 1996): 89–102.

Sedgwick, Eve Kosofsky. "Paranoid Reading and Reparative Reading, or, You're So Paranoid, You Probably Think This Essay Is about You." In Sedgwick, *Touching Feeling: Affect, Pedagogy, Performativity*, 123–51. Durham, NC: Duke University Press, 2003.

Self, Robert. *Robert Altman's "McCabe and Mrs. Miller": Reframing the American West*. Lawrence: University Press of Kansas, 2007.

Shumway, David. "Rock 'n' Roll Soundtracks and the Production of Nostalgia." *Cinema Journal* 38, no. 2 (Winter 1999): 36–51.

Simon, Alex. "Peter Bogdanovich's Year of the Cat." *Venice Magazine* (April 2002). Reprinted in *Peter Bogdanovich: Interviews*, edited by Peter Tonguette, 142–59. Conversations with Filmmakers Series. Jackson: University Press of Mississippi, 2015.

Sinnerbrink, Robert. *Terrence Malick: Filmmaker and Philosopher*. Philosophical Filmmakers. London: Bloomsbury, 2019.

Smith, Jeff. "The Auteur Renaissance." In *Sound: Music, Dialogue, Effects*, edited by Kathryn Kalinak, 83–106. New Brunswick, NJ: Rutgers, 2015.

Smith, Jeff. *The Sounds of Commerce: Marketing Popular Film Music*. New York: Columbia University Press, 1998.

Smith, Jim. *George Lucas*. London: Virgin Books, 2003.

Smith, Roche C. *Gaston Bachelard: Philosopher of Science and Imagination*. Boston: Twayne, 1982]. Revised and expanded edition. SUNY Series in Contemporary French Thought. Albany: State University of New York Press, 2016.

Sobchack, Vivian. "The Expanded Gaze in Contracted Space: Happenstance, Hazard, and the Flesh of the World." In Sobchack, *Carnal Thoughts: Embodiment and Moving Image Culture*, 85–108. Berkeley: University of California Press, 2004.

Sobchack, Vivian. "When the Ear Dreams: Dolby Digital and the Imagination of Sound." *Film Quarterly* 58, no. 4 (2005): 2–15.
Strouse, Charles. *Put on a Happy Face: A Broadway Memoir*. New York: Union Square Press, 2008.
The Swingle Singers. *Bach's Greatest Hits*. [Phillips, 1963] LP. American Release of *Jazz Sébastian Bach*. Phillips PHM 200-097.
The Swingle Singers. *Bach to Bach*. [Phillips, 1968] LP. American Release of *Jazz Sébastian Bach, v. 2*. Phillips PHM 200-097.
The Swingle Singers. *Jazz Sébastien Bach*. [Phillips, 1963] LP. Phillips 840.519 PY.
Symmons, Tom. *The New Hollywood Historical Film*. London: Palgrave McMillan, 2015.
Taylor, Greg. *Artists in the Audience: Cults, Camp, and American Film Criticism*. Princeton, NJ: Princeton University Press, 1999.
Thomas, Tony. *Music for the Movies*. South Brunswick, NJ: A. S. Barnes, 1973.
Time Magazine. "Double Vision." Review of *Butch Cassidy and the Sundance Kid*. August 26, 1969, 100.
Tonelli, Chris. "The Chiptuning of the World: Game Boys, Imagined Travel, and Musical Meaning." In *The Oxford Handbook of Mobile Music Studies*, Vol. 2, edited by Sumath Gopinath and Jason Stanyek. 402–26. Oxford: Oxford University Press, 2014.
Tweedie, James. *The Age of New Waves: Art Cinema and the Staging of Globalization*. Oxford: Oxford University Press, 2013.
Valck, Marijke de, and Malte Hagener, eds. *Cinephilia: Movies, Love, and Memory*. Amsterdam: Amsterdam University Press, 2005.
Vallée, Rudy. "Deep Night." Recorded February 6, 1929. Victor 21868. 78 rpm record.
Vallée, Rudy. *Vagabond Dreams Come True*. New York: E. P. Dutton, 1930.
Walker, Beverly. "Malick on *Badlands*." *Sight and Sound* 44, no. 2 (Spring 1975): 82–83.
Walton, Saige. "Air, Atmosphere, Environment: Folk Mood, Folk Horror, and *The VVitch*." *Screening the Past* 43 (April 2018). http://www.screeningthepast.com/2018/02/air-atmosphere-environment-film-mood-folk-horror-and-the-vvitch/.
Weis, Elisabeth, and John Belton, eds. *Film Sound: Theory and Practice*. New York: Columbia University Press, 1985.
Weschler, Lawrence Weschler. "The Brat's Tale: Roman Polanski." In Weschler, *Vermeer in Bosnia: Selected Writings*, 83–150. New York: Vintage Books, 2004.
Whittington, William. *Sound Design and Science Fiction*. Austin: University of Texas Press, 2007.
Wierzbicki, James. *Film Music: A History*. New York: Routledge, 2009.
Wierzbicki, James. *Music in the Age of Anxiety: American Music in the Fifties*. Urbana: University of Illinois Press, 2015.
Wierzbicki, James. *Terrence Malick: Sonic Style*. Filmmakers and Their Soundtracks. New York: Routledge, 2019.
Wolfman Jack and Byron Laursen. *Have Mercy! Confessions of the Original Rock 'n' Roll Animal*. New York: Warner Books, 1995.
Wood, Robin. *Hollywood from Vietnam to Reagan*. New York: Columbia University Press, 1986.
Yacavone, Daniel. *Film Worlds: A Philosophical Aesthetics of Cinema*. New York: Columbia University Press, 2015.

Index

For the benefit of digital users, indexed terms that span two pages (e.g., 52–53) may, on occasion, appear on only one of those pages.

absence, 5, 46, 47–48, 72, 103, 114, 120, 132, 149–52
actuality, 30–31, 32–33, 41, 51–52, 56–58, 85, 90, 123–24, 149, 217n.41
   See also presence
Adorno, Theodor, 63
affect, 39–40, 90, 105–6, 109–10, 195, 216n.35
   and the imaginal elements, 109
   See also elements: and direct ontology
Allen, Dede, 30–31, 203n.7
Altman, Rick, 61–63
Altman, Robert, 8, 19–20, 162–63, 165–66
   and realism, 85
   and sound design, 85, 86
   See also revisionism
American Graffiti (1973), 3, 5, 18–19, 23–24, 25–26, 126–28, 130–31, 132, 142–49
   compiled popular music in, 140–42
   critical reception of, 153–56
   as evoking fifties teenager films, 127–28
   and generational memory, 132–35
   historical breadth of source music in, 131, 140–41
   humorous moments of radio synchronicity in, 146–47
   and nostalgia in marketing, 147–49, 154–55
   prioritization of source music in, 129
   spatialization of sound in, 131, 144–45
   traditional musical interpretations, 128–29
animals, and their relationship to human ontological categories, 157, 159–60, 177–79
auteurism, 19–20, 31, 104–5, 133–34, 165
   as an influence on American film culture, 18, 31
   as a regressive ideological narrative, 10–12
   and the soundtrack, 21, 25–26, 67

Bacharach, Burt, 24, 65–66, 72–74, 81, 87–92
   and adult contemporary pop, 73
   and Brill Building songcraft, 72–73, 209–10n.21
   and historical pastiche, 73–74, 75–78
Bachelard, Gaston, 13–14, 24–25, 106–10, 123–25, 216n.36
   direct ontology and the imagination in, 106–7, 109–10
   earth, mud, and making in, 110–11, 119–20
   and the elements, 106, 107
   recently renewed scholarly interest in, 214–15n.27
   transparent water and deceptive superficiality, 114, 117–18
Badlands (1973), 26, 157–95
   and humor, 161
   musical eclecticism in, 162
   objects and objectification in, 164, 167–68, 175–76, 177, 179–80
   representation of the past in, 162–63, 164, 167–68
   the uncanny strangeness of contingency in, 178–79, 180–82, 188–89
Barnes, Ken, 141
Baroque pop, 76–77, 82–83, 89
Bazin, André, 13–14, 16–19, 34–35, 60
Beatty, Warren, 30–31, 39, 80, 202n.3
Beck, Jay, 15, 206n.41

Belton, John, 16, 95–96, 124
Benton, Robert, 28–29, 30–33, 59
Berliner, Todd, 95
Berrigan, Bunny, 111–13
Biancorosso, Giorgio, 139, 143–44, 214n.25, 221n.32
Bleek, Jennifer, 172–73, 189–90
blockbuster cinema, 9, 10, 20–21, 93, 133–34
bluegrass, 23–24, 30, 40–46, 54–55, 59, 98
    and hip culture, 55
Bogdanovich, Peter, 2, 19–20, 35–36, 132–35, 141–42, 153
Bonnie and Clyde (1967), 1, 2, 3, 8, 16, 18–19, 23–24, 28–59, 88–89, 90, 98, 164, 167–68, 188–89
    and Black militancy, 52, 53, 55–56
    countercultural reception, 50–59
    critical reception, 1, 40, 53–54
    as myth, 56–58
    orchestral scoring in, 46
    as pop culture fad, 52, 207n.51
    soundtrack album, 45, 48–49
Boym, Svetlana, 143, 155–56
Brackett, David, 136, 138, 154
breakdown, 28–33, 43–44, 59
    as a dance form, 28
    See also "Foggy Mountain Breakdown" (recording)
Brown, Royal S., 62–63
Brownlow, Kevin, 209n.19
Buhler, James, 63
Burgess, Jackson, 89–90
Butch Cassidy and the Sundance Kid (1968), 24, 60, 65–66, 67, 87–92, 97–98
    and musical-historical pastiche, 72–75
    silent film media in, 68
    and song sequences, 67, 87–88

Cantor, Eddie, 1, 2
Cavell, Stanley, 5, 167–69, 192–93
Cawelti, John, 58–59
Chinatown (1974), 24–25, 93–125, 164. *See also* elements; neoclassicism
    and jazz, 24–25, 98–99, 111–13, 116–17
    and contemporaneous jazz, 116–17
    solo trumpet, *film noir*, and masculinity, 111–12, 216n.39
    knowledge and its limits in, 95–96
    Latin music and percussion in, 115
    and musical modernism, 98–99, 111
    and mythic paranoia, 95, 97–100, 108–9, 122–23
    Noah Cross as a Bachelardian octopus, 216n.37
    pastness and presentness in, 98, 111, 116–17
    and sound design, 100–3
Chinatown (geographic location and ethnic community), 94, 97–98, 121–22
"Chinatown" (thematic worldview defined by mythic paranoia), 121–24
Chion, Michel, 139, 157, 178–79, 195
    acousmêtre and acousmachine, 38
    emanation speech, 47, 86–87
    theatrical speech, 37–38, 86–87
"Cinema of Poetry," 162–63
"Cinema of Sensation," 14, 19, 41. *See also* affect
cinephilia, 17–18, 90
classical Hollywood cinema, 2, 13
    and happy endings, 76–77
    and textual closure and openness, 13, 95–96
classical Hollywood film music, 29, 30, 40, 60, 65, 87–88
    increasing engagement with popular music, 21–22
    and modernism, 21–22, 64–65, 169
    and neo-Romanticism, 29, 65–66, 169
    neoclassical reimagining in *Chinatown*, 104
    and textual closure and openness, 13, 95
classical music in cinema, 162, 169
Cohen, Leonard, 24, 66, 78–81, 82–83, 87–92
    musical archaism and temporal ambiguity, 81, 211n.34
    songs in *McCabe and Mrs. Miller*, 81–82 (*see also* "Stranger Song, The")
    Songs of Leonard Cohen (album), 79–80
"Cold, Cold Heart" (song), 136
Collier, Peter, 52

INDEX 245

compiled music, 28–29, 135–39, 140–42
   See also classical music in cinema;
      pop songs
Coppola, Francis Ford, 19–20, 133–34
   Conversation, The (1974) and paranoia,
      surveillance, 99–100, 103
counterculture, 3–4, 24, 25–26, 29, 32–33,
   51–52, 55–56, 73, 81, 91, 174–75, 198n.6
country music, 128–29, 134, 138

Davis, Fred, 153–54, 223–24n.52
Days of Heaven (1978), 166–67, 194–95
"Deep Night" (song), 35
Deleuze, Gilles, 184–85, 200n.34
Deliverance (1968), 55
Dempsey, Michael, 155
diegetic music. *See* source music
Dillard, Doug, 30–31, 40, 55, 204–5n.29
documentary cinema
   direct cinema and *cinema vérité*,
      15, 29–30
   See also "New Hollywood Cinema and
      documentary influence"
Douglas, Susan, 141
Dream Life, the, 7–8, 30–31
Dyer, Richard, 67, 92
Dylan, Bob, 28, 50, 55–56, 64, 66

ecocriticism, 106, 168, 185, 192–93,
   226n.26
elements, the, 13–14, 24–25
   ambiguity and intertwining of, 96–97,
      101–2, 103–4
   as articulated through sound
      design, 101–3
   as direct ontology, 96–97 (*see also*
      Gaston Bachelard: direct ontology
      and imagination in)
   as imagined through instrumentation
      (*see also* musical instruments)
   muddy sounds, 119–20, 217n.45
   in relation to neoclassicism, genre
      bending, 96–97
   timbral imagery in musical score, 103–6, 110–16
   water and earth (wet and dry) in
      Chinatown, 95–98

embodiment, 171, 172–74
ephemerality, 34–35, 37–38, 39–40, 46,
   49–50, 51, 126, 132
   See also radio: and ephemerality
ethics, 107–9, 111–12, 123–24, 125
   Chinatown, paranoia, and the limits of
      critique, 124–25
   and violence in *Badlands*, 190, 191–95
Evans, Robert, 104–5, 214n.22
existentialism, 31–32, 170
exoticism, 63–64, 73
experience. *See* actuality

Farber, Manny, 18
Felski, Rita, 124–25
fifties (decade), 2–3, 5–6, 25–26, 132–33,
   142–43, 154–55, 158, 164, 186,
   187, 191
film music, 13
   and film philosophy, 194–95
   as foregrounded and backgrounded,
      36–37, 44–45, 182
   limitations of motivic analysis in, 139
   narratological versus imaginal analysis
      of, 109
   and representations of historical
      period, 35–37
   See also classical Hollywood film music;
      classical music in cinema; pop
      score; pop songs; myth in relation
      to film music
film noir, 24–25, 98–99, 213n.9
film philosophy, 17, 162–63, 166–68
   See also film music: and film philosophy
film theory, 13–14, 16, 34–35, 184–85,
   212n.50
Flatt and Scruggs (musical group), 28–29,
   41–42, 54–55
   and *The Beverly Hillbillies*, 54, 55
"Foggy Mountain Breakdown"
   (recording), 28–29, 30, 40, 41–43, 47–48
Frampton, Daniel, 13–14, 168–69, 184–85
Franklin, Peter, 13
French New Wave cinema, 15, 18–19, 42–43, 133–34
Fritzsche, Peter, 6, 7–8

246 INDEX

genre, 5–6, 14, 24–25, 61–62, 90–91
   genre "benders" and genre "breakers," 95
   semantic and syntactic articulation of, 61–62, 64–65
"Gassenhauer," (musical work), 160, 165, 169–74, 186–90, 193–94
Godard, Jean-Luc, 16, 28–29, 31–32, 42–43, 133–34
Goldman, William, 68–69, 76, 210n.29
Goldsmith, Jerry, 24–25, 98–100, 101–2, 103–6, 111–13, 114, 118
Golddiggers of 1933, 36–37
Gorbman, Claudia, 139, 165–66
Great Depression, 34, 36
Guffrey, Burnett, 46
Gustaffson, Henrick, 172–73

Hanlon, Ann Marie, 175–76
Hanson, Helen, 103
"Happening," 23–24, 33, 52–54
   as avant-garde theater, 30–31, 52–53
   as broad cultural metaphor, 30–31, 52–53
Heidegger, Martin, 166–67, 170
hermeneutics, 11–12, 26–27, 93, 109, 124–25, 170
history, 4, 6, 26–27, 29–30, 32, 49–50, 51, 61, 82–83, 87, 100, 124, 164, 191, 192, 198n.7, 222n.35
Hoberman, J., 7–8, 30–31, 52, 69, 154–55
Hollywood studio system. *See* classical Hollywood cinema
honky-tonk piano revival, 71, 209n.20
Hubbert, Julie, 25–26, 42, 129–30, 149

irony, 26, 31–32, 36, 40–41, 59, 88, 136, 139, 164, 167–68, 191, 194

Jameson, Fredric, 35–36, 148–49

Kael, Pauline, 1–3, 18, 89, 90, 203n.12, 223n.48
Keathley, Christian, 17–19
Keetman, Gunild, 26, 160, 161, 164, 165, 169–74, 178
   See also "Gassenhauer" (musical work)
Kershner, Irvin, 161
Killen, Andreas, 9–10, 218n.53

Last Picture Show, The (1971), 2, 25–26, 126
   and the absence of music, 151–52
   cinema exhibition culture and spectatorship in, 134–35
   compiled popular music in, 135–39
   critical reception of, 153–56
   as an emulation of classical Hollywood cinema, 127–28, 153
   and generational memory, 132–35
   historical specificity of source music in, 132, 134, 135–36, 220n.18
   humorous moments of radio synchronicity in, 146–47
   and nostalgia in promotional materials, 154–55
   prioritization of source music, 129
   and the unreflective mundanity of music, 132, 135, 152
Levi-Strauss, Claude, 61–62, 210n.32
   See also myth: musical and lyric images as "mythemes"
Long, Michael, 77–78, 128, 212n.50
Los Angeles, 93, 97, 110–11, 123
Lucas, George, 19–20, 132–35, 150–51, 153, 224n.57
lyrosophy, 168–69, 194–95

Magee, Gayle Sherwood, 80–81, 83–84
magic, 6–8, 51–52, 55–56, 62, 134, 147–49, 171
Malick, Terrence, 19–20, 26, 56–58, 157, 161–62, 164, 165–69, 170–71, 174–75, 185
   academic background and influence of Heidegger, 166–67, 183
   and characterization as a philosophical practice, 162, 191–92
   as a "melomane," 165–66
   philosophy as a topic in the critical reception of, 166–67
Marcus, Greil, 7–8, 50, 53, 154
Mast, Gerald, 14–15
materiality, 29–30, 46, 90, 125, 160, 164, 171, 226n.26, 227n.36
   See also Badlands: objects and objectification in; elements
McCabe and Mrs. Miller (1971), 8–9, 18–19, 24, 60, 66, 87–92, 97–98

clarity and comprehensibility of soundtrack, 85
music editing and synchronization in, 79–80, 84–85, 87–88, 211n.39
and psychedelic spatialization, 82–83
and song sequences, 67, 78–81, 85–87
media consumption, 73, 164
and selectivity (portable record players, jukeboxes), 137, 149, 220n.20
and television, 9–10, 16, 134–35
See also radio
melancholy, 5–6, 8–9, 12–13, 25–26, 45, 75–77, 89, 130, 131, 167–68, 174–82, 188–89, 192–94
See also melancholy; nostalgia; Satie: and melancholy reverie
Mickey and Sylvia (musical group), 187
Miklitsch, Robert, 100–1, 105–6
modernity, 6–8, 24–25, 63, 73–74, 97–98, 125, 171–72
Monaco, Paul, 14, 16
Morricone, Ennio, 75–76, 194–95
Morris, Mitchell, 9, 11–12
Murch, Walter, 20–21, 150–51
Musica Poetica (series of sound recordings), 183, 225–26n.17, 229n.56
musical instruments, imaginal readings of
muted bells in *Chinatown*, 114–15
piano in *Chinatown*, 113–14, 115
solo trumpet in *Chinatown*, 111–12
xylophone in *Badlands*, 172–73
myth, 5–6, 24–25, 26–27, 46, 56–58, 60–92, 163, 225n.14
definitions of, 60–67
and the film Western genre, 60, 86–87
as an imagined atemporal experience, 24, 56–58, 60, 67, 70–71, 82–83, 87, 90–91, 164, 167–68 (*see also* temporality: ambiguous or fluid)
ideological critique of, 61, 88–89, 108–9, 124–25
musical and lyric images as "mythemes," 79–80, 81
and paranoia (see *Chinatown* [1974])
political corruption and sexual violence as (see *Chinatown* [1974])
in relation to film music, 62–66
in relation to history, 58
religionist understandings of, 61–62, 208n.2

neoclassicism, 93, 95–96, 98, 100–1, 103–6
New Hollywood cinema, 3–4, 8, 9, 95, 133–34, 153
and cultural pessimism, 8, 9, 26–27, 95
definitional complexity, 197–98n.5
documentary influence, 15, 16–17, 19–20, 25–26, 129, 149
European New Wave influence, 13–16, 67, 133–34
and filmmaking technology, 15
and genre, 60, 62, 132
and incoherence, ambiguity, 11, 12–13
and the paranoia thriller (genre), 99–100, 103
prioritizing of source music, 25–26, 129, 149
and production trends, 19–20, 133–34
and reverie, 162–63
visual style, 37–38, 127–28
Newman, David, 28–29, 30–33, 59
New Sentimentality, 30–33
and Old Sentimentality in *Bonnie and Clyde*, 203n.12
non-diegetic music. *See* underscore
nostalgia, 2–3, 6, 8–9, 25–27, 88–89, 98, 142–49, 171–72
as an aesthetic, 128, 143
as a film genre, 132, 219n.10
and ideological critique, 142–43, 145–46, 148–49, 153–54, 155
and pop music revivalism, 73, 142, 154
as a popular culture phenomenon of the seventies, 153–56
spatio-temporality of, 130, 135–39
See also melancholy
nouvelle vague. See French New Wave cinema

O'Brien, Geoffrey, 73
Old Hollywood. *See* classical Hollywood cinema
"Old, Weird America", the, 7–9. *See also* Marcus, Greil

248 INDEX

Orff, Carl, 26, 160, 161–62, 165, 169–74
   choral compositions from the *Schulwerk*, 182–86
   Faust setting, 160, 186, 189–90
Orr, John, 56–58, 89–90, 162–63, 168–69, 211n.44

paranoia, 8, 10–11, 24–25, 97–100, 117–18
   and academic critique, 124–25, 218n.53
   sacred and secular, 99–100
   See also Chinatown: and mythic paranoia; New Hollywood cinema: and the paranoia thriller
past, the, and "pastness." *See* temporality
Peckinpah, Sam, 19–20
Penn, Arthur, 19–20, 30–31, 39, 47, 52, 56–58
phenomenology, 17, 24–25, 26, 41, 106, 107–8, 143–44, 146–47, 170, 184–85, 217n.46, 227n.36
photography, 33–35, 42–43, 49, 59, 73–75, 103, 187–89
   and contingency, 74, 187–85
   still images in contrast to moving images, 89
play, 26, 76–77, 159–61, 173–74, 179, 193–94
   and musical objects in *Schulwerk*, 170, 186
   See also violence: and play
Polan, Dana, 24–25, 99–100, 216–17n.40
Polanski, Roman, 24–25, 100–1, 104–5
   personal background and the ending of *Chinatown*, 123
   and sexual assault, 123
pop art, 1, 31–32
pop score, the, 19, 24, 40–46, 87–88
   and anachronism, 54–55, 98
   criticism of, 46, 65–67, 88, 129
   and expressive ambiguity, 35
   and historical setting, 25–26, 98 (*see also* "pop songs")
   marketability, 19, 65–66, 68–69, 87–88, 128–29, 199n.21
   mechanization and alienation, 40–41
   soundtrack albums, 21–22
   unique expressivity of, 45, 128–29
pop songs in cinema, 24, 83–84, 87–88, 128–29
   and eclecticism, 25–26
   and the emergence of "classic rock," 134, 141–42
   as markers of historical setting, 35–36, 126, 187
   music-video-style, montages, song sequences, 23, 65–66, 67, 77–78 (*see also Butch Cassidy and the Sundance Kid*: and song sequences)
   See also McCabe and Mrs. Miller: and song sequences
   as spatialized sonic objects, 129
presence, 2–3, 5, 18, 23–24, 25–27, 37–38, 41, 46, 109–10, 149, 150, 164, 172
   voices, non-human agency and, 183, 184–85
Proust, Marcel, 32–33
psychedelia, 64–65, 77–78, 79–80, 81–85, 212n.50

ragtime revival, 73. *See also* honky-tonk piano revival
radio, 25–26, 131, 136–37, 139, 140–42, 147–48, 155–56
   and automobiles, mobility, 137–38, 144–45, 150
   and ephemerality, 135, 141, 149–50
   imaginal spatiality of, 127–28, 129, 143–44, 148–49
   mystique, totemism of, 131, 134, 145–46, 149
   repetition, flow, and contingency, 136–38, 140, 146–47
Rasey, Euan, 111–12, 116–17
"Raindrops Keep Fallin' on my Head" (song), 65–66, 69–70
realism, 16, 25–27, 39–40, 85, 87, 129–30, 151–52
   and artifice, 2, 9–10, 18, 28–29, 49–50, 162–63
   and body noises, 47–48, 86–87
   and historical narrativity, 23–24
   and photographic indexicality, 16–17, 34–35 (*see also* photography)
   and subjective perspective, 100–1
   and violence, 43–44, 46, 151–52
   See also New Hollywood cinema: and prioritizing of source music

reality effects, 16, 23, 26–27, 29–30, 43–44, 46, 58, 149
    See also realism
revisionism, 5–6, 18–19, 24, 60–67, 87–88, 95, 109–10
    See also genre; myth; realism
Romanticism (aesthetic), 6–7, 31–32, 113, 190
Roszak, Theodore, 6–9
Rybin, Steven, 162, 167–68, 191–92

Sarris, Andrew, 2–3, 18, 223n.48
Satie, Erik, 26, 157, 161–62, 165, 169, 172–73, 174–82, 228n.45
    biographical periodization and reception, 174–75
    and gnosis, 180–82, 228–29n.55
    and irony, 162, 174–77, 192–93
    and melancholy reverie, 161–62, 177, 179–80, 186, 192–93
Schulwerk (pedagogical philosophy), 160, 162, 169–74
Sedgwick, Eve Kossofsky, 109–10
    "strong" and "weak" theory, 109–10
sensory immersion, 26, 46, 91, 125, 161
    and mystical experience, 26–27, 85
    realism and immanence, 85, 125
    superimposed with alienation, 162
seventies (decade), 4, 8, 11–12, 97, 146, 153–56
sexuality, 44–45, 47–48, 49, 91, 97–98, 116–17, 149–51, 206n.45, 223n.47
silent film music, 68–72
    historical revival, 71
    See also Butch Cassidy and the Sundance Kid: silent film media in
Sinnerbrink, Robert, 192–93
sixties (decade), 4, 5, 6–7, 30–31, 50–59, 91–92, 132–33, 145–46, 155
Sobchack, Vivian, 184–85, 215n.28, 227n.36
Smith, Jeff, 22, 128–29, 140–41, 205–6n.38, 223n.46
sound design, 19, 30, 37–40, 42–43, 46–50, 85–87, 194–95
    and the elements, 100–3
    and industrial training, 19–21
    and machine sounds, 37–40
    and magnetic tape recording, 21
    and the representation of surveillance, 103
    and stereophonic sound, 20–21, 194–95, 219n.8
    and violence, 39, 50–51
    and the voice, 37–38, 46–50
source music, 35–36, 86, 127–28
    edited akin to underscoring, 126–27, 144–45
    identifiability through aural distortion, 126–27
    See also New Hollywood cinema: and prioritizing of source music; pop score; pop songs
Stahl, Francis, 203n.7
"Stranger Song, The" (song), 78–81
    and film Western imagery, 78
    functionality and synchronization as compiled film music, 78–79
Strouse, Charles, 29, 30–31, 40–46
structuralism, 61–62, 106
stylization, 28–29, 39–40, 93
    See also neoclassicism; New Hollywood cinema
Swingle Singers (musical group), 76, 210n.28

temporality
    and alienation, otherness, 29–30, 46, 167
    ambiguous or fluid, 47, 87–88, 91–92
    and circularity, 97–98, 120–21, 122–23 (*see also Chinatown*: and mythic paranoia)
    diachronic and synchronic time in film music, 62–63
    imagined absence of mediation, 35–37, 47–48, 167–68, 191–92
    in New Sentimentality, 31–32
    and the pop score, 46
    and repetition, 37–38, 49–50, 136, 139
    and spatiality in "fantastic rock," 82–83
    and spatiality in the nostalgia film (*see* nostalgia: spatio-temporality of)
    and the soundtrack, 30, 98, 135–39, 140–42
    See also myth: as imagined a temporal experience

Thin Red Line, The (1998), 166–68, 192, 195
thirties (decade), 2, 35, 52, 100
timbre, 24–25, 71, 101–2, 109–10, 115–16, 118, 125
　See also elements: water and earth in *Chinatown*
Tipton, George, 157, 158, 165, 172–73, 185, 225–26n.17, 229n.56
　original music in *Badlands*, 179, 182, 189
　Satie arrangements in *Badlands*, 174, 177, 179–80
Towne, Robert, 93, 202n.3
Truffaut, Francois, 16, 29, 31, 133–34

underscoring, 21–22, 126
　choral music as, 182–83
Utopia (concept), 7–9, 26–27, 63, 88–89, 143–44, 148–49, 155–56

Vallée, Rudy, 35, 49–50
Vietnam war, 3, 4, 6–7, 32–33, 50–51, 64, 98, 130–31, 150–51, 190
violence, 1, 34
　and ethics (*see* ethics: and violence in *Badlands*)
　and fairy tales, 176–77
　and play, 160, 161, 192
　See also realism: and violence

Weber, Billy, 183, 225–26n.17, 229n.56
"Whiter Shade of Pale," (song), 76, 77
Wild Bunch, The (1968), 3, 4, 64
Williams, Hank, 126, 136, 138, 139, 152
"Winter Lady" (song), 83–85, 91
Wolfman Jack (Bob Smith), 131, 140–41, 143–44, 145, 146–47, 148–50
　and the historical role of the deejay, 141
Wood, Robin, 10–12, 13
worlds, 13–14, 23, 26–27, 39, 43–44, 46, 81, 82–83, 87, 95–96, 101–2, 117–18, 164
　and animism in *Badlands*, 184–85, 190
　as a concern of Heideggerian philosophy, 166–67
　diegetic spatiality of, 130
　and musical mundanity, 37, 139
　sound design as "worlding," 91–92

Yacavone, Daniel, 13–14, 184–85, 192–93, 229n.61

Zachariah (1971), 64–65